Greek W

Greek Weird Wave
A Cinema of Biopolitics

Dimitris Papanikolaou

EDINBURGH
University Press

Edinburgh University Press is one of the leading university presses in the UK. We publish academic books and journals in our selected subject areas across the humanities and social sciences, combining cutting-edge scholarship with high editorial and production values to produce academic works of lasting importance. For more information visit our website: edinburghuniversitypress.com

Edinburgh University Press Ltd
The Tun – Holyrood Road
12(2f) Jackson's Entry
Edinburgh EH8 8PJ

First published in hardback by Edinburgh University Press 2021

Typeset in Garamond MT Pro by
Servis Filmsetting Ltd, Stockport, Cheshire

A CIP record for this book is available from the British Library

ISBN 978 1 4744 3631 1 (hardback)
ISBN 978 1 4744 3632 8 (paperback)
ISBN 978 1 4744 3633 5 (webready PDF)
ISBN 978 1 4744 3634 2 (epub)

Contents

Figures

Preface and Acknowledgements

A few pages later, you will find a scene that, I have come to realise, could be used as a key to understand this book as a whole. In 2016, Yorgos Zois, a young Greek director, gave an interview to ARTE, the French/German art TV channel in 2016: 'The new Wave of Greek Cinema produces films that are as absurd as the financial crisis that has hit the country', begins the journalist. 'Welcome to Athens, the capital of Greece, the supposed weakest link of Europe'. As Zois's work came to international attention for its relationship to the socio-political situation that in recent years has come to be known as the 'Greek Crisis' all over the world, he is asked to speak about a controversial scene that he has directed, in which a young man is seen throwing a Molotov cocktail in an almost choreographed manner. While they were shooting, so Zois says, 'there was a real demonstration happening in the background',

– You used a real Molotov cocktail ?
  [He stops for a moment and looks at the camera, then laughs. He seems to have found the question awkward – which it is.]
– No, of course it was fake . . . When we are shooting something, it is a fake Molotov cocktail [that we use] . . .

So much in this scene – including the absurdity of the question 'you used a real Molotov cocktail?' – speaks to the questions that serve as a starting point for this book. What did an international and national audience expect from Greek Cinema during this recent turbulent period? How did it deliver? How can you make films with such expectations, but also *in* that socio-political context? How *real* should you be? How real*ist*? And also, how strange, how weird is it to be thrown into a predefined role and then to try, like the Greek director in this interview, to both stay on script, but also to showcase the levels of absurdity that that script has already reached?

The 'Greek Weird Wave', celebrated internationally after 2010, has been a national cinema movement that is not so much defined by the answers it might give to these questions, but by the questions themselves. From the outset, it was seen as the cinematic response to the Greek Crisis, sometimes in spite of the films themselves. It offered international circulation and production options to many Greek fiction films, although it has not altered the financial and institutional precarity of Greek Cinema as a whole. It became an easy reference point internationally; yet, it also remained contested. All its films were seen and treated as a closely related group, judging by their national and international reception, but what unites them remains difficult to pin-point.

One thing that surely brings these films together, so this book argues, is a culture of late capitalism, biopolitics and crisis neoliberalism in which they participate and which they often thematise. The analytical insights into biopolitics, as reformulated by Michel Foucault, become crucial for the argument in this book, as they focus on the management of human life from the large scale of a population – its categorisation, health, livability and/or proscription – to the minutiae of a human body, its functions and the ways in which it interiorises power and knowledge. Accordingly, a framework of *biopolitical realism* not only shows how the films of the Greek Weird Wave relate to each other, but it also allows viewers – and, of course, critical interventions, this book included – to appreciate and work with their political potential. The Greek Weird Wave today is not the only cinema of biopolitics, but it is certainly a paradigmatic one, and this is what the following sections and chapters will set out to show.

The final draft of this book was being reread while the whole world entered the biopolitically most acute period in recent history, with the global COVID-19 emergency, the lockdowns and the world health and economic challenges that ensued. Suddenly everyone started talking about biopolitics. To the researcher in Modern Greek Studies, this might feel like *déjà vu* – there was a time after 2010 when, in a similar way, you could find the word biopolitics everywhere in Greece.

Of course, the repercussions of the 2020 health crisis cannot be underestimated, and it will certainly take time for them to be fully apprehended. Until the very moment of completing this manuscript, I am not even sure whether this prolonged emergency will mark the end of what I describe here as biopolitical realism, only to introduce instead something much more radical and cruel, or whether it will lead to its mutation, further expansion and different critical openings.

This book has been a very long time in the making. I trace its first ideas back to a conversation I had with Dimitris Eleftheriotis in 2010 and then to a paper I gave at the University of Glasgow on his invitation. To Dimitris and his encouragement, therefore, I owe this book the most, as well as an apology that it was not finished earlier. The same gratitude and apology I extend to Gillian Leslie and the editorial team at Edinburgh University Press, for their amazing support at all stages and their trust.

As the reader will realise, this book has evolved alongside its subject-matter and while I was engaged in a number of different projects directly or indirectly related to the Greek Crisis – some of them academic, others political and activist. In many ways, *Greek Weird Wave* is as much about films as it is about that context, as well as the immense energy, the sense of potential, frustration and loss that the last decade has brought to many of us.

In the book's long period of development, I was fortunate to share my ideas on Greek Cinema and the Weird Wave with my students and colleagues at Oxford, and with audiences at the following universities: King's College London, Glasgow, NYU, Princeton, Columbia, UCLA, Rome La Sapienza, Geneva, Athens, Volos, Amsterdam, Sydney and Utrecht; and also at the Greek Médiathèque and the Greek Short Film Festival. Even though everything here has been written or rewritten specifically for this book, ideas and different versions of short sections from Chapters 1, 4, 5, 6 and 7 have appeared in Papanikolaou 2012; 2018a; 2018b; 2019a; 2019b; 2020. I am grateful to all editors and publishers for the permission to use this material and to Konstantinos Matsoukas, who allowed me to consult his English version of Papanikolaou 2019a before rewriting Chapter 1.

Research support has been provided first and foremost by the Faculty of Medieval and Modern Languages at the University of Oxford, the Oxford University Fell Fund and the Oxford Strategic REF Fund, as well as a 2012 Remarque Fellowship at NYU.

The amazing Kristina Gedgaudaite has been an ideal research assistant and my teaching *alter ego* while I was on leave. Afroditi Nikolaidou has been the most ardent and crucial supporter of the project overall. Spyros Chairetis, Elliot Koubis and Geli Mademli have provided crucial research, translation and editing support, as well as important advice when my ideas became too awkward.

Previous drafts of the book were read by Maria Boletsi, Janna Houwen, Athena Athanasiou, Dimitris Eleftheriotis, Vaskos Demou, Kyveli Short, Reidar Due, Dimitris Plantzos, Sotiris Paraschas, Grigoris Gougousis. I offer them my sincere thanks for their generosity and note that their comments have had a significant impact on the final outcome. Konstantina Kotzamani has kindly given me permission to use a screen capture from *Washingtonia* on the cover. And Nina Macaraig was the copy-editor I could hope for: caring, insightful, engaged.

William McEvoy has been there – always, as always – supporting, discussing, reading, rereading and every time being able to find a reason why this was a book worth writing. As with the rest of my writing, this one is very much his, too.

Among the many friends and colleagues who have stood by me during this period, I should mention in particular Eleftheria Ioannidou, Anna Papaeti,

Elena Tzelepi, Liana Theodoratou, Guido Bonsaver, Almut Suerbaum, Karen Leeder, Catherine Pillonel, Wes Williams, Philip Rothwell, Mihalis Dafermos, Ipek Celik, Nick Rees-Roberts, Fiona Antonelaki, Jessica Kourniakti, Anna Poupou, Costas Douzinas, Joanna Bourke, Helen Swift, Caroline Warman, Sotiris Mitralexis, Maria Komninou, Deborah Philips, Peter Jeffreys, Vrassidas Karalis, Giorgos Korakianitis, Vargias Karavas, Alexandre Collet, Claudio Russello, Loukas Triantis, Iro Tagkalou, Antonio Hernandez, Kostas Skordyles, Konstantina Nanou, Eleni Syminelaki-Nanou, Ludovic Malbet, Marcus McAllister and, last, but certainly not least, my wonderful Jean Michel Clément, who now knows more about biopolitics (and Greek Cinema) than, I suspect, he ever wished. This book started with the aim to understand the unhomely at a time of biopolitics; it ends with the thirst for home, and its weird realisations.

Note on Transliteration

Transliterations from the Greek language follow the conventions of the *Journal of Greek Media and Culture*.

Introduction

WHAT'S IN A NAME:
THE GREEK WEIRD WAVE AND THE CONTOURS OF INTERPELLATION

'*Attenberg, Dogtooth* and the weird wave of Greek cinema' – this was the unassuming title of the two-page spread published in *The Guardian* to coincide with the British release of Athina Rachel Tsangari's *Attenberg* in August 2011. Written by the critic Steve Rose (2011), it started by asking: 'Are the brilliantly strange films of Yorgos Lanthimos and Athina Rachel Tsangari a product of Greece's economic turmoil? And will they continue to make films in the troubled country?'

This is how the Greek Weird Wave gained momentum, as a name and as a concept: From the beginning, it was related to the question of how the socio-economic crisis was affecting recent Greek Cinema, and whether the latter would survive 'in the troubled country'. As a matter of fact, in the years after Rose's article, Greeks did, indeed, continue to make films; the country continued to be troubled; and the term Greek Weird Wave somehow stuck, to denote for world cinema, a full-fledged cinematic movement.

In 2011, when this *Guardian* article was published, Yorgos Lanthimos's film *Dogtooth* (2009) had just completed an impressively successful international run that included a nomination for the Oscar for Best Foreign Film, the Un Certain Regard prize at Cannes (billed as 'the true Cannes discovery of the year'),[1] various other accolades and, most importantly, distribution in more than twenty countries around the world. Lanthimos's subsequent film, *Alps*, was to follow suit in the winter of 2011; in the meantime, his close collaborator Athina Rachel Tsangari's second feature film, *Attenberg* (2010), won two awards at the Venice Film Festival and was also receiving distribution in many European and American countries, to very positive reviews. A number of other films had also received coverage in the international press, among them Panos Koutras's *Strella: A Woman's Way* (2009), Filippos Tsitos's *Unfair World* (2009), Yannis Economides's *The Knifer* (2010) and Syllas Tzoumerkas's *Homeland* (2010), frequently inviting comments about how they all seemed to belong to the same 'wave' of Greek filmmaking.

Apart from the fact that suddenly and in quick succession Greek films were catching the eye of international critics, film festival juries and publications, something virtually unheard of for decades in the context of this national cinema, also noteworthy was the close affinity that some of these films and many of these filmmakers seemed to have with one another. Lanthimos starred in and co-produced Tsangari's *Attenberg*; conversely, Tsangari had co-produced his *Dogtooth* and *Alps*. Actress Arianne Labed (soon to be Lanthimos's wife) starred in both *Attenberg* and *Alps*, and she had been a key member of the Athenian avant-garde performance scene which also featured Angeliki Papoulia, the protagonist of *Dogtooth* and *Alps*, Christos Passalis, the protagonist of *Dogtooth* and *Homeland*, and Mary Tsoni, the third protagonist of *Dogtooth*, for whom the main role of *Attenberg* was originally written.[2] A host of other actors, producers, screenwriters and directors similarly were in close contact, sharing platforms, publications and sometimes also creative choices. Something was going on – even though, admittedly, international critics told their audiences that they did not understand what exactly it was.

> In recent years, Greece's global image has been jolted from Mediterranean holiday idyll and home of big fat weddings to fractious trouble spot. And not just in economic terms; let's not forget Greece had its own street riots in 2008. So perhaps it's to be expected that the country's cinema is chang-ing, too. The growing number of independent, and inexplicably strange, new Greek films being made has led trend-spotters to herald the arrival of a new Greek wave, or as some have called it, the 'Greek Weird Wave'. [...] Is it just coincidence that the world's most messed-up country is making the world's most messed-up cinema? (Rose 2011)

A 'messed up country', a 'messed up cinema' and 'a scale of strangeness' catch the eye here.[3] The *Guardian* article undeniably uses phrases that conjure up a certain orientalist viewpoint (cf. Nikolaidou 2020; Kourelou et al. 2014; Galt 2017). Yet, it also tries to point to an undeniable convergence of factors. The period when new Greek films started receiving notice in international fora in the late 2000s coincided with socio-economic turmoil in the country itself. As I will explain in more detail below, in May 2010 Greece officially agreed to its first Memorandum of Understanding (MoU) with creditors, one of several to follow. The country had become synonymous with the inter-national financial crisis that hit interrelated world economies after the 2008 collapse of the American bank Lehmann Brothers. The massive demonstra-tions, police mobilisation and images of destruction that hit world screens in December 2008, when the Greek capital was rocked by weeks of civil unrest following the police killing of teenager Alexandros Grigoropoulos, were repeated time and again after 2010, making the earlier events look more like a preamble. Demonstrators regularly took to the streets of Athens and other big cities, as new austerity measures were being announced and presented as non-negotiable. In the summer of 2011, the period just before Rose's article in the *Guardian*, demonstrators occupied Athens' Syntagma Square and eventually other central squares of the country, in an exercise of direct democracy, sit-ins and new political mobilisations that has since been both mythologised and deconstructed (cf. Dalakoglou and Angelopoulos 2018; Douzinas 2013b; Butler and Athanasiou 2013; Gourgouris 2011; Kioupkiolis and Katsambekis 2014; Papapavlou 2015; Stavrides 2016). The Greek *indignados* movement – which would see similar events spread around the countries of the Mediterranean South and in itself was reminiscent of the Arab Spring and the Occupy movements – became a reference point for Greece, creating a rallying point for the symbolic imagery of the resistance to the Greek Crisis (Dalakoglou and Vradis 2011; Panourgia 2011; Papanikolaou 2014).

By 2011, the Greek Crisis had, therefore, already developed its own visual economy; it had become iconic, iconoclastic and ethnographic all at once (Basea 2016). A palimpsest of images of demonstrations, the burning of public buildings, people's assemblies and the sudden impoverishment visible in the big Greek cities constructed a rich iconography which circulated across international media and often found its way into Greek cultural expression, in art photography, installations, theatre and sometimes in cinema, too. Films such as *Wasted Youth* (Argyris Papadimitropoulos, 2011), *Congratulations to the Optimists* (Konstantina Voulgari, 2013), *Homeland* (Syllas Tzoumerkas, 2010; analysed in Chapter 6), *Xenia* (Panos H. Koutras, 2014), Thanos Anastopoulos's *The Daughter* (2012) and Alexis Alexiou's *Wednesday 4'45"* (2015) all incorporate this visual iconography of crisis, as do the commercially successful melodramas by Christophoros Papakaliatis, *If* (2012) and *Worlds Apart* (2015).

I start this introduction with this *Guardian* article because it named a local movement and, in the process, ended up performatively shaping it, at least at an international level. But I do so also as a reminder that the term 'Greek Weird Wave' was from the very beginning used to describe different styles and political strategies for representing the Greek Crisis.[4] For many critics who adopted it immediately, the reality of the Greek Crisis was already cinematic, and its 'weird' realism seemed to be engulfing everything, from documentary footage to complicated allegory. It might all have started with Lanthimos's largely allegorical films and their impact on international audiences and critics. Yet, even in its first appearances, the term 'Weird Wave' was much less about Lanthimos's *mise-en-scène*, and much more about the feeling of unease provoked by the Greek Crisis and the ways in which diverse Greek cinematic productions captured that unease. Even in its first use as a new term in the world cinema lexicon, 'weird' seemed malleable, pointing the discussion to audience and critical response, to different directors 'somehow' working with each other, and to the terms of recognizability and recognition that the cinema of a small nation was reinventing for itself. Of course, 'weird' is a very problematic term. Yet, it is also a term that is able to unlock the very social, cultural and power dynamics that put it in use in the first place. The rest of this introduction aims to explain why and how.[5]

THE TIMING OF A NEW WAVE

Soon the 'Greek Weird Wave' became a tag, an easy reference, a bibliographical entry, a festival genre, a bandwagon for new productions, a keyword for script-optioning and a world cinema analytical concept.[6] It also became highly contested; after all, Greek directors had not created a manifesto (as, for instance, the Dogme directors had done in Denmark in 1995),[7] nor did they have one collective publication around which they clustered (as in the case of the French Nouvelle Vague and their connection with the *Cahiers du Cinéma*). And crucially, as many critics have pointed out since, they kept creating extremely diverse films.[8]

The Greek Weird Wave was received in the context of what we are used to calling world cinema – a diverse body of films mainly produced outside the big film industries, defined by its presence on the international film circuit and at festivals, mingling national reference with transnational aspirations, often with small budgets and inventive production and release strategies, as well as constantly open to new (and cheaper) technologies (Elsaesser 2009; Nagib et al. 2011). As a world cinema movement, then, the Weird Wave is not the first that was named, if not performatively shaped, by curatorial work at international festivals and by a couple of journalistic articles. Other recent examples include New Queer Cinema (Rich 2013; Aaron 2004) and New French Extremity (Quandt 2004; Horeck and Kendall 2011). In all those cases, the initial text that popularised the name in question was a somewhat descriptive account of recent filmmaking or of specific films, and the films mentioned were very different from each other and certainly did not emerge from any concrete movement or school.

Such 'labels' perform not only the work of classification, but have a wider cultural impact: They steer the production of certain films but not others, creating access to markets otherwise closed to representatives of world cinema, and they certainly provoke debates, both in the country of origin and in international sites such as film festivals and specialised media (Elsaesser 2018). They create a certain framework that suddenly turns a local, world cinema production, into a paradigmatic moment of wider cinematic movements, their production and consumption. Suddenly, for instance, Yorgos

Lanthimos's *Dogtooth* and its 'weirdness' became a (post-)identificatory space for a new type of cinema. During the research for this book, I often saw stills from this film used to promote new art channels, new magazines on media and culture in Greece and abroad, new art film streaming websites and so on.[9] That identificatory space of weirdness was not merely a defining moment for Greek Cinema; it also pointed towards a larger cultural momentum.

It is not surprising, therefore, that in subsequent years the term Weird Wave eventually stuck – even though not without problems, surprises, or protests by the interested community of artists, critics, academics and cinema-goers, some of whom prefer the term 'Greek New Wave' instead. Still, even in Greece the term 'weird' started to be used, also for a cultural production beyond the cinematic: Novels, plays and music albums were now identified as part of a general Greek Weird Wave (Dimadi 2013; Hulot 2014).

This book, as have done others in the past (Calotychos, Papadimitriou and Tzioumakis 2016; Psaras 2016), engages with the challenge of the Weird Wave, while it also holds on to the debatable term. It is not a full, close, or even adequate description of the filmmaking that has emerged from Greece in recent years. The problems with the term are clear: The most iconic of the films of the Greek Weird Wave were planned (and some even produced) before the Greek Crisis became evident (Chalkou 2012); 'weird' seems to apply to and describe only some films, mainly those by Tsangari, Lanthimos and Makridis (Karalis 2012); and that the very word 'weird' smacks of a somewhat patronising, even orientalist, framing – weird, after all, is an adjective often used to describe acts simply misunderstood by those who feel they are privileged to know better (Galt 2017). Finally, names such as these always run the risk of becoming a form of self-exoticisation as well (Kourelou et al. 2014; Nikolaidou 2020; Panagiotopoulos 2020).[10]

At the same time, I see the analytical benefits of the term 'weird', and I treat it also as a reminder, an opening to review precisely those diverse challenges inherent in the production, distribution and global circulation, as well in the sharing, watching and analysis of more than a decade of Greek Cinema. As Afroditi Nikolaidou and Anna Poupou remind us in a recent article titled 'Post-Weird Notes on the New Wave of Greek Cinema' . . .

> The fact that the term weird wave was coined by international critics and festival programmers, as well as the subsequent involvement of Greek directors and producers in the cross-national processes of the European film market, pose the question of self-determination, self-representation or even self-exoticism. Nowadays, new waves or movements, such as Dogme 95 or the Romanian new wave, are created more by extra-cinematic processes (such as the production, promotion, and reception conditions of these films), by the performative capabilities of the directors/filmmakers themselves, and less by

shared morphological and thematic elements. However, the fact that these processes are linked to the history and culture of each country is the reason why each movement ultimately draws on the specific pools of aesthetic tools: Greek new-wave films do not have affinities with each other – what they share is a common political and cultural stance. (Nikolaidou and Poupou 2017: 91)

In line with this, rather than speaking about common features (or even thinking of them as weird), what I am setting out to do is to talk about a cinematic wave based on the contemporaneity of its engagement. I use 'contemporaneity of engagement' as a concept able to question the politics of the image together with the politics and politicisation of viewing, thereby facilitating an investigation of the context towards which a film gestures, as well as of the context into which it is thrown. Engagement also points to the fact that a new generation of films and filmmakers from Greece during a difficult period had to measure up to an extraordinarily complex and often hilarious set of expectations. One needs to be able to see also this as a weird setting, so as to be able to engage with its deconstruction.

WEIRD RECOGNITIONS: *CASUS BELLI*

One of the most celebrated short films to emerge as the term 'Weird Wave' started to circulate is the eleven-minute *Casus Belli* by Yorgos Zois. Made in 2010, it premiered in Venice in 2011 and then was presented for years at festivals and in TV specials on Greece around the world.[11] I draw attention to it because it takes the expectation of a 'weird Greek film on the Crisis' as its main *raison d'être* and playfully responds to it. It is not coincidental that, in order to do so, the film weaves together realism, direct reference to social context, image manipulation, allegory and iconicity. In many ways, *Casus Belli* is an extended comment, on living under austerity in contemporary Greece, as well as on the visual and cinematic economy that this context produces. Like most of its director's other work, *Casus Belli* exemplifies the dialectic that developed between Greek filmmaking and the international expectations from 'a country in crisis'.

The film starts by following a queue in a supermarket. As the camera pans from left to right, we slowly pass by all the people standing in this queue. Once we reach the person standing first in the queue and paying at the till, we follow them as they move on and join the next queue, now in a nightclub. This queue will then lead to another in a church and so on. In the next series of long tracking shots – which are digitally edited to give the impression that we are seeing actually one single, very long, continuous take – more queues are collated, one after the other. Each queue weaves into the next, with the

Figure I.1-3 *The queue in front of the Panathinaikon stadium and a trolley falling on the staircases of Parliament Square, Athens, digital stills from* Casus Belli *(Yorgos Zois, 2010).*

movement of the camera linking them together. It is an aesthetics that, for good reason, reminds the viewer of TV commercials, while at the same time perhaps referencing the old credo originally employed by the *Cahiers du Cinéma* critic Luc Moullet (1959: 14): 'Morality is a question of tracking shots', famously rephrased by Jean-Luc Godard as 'the tracking shot is a question of morals'.[12]

We follow this digitally 'enhanced' continuous sequence of tracking shots until we reach the last queue, at a soup kitchen in front of the Panathinaikon Stadium in Athens (known for hosting the whole of the 1896 and a small but significant part of the 2004 Olympic Games). There, a lonely old man, who is denied access to the soup kitchen when it is his moment to be served, turns abruptly to the queue behind him and violently pushes it back. Now the camera starts panning right to left, as all the queues we have seen so far start collapsing in a domino effect, with every person falling backwards. When we reach the very first queue in the supermarket, a supermarket trolley full of products joins the camera's fast back-travelling. It now starts to travel throughout Athens. It hits the steps of Syntagma Square, and fruit and vegetables scatter as the trolley rolls down the stairs, in an amusing reference to the famous pram scene in Eisenstein's *Battleship Pottempkin*. As it leaves the city for the countryside, the trolley stops in an empty landscape, where it is awkwardly reunited with the old man who had started the domino effect. He approaches it, looks at it, then looks at the camera. End of film.

We have here a very straightforward mix of realism (soup kitchens, people waiting in queues to pay at the tax office), metonymic referentiality (each queue stands for a larger social issue: the soup kitchen for poverty, the supermarket for the world of consumption, the church for religion and so on) and allegorical potential (the very image of the queue, the domino effect, the final scenes, the trolley falling down the stairs). There is also a very readable effort to capitalise on this mix in terms of film form: Digital editing, shot construction, rhythm and camera movement, as well as the occasional reference to film history seem to underline both the realistic/indexical and the analogic/ allegorical planes of reference.

Zois himself was often asked to explain these conjunctions to international audiences during the numerous times the film was shown in theatres and on TV channels around the world, often accompanying special events on the Greek Crisis, or programmes on the 'Greek Weird Wave'. The following extract comes from one of these interviews:

> [In recent years] if you were walking on the streets of Athens or reading the news, you would have the feeling that a crisis was about to happen. [. . .]
> As I was watching all these things, I was smelling it in the air, in the atmosphere, that something huge was about to happen. [I thus decided to make

Casus Belli], I thought it was the most direct way to show the whole of society in those seven queues. My point was to show that we are all connected. If one falls, everyone falls. It is like in Europe at the moment. We are all connected. If one collapses, everyone will collapse. Every queue has someone who walks from it to the next – they are the pure survivor. But even that person will fall at some point.

[In Greece], it is very difficult not to be influenced by the violent images that are multiplying every day. So, this is my way of expressing myself. And sometimes I feel this is my way of personal resistance. Until we get to a point where a massive resistance comes, this is my way of doing things. (Zois in Arte 2011)

A similar take (and an aesthetics that self-consciously references music videos and advertising) was adopted by Zois in the advert that he directed for the Third Biennale Art Exhibition in Athens. It shows a masked man, almost in choreographed slow motion, throwing a molotov cocktail in front of the neoclassical buildings of the Academy of Athens and the old Greek National Library. Made in 2011, the Biennale promotional video became the talk of the town in the Greek capital and further afield. In an interview for French television in 2016, Zois was filmed in the same location as the choreographed man throwing the Molotov cocktail in the video five years earlier. While also discussing his first feature-length film *Interruption* (2015) – which is about a stage performance interrupted by a group of terrorists who hold the audience hostage – Zois was eager to expand on the issue of 'interruption' more broadly. His generation, he said, had wanted to underline how art is interrupted in Greece and elsewhere. 'The new Wave of Greek Cinema produces films that are as absurd as the financial crisis that has hit the country', says the journalist in voice-over, as an introduction to the interview. 'Welcome to Athens, the capital of Greece, the supposed weakest link of Europe'. He then calls on Zois to talk about his notorious Biennale video. 'When we were shooting the scene, there was a real demonstration happening in the background', he responds.

> – You used a real Molotov cocktail?
> [Zois stops for a moment and looks at the camera, then laughs, as he seems to have found the question awkward – which it is.]
> – No, of course, it was fake . . . When we are shooting something, it is a fake Molotov cocktail [that we use] . . .
> [He turns and points to a demonstration passing by on the other side of the street while the interview happens.]
> Ah, you see now, these are demonstrators, they are marching.
> It is a typical situation in Greece, life interrupts art, art interrupts life, and the two are really mixed. (Zois interviewed in Arte 2012)[13]

As he points to the group of activists passing by with an enormous banner from the other side of the street, the camera performs a 180-degree turn and we see the banner and the activists moving, while the interview continues and Zois discusses cinema. He is on script: A young Greek filmmaker, in 2016, years after his first short films gave him peer and international festival recognition, explains how the Crisis has entered his films (and how they, subsequently, reached the international market). We have a filmmaker wanting to be indexical – here I use the term in the sense of 'deictic' (Doane 2007) – and eager to point out and show, to give form and semantic presence to a specific reality. But then there is also the unexpected, that most awkward moment of all: Not the presence of the demonstrators while the interview is taking place (*that* is quite an expected part of such an interview), but the French journalist's question, whether they had used real Molotov cocktails while shooting the 2011 video.

What makes this moment so striking is that the international media crew are treating Zois and his own team (and, synecdochically, the films they make) not just as agents of representation, but also as dynamic participants in the ecology of social unrest and protest that an international audience, perhaps with a degree of exoticisation, observes in 'the weakest link of Europe'. Are the directors not 'producing films as absurd as the Crisis that hit the country' with themselves as observers of the 'messed-up country'? How much part of 'all this' are they? What and how do *they* demonstrate?

A moment of silence, a look back in disbelief, a little laugh – then, regaining composure, the realisation that both are true: The Greek director is an active agent of representation, but s/he is also responding to a predefined role, a prepackaged system of signification. And finally, the answer: 'No . . . you know . . . when Greeks make films about demonstrations, even *they* need to use props'.

All of *that*, I call weird. Weird, as in a shared feeling produced by (and producing) awkward questions such as: Are these brilliantly strange films a product of Greece's economic turmoil? Will they continue to make films in the troubled country? Weird, as in a shared feeling produced by the awkward ways in which Greeks (including Greek directors) are trying to provide answers. But also, weird as in that moment of disbelief, and that awkward moment of realisation that agency is both predefined and subtly reconfigured, that sense of ill-fitting that ends up being played with and assumed as a position.

As Mark Fisher so aptly says, 'the weird is that which does not belong. The weird brings to the familiar something which ordinarily lies beyond it, and which cannot be reconciled with the "homely" (even as its negation)' (Fisher 2017: 10–11).

In other words, the term 'weird' may have started as a critical misrecognition of what was happening in Greek cinema *circa* 2011; yet, it still has the potential to unlock moments such as the one in Zois's interview. It has the potential to help us think through the weirdness in those moments of (mis)recognition and non-belonging where you realise that you adhere to the script while also being somewhat out of line. It is for this reason that I want to reclaim such weirdness, not as a tag, but first as an analytical position; not as any sort of answer, but as a starting point for questioning the thematic and stylistic traits that developed in Greek narrative cinema during the first decade of the Greek Crisis.

WEIRDING ALLEGORY

In the previous pages I have broached the two main questions with which I started collecting material for this book. On one hand, I had wanted to discuss the films made in Greece during a difficult decade and to assess them, as much as possible, as a group. How did this period (and the discourses) coinciding with what was globally referred to as the Greek Crisis influence Greek cinema?

On the other hand, the purchase of the term 'weird', as it named and framed the reinvigorated international interest in Greek Cinema, seemed symptomatic of larger movements in world cinema during a period of rapid economic, cultural, social, as well as audiovisual change. How far can the concept of 'weird', *pace* its initial use, serve as a sensor alerting us to the shifts and movements in a larger socio-cultural setting? For the period I had set out to review, weirdness became something akin to what Raymond Williams (1961) has called a 'structure of feeling', an expansive affect that alerts to the existence of an emergent culture.

Two further interrelated issues emerged as my inquiry continued. The first was that of national allegory. From the ancient Greek for 'speaking in public otherwise' (*allos agoreuein*), allegory bridges the personal and the public, the individual and the collective, as a rhetorical trope in which one set of references stands for another. To put it more simply, one story is presented while another is inferred. Allegory, thus, produces two orders of signification: one 'literal' and the other to be deciphered – and, hence, largely dependent for its impact on the act of allegorical reading, the allegoresis.

In that manner, I could see how critics, especially those outside Greece, were eager to read an allegory of the contemporary nation (and of *the* Crisis, by that time widely written with a capital C) in most Greek films of the period. As is evident from the discussions that shaped the Weird Wave (see Chapter 1), national allegory became a useful motor for the international circulation of these films, the individual/family narratives in the films being read as allegories of the very public and recurring story of a people and a nation (cf. Larkin 2009: 165).

Some films, to be sure, were more susceptible to these readings than others, and some directors were more eager to encourage this discussion, while others felt extremely constrained by the national allegory placed upon them.[14] This should not come as a surprise. From its popularisation in Fredric Jameson's essay on 'third world literature', it has become evident that the dynamics of (reading for) *national allegory* are themselves caught up in networks of power and ring-fencing, bound to be controversial but also critically productive (Jameson 1986; Ahmad 1987; Szeman 2001; Jameson 2019; Larkin 2009). The term has been vehemently criticised, especially in Film Studies, even when it was widely used and when scholars engaged with it (Xavier 1999; Tambling 2003: 9–21; Shohat and Stam 2014).

In his original essay, Jameson argued that 'third-world texts, even those which are seemingly private [. . .] necessarily project a political dimension in the form of national allegory. *The story of the private individual destiny is always an allegory of the embattled situation of the public third-world culture and society*' (1984: 69). The sweeping and prescriptive force of the argument immediately invites its deconstruction. All texts (and, in our case, all films)? 'Always'? Only from 'third-world countries'? All genres? All types of stories? Is this a fact, or a recipe for well-wrought revolutionary 'third-world' cultural texts? And where exactly is this 'third world'? Who defines it, and how prescriptively? Last, but not least, what if we read oppositionally: not for the allegorical, but for the affective intensity of the literal in the text (cf. Attridge 2004: 32–64; Van Alphen 2008; Boletsi 2018) – how radical and how political can *that* be?

That said, as Joanna Page reminds us, one cannot underestimate how much allegory still 'stages the relationship between personal and political, private and public, which is often central to the production of political meaning in art' (2009: 182). Certainly, it is equally productive to think of the term beyond the confines and definitions of a 'third world'. Let us not forget that in countries such as 1990s Argentina (Page's example) as well as in Crisis-Greece an oxymoronic classification develops in any case. While their cultural products, especially 'their films and their success on international screens, become fully associated with [the country's] "First World aspirations", there is a lot in their financial situation that makes critics think of them as close to "third world status"' (Page 2009: 199).

Even though the term 'third-world(ing)' was used for Greece in the years of the Crisis (cf. Rajagopal 2015), I certainly do not want to engage in such a discussion, as I find it counter-productive. I prefer to reread Jameson's argument as an incitement to see the workings of allegory in critical times/ places and historico-political settings. To do so does not signal an easy way out of the intricacies of cultural texts and their specific materialist relation to the society whence they come, but a reminder of how present allegory is in the everyday reality of the social, in the everyday experience of the political, the psychosocial and (of course) the national.

Take a brief example from Greece and from a previous 'critical moment' in its history: The most celebrated case of literary resistance to the Greek dictatorship of 1967–74 was an allegory titled *The Plaster Cast*, published by author Thanassis Valtinos in 1970. It is the story of a hospitalised patient being put in a plaster cast until he suffocates, and this was read as a powerful denunciation of the regime's oppressive policies and widespread torture. The allegory was so transparent and readable by its target audience precisely because it was based on the regime's own cautionary discourse. Indeed, the dictator himself had made a habit of referring in his speeches to Greece as a patient in need of urgent hospitalisation (and also a plaster cast). This was not simply the case of an individual's travails standing for the country's embattled situation. The allegory had already been part of a system of policing and abusing; it had been part of the battle already (see Van Dyck 1998: 16–17.).

In a very similar fashion, what became characteristic in the case of the Weird Wave – much like national allegory, a term immediately garnering resistance, even though also widely used – was not the question of whether these films were allegories and of what exactly. It was, instead, the playful way in which they included, played with and deconstructed the allegories already circulating in and about the nation.

In some of the films I analyse in this book, such as *Suntan* (Chapter 1) or *Pity* (Chapter 4), it is precisely the impulse to national allegory that is being ironically revisited and undermined. Others, such as *Attenberg* (Chapter 4) or *Third Kind* (Chapter 2), reconfigure allegory's visual politics by revisiting the empty sites that have represented the imaginary space of the nation: a modernist industrial town in the former, a national airport in the latter. Last, but not least, in the films of Lanthimos, which play a recurrent role in this book, allegory is present as a disciplinary tool, notably in *Dogtooth* (see Chapter 5), and as a diffuse disposition that engulfs the viewer.

A theme common to Lanthimos and most other directors of the Weird Wave – that is, the oppressive or dysfunctional family (see Chapters 1, 5 and 6) – was also bound to confront the spectator with the porous boundaries of allegory. Why did these stories of locked-down families suddenly start filling the storyboards of Greek Cinema? Why were they so affective? Were they realist representations of family/gender violence rife in Greek society, or allegories for a nation in crisis? What is the family in the end: a small molecule of the nation, a workshop of its ideologies and disciplinary tactics, its most transparent form of allegory, or all of these together?

Early on I noticed the extent to which the allegorical reception of such films was not necessarily positioned against a possible affective/literal reading. Somehow, as I go on to analyse in Chapters 1, 2 and 5, the literal, the affective and the allegorical can all work together in these films. This is the case, even if it entails, as I will explain, a somewhat different understanding of allegory, one that exploits metonymic displacement within the allegorical and undermines the view of allegory simply as an extended metaphor.

As I return to discuss often in this book, and especially in Chapter 3, there was not one but many allegories that developed in, around and with the Greek Weird Wave. The most peculiar of them is a form of reverse allegory: It was the Greek Crisis that in the end became an allegory for the world – an allegory of lost agency, of late capitalist disempowerment of polity, of undermined sovereignty, of the undoing of the demos. Greek films were caught up in that process. For them, allegory became an inescapable context – but not, as Jameson would have it, because their protagonists' hazards necessarily stood for the national travails. Instead, the films were seen as part of a national situation that was becoming a global allegory for the new way of the world. In Chapter 3, I dedicate a lengthy analysis to a 2011 special French/German TV programme on Greece, with Lanthimos as its main guest. In that programme, the tropes of national allegory are exposed from start to finish, and so are the efforts of artists to both exploit and deconstruct them, offering their everyday reality as an alternative platform from which one can think through the cultural expression of a small nation in financial and social crisis. While interviewed, these artists have to act within a context and an allegory placed upon them; what they offer in response is a persistently renegotiated (and thus weird) realism. This distinct realism that emerged in Greece during the period in question – a realism that among others also engaged with allegory, its negotiation and sometimes its playful unravelling – I will call here a *biopolitical realism*. As I will explain below, among the other things it targets, biopolitical realism also questions, displaces and reconfigures the impulse to allegorical reading. It uses the 'not quite rightness' of weird affect to problematise the transitions between the real and the allegorical. I will now briefly turn to this term to explain why and then expand on it in Chapter 4.

WEIRD BIOPOLITICS

Asked to provide the main characteristic of the films made by him and his peers, Yorgos Lanthimos during an interview came up with the sentence that will serve as focal point in my third chapter: 'What interested us were the ways in which a family or a group is governed and what kind of impact this has on every member of the group'.

This phrase introduces (after allegory) the second issue I had to tackle as my inquiry grew larger. What I could see in all the films under study was their particularly persistent engagement with a certain type of *governing life*, of *politics over life*. Films such as *Dogtooth, Alps, The Lobster, Miss Violence, Attenberg, Suntan, Homeland, A Blast, Oiktos (Pity), Boy Eating the Bird's Food, Strella, Xenia, The Knifer, Washingtonia* and others mentioned briefly or analysed in this book were part of a broader arena of cultural production that registered a deep unease with the modern politics of surveillance, austerity management, control over life, state of exception and moral panic. To be sure, while this is a politics that characterises much of the contemporary world, it was particularly intensely felt in Greece and became the main topic of discussion there from 2008 onwards. During that long decade, one word kept cropping up in the Greek public debate to describe all this. It was a concept much debated after Michel Foucault had reintroduced it in the 1970s, and it has now become almost a household term (helped by the fact that it is based on two Greek words): βιοπολιτική, or biopolitics.

Foucault's understanding of the difference between a classical *sovereign power* and those forms of power that become more dominant in modernity (that is, the *disciplinary and the biopolitical power*) underlines how the latter two take hold of life in new and innovative ways: 'In the classical theory of sovereignty, the right of life and death was one of sovereignty's basic attributes [. . .] The right of sovereignty was the right to take life or let live. And then this new right is established: the right to make live and to let die' (2003: 240–1). This very modern conceptualisation of *biopower* – that form of power whose aim is no longer the sovereign's 'take life or let live' [*faire mourir ou laisser vivre*] but, on the contrary, 'to foster life or disallow it to the point of death' [*faire vivre ou laisser mourir*] (Foucault [1976] 1998: 138) – does not merely describe the intensification of power's concern with the health of the population as a whole and as a result also of the individual (Taylor 2011: 41–54). Rather, it points to a change by which politics over life *becomes* politics, redefines the political and reassesses its scope (Prozorov 2017: 328). Biopolitics describes a set of social and political practices that focus 'on disciplining the living being, on optimising its capabilities and extorting its forces so as to integrate corporeal life into systems of efficient and economic controls' (Väliaho 2014b: 105). It is actually this productive over-controlling of human life – and thus of diversifying the types of control in order to taxonomise, to marketise, to place within borders, frames and systems of reference, and to optimise it – that today has reached such a point of intensification that it might be said to characterise the historical period in which we live and perhaps even the very 'cultural logic of contemporary capitalism' (cf. Baumbach, Young and Yue 2016). This does not mean that there is a clear root, an announced rationale, an identifiable centre of biopolitical control: Instead, there is an archipelago of measures, points of incitement, control and calculation, systems of prediction and normativity. Contemporary biopolitics is not a global localisable power of oppression; it is an over-expansive and dominant logic of governance.

Most of the films I analyse in this book address the diffuse biopolitical nexus of power and thus do not aim to confront it directly as a localisable centre of control. Instead, they offer the opportunity to reflect on what develops (as a reaction, as a mode of address, as an ethics of relation and as a form of representation) when biopolitics entirely becomes the general context, the permanent background, the only way. This is how, I will argue, the Greek Weird Wave became a spectacular world example of *a cinema of biopolitics*. This is a type of cinema that we can see at the moment emerging also elsewhere – in Latin America, for instance, or in Southern Europe – adopting similar or different patterns, but certainly engaging as a cultural product of *our biopolitical present*.[15]

A cinema of biopolitics can undoubtedly be a term that covers not only other examples and types of world cinema, but also areas of cinema production beyond the fiction film – the documentary or the film essay are obvious examples. Even though I will briefly point to such examples as well (for instance, the documentary series *Microcities*, in Chapters 2 and 3), I mainly confine myself to an analysis of fiction films. I do so, first, for the sake of consistency and, more importantly, in order to follow the particular story of the Greek Weird Wave, which was identified as a new wave of fiction films. Nevertheless, it is my conviction that the triangulation allegory/biopolitics/weird has the potential to tell us something more, not only about the Greek Weird Wave, but also about the concept of Crisis and the larger cultural expression of our intense biopolitical present.

Biopolitics – in its various definitions, pathways and iterations – is a toolkit that will allow me to enter a new dialogue with the films in question, as well as their creative and cultural context. Yet, I also consider the biopolitical more broadly a dynamic constituting the political today and inflecting political art. This is what I will call throughout (and analyse in Chapter 4 as) the expansive socio-cultural modality of *biopolitical realism*.

Even though my use of the terms 'intense biopolitical present' and 'biopolitical realism' might seem like a sweeping attempt at periodisation, my description of a certain biopolitical present is intended to be heuristic. Rather than nominating a genre, a period and a specific chronology, I start from a very specific cultural example and specific time-span for one country. The biopolitical aspect of power has not only been intensely felt in this time and place, but it also seems to relate it to the world and provide its major cultural logic. In Chapter 2, I will relate this discussion to more specific debates about culture, politics and critique in our contemporary world of constantly mutating neo-capitalism and forms of control.

However, equally important for my discussion is what I have already tried to describe as a logic of counter-conduct: a much more diffuse, yet also much more pervasive, affective, playful and pensive reaction to an ill-fitting context. It is that feeling, after all, that draws me to a term such as 'weirdness'. As the anecdote about director Zois makes clear, I hope, I want to claim 'weirdness' as the very (affective, situational, experiential) state that results from the fact that one is very much governed by a script, yet also finds oneself somewhat lagging behind, being a little off-kilter, while at the same time being in constant and multiple frames, delimited, constrained and contained. I also claim 'weirdness' as the necessary emotional and affective outcome of the effort to interact with and speak about a biopolitical present.

As was the case with the framing of national allegory, weirdness as a counter-conduct in biopolitics should not be thought of as a denial of the historical moment or an escape from it. History makes a spectacular entry in the frames I am discussing, often unexpectedly, and often spectrally. The films of the Greek Weird Wave are not only found in an intense biopolitical present; they are also registered in a political, social and historical archive which is thrust upon them, even when they try to avoid it. I see this as the 'inescapable political and historical context' of the Greek Weird Wave and will thus analyse it in Chapter 3, where I also assess how this latest wave of Greek films performatively rearranges the existing narratives of Greek film history.

Throughout this study, my efforts are towards providing a close analysis of films, together with an exploration of their cultural context and their theoretical ramifications. Film Studies, Cultural Studies, as well as a style of participatory cultural observation that one could characterise as auto-ethnographic – these all play a methodological role in the book, which also owes a lot to specific debates in cultural, gender and social theory conducted in Greece and beyond over the past few decades.

DOING THE LAUNDRY: EMBODIMENT, METONYMY, ASSEMBLAGE

Since 2015, the national daily *Efimerida ton Sintakton* (*Newspaper of the Journalists*) publishes in its Saturday edition a cartoon under the banner 'The Dictionary of the Crisis'. According to the editors, it is an effort to 'dispel with cartoons those words which bombard our everyday life as a result of the Crisis' (Koukoulas 2015).[16] Every week, signed by a different cartoonist, the 'dictionary' is expanded by a visual take on a new word from contemporary Crisis

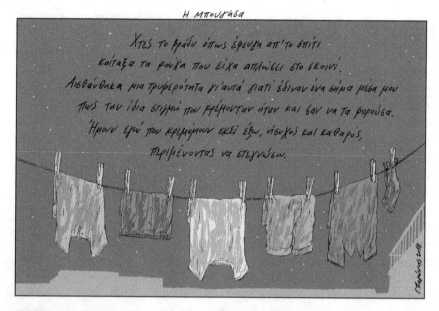

Figure I.4 *Gavriel Pagonis, 'The Laundry'. Copyright Gavriel Pagonis and* Efimerida ton
Sintakton.

politics: 'Privatisation', 'foreign investment', 'banking', 'European values',
'exit', 'anxiety', 'memory', 'waiting' and so on. On 7 July 2018, the word of
the week was 'The Laundry' (Η μπουγάδα). The one-panel cartoon, signed by
Gavriel Pagonis, showed a line of T-shirts and shorts hanging on a rooftop.
There was one long caption in the frame, which read:

> Yesterday evening, as I was leaving my house, I looked at the clothes I had
> hung on the washing line. I felt a tenderness for them; they were giving out a
> sign of life; as they were hanging it was almost as if I was still wearing them.
> It was me hanging out there, docile and clean, waiting to dry. (Pagonis 2018)

The humorous effect first rests on the over-appropriation of a metaphor
widely used during the financial crisis: Cleaning, clearing, sorting out and
tidying up have been central to the vocabulary of the Greek Crisis, as they
are also central to global neoliberal governmentality more generally. Yet,
this cartoon is extremely powerful in that we see in the picture and read in
the caption not merely a distanced visual metaphor. Somehow, a connection
of proximity, an experienced situation, one's body has entered the picture.
There is a disquieting suggestion that an impact on bodies and people has
been the aim of doing this type of 'laundry' all along. When new 'Crisis policies' talk about cleaning, they ultimately manage lives, create docile subjects
and hang bodies to dry.

The trope that helps this cartoon make a powerful point about the contemporary biopolitics of crisis is no longer a metaphor; rather, it is metonymy. The clothes lying 'out there', able to recall the body they contained, as well as the feeling of hanging, pending, being in suspension, create what a semiotician would call a long metonymical sequence, a chain of references that relate to each other through their proximity, their contiguous placement.

In the course of putting this book together, I realised that this move towards metonymy is much more extensive and plays a much more crucial role in my case-studies than I had first thought. As the following chapters will show, what emerges as a link between crisis, weirdness, allegory, biopolitics and biopolitical realism is a certain tendency towards metonymy that follows a pattern very similar to the one described in the newspaper cartoon: It becomes an expansive impulse. More precisely, it becomes a metonymical impulse towards assembling and collating references, reactions, gestures, embodiments and representations on the basis of their proximity, their seriality, their experience and their touch.

One of the tropes of ancient rhetoric – discussed in some ways by Aristotle, formalised by Quintilian and given a new life in modern theory after Roman Jakobson used it as the centre of his analysis of aphasia – metonymy is the rhetorical sibling of metaphor (Jakobson and Halle 1956: 90–96; Jakobson 1971; Matzner 2016). We tend to think of metaphor as a rhetorical and signifying trope where substitution (of a word, a concept, or an image) is based on analogy; something stands *for* something else on the basis of some sort of likeness. As many theorists have reminded us, the word comes from the Greek verb 'μεταφέρω', to carry over, and metaphor (μεταφορά) in contemporary Greek also means 'transfer'.

However, we tend to think of metonymy as based on contiguity and seriality; something stands *next to* something else in a signifying chain, on the basis of some form of proximity (cf. Jakobson and Halle 1956; Lodge 1977). As Barbara Johnson (2014) explains, 'in metonymy, substitution is based on a relation or association other than that of similarity (cause and effect, container and contained, proper name and qualities or works associated with it, place and event or institution, instrument and user, etc.)' (108). The word in Greek roughly translates as 'giving another (related) name'.

Of course, as happens in the laundry newspaper cartoon, metaphor and metonymy are seldom pure. They relate to each other on a continuum (cf. Dirven and Pörings 2002), which means that for the most part they come to be entangled and intertwined (cf. Genette 1972: 41–63; Culler 2001). Nevertheless, a push towards the metonymical side of this continuum often belies a radical historical and political possibility (Laclau 2014: 53–78; Greenfield 1998: 113–24).

As Brenda Machosky points out, within the hermeneutic process, 'metonymy is not primarily about "finding meaning" (by interpreting words); it is about understanding the structure of meaning (by focusing on words themselves)' (Machosky 2009: 194). In its wider cultural ramifications, this means that metonymy exposes and exploits differential meaning, networks, associations and the work of signification as it happens and is experienced; it also promotes non-resolution, process and chains of association, rather than a stable map of signification. A metonymical positioning and point of view often seems weird, precisely because it so very much foregrounds the frames and structures of meaning, as well as of the meaningful, of life and the livable. By showing the way in which they are imposed and standing at an (ironic) angle to them, it ends up destabilising them, too. Nevertheless, the structure of meaning and of sorting out is not the only thing foregrounded in this process. As the chapters of this book progress, another element will also become evident. Metonymy not only foregrounds signifying chains, but it also works *on* bodies and lives, *in* the biopolitical present. We as viewers are touched by the metonymies on screen; we are touched by a trope that functions by way of touch/proximity/adjacency. Furthermore, in the workings of the biopolitical present, the body, the population and the territory are (among other things) continuous and contiguous, yet (partly) in purely physical, non-figurative ways; we can say, for instance, that borders affect and mark bodies in literal, material and physical ways.

Most, if not all, of the film scenes that I will analyse in the following chapters employ metonymy at different levels – from the story to the *mise-en-scène*. They represent and invite metonymical readings. They are positioned in metonymical chains and focus on characters who find themselves in similar positionalities. At the centre of these films often appear characters for whom metonymy is, weirdly, the most political reaction that they can articulate, as they find themselves on stand-by, stranded, wandering, waving and exploring lines, (empty) structures, paths, walks and connections. This is exactly what the two characters played by Makis Papadimitriou do in *Letter to Yorgos Lanthimos* and *Suntan*, in the examples that I use in the opening chapter. It equally happens with the protagonists of the two films that close the book, *The Distance between Us and the Sky* and *Winona*. I use them as triggers to first tell the story of a biopolitical cinema in a linear fashion (background, emergence, first films and reactions) and then reposition the Weird Wave as a recurring question and continuing, unfinished process. The films on which I focus in the second chapter are the medium-length *Washingtonia* and *Third Kind* (again, with their characters stranded, wandering and exploring metonymical connections, as does the films' editing). They allow me to provide a lengthier analysis of biopolitics and the analytical possibilities that it offers for contemporary (Greek) cinema. Chapter 3 opens with a scene from *The Lobster* and then continues with a scene of Yorgos Lanthimos being interviewed for TV under the Parthenon. He finds himself in a position similar to that of Yorgos Zois in the interview I described in the previous section: a little lost and having to account for the Weird Wave's relationship to the socio-political context. He equally opts for a turn to metonymy, pointing to unexpected links and structures: not only to films hanging on the line, but also to people, to a community of artists and filmmakers who operate in Greece, making do with what is available and reflecting on this as a cultural practice. The chapter follows Lanthimos's cue and retells the story of *The Lost Highway of Greek Cinema*, an Athenian cinema collective that can be seen as exemplary of the groups and activities that supported the Weird Wave in its emergence and development.

If the first three chapters aim to tell (and retell) the story of the Weird Wave as a cinema of biopolitics, the remaining four propose keywords for further analysis: biopolitical realism (Chapter 4, with a focus on the films *Pity*, *Attenberg* and *Alps*); discipline and allegory (Chapter 5, with a focus on *Miss Violence* and *Dogtooth*); archive trouble (Chapter 6, with a focus on the stage multimedia production *The City-State* and the film *Homeland*); and assemblage (Chapter 7; on the films *Mum, I'm Back* and *Strella*). The way in which these keywords are presented is not coincidental. In the earlier chapters, the world of biopolitical realism looks impossible to break, and a metonymical impulse seems to be either a cry of desperation or an (equally desperate) ironic reflex. Yet, in the later chapters, metonymy becomes the trope for the more productive poetics described as 'archive trouble' and 'assemblage'.

All these keywords reflect on a world of biopolitical realism and thematise the impulse towards framing and reframing, collecting, collating and assembling. If biopolitical realism looks weird, it is precisely because of its unexpected touch, its sudden push-back against the endless metonymies constituting the real. This goes some way towards explaining why metonymy itself is not given a chapter of its own – simply because, like biopolitics and the concept of the weird, metonymy is everywhere.

I have started my inquiry by following the weird as an analytical, conceptual and largely cultural challenge that a type of filmmaking in biopolitics produces. As the first chapters will explain, this means that the main argument develops processually. Metonymy emerged as an overarching mode, and even as a mode of writing and movement from one theme to another. Therefore, one of the last questions binding this book together became the following: How does metonymy relate to the weird and the allegorical, and why is this important in a culture of biopolitics?

'WHY DO YOU TOUCH ME?' METONYMIC INTIMACY

In the next chapters I repeatedly underline a personal question that I have always had while watching these films: Why do they affect me so much? Why do even their most absurd, idiosyncratic, unexpected and intellectually difficult gestures move me? How do they touch me?

I soon realised that this was a question shared by many around me. Why and how did these films draw us in? My tentative answer, and one that slowly developed as an argument over the course of this book, is that their metonymic chains, especially as they are often weird and hard to make sense of, foreground principles of continuity for the spectator. This leads to a sense of (or questions about) contiguity/continuity between the film/viewer/biopolitical life, a feeling of being inside that triangulation.

'This is not a scene I have ever experienced; this is too far from my own life; yet, why does it touch me?' This question, which I often repeated while watching these films and which I will also repeat in this book (see, for instance, Chapter 5), is another way of saying that there exists a certain metonymic relation, that I am becoming alert to the fact that the world on screen, the world outside, and the viewer in time and space in front of the screen all touch each other.

Classic film semiotics, starting from a point made by Jakobson, has often associated metonymy with (some types of) montage and, eventually, with the film narrative, the way in which the story is propelled forward on a syntagmatic horizontal axis along which shots are combined (Jakobson and Halle 1956: 92; Metz 1977: 197–206; Andrew 1984: 164–71). Interestingly, theorist Mark Fisher has also associated montage with the weird as a concept. 'The form that is perhaps most appropriate to the weird is montage', he maintains, 'the conjoining of *two or more things which do not belong together*' (Fisher 2017: 11). There is, certainly, something weird and powerful in collating – as classic semiotic analysis of surrealist film or of assemblage art would underline. But I consider the point as having a more general value. There is a sense of the weird when conceptual and/or visual montage is underlined as such, or when contiguous relations are emphasised, and even more so when they are proposed as possibly rearrangable. In this study I underline films where weird metonymies come to play a major role through cinematic montage (such as *Washingtonia*, in Chapter 2, or *Country of Origin* in Chapter 6). However, I am also following metonymy as it works on other levels (and not necessarily based on montage): in shot construction (as in *Dogtooth*, in Chapter 5, or *The Distance Between Us and the Sky* in the Epilogue), in the way in which characters place their body in space (as in *Attenberg*, in Chapter 4), in the way in which sites are being used (as in *Third Kind*, in Chapter 3), in the way in which framing operates in the films (for instance, in *Oiktos/Pity*, in Chapter 4, and *Miss Violence*, in Chapter 5)[17] and in the way in which the family dynamic is positioned as a synecdoche of the social and the national (in *Miss Violence*, *Country of Origin*, *Mum, I'm back* and *Strella*, in Chapters 5, 6 and 7, respectively). Last, but not least, I follow it in the way in which metonymic poetics replicate strategies of governmentality in a biopolitical world, inviting the viewer to contemplate these connections, as I suggest more prominently in the last chapters. Weird poetics is not simply a *mise-en-abyme* of weird biopolitics (the film thus reproducing *in vitro* the power structures of the world whence it comes), but a more complex entanglement also based on contiguity.

To put it in another way, there is something in the biopolitical world that makes weird engagement a productive position. There is something in the biopolitical that turns forms of metonymic positioning into a productive arrangement: from cinematic montage to assemblage as an artistic or as a post-identitarian or critical practice; and from rearranging an archive to reperforming assembly in public space. With 'productive arrangement' I describe a survival tactic, a form of making do, a way for one to be realistic about biopolitics, as well as a survival tactic to do realism in biopolitics, to do biopolitical realism. This might come as a surprise to the remaining few followers of classic models of cinematic realism (for example, Andre Bazin's) which tend to see montage-driven narratives (for instance, the early Soviet films or Hollywood action films) in some ways as the opposite of a cinematic realism exemplified in Bazin's reading of Rossellini and Italian neo-realism (see Nagib and Mello 2009: xiv–xxvi, for a brilliant explanation of how complicated the picture is). Yet, this is exactly the point I am making in Chapter 3, where I introduce the concept of biopolitical realism – playing, as I have already done here, with the idea of 'being realistic' with an intense biopolitical present, as well as proposing it as a different attitude towards both the concept and the doing of realism.

In biopolitical realism, it is easy to see why metonymy is associated with montage and framing, with the weird, with allegory, with biopolitics. This is what I am trying to foreground in my last two chapters. The cultural poetics of *archive trouble* that I discuss in Chapter 6 is a metonymic poetics that engages creatively with the biopolitical present. This is also the case with *assemblage*, with which I conclude my analysis in Chapter 7. Following a discussion that I can only briefly indicate here, I introduce assemblage as a cultural poetics in/for/of biopolitics which, precisely because of its metonymic dynamic, can also offer unsettling, potentially radical positionalities.

Even though every chapter analyses one or two well-known films from the Weird Wave, it does not rest solely on them (nor does it aim to offer their full analysis). It often counterposes the analysis of other, lesser-known or -circulated films and videos. Nevertheless, the structure is not determined by these case-studies. Instead, I often return to the same films or move the discussion to other types of material, including theoretical works, other cultural and social trends, as well as types of cultural text of the past or present. Metonymy as a mode, and the cultural/social practices analysed in the last chapters as archive trouble and assemblage, might perhaps also offer a way of reading how this book has been put together: in the effort to show not only connections, but also to underline how these cultural texts are contiguously related, how they touch each other, how they are touched and touching, how an affective contiguity binds this material together. This is a very personal, very idiosyncratic, very weird history of the Weird Wave. It does, therefore, propose itself as standing in a symbiotic relation with other studies that in recent years have appeared on the same or other important Greek films of the twenty-first century.

Last, but not least, my present approach goes against understandings of the Weird Wave as too intellectual, dissociated, or even heartless and 'unloving', as a comment I quote in Chapter 1 suggests. I beg to differ. Biopolitical realism means that metonymic chains such as those I will trace in the following pages are not only the ones already organising 'reality'; they also unlock, as they weirdly develop, a much-needed intimacy. Even though not yet a full-fledged revolutionary affect, this is an intimacy able to exploit the fact that it overflows from (and thus can stand as something more than) a (bio)political project.

Notes

1. Available at https://www.thewrap.com/dogtooth-drama-takes-cannes-prize-un-certain-regard-3270/ (last accessed 16 June 2020).
2. A piece of information that was lost, at least initially, in the international reception of the Weird Wave was that many of the actors who played a prominent role in its first films were also key figures in a newly emerging physical and avant-garde theatre scene in Athens after 2004. Arianne Labed was a co-founder of the theatre group Vasistas (and the screenwriter Efthimis Filippou was a frequent collaborator), while Angeliki Papoulia and Christos Passalis were key members of the group Blitz, and Mary Tsoni was one half of the avant-garde performance duo Mary and the Boy, the other half being Alexandros Voulgaris, whose cinematic work I will discuss in the Epilogue of this book.
3. Rose's article is an impressive piece of journalistic writing, but several of its assertions do not survive critical scrutiny –for instance, the matter-of-fact mention of Panos Koutras's new queer films as high up on 'the strangeness scale'. It is clear from the way in which I discuss this article that I do not share its views. What I find worth pursuing is the 'weird feeling' it describes as the critic's response to these films, as well as the article's own, plentiful awkward moments.

4. Apart from *Dogtooth*, *Alps* and *Attenberg*, Rose mentions in his article a series of completely diverse films: *Wasted Youth*, *Homeland*, *The Knifer* and *Strella*.

5. Marios Psaras in his accomplished *The Queer Greek Weird Wave* (2016) does something similar, by exploring the semantic affinities of the concepts 'queer' and 'weird' – an opening that allows him to pursue a valuable exploration of the films of the Greek Weird Wave through the optics of Queer Theory.

6. There already exists an entry on Greek Weird Wave in the IMDB list (https://www.imdb.com/list/ls025579433/), countless lists of 'Top Greek Weird Films' online (see, for instance, http://www.tasteofcinema.com/2016/the-10-best-movies-of-the-greek-weird-wave/), international festival retrospectives (see, for instance, http://www.mumbaifilmfestival.com/blogs/getting-to-grips-with-the-greek-weird-wave/) and a number of focused university syllabi. For a precise mapping of the use of the term 'weird wave' in criticism and the media, see Sifaki and Stamou 2020.

7. Available at http://www.dogme95.dk/the-vow-of-chastity/ (last accessed 16 June 2020).

8. Nikolaidou and Poupou (2018: 19–20) have recently developed a persuasive counter-argument. They point out specific formative moments that allow us to talk about a cinematic movement in this case, too: the founding of the group 'Filmmakers in the FOG' which I discuss in Chapter 1; the collective text 'Who is Fucking Greek Cinema?' distributed by the Greek Film Directors and Producers Guild in the 58th Thessaloniki Film Festival (2017); and the establishment of new international journals that focus on Greek cinema and put together early special issues on the New/Weird Wave, such as *Filmicon* and the *Journal of Greek Media and Culture*. Last, but not least, 'the various texts and interviews of a number of directors (such as Syllas Tzoumerkas, Babis Makridis, Alexandros Voulgaris) can be seen as parts of an informal manifesto, whose shaping is processual and happens mainly online and in the social networks' (20).

9. A good example is the streaming channel MUBI, which in 2018 ran for several months its own promotional campaign with a still from *Dogtooth* as its central image. A major supporter of recent Greek Cinema, MUBI tends to call almost all the new Greek films it distributes 'Greek Weird Wave examples'.

10. Olga Kourelou rightfully claims that in the 1960s, another period when Greek Cinema became international, it eventually faced the accusation that it promoted an exoticised version of Greece (with films such as Michael Cacoyannis's *Zorba the Greek* and Jules Dassin's *Never on Sunday* with Melina Mercouri). The Greek directors of the 2010s run a similar risk – that is, 'the danger of fetishising a post-industrial primitivism, embodied by the corrupt and abusive patriarchs that populate their films' (Kourelou et al. 2014: 142).

11. The global distribution of *Casus Belli* after 2011 very clearly shows the level of expectation for that type of a 'cinema of the Crisis' from Greece. The film was shown at numerous festivals, and its broadcasting rights were bought by TV channels around the world. In the period between April and December 2012, *Casus Belli* was shown on the French-German channel ARTE no fewer than five times.

12. Originally a phrase to describe Sam Fuller's filming of the concentration camps (see Nagib 2011: 10 and 28–29, on the origin and history of both Moullet's and Godard's phrases).

13. The French-German channel ARTE has been one of the most consistent supporters of the Greek Weird Wave in terms of production and promotion, and it can be considered one of the shaping forces for its European reception. This is one of the reasons why I often quote from its programmes and interviews with Greek directors.

14. As Ismail Xavier has memorably described, 'allegories usually rise from controversies' and moments of crisis (1999: 334). Even though it is possible to distinguish between an allegorical work (where the allegory is integrated in the structure, provoked, anticipated) and allegorical readings of works 'that do not specifically encourage such deciferement' (343), more often the line between the two cannot be easily drawn. This will be the case with most of the examples in this book (see, for instance, the discussion of *Washingtonia* in Chapter 2, *Pity* and *Attenberg* in Chapter 4, or *Dogtooth* in Chapter 5): In their case the chain of allegorical 'intention-utterance-interpretation is so complex', that one cannot discuss allegory 'without dealing with both the structure of texts and their reception within specific cultural and social contexts' (337, 335).

15. I reread these paragraphs while observing the global reaction to the COVID-19 emergency and the novel forms of social life and politics over life that the new management of populations brought about in 2020. The phrase 'our intense biopolitical present' no longer seems in need of further explanation. Yet, what happened globally in 2020 also felt like a *déjà vu*, a scenario for which we were already prepared by a wide and diverse cultural engagement with the biopolitical aspects of our societies over the last few decades.

16. In the special supplement on comics and the graphic novel, which the *Newspaper of the Journalists* publishes every Saturday, the Crisis has been an ongoing major focus. Between 2013 and 2015, for instance, a special page was devoted to documenting the Μέρα της Κρίσεως, a phrase that in Greek can mean both 'Judgement Day' and 'The Day of the Crisis'.

17. I mention framing specifically because it sits awkwardly with a post-Metzian semiotic analysis that tends to see this level of the film – shot composition, *mise-en-scène* and so on – as the domain of the metaphorical. Of course, there already exist numerous different approaches to framing and the axis of metaphor/metonymy, starting with Metz's own diverse positions.

Part I

Process:
The Weird Wave of Greek Cinema
and the Cinema of Biopolitics

'There Are No Words to Describe Our National Pride': Weird Walks, Awkward Crisiscapes and the Most International Moment of Greek Cinema

LETTER TO YORGOS LANTHIMOS

Dear Yorgos, there are no words to describe the national pride we all feel these days . . .

In the week leading up to the Ninety-First Academy Awards Ceremony in 2019, the Association of Greek Cinema Directors and Producers (ESPEK) released a video to wish Lanthimos good luck. His third English-language feature film, *The Favourite*, had been nominated for ten Oscars, the culmination of an international reception that included the Grand Jury Prize at the Seventy-Fifth Venice Film Festival, an array of Golden Globes, Baftas and other mentions during that 'award season'. The film eventually won Olivia Colman the Academy Award for the best performance by an actress in a leading role.

The Greek Cinema Association's video is titled *Letter to Yorgos Lanthimos*,[1] and it was filmed in the seaside town of Kinetta, the location of Lanthimos's first feature-length film of note in 2005, *Kinetta*. It starts with actor Makis Papadimitriou, well-known from a spate of recent Greek films such as *Chevalier, A Blast* and *Suntan*, reading the first lines of his 'letter' to the famous director while on a coach heading to Kinetta. He continues via voice-over while we see him wandering through empty streets, beaches and hotels.

> Dear Yorgos, there are no words to describe the national pride we all feel these days. We are counting your Oscar nominations over and over again and cheering out loud. And yet, you see, I always expected it because I always believed in you and in Greek Cinema. You may now be walking around Santa Monica, surrounded by glamorous stars and relentless paparazzi. But I always remember that things had their beginning on another, more humble beach. A beach by the name of Kinetta . . .
>
> Above all else, Greek Cinema needs love. You know this better than anyone, Yorgos. And, of course, while you make Greek Cinema famous around the world, we remember all the reasons that are keeping you away [from Greece].

At that point, trailers file past at the bottom of the screen, listing the reasons that might cause a Greek director to be disillusioned with the state of Greek Cinema: 'Lack of strategy. Lack of coordination. Lack of funding. Inefficient institutions. Lack of support by the Ministry of Culture. The indifference of the Greek state'. It ends with a slogan addressed to all these institutional figures, but, in a way, also to spectators: 'Give a Little Loving to Greek Cinema'.[2]

The association's video, therefore, may have started as a celebration of their most famous colleague's international achievement; yet, it ends as a tongue-in-cheek reminder of the current state of Greek Cinema. The viewer is reminded that this is a national cinema which, at least since 2009 – in the years coinciding with what the Greek and international press has called 'the Greek Crisis' – has . . .

- not ceased making films invited to (and frequently given awards at) international festivals;
- seen the emergence of a new generation of filmmakers (the community 'speaking' to their peer Lanthimos in the video) who are regarded by international as well as national critics and informed audiences as a closely-knit group, although this may not be quite the case;
- created a clear point of reference with milestone films that have already produced a canon of sorts: *Dogtooth* (2009), *Strella* (2009), *Attenberg* (2010), *Homeland* (2010), *Alps* (2011), *Boy Eats the Bird's Food* (2012), *Miss Violence* (2013), *Chevalier* (2014) and *Suntan* (2016);
- become the platform for the emergence of local production companies with a significant international presence in World Cinema after 2010 (Faliron productions, Haos films, Homemade films, Heretic);[3]
- used a number of actors who are now recognizable to the general public in Greece and abroad for their participation in characteristic roles (Angeliki Papoulia, Makis Papadimitriou, Arianne Labed, Vangelis Mourikis, Sofia Kokkali, Errikos Litsis); and, last but not least,
- had to face a number of problems, including the lack of institutional support and funding, issues very typical of what has been called 'the Cinema of Small Nations' (Hjort 2005; see Chapter 3).

The video-letter to Lanthimos makes apt reference to two further, less obvious issues. The first is the gap between the international recognition that Greek Cinema is receiving and the relatively low appeal of these films in Greece itself. The 2019 campaign to 'Give a Little Loving to Greek Cinema' (of which this video became the most notable moment) was aimed not only at state and cultural institutions, but also at the Greek public, which, at first glance, does not seem to have embraced very enthusiastically the most famous cultural product of Greece during the years of the 'Greek Crisis' – namely, its cinema (cf. Flix Team 2018).

'You are lying to your friends, ashamed to confess that you have not seen *Dogtooth*? There is no reason anymore, because we are now offering all of the famous director's films for free on our Films on Demand platform'. This was the main slogan of an advertising campaign to attract new subscribers to a Greek mobile phone network after the release of *The Favourite* in Greece (Politakis 2019). It demonstrates in practice the shared feeling that the most recent Greek Cinema has not had as many viewers as it should have, but it also exploits the opposite idea: that it enjoys very wide recognition and is still today being watched and promoted on channels other than the traditional cinema distribution network.[4]

At the same time, the *Letter to Yorgos Lanthimos* appears to be something of an inside joke, too, as it directly refers to the style and setting of several well-known recent Greek films and playfully reenacts specific scenes. Kinetta, the area where Makis Papadimitriou walks as he reads his letter to Lanthimos, is a lower-middle-class tourist resort a short distance from Athens, characterised today by environmental neglect, abandoned buildings and ample evidence of underfunding, largely resulting from a previous period of over-development as well as a decade of austerity that has hit the lower middle class particularly hard. A scene with someone walking in the empty streets of Kinetta, especially in winter, in front of closed-up houses, run-down sidewalks and badly maintained cement structures, feels suddenly imbued with a sense of allegory – or, more precisely, a national allegory. Add to this a number of strange moments: characters wearing clothes that do not fit, the film's rhythm unexpectedly slowing down, the camera adopting peculiar angles and often ending up fragmenting bodies and objects or turning them upside down. In this weird scenery, a weird monologue is presented as a letter and weirdly filmed. Even if one is reluctant to do so, even if one maintains adherence to the video's obvious realism, one has already begun to watch allegorically what is on screen. The desolate and abandoned landscape makes one think of the country; the more the framing becomes precarious, the more one thinks of the country in Crisis.

The story that this book narrates is called (depending on the occasion and who is doing the telling) 'Greek Weird Wave', 'Greek New Wave', or 'The Greek Cinema of the Crisis', and this is exactly what is being invoked as the background to this *Letter to Yorgos Lanthimos*. The story begins a few years earlier and, for the sake of context, it is worth picking it up from that earlier moment.

Figure 1.1a–b *Makis Papadimitriou weirding it up in* Letter to Yorgos Lanthimos *(Vassilis Katsoupis, 2019); digital stills.*

STORM IN A MATCHBOX

Matchbox, the eighty-minute film by Yannis Economides, was made in 2001. It first appeared as a work in progress at the Forty-Third Thessaloniki International Film Festival in November 2002 and was released in Greek theatres in March 2003. Subsequently, it won the 2003 Greek Film Critics Association Award. At that point, it remained almost unnoticed by the Greek public or international festivals. Today, however, it has achieved cult status, and Greeks, especially younger generations, often make jokes based on the film's central scenes.[5] This reputation is largely owed to the film's continuous circulation in DVD format and as television reruns in the years after its initial release, to scenes having become online memes and samples in popular songs, and to later theatrical versions that attracted considerable coverage.[6] It would not be an exaggeration to say that even the word 'matchbox' has become synonymous with a particularly Greek family dynamic; for some, it has also become a keyword for a turning point in Greek Cinema.[7]

I do not know if *Matchbox* emerged, as one might put it, 'ahead of its time', but it is clear that many of its early viewers undoubtedly felt they did not really understand what the film was about. One critic told me years later:

> I remember watching it at a festival and most of the people were leaving the room after the first scenes; only the Greeks in the audience remained, alongside a couple of Japanese critics, who kept asking us whether all Greek families were like that. It was very difficult for them to take in a film where nothing happens apart from yelling, bullying, cursing, and a constant exchange of emotional attacks and extreme psychological violence between the members of a family inside their home.

Indeed, even today it is difficult to watch *Matchbox* without experiencing a strong reaction. In the film, a petty bourgeois family finds itself stuck at home during a heat wave and, for eighty minutes, devours its own flesh: without much of a plot, the whole film is taken up by each sweating family member relentlessly shouting abuse at every other member. The claustrophobic atmosphere continues to the end, without even a door opening to allow some air into this family's closed-off *nouveau riche* house.[8]

Matchbox premiered in Greece at a time when nearly everyone was still preoccupied with the coming 'miracle of the 2004 Olympic Games', fixated on what the country would be showcasing during those games. What eventually took place in the summer of 2004 was, to a large extent, based on last-minute make-overs and overspending on projects that would be abandoned soon after. Everywhere in Athens trees where planted to grow during the summer of 2004, but they would dry up within a few months. Many of the illustrious sports venues would stand dilapidated within a few years – becoming the ideal setting for films about social stagnation, marginalised youth and national decline, such as Sofia Exarchou's *Park* (2016; cf. Barotsi 2016). Yet, such imagery was at that point far in the future, still unthinkable at the time when *Matchbox* hit Greek screens.

At the start of the new millennium Greece seemed to be prosperous and, crucially, united in a spirit of national buoyancy which it had not experienced for decades. A national revival was being celebrated, with flags on buildings and people taking to the streets on every possible occasion to bask in national pride. The nation celebrated events such as the homecoming of athletes who had won medals in international competitions; the Greek team winning the Euro 2004 football championship in June of that year; eventually all the key moments of the 2004 Olympic Games (and certainly those that included Greek medals); and even Elena Paparizou's victory in the 2005 Eurovision Song Contest with the song *My Number One*. With a nation in such high spirits, there was not much cultural space for a film set inside four walls, portraying a Greek family far removed from the stereotype of the 'Holy Greek family' (Papanikolaou 2018a). In *Matchbox*, viewers were confronted with a family in strife and panic, constantly at war with itself and bragging about its newly acquired material wealth. None of this exactly fit with the projected image of Greece and Hellenism that was being actively promoted and performed at the time.

There were undoubtedly some people who thought that the nervous and excessive atmosphere of *Matchbox* offered a realistic glimpse of the rifts found behind closed doors in Greek homes (Katsounaki 2003). But even they would have agreed that it was not a suitable image for international circulation. Certainly, no one at the time, at least publicly, was ready to see this image of a profound, persistent and painful inner crisis as an allegory of a whole country.

A few years later, however, after December 2008, many had cause to think back to that tension, perhaps even to *that* film. On 6 December 2008, fifteen-year-old Alexandros Grigoropoulos was shot in the central Athens neighborhood of Exarcheia by an on-duty policeman; he died on the spot. The event acted as the spark that threw the country of 'national revival' and of clean and well-kept bodies (of sportswomen and sportsmen, or of tourists bathing on its shores) into disarray. Immediately following the killing of Grigoropoulos, Greece's youth took to the streets to demonstrate, energetically demanding the right for their voice to be heard in the public sphere, calling for a general strike and denouncing the entire social structure as corrupt (Tsilimpounidi and Walsh 2014; Dalakoglou and Vradis 2011). The country that wanted to be internationally associated with the choreographed ceremony that marked the lighting of the Olympic flame (cf. Plantzos 2012) suddenly became the country whose streets (with names equally taken from ancient Greek history and mythology) would burn uncontrollably. In December 2008, images of the Athens' Christmas tree burning on Syntagma Square, a culmination of the demonstrations as well as of days of looting and burning, were seen around the world. These images of Athens experiencing extreme unrest would often be repeated and internationally circulated in the years to come (Papanikolaou 2014; Poupou 2019; Plantzos 2019b; Kalantzis 2016). They would attain a symbolic power, at times aestheticised as revolutionary imagery, as in Chris Marker's *December Seeds – A Short Film on the Greek Revolt* (2008).

FILMMAKERS IN THE *FOG*, *STRELLA*, *DOGTOOTH*

After December 2008, everything in Greece was suddenly being called into question, and the international financial crisis, which had slowly started becoming a national one, paradoxically seemed to amplify this more general movement of contestation and anti-authoritarian protest. In this atmosphere, a new generation of Greek filmmakers, most of them in their thirties and forties, decided to take action. They argued that the traditional financing, production and support systems of Greek Cinema had been the major reason for its stagnation and introversion, and so they called for change. They labelled themselves *Filmmakers in the Fog* (Κινηματογραφιστές στην Ομίχλη), playing not only with the acronym FOG – Filmmakers of Greece – but also with the title of a 1988 film by the modernist master director Theo Angelopoulos, *Landscape in the Mist* (Τοπίο στην ομίχλη). In that earlier Angelopoulos film, two children are crossing Greece in search of their father; yet, what they finally find – at the border, in the eponymous mist, in the new, or in another, world – is a tiny piece of undeveloped celluloid. In their first meetings and their initial official statements, *Filmmakers in the FOG* underlined their wish to shape a new period of Greek Cinema without the patronising presence of 'forefathers' and the suffocating control of old production networks. Moreover, they wished to find, not unlike the children in Angelopoulos' film, a lost link, not so much to the past, but to the future.[9]

Two very different fiction films that appeared in Greek theatres almost simultaneously in the winter of 2009 became the iconic representatives of this new movement. Interestingly, they were both films on (different Greek) families and seemed to pick up the thread from where *Matchbox* had left it a few years earlier. The first was *Strella: A Woman's Way*, directed by Panos Koutras, with a script co-written with author and queer activist Panagiotis Evangelidis. It tells the story of an optimistic and resourceful trans woman and her passionate and traumatic love affair with an older man just out of jail who, over the course of the film, is revealed to be her abusive father. It premiered at the Panorama Section of the 2009 Berlin Film Festival – the very year and place where, as it turned out, Theo Angelopoulos would show his last completed film, *The Dust of Time*, out of competition. *Strella* soon became a platform for gender and queer identity and politics in Greece; the debate around it focused not on the scandal of incest, but on alternative kinship, sexual citizenship and the secretive, oppressive mechanisms of the Greek family.

The other film of the year was *Dogtooth* by Yorgos Lanthimos, based on a script co-written with Efthimis Filippou. It premiered in May 2009 in Cannes where it earned the prestigious 'Un certain regard' prize. In *Dogtooth*, a family of five lives cut off from the rest of the world in their comfortable suburban home. They are all under the absolute authority of the domineering father, who is the only one who can leave the enclosure and who provides (literally, symbolically and in the grey areas that lie between) for all the members of the family. The children have been barred from going outside and have never seen the world beyond their garden fence. Their life consists of the indoctrination, training, disciplining and 'caring' regimes organised by the patriarch with the help of his wife. It is a life seemingly unperturbed, until the eldest daughter starts breaking ranks with the children's induced docility.

Strella and *Dogtooth* were very different in terms of form, storyline and directorial style. Both, however, placed the family at centre stage. They presented it, once again, more than seven years after *Matchbox*, as a site of hidden trauma and violence. Yet, in both films, at least one protagonist was shown as trying to break out and escape from the suffocating environment – prompting critics here to discern a new 'cinema of emancipation' (Chalkou 2012). With their successful runs on the international festival circuit also ensuring a wide distribution in countries outside Greece, these two films did something that Greek cinema had not seen for years: They created a buzz and provoked international debate.

In those same months, Greece was entering the period that would soon be formally known as 'the Greek Crisis', the local variant of the international financial crisis triggered by the 2008 collapse of the Lehmann Brothers' international financial services firm and the subprime markets, which kickstarted a chain of events around the world. A sovereign debt crisis in Greece followed, bringing the country to the verge of bankruptcy and eventually causing one of the most dramatic drops in living standards, wages and pensions seen in Western Europe since World War II, as well as an enormous increase in taxes and unemployment. Throughout the winter of 2009–10, as *Strella* and *Dogtooth* were still on their screens, Greeks kept hearing about economic failures, big hurdles difficult to overcome, thresholds that had been exceeded, European partners pushing for drastic solutions and a society about to explode. While during those months two prominent films in the theatres were about families at the point of a meltdown, at the same time the Greek prime minister and the 'European partners' were talking about the need to save the country, all together, like one big family.

In the most iconic media event of the period, on 23 April 2010, then Prime Minister George Papandreou gave a dramatic televised address to the nation, from the border island of Kastelorizo. He announced that he would resort to the EU and IMF's support mechanism 'so that Greece could stand on its own

Yesterday the facts about the real magnitude of the deficit of 2009 were made public.

Figure 1.2   Prime Minister Papandreou announcing on national TV Greece's official application to the IMF. Source: Vimeo; digital still.

feet' and be offered 'a sheltered harbour'. Watching him give his speech that day, it was not difficult to think that he was assuming the posture of a caring father; that the small port of Kastelorizo where he was filmed delivering his address looked like an enclosure, a desperately narrow strait, symbolising the idea that no escape was available; and that the colourful, picturesque houses and the blue waters of the scenery behind the prime minister were carefully chosen in order to reassure viewers that everything would be fine. Watching George Papandreou speaking that morning in the port of Kastelorizo, many people did, in fact, think of images of the father in *Dogtooth* gazing straight at the camera while preparing to address the members of his family.[10]

Two weeks later, on 10 May 2010, the Megaron Concert Hall in Athens hosted a modest ceremony to hand out their first 'Greek Film Academy' awards. The academy was the brainchild of the *Filmmakers in the FOG*, and its awards were meant as a sign of their independence and the fresh air they wanted to bring to the production, distribution and recognition of Greek Cinema. Unlike previous generations who had relied for recognition on the main state-run film events of the country, the Thessaloniki Film Festival and the State Film Awards (Chalkou 2008: 31), this new generation of filmmakers was ready to rewrite the rules and organise its own 'Film Academy' and annual awards, which in the following years would become more important

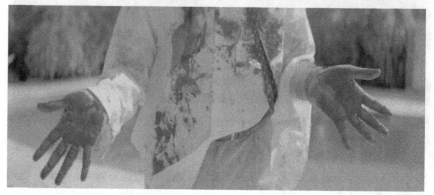

Figure 1.3a–b *Christos Stergioglou as the father in* Dogtooth *(Yorgos Lanthimos, 2009); digital stills.*

than all the other accolades awarded for Greek Cinema. The two films that emerged triumphant at that year's First Greek Film Academy Awards were, predictably, *Dogtooth* and *Strella*.

On the very same day as the FOG Academy Awards were being held, Greece also formally submitted its application for membership in the 'financial support mechanism', a move that would pave the way for a long series of rescue packages and extreme austerity programmes known in the country as *Mnimonia* (Memoranda of Understanding between Greece and the lenders).[11]

THE ACCIDENTAL BIRTH OF A NEW WAVE

Even if all these events were a series of coincidences, they were nevertheless enough to establish a lasting connection between the 'Greek Crisis' and these two films, *Dogtooth* and *Strella*, as well as a new wave of Greek Cinema which they now were seen to be spearheading. This was especially true for international critics and the media, who were eagerly searching for visual narratives and symbolic images in order to illustrate the events unfolding in the country. Alongside the graffiti on the iconic buildings of Athens and streets filled with demonstrators, a central photo from *Dogtooth* – in a scene at once familiar and paradoxical, the children are lined up in a room specially decorated for a family celebration – for years remained a widely used symbolic illustration of the cultural, economic, social and political state of Greece.

The idea of the 'short-circuiting' family at the centre of these films became thus intertwined with the period as its most iconic subject-matter: 'Is the family the seed of evil in Greek society? Is it a rage-breeding machinery, which is piling up its produce from one generation to the next?' (Katsounaki 2010). This is what Greek journalists and critics wondered, as films (and soon also theatrical plays, art exhibitions, novels and poetry collections) about the family started accumulating. As new films kept gaining international distribution, *The Guardian*'s cinema critic Steve Rose, in the text that I discussed above and as one of the earliest to use the term 'Weird Wave', concluded with the rhetorical question: 'Is it just coincidence that the world's most messed-up country is making the world's most messed-up cinema?' (Rose 2011).

In the following years, partly relying on this international interest, Greek Cinema produced some of its most debated (and award-winning) films. A circle centred on the directors Yorgos Lanthimos, Athina Rachel Tsangari, Babis Makridis and the scriptwriter Efthimis Filippou created films that appealed to international film audiences precisely for their awkwardness: *Dogtooth*, *Attenberg*, *Alps*, *L*, *Chevalier*, *The Lobster* and *The Killing of a Sacred Deer*. All these are dominated by irony and the filming of empty (often urban) spaces. Paradoxical or absurdist moments of storytelling, open endings, sudden scenes of violence and a tendency towards visual allegory are combined with a deadpan delivery by the actors, mechanical or distanced acting and sequences in which someone tries to assert complete control over others' bodies and/or consciousness (hence the many scenes in hospitals and educational settings, as well as the many scenes of training . . . dogs). When international critics refer to the 'Weird Wave of Greek Cinema', they mostly have these elements in mind; interestingly, this association occurs even when these characteristics are not present in the Greek films they watch. 'Weird' may have started as an effect that some directors (especially Yorgos Lanthimos and Babis Makridis) were eager to provoke. However, it now seems to have become less of a label and more of an umbrella term, a way to introduce the Greek Cinema of the period and the films of many more filmmakers, to see it as a collective effort and in context (see Mademli 2018; Nikolaidou 2020; Nikolaidou and Poupou 2017; Westlake 2014).

Of course, not all the Greek films of the last fifteen years were made in the form just described. Yannis Economides, after *Matchbox*, continued to create films (and directed theatre performances) in which overblown violence questioned the kinship and social foundations of Greek society (*Soul Kicking* [2006], *The Knifer* [2010] and *Stratos* [2014]). Panos Koutras complemented *Strella* with *Xenia* (2014), another new queer film about Greek society, belonging and the challenges of ethnic and sexual citizenship (Papanikolaou 2020). Syllas Tzoumerkas, Filippos Tsitos, Konstantina Voulgari, Thanos Anastopoulos, Ektoras Lygizos and Yannis Sakaridis worked within a complex social realism and a more straightforward thematisation of Greek society during the crisis, often with an emphasis on the subcultures and social movements created during these years in the bigger cities. Elina Psykou, Alexis Alexiou, Angelos Frantzis, Alexandros Voulgaris, Giorgos Georgopoulos and Yiannis Velsemes explored film genre, often in an overtly allegorical mode.

Not all of these films were centred on the Greek family, as *Matchbox*, *Strella*, *Attenberg* and *Dogtooth* had been. Still, kinship networks and the system of gender and sexuality have more often than not been one of their main subjects, especially the power structures that make up these areas of human life and the various economies of violence and affect that support them.

Were all these films about the Greek Crisis? Did they have a direct and immediate relationship with it? Not necessarily. However, the context of the Crisis, often indirectly, ended up becoming inescapable, in a way similar to what had happened with *Dogtooth* and *Strella*. The Crisis ended up framing the way in which these films were received at international festivals and by those audiences, and ultimately by the public in Greece. As Geli Mademli has noted, 'the most prominent feature of Greek films when presented abroad was the label of the cinema of "crisis", which was attached to every exportable cultural product in this field' (Mademli 2016: n. p.; cf. Papadimitriou 2014).

Is it correct to group all these films under the title 'Weird Wave' and that problematic understanding of 'a messed-up cinema from the world's most messed-up country'? Many Greek directors and critics have argued at length about the inaccuracy of this phrase (see Chalkou 2012; Kourelou et al. 2014; Mademli 2015; Nikolaidou and Poupou 2017). What exactly does 'weird' mean, anyway, apart from the inability to understand why something is happening? However, this term has survived the day, and it has survived well, as a simple internet search would show. Under the term 'Greek Weird Wave', international subscription-based TV channels still make extensive tributes; books and chapters are published; and special screenings are organised at festivals and by film groups. More importantly, as I argue in this book, talking about a Weird Wave allows one to reflect on the complex dialectics of (international) reception and production of these films, as well as on their critical and social context.

It should also not be forgotten that, since 2008, the production of Greek Cinema has changed dramatically. For at least three decades before that moment, Greek Cinema was mainly clustered around a small number of production companies that primarily tried to secure their funding from the Greek Film Centre, the Greek state TV channels, the state-owned Hellenic Broadcasting Corporation (enforced by law to dedicate some of their income to Greek film production) and several European Cinema Funds (such as Eurimages). Even though after 2008 most of these institutions and arrangements remained in place, their funding capacity became more and more precarious. The meager income that could be sourced from TV networks collapsed. What replaced these sources were more diverse and energetic production networks, eager to find funding (and sometimes partial funding) from new, international sources. This is a story characteristic of many other 'small nation' cinemas since the end of the twentieth century, and it has been very well told in the case of Greek Cinema in recent years, by Lydia Papadimitriou. As she astutely remarks in her discussion of the international co-production networks that have increasingly financed Greek films, '[recent Greek cinema's] international trajectory and recognition is [now] not just a desired extra, but a fundamental condition of possibility [. . . T]hese films, in other words, are crucially dependent on international circulation in order to exist' (Papadimitriou 2017: 148; cf. Papadimitrious 2018a).[12]

Framing the reception and production of Greek Cinema in this way has also resulted in certain strong, even if debatable, critical patterns. As I have already mentioned, the 'weirdness' of these films has been considered an all-encompassing characteristic, somehow directly reflecting the country's socio-political problems. In a similar manner, the presence of violent and sexual scenes is taken as an emotional release or a cry of desperation, and the insistence on the topic of family dynamics has been widely interpreted as a reference to an educational system, a state and a society gone awry. These thematic, visual and critical patterns have even provided their own anti-narrative in the form of certain directors' ironic meta-cinematic commentaries.

Take, for instance, *Oiktos/Pity* (2018), directed by Babis Makridis from a script by Efthimis Filippou, the scriptwriter best known for his work with Lanthimos. In *Pity*, the central character is so closely identified with the pity he receives while his wife lies in a coma in hospital that he keeps lying about her condition even after she finally and unexpectedly wakes up. Eventually, he decides to kill her alongside the rest of his family, in an effort to restore the original economy of pity that he had enjoyed until that point. Family violence, off-tone script delivery and awkward framing all help to develop a labyrinth of meta-cinematic comments on the Greek Weird Wave. The joke, one might suppose, works against recent Greek Cinema, implying that, like

Pity's unnamed central character, it is now overeager to meet specific frames of expectation in order to keep enjoying the positive international response to which it has become used.

At this particular juncture, as austerity measures and the precarity of national finances are becoming the new norm in Greece, a new generation of filmmakers and critics gives the impression that the Weird Wave is now a standard point of reference, an achievement with undeniable status and impact, but also a phase coming full circle, forcing artists to think 'what next', as I will explain in the Epilogue. This is precisely the juncture occupied by medium-length and feature-length films presented after 2014 by younger Greek directors such as Konstantina Kotzamani, Jacqueline Lentzou, Yorgos Zois, Rinio Dragasaki, Vasilis Kekatos, Zacharias Mavroides, Dimitris Katsimiris and Christos Massalas, mentioned at various points (often as counter-points) throughout this book.

THE ODD ONE OUT: *SUNTAN*

In the film *Suntan* by Argyris Papadimitropoulos (2016; script co-written with Syllas Tzoumerkas), Makis Papadimitriou – an actor well-known for his 'weird wave' roles, whom we have already encountered in his delivery of the 'Letter to Yorgos Lanthimos' – plays a displaced doctor. Driven by unemployment and previous professional mishaps, he decides to accept a post to work as the sole general practitioner on the small and picturesque Cycladic island of Antiparos. During the winter, locals live alone in a close-knit community, and almost nothing ever happens. In the summer, however, the island fills up. Tourists of all ages, especially young people from all over the world, come to this small earthly paradise to acquire the celebrated suntan of the film's title, offering in exchange the economic fuel needed for the survival of this small society. Curious, trapped, feeling a failure and trying to hide his past, the doctor's first winter on the island passes quietly. But in the summer suddenly everything turns upside down. He falls in love with a young female tourist. He is at a loss. He starts following her group of friends, not knowing how to fit in and make himself liked. He is an obsessive stalker and willing joker, the odd one out in the group, what some people might call a 'weirdo'. He is also the one who daydreams about escaping his everyday reality – he is a dreamer in need.

From the middle of the film onwards, what we see might be either an unmarked dream or a totally surreal epilogue that plays with cinematic genre. After wandering the island in a frenzy (viewers get to see one of the most debunking sequences of 'partying' on a Greek island in August), the doctor abducts the girl he 'loves', drugs her and carries her to his surgery. The film

Figure 1.4   *The doctor (Makis Papadimitriou) standing over his victim's body, in the closing scene of* Suntan *(Argyris Papadimitropoulos, 2016); digital still.*

ends with a medium shot of him standing over his victim, surveying her unconscious body, just as he did when he first met her, several days earlier, in his role as her doctor.

One might think of *Suntan* as a strange film that does not know how to end; as a film not ready to take responsibility for the allegories it builds; or as a free-wheeling joke on splatter movies. One might think that the gender violence in the last scenes is satirised in a politically incorrect way and therefore potentially take issue with it; but also that we are seeing a hilarious, although somewhat shallow conceptual and visual subversion of every speech about 'commitment', 'salvation', 'assistance' 'development' and 'salvaging' with which Greece has grappled in recent years.

Some of the film's comic effect derives from the discrepancy between the image that the central character has of himself and what others think of him. Its comic value also relates to the fact that, from one point onwards, the film can equally be seen as an allegory of the small national cinema whence it comes, an impression strengthened by the appearance of directors of the new generation of Greek Cinema in cameo performances throughout. *Suntan* does not simply rely on the exchange and 'gift economy' characteristic of cinemas of small nations, an informal system in which various people work for free or for scale in each other's productions. Out of this gift economy, it also creates a visualisation of Greece as a heterotopia, and then as a heterotopia gone awry, gone wrong, gone mad, gone sad – in that order. This satire of national representation and national allegory happens, let us not forget, as the central character, everything that happens to him and everything he does is presented as more and more awkward, mismatched and out of place. As it self-consciously turns to mix genres and to weird things up, *Suntan* not only becomes a Weird Wave film, but it also shows how to make one.

Excessive, eclectic, defamiliarising and 'weird' – this is how *Suntan* builds a parody of the cinematic representation of Greece as a 'summertime paradise' (from *Shirley Valentine* [1989] to *Mamma Mia* [2008]) *and* an ironic comment on recent Greek Cinema's critical turn. A story that verges on the surreal thus ends up providing an indirectly illuminating picture of what is happening in the country, for instance, during the summer holidays on 'paradise islands'. At the same time, a collection of scenes that could be thought of as realistic representations ends up asking the viewer to also think of them as ironic allegories. It is even possible to see the doctor's character as standing for this whole new turn of Greek Cinema, singled out, uneasy, spotlighted: not so much waving, but weirding.

The story of the recent 'Weird Wave of Greek Cinema', which started with a family screaming inside the four walls of a *Matchbox*-like apartment, might actually end with scenes such as this, in a doctor's surgery, with the body of a woman lying on an examination bed and a strange, awkward man standing and looking at her, the viewer uncertain as to how far (and against whom) the irony reaches and whether the social criticism in the film (including criticism of the casual representation of gendered violence in film) is intended to be serious or just another ironic pirouette.

Greek Cinema in recent years appears to have expressed a creeping violence, a disruption of institutions and traditional systems of identity and community (such as the family), a discomfort with old systems of reference and established cultural archives (including of the old Greek Cinema and its iconography), a desire to review the way in which one speaks of a modern reality in crisis, a willingness to find an international audience and new ways and channels of production and distribution, as well as a reflection on how this could all work out. All these tendencies are still there, but as the recent video by the Association of Greek Cinema Directors/Producers I described at the beginning of this chapter reminds us, Greek Cinema is also now left with a different set of questions which it needs to answer. These questions have to do with its political and ethical stance; with its next steps; with its funding sources and target audience; and with the aim of its critique. Last, but not least, is the question that lays behind the petition to 'Give a Little Loving to Greek Cinema': How can Greek Cinema now move on and manage to transform a frenzy of mobility, of analytical insightfulness and critical over-drive, into a more sustainable affective engagement?

EXCESSIVE ALLEGORIES, BIOPOLITICAL ANXIETIES, TRAPPED BODIES

The early international success of *Dogtooth*, as well as the spate of Greek films that attracted international attention, especially during the years 2009–13, created a momentum that went on to affect the subsequent international reception of Greek Cinema, its production and funding opportunities, as well as the critical reflection dedicated to it, at all levels. Undoubtedly, this 'golden age of the Greek Weird Wave' and the opportunities it created are often exaggerated. Lanthimos has always maintained that, even two years after *Dogtooth*, he still could not properly fund his next film *Alps* (and this was partly the reason why he eventually decided to seek international co-productions and settled outside Greece). Meanwhile, for all the international appreciation of Greek Cinema, a decade later, the actual production of critical texts and academic analysis may be significant, but it certainly is not enormous.

Some critics have gone so far as to argue that the Weird Wave was an idiosyncratic gesture, a formal game that happened to find an international audience, but now 'has to "grow up", to show some depth, to take, while also giving back, some "love"' (see Politakis 2019). While explaining that once again it had become difficult to secure international funding for new Greek films, a Greek film producer told me late in 2018 that 'it is high time we now get serious and see how we can make Greek cinema survive; the Weird Wave was just a parenthesis' (see Vourlias 2020).

This is exactly the point and the argument which this book aims to debate. I would certainly argue that only looking at Lanthimos's films and their poetics misrepresents the much more fluid and multi-layered developments in the Greek Cinema of recent years. But at the same time, not theorising the Weird Wave (and Lanthimos's crucial, even if somewhat unwilling, influence) *enough* would also be a missed opportunity to examine a specific period of Greek cultural history. As I have already mentioned in the Introduction, what I understand as the Weird Wave is not so much a specific cinematic form or a finite set of thematic traits; rather, it is more of a process that characterises cultural production in the current moment. It is in these terms that I want to argue once again for the cultural and socio-historical importance of cinema in Greece during the period we now customarily refer to as the Crisis. It would be a grave mistake, I suggest, not to see the bigger picture into which the Weird Wave (even with its highly debated title) fits and not to examine it as a key example of a larger and politically fascinating cultural landscape responding to an intense biopolitical present. Instead of seeing the Weird Wave simply as the successful sub-genre of a much wider cinematic production (which, of course, it was), I propose to consider it as a key to understanding a series of cultural, social and political developments. Seen in this way, I propose to consider the Weird Wave as the cultural product of a specific, and very intense, historical moment. For reasons that will become obvious, I call this moment an *intense biopolitical present*, and I frame this book's exploration of Greek Cinema as one of the many cultural projects that emerged within it.

As I have already mentioned in the Introduction and as I will explain in detail in the chapters below, Greece is a very good example of how, in the context of a late capitalist twenty-first-century democratic state in economic crisis, the intertwinement of politics with life becomes ever more pronounced and obvious, as it spectacularly reframes which lives matter and how. From whichever perspective one wishes to see it, however sensitively one approaches it, there has been a lot going on in (and about) Greece in the first decades of the twenty-first century to make one think about *biopolitics*. Biopolitics is a concept revisited by Michel Foucault in his lectures in the late 1970s, when he wanted to reflect further on those forms of power and knowledge that intensify in modernity, focusing on the management of human life from the larger scale of a population, its categorisation, health, livability and/or proscription, to the minutiae of the human body, its function and the ways in which it interiorises power and knowledge. If disciplinary mechanisms take care of the latter, it is their projection and organisation at the level of the population that guarantees their longevity and constant reinvigoration. Not coincidentally, biopolitics as a term is not only widely deployed today as one of the most powerful tools to conceptualise political developments over the past three centuries, but also, very intensely, marks the contemporary moment.

The 2010 address by Papandreou in Kastelorizo was just the tip of the iceberg. From that time onwards, the Greek public sphere became saturated with narratives of a state of emergency, national salvaging and survival, framing, bordering, training, retraining and disciplining. Greeks became accustomed to the idea of their country as 'the big patient' of Europe, of the austerity measures as 'a necessary and powerful medicine'. They faced stereotyping as an everyday reality in their country's international relations, as well as in their own everyday experience. They also became used to discussing on a daily basis monetary figures and projections that kept relating the individual (and the individual's survival) to a population (and its economy). They debated political decisions and negotiations alongside stories of individual and collective hardship, everyday failures to make ends meet, alongside rising suicide rates. With a migration and refugee crisis also reaching its peak during the period, especially after 2014, Greece was seen as one of the major European sites of/for holding people, moving people *en masse* and witnessing people moving *en masse*, as a place for the organisation, detention and deportation of people, for the construction of camps for people. Population became an issue constantly recalled, discursively and physically mapped onto people's bodies, related to life, livability, precarity and more generally the politics of life and death. To paraphrase a well-known Foucauldian expression (see Foucault [1976] 1998), the bodies of people, their disciplining and function, the anatomo-politics of the human body, in a spectacular and very public fashion came to be intertwined with the metaphorical constructions of the national body in crisis and with the biopolitics of (a) population.[13]

I do not want to imply here that the economic and socio-political crisis in Greece after 2008 created a monolithic, concrete historical period. What we understand as the 'Greek Crisis' was a much more diverse time, containing different turns, moments of social uprising and capitulation, extreme political instability and stabilisation, instances of insolvency felt in the everyday and periods of a seeming 'return to normality'. This series of developments continues to this day, even if the Greek Crisis as a period has been officially declared to be over. Talking about the period of 2008–2018 as that of the 'Greek Crisis' does not mean, therefore, that I consider it as either unified or concluded. Having said that, Greece has certainly experienced a prolonged state of emergency, a political debate about it, and a certain understanding of it as a historical moment and an iconography, which have resulted in shaping a narrative of the Greek Crisis. It is to this diffuse yet impactful and continuing narrative of our lives that I, along with many others, refer to as the 'Greek Crisis', with a capital C.

This is the context in which Greek films have been made, watched, rewatched and critically debated in Greece and abroad. The context is one to which I return, in this book, to rethink the films' engagement with the domains of the public and the private; their investment in the theme of the 'Greek family'; their portrayal of violence (and their insistence on the systematic nature and economy of violence); their screening of the body, of scenes of education and induced docility, or of scenes of eruption and disarray; their approach to gender and sexuality; their screening of landscape, including the landscape of development and uneven modernisation; and their reception and use, by communities of viewers, as a platform to create new cultural genealogies and to tell new histories of Greek Cinema. Most importantly, it is in this context that I want to review these films' insistence on weaving realism with allegory and on developing a poetics of metonymy – in ways that demand the engagement and investment of the viewer, reflect on relations of proximity and contiguity, and revisit both realism and allegory as critical tropes.

In short, what I want to do is consider the Greek Weird Wave as a challenge: an analytical, conceptual, cultural and historical challenge that develops alongside what I call 'a culture of biopolitics' and replicates its main modes of engagement. As will become obvious, one of the key characteristics of biopolitics, as a politics operating over and through (human) life and bodies, is its expansiveness as well as its tendency to be interiorised. A characteristic of biopolitics is that it orders a politics of life and death *already*: once you have started analysing its intricacies, you already are within its economy. In a similar vein, a culture of biopolitics cannot avoid denoting a culture that tends to develop concepts, analytical terms and critical discourses from within, no matter how much they also try to destabilise this within. A culture of biopolitics means a culture of making do, of doing and using, redoing and reusing, or, in terms that sit well with a Foucauldian vocabulary, a culture of usages and practices. The last decade of Greek filmmaking presents us with a cinema of biopolitics also because it helps develop concepts, ideas and critical stances in order to understand this wider and very contemporary culture of biopolitics on its own terms.

My argument about the Greek Weird Wave follows the logic of what Martine Beugnet, in a very influential essay, has argued about the films of the French New Extremism. Reviewing a well-known series of films from the 1990s and 2000s by directors such as Olivier Assayas, Catherine Breillat, Claire Denis, Marina De Van, Bruno Dumont, Philippe Grandrieux and Gaspar Noé, Beugnet argues for our need to see them not necessarily as products of, but as enmeshed *in* their specific socio-cultural context. She also maintains that we need to do so in a way that would be more complex than considering them as expressions (and efforts to engage the audience's feelings) of loss, disappointment and nihilism. Beugnet, following Kristin Ross's classic analysis, reminds us that in the wake of decolonisation and the trauma of war in the late 1950s and 1960s 'fast cars – clean bodies' had become the dominant image to dispel the ghosts of the recent past. This exact paradigm is now being reversed, she says, and it is being reversed in a pointed, calculated way. In the France of the early twenty-first century, broken cars/unclean bodies have been the way to engage with an uneven, insecure national and global present, and 'to sense it' before 'we can make sense of' it (Beugnet 2011: 31).

In a similar way, and in agreement with a host of other critics who have recently turned to these works, I argue that the films of Lanthimos, Tsangari, Tzoumerkas, Koutras, Economides, Kotzamani and so many others under study are themselves invested – and, directly or indirectly, aim to engage the viewer – in a deep contextualisation and feeling of their socio-cultural contemporaneity. They do so by reversing previous narratives of national propriety and belonging, as well as the more accepted modalities of national allegory (see Psaras 2016; Lykidis 2015; Aleksic 2016). Instead of allegories largely conceived on the basis of metaphor, these films work with metonymy, making unexpected connections and emphasising the critical potential of proximity, contiguity and touch. Their violence often emanates precisely from the way in which they thus dislocate the allegories that support national and cultural (psycho-social) belonging.

I also make the further claim that what binds this disparate group of films together is their willingness to talk biopolitics, to engage in biopolitical think-ing, as well as to screen (and affectively [re]produce) biopolitical dissonance, noise and resistance. Allegory is shown to be very much part of the biopoliti-cal present (as a tool and/or its representation) in these films; and violence is present and pervasive. Sometimes, it disturbs the allegorical taxonomisa-tion and production of 'naturalness'; at other times, it acts as a metonymic wake-up call for the viewer to think about context where it was (through metaphor) airbrushed out; and often it comes as the excessive flooding of the real where the symbolic had been.

Excessive allegories, biopolitical anxieties, trapped bodies: this is the script that many Greek cultural texts have tried to perform in recent years. And if this is an important and more obvious background to the films of Lanthimos that have tailored this exploration (and expectation) to more mainstream audi-ences, it is also a key aspect of a much larger filmmaking activity in Greece of the last two decades and one that makes more palpable their political critique, radical positions and connection with other, equally active cultural scenes in Greece and beyond.

In what follows I pursue the connections, try to see beyond the jokes and the easy references, often counter-pointing my own politics (and that of the communities to which I belong) to the biopolitics made evident on screen. Often, I propose more than one reading of one film or one scene and insistently try to relate them to a larger context. I have already done so in this introductory chapter, for instance, pairing the last scene of *Suntan* with the scenes of the same actor in the promotional video-letter to Lanthimos, elaborating not only on the humour and irony of the film, but also on its visual associations and its overall arguments about filmmaking at a site of crisis and biopolitical intensification. I have also tried to see the anxiety that *Suntan* projects in its final scenes, that overall feeling of failure, as a productive position of critique, set in motion, if not in, then at least with the film.

It is in the same vein that I want to turn to a celebrated medium-length film which, I argue, provides a self-conscious commentary on recent Greek Cinema as a cinema of biopolitics. In Konstantina Kotzamani's *Washingtonia*, with which the next chapter begins, people, plants and animals are sorted and surveyed, their stories intermingled, managed, as well as undercut and frag-mented, in an Athens visibly in trouble. What can one do with this awkward assortment but to try to look out for, if not invent, continuities? The anxiety to do so is calculated to provoke in the viewer an impulse to connect the dots lying in and outside the film; this is what the next chapter itself will also try to do.

NOTES

1. Available at https://www.youtube.com/watch?v=5FsTwViXuNw (last accessed 16 June 2020). *Letter to Yorgos Lanthimos* was directed by Vassilis Katsoupis, with a script by Sotiris Krimpalis and Zacharias Mavroeidis, all members of ESPEK.

2. This was also the title of a larger campaign organized by ESPEK in 2018–19. See https://www.greeknewsagenda.gr/index.php/interviews/filming-greece/6899-filming-greece-%E2%80%9Cgive-a-little-loving-to-greek-cinema-%E2%80%A6-aka-the-need-for-a-single-cinematic-policy%E2%80%9D (last accessed 6 June 2020)

3. For an analysis of how these new companies operate, see Papadimitriou 2017; see also the discussion of gift economy in Greek Cinema here, pp. 86–8, as well as in various interviews by key players, for instance, Kekatos in Kokkini 2019 and Exarchou 2010. This issue often comes up in the interviews with young filmmakers published online in the series 'Filming Greece' https://www.greeknewsagenda.gr/index.php/interviews/filming-greece (last accessed 6 June 2020).

4. Available at https://www.lifo.gr/print/shortcut/227999/theloyme-ki-emeis-ligi-agapi-apo-to-elliniko-sinema (last accessed 16 June 2020).

5. Examples include, among many others, the following videos: https://www.youtube.com/watch?v=JgemRu0AQuY and https://www.youtube.com/watch?v=lpqKLqLx9fQ. Each has more than 300,000 views.

6. On adverts based on *Matchbox*, see https://www.lifo.gr/videos/lifo_picks_planetearth/112371. On the larger cultural impact of the film, see the interview by its protagonist Errikos Litsis at https://www.lifo.gr/articles/theater_articles/179882/errikos-litsis-an-ego-os-ithopoios-eniotha-kindyno-o-kardioxeiroyrgos-ti-tha-eprepe-na-niothei (last accessed 16 June 2020). The exact channels of circulation and the cultural significance that *Matchbox* acquired over time can be used as a way to rethink the question of Greek art cinema's national impact in the twenty-first century. Measuring this impact only in terms of tickets sold upon the film's first release in the major Greek cities is inadequate, as the example of *Matchbox* shows quite well. Therefore, a reading based on more diverse data will be required to measure the Weird Wave's reception in Greece, especially what Lydia Papadimitriou has aptly called its much more complex 'economy and ecology' (Papadimitriou 2017).

7. In a very interesting project that takes the direction opposite to mine, Tonia Kazakopoulou has argued that, instead of focusing on the 2000s and trying to locate turning points and blasts of iconoclastic energy in Greek Cinema (as I do here), we should rather review a longer period and discern slower and lengthier developments. Greek popular cinema of the 1990s, she reminds, was already full of moments of contest and critique, only articulated in a different key (see Kazakopoulou 2017b).

8. Large parts of the low-budget *Matchbox*, shot with a handheld camera and natural light, with actors' lines finalised in rehearsals, seem influenced by the Danish

Dogme manifesto. Similarly influenced by Dogme were the films by Costas Zapas, a director whose work was also partly financed by Lars von Trier's company Zentropa. See, in particular, *Uncut Family* (2004) and *The Last Porn Movie* (2006). For more on Zapas, see Karalis 2017: 233–38.

9. With a name that some commentators interpreted also as a reference to the film *Guerillas in the Mist*, the *Filmmakers in the FOG* first started as an unofficial discussion group in 2008–9; they eventually turned into a concrete protest movement within the Greek film industry, with specific demands from the Ministry of Culture and its own public screenings and events (see Antiohos 2009; Flix Team 2018).

10. As Geli Mademli has so aptly pointed out in her discussion of the same national address by Papandreou, '[t]he severity of this speech was ironically counterbalanced by the serenity of the natural background of the picture – the coast of a remote Greek island, which could have emerged from a whimsical storyboard drawn by a professional production designer. [. . . T]he evolution of the crisis would not be just televised: from that moment in time it was something divertingly cinematic in its groundings' (Mademli 2016: n. p.).

11. These were long legal texts, often followed by annexes and later additions, which expounded on the details of the austerity measures that needed to be implemented, but often also branched further afield, giving the impression that they were a full mapping of the (future) life of the Greek population, a detailed biopolitical organisation and projection.

12. The rapidly changing funding landscape – which the FOG filmmakers had to face from the outset – alongside the technological changes that have allowed for cheaper production, diverse distribution and appreciation of the cinematic product, indirectly reinforced their group identity to a certain extent (see Kontakos 2009).

13. A very well-known indication of that interweaving is to be found in the discourse of the neo-fascist group Golden Dawn, which supported outright racist politics, glorified the bodies of 'Greeks' and targeted the bodies of 'others', spectacularising its 'right to maim', especially racially marked refugees and migrants. However, Golden Dawn's discourse (and its significant sudden popularity among a part of the population) is not an isolated phenomenon. It fits in with a larger biopolitical discourse that made its presence felt in Greece especially after 2009, often also articulated by more mainstream politicians and official policies.

CHAPTER 2

Why Biopolitics?

WASHINGTONIA: A SHORT HISTORY OF METONYMIC CONNECTIONS

Big dogs and small dogs. Dogs in cages, dogs being trained, dogs with hairstyles that look like people's hairdos. An Athens that is not exactly recognizable: the unfamiliar setting of a park, a museum of stuffed animals, a suburban house with a big grassy yard and a swimming pool, an empty industrial space and an old bourgeois home past its prime. Characters who speak with what could be called a deadpan delivery, a certain coldness or ironic distance, even though every single time the way in which they speak can actually be attributed to the specific circumstances in which they find themselves: a boy who lives alone without friends, a blind elderly woman alone in an empty house and so on. Scenes of training that somehow goes awry, to tragicomic effects. Awkward camera framing, often cutting off the top and bottom parts of humans and animals. Stasis and only occasional movement, in both the storyline and (it seems) people's lives. Chains of scenes that first fit together visually before one realises a possible narrative connection. Metonymical chains of signification that ask for an effort (by the characters in the film, but also by the film's viewers) in order to see where they are going. And, more often than not, chains exceeding the frame.

The very first image of this film features the long neck of a giraffe, with both its head and the rest of its body outside the frame. As the voice-over is telling us in French at the beginning of Konstantina Kotzamani's *Washingtonia* (2014), the giraffe has the biggest heart in the animal kingdom. Otherwise it could not pump the blood three metres high to reach the giraffe's head. 'When the giraffe is flat on the ground, one can hear the beating of its heart, which reverberates through the earth, and all the animals synchronise themselves with the heart of the giraffe'. In the middle of the summer the heart of the giraffe stops beating so fast, and this means that all animals are somewhat disorganised. 'And here comes the most bizarre moment of all. The last days of the summer, when the first headwinds arrive, we can hear the heart of the giraffe again'.

The shots of giraffes are accompanied by the voice-over of Mamadou

Diallo, an African immigrant living in Athens. At one point, the screen is filled with the colour yellow, as if the camera has suddenly turned to the sun, and here the voice-over changes and a woman's voice starts speaking in Greek: 'Have you seen the African dust? It is like a form of blindness'. Cut to a close-up of her: She is an elderly blind woman, often turning to the camera while speaking about love and togetherness. The scenes will go on being collated in that manner, following an unfamiliar visual or lexical, rather than narrative continuity.

We will eventually hear and see fragments of a number of stories: the life story of blind Ms Elly, narrated to Mamadou; Mamadou's everyday life and work in a patisserie shop, of which Ms Elly is a client, where we see him constantly framed by the windows and the refrigerators containing the cakes; his efforts to rescue Ms Elly's favourite palm tree, given to her once as a wedding present, which has now succumbed to the red palm weevil that has been infesting southern European palm trees in recent years and as a result is slowly dying (as are, it seems, both Ms Elly and the small yukka plant we see at some point in her lounge);[1] the story of a young boy living in a strangely deserted suburban home with his mother and their dogs, which are being trained, and which he will eventually release in order to annoy his mother; the story of a loner living in an empty warehouse who eventually buys the boy's trained poodle ('. . . this is a love dog!') and takes it with him pole-dancing.

One might think that this is an absurdist take on contemporary urban life, unrelated to life in contemporary Athens. Yet, the point of *Washingtonia* is that, taken as a whole, it is not absurd at all. The stories eventually start making sense, especially as they connect. Mamadou has met Ms Elly in the past, in the patisserie where he works, and the same patisserie is visited by the mother and the lone child to buy a cake for his birthday. The child has sold his mother's poodle to the loner on a whim, because he is bored on his birthday, and so on. At another level, the story of the palm trees dying because their heart is being eaten by the red weevil is connected to all those other stories of humans and animals that are, in some way, stories of the heart, stories of love, but also stories of something going wrong.

The link between all these stories can best be described by the trope of metonymy. We think of a metonymical chain as one that is based on contiguity, a relationship forged on the proximity of its elements, a proximity of notions, locations, objects (in a list or a museum), words and concepts and/or, as in this film, of edited frames. To an important extent, then, metonymy in *Washingtonia* becomes the motor of the film's storytelling. As I explained in the Introduction, unlike metaphor, in which substitution is based on analogy or similarity (something is like something else), metonymy is based on the way in which two elements are combined along a horizontal axis: One stands for (and eventually could link to) another because they are close, because they touch, because they belong in a list or an assortment or an entity, or because they are related through a line of cause and effect, container and contained, and so on.

For instance, the shot of a giraffe's neck with which the film begins turns out to belong to a stuffed giraffe, an exhibit in a museum of national history. From this museum, a place of cataloguing and sorting plants and animals, the voice-over introduction will expand to the animal kingdom (the animals linked, so the voice-over implies, through touch, rhythm and feeling); then to space and geography, to the continent of Africa, where the giraffe originates from, and to a characteristic plant of the continent, the palm tree. All these are metonymical relations. Editing underlines this, creating its own metonymic poetics and propelling the narrative forward along the syntagmatic axis, even if at the same time it draws attention to connections and undermines the smoothness of this process. We see shots of palm trees whose tops are chopped off, while we hear how the trees have been destroyed by the pest of the red weevil, resulting in them dying slowly from top to bottom. Palm trees were transferred *en masse* to mainland Greece after the 1970s, to embellish its coastlines in the period of the tourist-industrialisation of the country (and of the European South in general). Many of these are the palm trees that haven now fallen sick.

The connections between these micro-storylines are defamiliarising because they are first based on unexpected metonymical chains (the neck of the stuffed giraffe – the full giraffe – the giraffe as a species – the animal kingdom; the African desert – Africa; the palm tree – the red weevil). Note also how, with metonymy established as a connecting gesture, analogy and metaphor are also allowed in, mostly as an afterthought. The palm trees, we are reminded, are tall, as are giraffes (and visually cut, in this film, in a similar way, as the body of the tree visually reminds us of the neck of the giraffe). Also, they are as sick as the Greek economy.

As these images and fragments are stuffed into the cinematic sequence one after the other, the result becoming more and more awkward, one realises that the awkwardness also comes from the fact that every image, every frame, every voice-over or dead-pan phrase said on camera may lead the viewer to a whole new story, a rich archive of contexts and backgrounds and substitutions that are here just alluded to and threaded together by implication. What started as a metonymical expansion has interestingly now been transformed into a rhizome.

In this way, *Washingtonia*, as a film, seems positioned in a metonymic relation to more documentary depictions. It points to the possibility that these potential stories, here only excerpted in fragments and awkward connections,

Figure 2.1a–d   *Framing, imitating, observing, training people and animals in* Washingtonia
(Konstantina Kotzamani, 2014); digital stills.

could expand, visually, somewhere close-by. This is how many scenes in this film, especially the interaction between the migrant worker and the old Athenian lady, bring to mind, at least for me, documentary series such as the fourteen-episode *Mikropoleis/Microcities*, directed by Thomas Kiaos, Giannis Gaitanidis and Persefoni Miliou. The latter was produced in 2011–12 by the national broadcaster ERT, and it was shown and debated widely beyond the episodes' initial broadcast, in public projections, exhibitions and other settings. The series had the express aim of depicting Athens 'as it is now' and the implied willingness to talk about the chain of details, the 'microcosms' of the Athens of the Crisis. The narrative syntax here, too, was mainly based on metonymy. Each episode focused on one neighbourhood and one particular location. For instance, in the first episode of the series with the title *Kypseli - The Basement* (directed by Persefoni Miliou) the main narrative involves the cohabitation of a group of African migrant workers who live in the basement of a block of flats and a couple of elderly Athenian ladies who have always lived in the penthouse of the building in question. The two stories do not so much intersect as they, quite literally, stand next to each other – or, rather, one above the other.

Trained by such documentaries which presented the contemporary moment in the 'micro-cities' of Athens as a confluence of diverse peoples, crises, histories and archives, the viewer of Kotzamani's film is led to wonder: What is the story of this immigrant man, and how does he live in Athens? What is the story of the elderly woman and of her beautiful house and garden? How does the surrounding area look today? What kind of micro-city is this? From which other story (or, other genre and other film) does the character of the loner come? Is the feeling of awkwardness, this pervasive weirdness that binds the film together, the outcome of the fact that so many fragments from different stories are intersecting? Is our tendency to see these characters as acting out of place and these settings as weird, the result of our limited access to the whole picture, our fragmented confrontation with these intersecting stories?

A VIEW OF RECENT GREEK FILMMAKING AS A RESPONSE TO BIOPOLITICS

If *Washingtonia* creates estrangement through its metonymical impulse, it also implies that its result, *this* weirdness, is a way to navigate a wider net, a network of significations which incorporates the position of the viewer trying to make sense of it. Metonymy in the film is not only an aspect of its poetics, but it also characterises a relationship to the viewer, who is provoked to contemplate how these metonymical chains continue, even beyond the screen. Progressively, one realises that this larger network of signification in often unexpected ways engages directly with life and its politics, as well as politics over life – the more you try to make sense of these metonymical chains, the more you realise you are *in biopolitics*.

In the first instance, the film obsessively references training, affect and health, both at the level of the anatomy of single humans/animals and at the level of populations. It talks about (and shows) framed habitats where everyone's relations seem to be formed and organised according to protocols of interaction: a park, the jungle, various micro-sites of an urban centre, a museum. It talks about maintaining bonds, bodies and rhythms. Biopolitics as a theoretical tool alerts us exactly to the ways in which a certain politics over life establish and maintain which lives are livable and how, how disciplinary regimes interact with health provision and the maintaining of environment, in order to create a politics of life that works both at the level of the individual (an 'anatomopolitics of the human body') and at the level of the group ('a biopolitics of the population' – both Foucault's famous phrases in one of his earlier and most influential passages on biopolitics; Foucault [1976] 1998: 139–56). The constant mention of regimes of observation and health maintenance in *Washingtonia* serves exactly this aim. The recurring scenes in museums, as they intercut with scenes of humans interacting with each other and/or with animals, remind us of the role of sorting, cataloguing and exhibiting that underpins the act of nominating forms of life and preparing frames of livability. So does a constant effort to draw attention to the role of the camera in this context. In the film, there is an obsessive and self-conscious underlining of (observational) framing, either through producing those awkward framings of human and animal figures and extreme close-ups, or by filming figures in a way aimed at the frame-within-a frame effect – a window, the panel in a museum, the door frame and so on. There is even a dog walking on a treadmill at one point (Figure 2.1d) – is it being trained or observed for health reasons? The scene may be connected to a similar one in the *Microcities* documentaries, where it was used even for the overall trailer of the series. Yet, the image of the dog running while the camera stays still also creates an eerie cinematographic effect, bringing to mind pre-cinema and early cinema experiments with capturing the movement of animals (such as the 1878 'race horse' series of photographs by Edward Muybridge, both a cinema precursor and 'a major contribution to anatomical science') (Bordwell and Thompson 2003: 15–16).[2]

The irony of a Greek filmmaker in 2014 providing an assortment of images of training, museums of the living and the dead, palm trees infected and dying out, and giraffes' hearts obstinately pumping, is not meant to be lost on the domestic audience, nor on the international audiences of cinephiles who warmly welcomed the film. *Washingtonia*'s visual resonance was certainly not coincidental. Greece, as mentioned earlier, was already widely talked about as the 'great patient of the European Union', 'almost alive', in need of urgent 'special measures' and 'a certain disciplining'. At the same time, migrants and refugees who found themselves in the country became a part of the population that largely fell outside this austerity-driven matrix of recognition (Rozakou 2012). As a new 'migration crisis' developed from 2011 onwards and more intensely after 2014, migrants and refugees became a necropolitical spectacle, a constant reference point of people *ante portas* (or in camps within Greece, or passing through in transit, or losing their lives in their effort to cross), groups whose lives, but also whose death, mattered differently (Davies et al. 2017). With the constant mapping of the refugee crisis at the double level of individuals' bodies and their plight, and at the level of the whole country and the 'numbers it can currently contain' (or 'not contain', as phobic discourse often had it), biopower was underscored as the very central issue and structural question underlying all developments. Austerity and discipline, the politics over life and the discourse about the population became an everyday affair – or, rather, the way to understand the national everyday.

In a second reading, therefore, *Washingtonia* critically alludes to the very specific experience of talking about health, migration, movement and belonging, family and/as nation, discourses of public health and self/collective reeducation in the Greece of a dramatic period after 2008. It does so indirectly perhaps, certainly metonymically, but because of that no less powerfully.

Yet, in a third reading, this film also provides an in-joke, an almost generic apology, as it very much looks like a pastiche of scenes from Lanthimos's *Dogtooth* (2009) and *Alps* (2011), Makridis's *L* (2012), Economides's *The Knifer* (2010) and Tsangari's *Attenberg* (2010). Elements from all these (and many more) films are crammed into *Washingtonia*, as if they had been material in a developing cinematic archive. In a scene early on, we see the shot of a grassy garden being watered and the strange black and white mass of a body hopping over it in the direction of the camera. With gestures neither human, nor animal, but in a mimicry of both, this is the boy wearing a strange costume and making strange body postures in order to relieve his boredom and feeling of enclosure. Anyone who has seen *Dogtooth* or *Attenberg*, which start with similar shots of gardens, is immediately alerted to the reference here, and to what is happening in *Washingtonia* as a sort of meta-explanation of the earlier films' poetics. The direct references multiply. The blind lady acts and looks like the blind lady in Lanthimos's *Alps*; the constant mention of dogs being trained brings to mind similar images in Economides's films, as well as Lanthimos's *Dogtooth*. So do most of the characters: The boy, as he adopts peculiar poses in his garden, brings to mind the heroine of *Attenberg*, and as he talks about his birthday, he reminds us of Stergios, the main character in Syllas Tzoumerkas's *Homeland* (2010).

Washingtonia provides a narrative frame for all of them, a certain explanation of how they, in diverse ways, also relate to a very specific, very experienced and very pertinent biopolitical present, to which the viewer needs to be alert, to react and to make connections in order to comprehend. It is as if the director wants to explain (with an even shorter and much more opaque film) why these other films were made in the way in which they were, and how they are connected to their contemporary social and cultural context. The fragments of cinematic references are edited together, as are the different fragments of the narrative, in metonymical chains. Metonymy is thus proposed as the mode for understanding the relation among the Weird Wave films, as well as the qualifier 'weird' itself. Kotzamani, a socially engaged filmmaker who studied at the relatively new Greek Cinema School of the University of Thessaloniki during the years of the Crisis and the emergence of the Greek Weird Wave, is here proposing a concise guide to recent Greek filmmaking as both a weirdly metonymical undertaking and an engagement with biopolitics.

Is metonymy a mode that enables a creative and critical reaction to an intense biopolitical present? Is a metonymical chain (of concepts, images, stories) weird? Does weirdness, therefore, indicate a creative response to biopolitics? *Washingtonia* neither explains, nor answers these questions. But in posing them in quite memorable ways, it presents a link between the (bio) politics of austerity and its own poetics of metonymy, thus proposing what could be a cinematographics of biopolitics. *Washingtonia*'s main story is the one that is the most pressing yet elusive to tell: It is the story of a cinema of biopolitics.

BIOPOLITICS FOR FILMMAKERS

One could argue that there is something inherently biopolitical in cinema. It not only follows, but also produces (a vision of modern) life. It not only observes, but also regulates movement and the body. Cinema '(re)animates' life and 'reframes' bodies. This is exactly what biopower is about.

Film Theory and Film Studies have therefore understandably been characterised by works that focus on power and the body, screening groups and crowds, the intertwinement of observation with surveillance and the use of the camera as a disciplinary tool – in a sense, this has been a field speaking about the matter of biopolitics before a theory of biopolitics was ever developed. This might also be the reason why film critics did not immediately turn to the use of the actual term biopolitics, as it happened, for instance, in literature, postcolonial or gender studies. Having said that, over the last decade much has changed. At the risk of over-simplification, there are at least five ways in which recent film scholarship has turned to the more specific theoretical vocabulary of biopolitics.

Biopolitical Worlds

A number of critics have focused on how specific cinema and TV genres, especially science fiction and fantasy film, construct dystopian worlds whose central characteristics relate to an intensified biopolitical governmentality. This is what has been argued, for instance, about *Gattaca* (Frauley 2010; Whitehall 2013), *Children of Men* (Žižek, on the DVD jacket notes: 'And my god, this film literally is about biopolitics [. . .]: how to generate, regulate life' [Žižek 2007; cf. Latimer 2011; Whitehall 2013]), *Never Let Me Go* (Pisters 2014; cf. De Boever 2013; del Valle Alcalá 2019), as well as novels widely read as biopolitical fictions and recast as TV series that comment on the contemporary moment, such as *The Handmaid's Tale* (2017–20) based on the novel by Margaret Atwood (1985). Works such as these become preeminent demonstrations of biopolitics at work, of regimes that organise the very minutiae of life, taking biopower to its extreme deployment in eugenics, security states, bioindustry and bioethics, and so on.

Even though this is the most straightforward way to bring biopolitical theory into cinema criticism, it is also one of the most engaging, especially when it questions why a certain representation of a biopolitical regime is constructed, circulated and ends up having an impact as a cultural text at a certain moment and place. A good example here is the discussion about biopolitics in zombie films (Domingo 2018; Pokornowski 2016). Part of my discussion in the chapters that follow is influenced by this aspect, allowing me to think of the dystopian and/or heterotopic world of many a Weird Wave film as an indirect commentary on contemporary Greece and its biopolitical experience.

Biopolitical Screens

If the previous category of studies investigates how a regime of biopolitics is depicted on screen, another group of theorists is more engaged with *how* biopolitics intertwines with forms and strategies of visual representation, how it affects and is in turn affected by them. Following here the catchy title of Pasi Väliaho's highly influential work (2014a), one may group together a number of studies that try to think through the relationship between the surveillance of 'screening', the development of optical apparatuses and new media, on the one hand, and people's engagement with them and with the politics of life, on the other. In these works, biopolitical worlds emerge as governed, not by a panopticon, but by a biopolitical gaze, one internalised in the process of subjectivation, through the regulation of (un)belonging and (de)bordering. As Väliaho points out, we live in a culture of biopolitical screens, and the critical focus here 'seeks to shed light on how images today plot the organisation of our sensory apparatus, on the movements and interplay of the heterogeneous but often muddled audiovisual mediators that work to define both our individual and our social realities' (Väliaho 2014a: x; cf. Neroni 2015, Ball et al. 2012).

Biopolitics and the Gesture

In a similar fashion, another avenue for research has been the more philosophical and historical engagement with cinema as an apparatus that evolves alongside modern techniques of biopolitics. After Foucault, we tend to understand biopolitics as a type of power that became more and more visible in the late nineteenth century, a moment we also associate with the long invention of the cinematographic image. Film historians have not underestimated the coincidence: The birth of cinema historically came at a moment when biopolitical governmentality took its more developed form (Muhle 2012; Väliaho 2014b).

Thus, the modernity of cinema and the biopolitics of the modern era may be seen as inseparably connected from the outset. This, at least, seems to be the main point that Giorgio Agamben makes in one of his most famous short essays, 'Notes on Gesture' (Agamben 2000: 48–59). Thinking of the gesture as an incitement to move, a posture that already has movement in itself – and, thus, an image that is already proposing itself as a duration and an expansion in movement – Agamben implies that modernity, by definition, undermines the self-reliance of the gesture, disrupts its rhythm and emphasises its mediality. No wonder, then, that in the late nineteenth century so much discussion (and so much description and photographic illustration and sequencing) has been on the subject of uncontrolled movements – for instance, those of the psychiatric patients in the Salpêtrière hospital in Paris, studied by Gilles de la Tourette. Are these images not eerily reminiscent of (or, rather, are they not predating) the syncopated movements of the first human figures to be filmed moving? 'This is the impression, at any rate, that one has when watching the films that Marey and Lumière began to shoot exactly in those years' (Agamben 2000: 52).

Agamben argues that cinema was both a way of compensating for 'a society that had lost its gestures' in the late nineteenth century and, in the long run, the medium to deal with this loss: 'In the cinema, a society that has lost its gestures tries at once to reclaim what it has lost and to record its loss' (53). Agamben's point becomes clearer when contrasted with the historical moment he describes and the use to which the very first photographs of 'a society losing its gestures' had been put. The photographs of the Salpêtrière, for example, are only some of the many 'indocile bodies' photographed and published in similar medico-legal examinations throughout the second half of the nineteenth century. They came to complement the enormous efforts of cataloguing and taxonomising that had gone on, with the help of photography, to support such wide biopolitical projects as eugenics, physiognomy, criminology, racial profiling, ethnography and sexological study. Thus, the 'society losing its gestures' that Agamben refers to here points to the saturation point of a society cataloguing and fixing its subjects in order to further develop wide-spread biopolitical mapping and disciplinary management. Cinema eventually becomes the means to both record this un-gesturing and come to terms with it, to react and to counter-point. It is not coincidental, Agamben reminds us in another legendary essay, that contemporaneously with cinema developed the work of two philosophers and historians who became obsessed with the post-life (*Nachleben*) and the dialectics of the image, Aby Warburg and Walter Benjamin. Cinema came at a moment when all new technologies were pressed into the service of measuring, controlling and shaping the human body as part of a managed population, as both Warburg and Benjamin, lifelong opponents of racism, eugenics and fascism, were painfully aware. But if photography seems, at least momentarily, to be exhausted by the biopolitical project of modernity,[3] cinema gives the impression of safeguarding the lost potential of the image, its potential for duration and movement, its gestural quality, its potential of a *Nachleben* that is not wholly predefined by the modern use of images in order to map, shape and control (Agamben 2011; cf. Agamben 1998).

Agamben's powerful argument has given rise to a fascinating and distinct engagement with biopolitics and film, one that investigates the theoretical ramifications of this historical intersection and the analytical legacy it leaves behind as both cinema/visual culture and biopolitical governmentalities evolve in the twentieth century (Gronstad and Gustafsson 2014). For Olivier Roland, for instance, cinema fundamentally changes the way in which bodies are perceived, in motion but also as entities to be governed in life, and it is exactly this cinematic revision of the object of biopolitics that is then taken up (and shaken up) in the long twentieth century by authors such as Artaud or Bataille, before being reworked by entire cinematic movements such as the French New Wave (Roland 2013). My views on biopolitical realism (see Chapter 4) are particularly influenced by this train of thought.

Biopolitics, Genre, the Body (and the Nation)

Since biopolitics is a theory that so much reflects on the government of (and the care of and effects on) the body and the government of a population, a number of critics have returned to national cinemas and to the importance that specific genres, or themes developed by the film industry, have had in the biopolitical taxonomy of the nation. Robert A. Rushing's work on the peplum genre is indicative here. In his *Descended From Hercules: Biopolitics and the Muscled Body on Screen* (2016), Rushing focuses on the diverse reinventions of films set in Classical and Post-Classical Antiquity and featuring strong central characters (mainly muscled men). According to this analysis, the peplum expresses, mediates and polices biopolitical anxieties; thus, even though not made to be viewed within one single national context, it can also function as a direct ideological mechanism for the state-supported monitoring of life and, more generally, for the discursive coherence of a national and/or racial taxonomy. This explains, for example, the use of Maciste Italian films as national allegories in the 1910s and 1920s (Rushing 2016: 8–12), or body-builders who became peplum stars before entering American politics (138–40). This is a biopolitical nationalism of the powerful male cine-body that produces transnational effects.

Other works, such as those on melodrama in a national and a post-national context (Marcantonio 2015; Muhle 2012), have made a similar argument about specific genres' biopolitical interventions, a discussion to which I will return in my analysis of the film *Strella* in Chapter 7.

It is exactly because of the modernity and the overmediatisation of discourses about the 'health, the life range [. . .] and the vitality of the nation' (Rushing 2016: 3–4) – including their excessive screen mediatisation – that biopolitics intertwines so much in late modernity, not only with the nation state, but also with national culture and our concepts about national culture. There is something inherently biopolitical in our thinking about national culture, modernity and visual culture, modernity and the nation, cinema and national allegory. The confluence of these diverse discussions has paved the way for recent, more positive takes on cinema and biopolitics, which mainly focus on a biopolitics of emotions able to move beyond the confining categories of nation and national culture.

Biopolitics and/of Affect

This is the last category I discern in recent criticism. It is not the easiest to summarise, yet consists of efforts to respond positively and creatively to a generalised biopolitical climate, inspired by the art of self-constitution and the very poetics of holding on and investing scenes of belonging with affect. For instance, the editors of a volume on *Poetic Biopolitics* describe their project as follows:

> Through the poetic modes of artifact, image, installation and word, this book seeks to reveal the complex relations of physical and psychic lives that exist in biopolitical culture. [. . .] By showing how aesthetic and political expressions interact, ethical relations can be composed transversally in idioms where aesthetics and ethics combine. (Rawes, Loo and Mathews 2016: 4)

A more focused employment of this agenda has been the organising principle behind Timothy Campbell's *The Techne of Giving: Cinema and the Generous Forms of Life* (2017). There, Campbell, an intellectual known for previous work on the theory of biopolitics, decides to turn to the cinema of Visconti, Rosselini and Antonioni, because what these films have to say about holding on, being attached and being together provides, so he maintains, an answer to the riddles of 'contemporary life in both its political and less political forms' (Campbell 2017: vii). Film viewing, film criticism and filmmaking are here seen as inseparable forms of reacting creatively to a culture of intensified biopolitics. Campbell sees the twentieth-century films he reads in the early twenty-first century, therefore, as 'ethical enterprises': While showing how biopower works in a certain social setting, they also 'continually show us how important it is to extend the meaning of holding, be it of ourselves, our ideas, or each other' (ibid).

AN INTENSE BIOPOLITICAL PRESENT

It is true that the very partial mapping I have attempted to present here is somewhat calculated to follow the route taken by Michel Foucault himself in his treatment of the concepts of biopolitics and biopower; to an extent, it also follows the criticism that came on its heels. Starting from a general depiction of biopolitics as a very modern form of surveillance and of imposed, extensive and internalised power over life, Foucault moved to a more complex thinking about biopower. He analysed how it affects and is affected by the material conditions that surround it, how it takes hold of life, while also reformulating its object, reformulating the very meaning and framing of life. From this perspective, in Foucault's last works and political/social commentaries, one can discern a certain space for the development of a care and an ethics of the self, durational attachment and a bio-aesthetics.

When referring to Foucault's own engagement with biopolitics, I have in mind criticism ranging from *Discipline and Punish* ([1975] 1991) and the first time he developed a concrete use of the concept in the last part of *The Will to Knowledge* (1976), a reference that I have already made repeatedly, to the development of the concept in his Collège de France lectures (*Society Must Be Defended*, 1975–76; *Security, Territory, Population*, 1977–78; *The Birth of Biopolitics*, 1979–80), and leading up to the last contours of his thinking and teaching, evident in shorter texts he wrote in the last years before he died, as well as in his lectures between 1980 and 1983 (*On the Government of the Living*, 1979–80; *The Hermeneutics of the Subject*, 1981–82). However, I could equally have referred to the waves of criticism on biopolitics, representing different major voices (from Giorgio Agamben's negative conceptualisation of biopolitics as oppression, to Toni Negri's positive take on a politics of life as a creative response) and different communities of debate.[4] These different optics are, in a somewhat more eclectic manner, represented in the visual studies criticism on biopolitics that I have summarised in the previous section – from 'biopolitical screens', which takes a largely negative view of biopolitics as surveillance and internalised control, to 'biopolitics and/of affect', which opens the door to an analysis of positive and engaged bio-aesthetics. My own discussions in this book will follow a similar trajectory, from a vision of biopolitics as enclosure and inescapable context, to a consideration of ways of inhabiting contemporary (socio-political) space, as Lauren Berlant has it, with 'the desire to have an impact on it that has some relation to its impact on us' (Berlant 2011: 12).

The very stuff of the present, the rule book, the matrix, the screen, the analytical vocabulary, the inescapable political framing, the grammar of sorting out the livable from the non-livable, the living from the dead(ly), the now from the (archives of the) past and the (fantasies for) the future – this is what I call an intense biopolitical present. I have seen this intense biopolitical present unfold (and fold us in) in Greece, at least during the period to which this book mainly refers. My continuous attempt to position the films of the Greek Weird Wave in a larger cultural and socio-political context is not simply a methodological decision of a Cultural Studies approach. It is an effort to present them from within this intense biopolitical present, in terms developed in interaction with it.[5]

I am certainly not alone in considering the biopolitical aspects of the contemporary moment in Greece, or more widely in the world. A much shared opinion, with which I concur, maintains that the post-2008 global financial crisis is not simply a crisis of capitalism, but one whose force and specificity relate to the extensive prevalence of the new market products and the full neoliberalisation of socio-economic governance (Streeck 2016). It is the extreme neoliberalisation of society, what Pierre Dardot and Christian Laval ironically call the 'new way of the world' (2017), that makes biopolitics so central to our experience of the social, the political and the everyday.

Foucault himself had expanded significantly on the link between biopolitics and liberalism, ordoliberalism and neoliberalism. He had seen how a biopolitical form of governance fits well with (and is further developed by) the main premises of neoliberal governance, the marketisation of all aspects of life and the reinvention of the self as enterprise. Critics are still puzzled by Foucault's seeming unpreparedness to outrightly condemn neoliberalism; at times, especially in his 1979–80 course entitled *The Birth of Biopolitics*, he seems to serve almost as an apologist for it, admiring neoliberalism's inventiveness (Zamora and Behrent 2016, especially Behrent's article; Audier 2015; see also De Lagasnerie 2012; Revel 2005). Yet, it remains undeniable that he also offered the main tools to analyse how, through biopolitical governmentality, neoliberalism 'undoes the demos' and creates new models of citizenship and social contract, while also aiming to change older liberal views regarding 'fundamental human rights' such as health, education and the very idea of freedom (Brown 2015). With even those ideals – rights, freedom, education, health – now becoming less aspects of a shared humanity and much more part of a larger enterprise of 'sorting out' who can have which of their marketised versions, an analysis of the biopolitical common ground linking the strategies behind those deep and sudden changes can, at the very least, provide us with a starting point for resistance (De Lagasnerie 2012; Laval 2018). As Pasi Väliaho points out, . . .

> [t]his direct capture of our lives by the machinery of profitability is what Michel Foucault described as 'biopolitics', a process historically rooted in the birth and dominance of liberalism. In the emergence of biopolitical modes of thinking and doing, Foucault observed, populations were for the first time considered 'a sort of technical-political object of management and government'. As a result of this process, today's neoliberalism – broadly understood as an 'apparatus' comprising different practices and modes of thought, spanning political agendas, governmental techniques, military operations, scientific rationalities, logics of finance, and the like – amounts to the instrumentalisation and commercialisation of virtually all domains of existence, from the personal to the social and from the biological to the mental. By means of scientific, governmental, and military administration, and under the market logic that promotes risk, competitions, and crisis, life and the unknowability of life's becoming are turned into a source of value. It is in this sense, as Melinda Cooper points out, that life is 'surplus' in the neoliberal era. (2014b: xii)

Organising life as 'surplus value' does not mean liberalising attitudes towards institutions and forms of life, quite the opposite. In her recent marvellous account of the strategies of neoliberal politics and theory regarding 'family life', for instance, Melinda Cooper (2017) painstakingly explains how, since the late 1960s, neoliberal theorists and then decision-makers redefined versions of propriety, stability, security and family life, not only in order to better suit their market-oriented economic plans, but also to strengthen a core ideology that would present these plans as inevitable and obvious. Interestingly, these new versions of propriety and family were the ones that eventually synchronised traditionalist, racist and neopatriarchal ideologies with the market, preparing (rather than preventing) the rise of neoconservative (and often neofascist) ethnopolitics around the world.

In this context and in her work that also builds on extensive research by many other scholars on Greece, Dimitra Kotouza explains how the Greek economic crisis precipitated an extensive 'biopolicing' that cannot be fully understood unless we take into account the biopolitical aspects of its employment. Kotouza focuses on the way in which moral panics related to immigration, gender and sexuality were instrumentalised in order to support a view of the Greek population as being under threat by disease and from outsiders. Unless one takes into account that the biopolitical austerity *management* of the Greek population also entails the creation of a more general climate of enclosure, fear and covert racism, one cannot comprehend 'why specifically *the border* and *sexuality* have been the major points of governmental concern with regard to the population in this moment of crisis' (Kotouza 2018; see also Athanasiou 2012; Carastathis 2015; Dalakoglou and Agelopoulos 2018).

Similarly, archaeologist Dimitris Plantzos has argued at length about the logic behind using images of antiquity (such as the Acropolis or statues, for example, the Keratea Kouros), words referencing ancient Greek culture (such as the naming of the various police raids against immigrants as Xenios Zeus) and the materiality of antiquities (such as the excavation findings in the northern town of Amphipolis, among others) in order to strengthen a view of the Greek population both as under threat of extinction and as an object of care, cleansing, ordering and surveillance (Plantzos 2017b; see Hamilakis 2016). Plantzos reminds us how much archaeology in Greece can become an allegory, an ideological frame and an apparatus of biopolitical management, all at the same time. Against this background, the prime-minister-as-archaeologist (a position exemplified by the image of Prime Minister Antonis Samaras visiting the archaeological sites of Amphipolis in 2014) is one of the most telling symbolic evolutions for the Greek head of state during the years of the Crisis: from the symbol of pastoral care to that of a complex and self-congratulatory biopolitical agent.

These examples, among many others, essentially show how an understanding of the biopolitical in contemporary Greece can help discern the motives and discursive strategies of specific policies and their results, as well as the role they played during the Greek Crisis. Social movements in Greece, investigative journalism and cultural fields and genres such as theatre (Hager and Fragkou 2017; Zaroulia and Hager 2015) have developed precisely this point in recent years. Some of the best examples of 'documenting the Greek Crisis' have come from devised performances and documentary films specifically targeting the following areas as aspects of biopolitical management during the Crisis (see Ponsard 2014; Papadimitriou 2016): gender/sexuality (*Faster than Light*, directed by Kentaro Kumanomido and Thomas Anthony Owen, 2018), border controlling (*Specters are Haunting Europe*, Maria Kourkouta, 2016; cf. Giannari and Didi-Huberman 2017), financial management and employment (*The Prism*, directed by Nikos Katsaounis and Nina-Maria Paschalidou, 2011; *Next Stop: Utopia*, directed by Karakasis 2015) and their ideologies (*Agora: From Democracy to the Markets*, directed by Yorgos Avgeropoulos, 2015, second part 2020; *Debtocracy*, directed by Kitidi and Chatzistefanou, 2011).

Moreover, a number of debates that happened in public events in Athens, often involving well-known thinkers associated with the theoretical arguments I have been sketching out so far (such as Agamben, Žižek, Butler, Brown, Rancière, Spivak, Didi-Huberman, Berardi and Preciado) had an impact on the Greek public sphere, further aided by their wide circulation on the internet. [6] Audiovisual culture, therefore, already plays a key role in addressing contemporary biopolitics in Greece and uncovering its collusion with neoliberal governmentality and austerity measures.

There is, however, a larger cultural engagement with biopolitics, neoliberalism, the Greek Crisis and, indeed, Greek politics, which does not have the same claim to realism and immediacy projected by documentary film, devised theatre, political public speaking and activist writing. Or, rather, whose claims to realism and immediacy are of a different nature. The films of the Weird Wave are the most obvious example. They often take the cultural negotiation with the biopolitical present onto different terrains, while engaging, as was the case with *Washingtonia*, in complex reflections on form and genre, cultural production and the ethics of representation and engagement.

What happens when the politics of/over life become such a common feature of everyday discourse that even escapist cultural representation is drawn into the discussion? What happens when the very context films are made of/in is always already biopolitical? What happens when the location of films already contains a rich archive of biopolitical management? In a 2018 film that attracted a lot of international attention, *Third Kind*, Yorgos Zois once again seems to be providing some of the answers to such a set of questions. It is to this film that I will turn in the following pages.

RE-ENCOUNTERS OF A *THIRD KIND*:
THE BIOPOLITICAL SPACE REVISITED

In Yorgos Zois's medium-length film *Third Kind* (2018, based on a script co-written with Konstantina Kotzamani), a group of three characters in spacesuits disembark in the old Athens International Airport in the area of Ellinikon, in what at first sight looks like an exercise in film genre. Everything in *Third Kind* – from colours, to props, to camera angles and the spacesuits – is designed to evoke an intertextual reference. The cameras, for instance, were old models manufactured in the Soviet Union, employed here with the express aim to have the final cut reminiscent of Andrei Tarkovski's *Stalker* (1977) and *Solaris* (1972). The title (as well as several scenes at the end of the film) makes a direct reference to Spielberg's *Close Encounters of the Third Kind* (1977). This is a low-budget meta-sci-fi film, bringing to mind Fredric Jameson's argument that Science Fiction does not really aim to give us images of the future, but 'rather to defamiliarise and restructure our experience of our own present' (Jameson 1982: 151), thus presenting 'the future as history' of the present (Vint 2011). In that mode, Zois sets out to problematise the very experience of the present, by recasting one of its sites as the future's past.

Nevertheless, the main political gesture here comes not so much from cinematic references and genre, as from the actual site and the 'real-life' signifying chains energised by its employment. I remind that metonymy is a trope of contiguity, and *Third Kind* is, among other things, an exercise in contiguity (as well as contact, contagion and confinement). The film, as the director would explain time and again during its much anticipated presentation at the 2018 Cannes Film Festival, was shot in 2017, just days after the old Athens airport had been evacuated of its erstwhile inhabitants, groups of migrants who had for years found refuge in the buildings, in the open areas and semi-open spaces of the abandoned Elliniko Airport. This is one of many films, fiction and non-fiction, that had been made in that very evocative location since 2000; if anything, Zois's work also seems to be a commentary on the tendency of directors to revisit that space.[7]

The film, he explains, came together as an idea the very moment the old airport was evacuated to 'clear' the space for its eventual commercial 'regeneration'. His crew was given access to what had effectively been a makeshift refugee camp immediately afterwards, and '[we realised that] all their stuff was there, just like civilisation had stopped'. He explains that, rather than the idea for the film, what came first was 'the rhythm of the film; [it] is similar to what I had experienced the moment when I first experienced that site. We were walking slowly, we were taking photos, watching what was like the remnants of an almost gone civilisation' (Zois 2018).

The three cosmonauts, speaking different languages throughout, but still somehow understanding each other, disembark and walk slowly through the abandoned airport. The camera follows them and rests on the old airport's modernist architecture, itself a fragment of the past. But then, when the cosmonauts enter the different parts of the building, the references to its later, more recent life become more concrete. At one point, the cosmonauts find a pile of papers and a postcard. It is written in German, and the text is seen and read out on camera: 'Everyone in the morning is searching for food; everyone is going a little crazy here'. From which camp is this phrase, this voice coming? From what part of the historical record? Which archive? The slippage, that uncertainty, is painful and remains thus until the voice-over reads the signature on the postcard: Atifa, an Arab female name.

As the cosmonauts move on, the references become clearer. When they enter the toilets of what was once the main Departures hall, they stumble across walls full of graffiti conveying humour, a sense of desperation, the feeling of enclosure, and demands and cries for help: We are the last 3,000. Tourism in Syria. This is not my home. This is not an airport, it's a camp. No more tears. Give papers. Love you, Rosie. No Future.

'This is not an airport, it's a camp... No Future'. To this day, I have not attempted to learn whether all the wall scribblings that the camera captures in Zois's film were originally there, in the toilets of the abandoned airport, when the cinema crew first surveyed the location, or whether they were added as part of the setting by the production team, conveying thus their own experience of austerity-related graffiti, of the kind that has filled the walls of Athens since 2009 (cf. Boletsi 2016; Alexandrakis 2016; Boletsi and Celik-Rappas 2020). Either way, this rich archive of representation, assembled as it is in this setting, points to what a camp is and what it means for biopolitical management, as well as to the complex debate around this ontological condition. It is there, 'fictional', a remnant of actual slogans written during a certain period, or something between the two. It is there as a discursive and filmic reaction to a camp, remaining as an archive on the walls of a site that was used as a makeshift camp, nominating the space as it records its use.

Later, the cosmonauts will listen to a 'found' recording by a doctor, a voice testimonial describing a medical visit to immunise the population of refugees who had assembled there:

> 3/7/2016, today we vaccinated more than 1,000 people. More than 600 men and 200 women, the rest were children below the age of 18. We gave a double dose of MMP, the triple anti-tetanus and diphtheria vaccine.
> There was no time for more.
> A woman was fainting in our hands with strong splanchnic pains.

Figure 2.2a–d   *Biopolitical space revisited: The airport, the camp, the screens in* Third Kind *(Yorgos Zois, 2018); digital stills.*

They walk further, in choreographed movements meant to underline the fictional and genre-evocative treatment of the space in this medium-length film, but they keep stumbling upon remnants of the real. At one point they enter a room full of tents, abandoned clothing and furniture, the debris left behind after the long occupation by people in need, now indicating their fast departure. This is not (just) fiction, and what we watch is not a place that looks *like* a camp. It is a space that was used as a camp by people in transit, dismantled by the authorities using police force, with many of the people whose belongings we see on screen quite possibly being in another similar (more official, more secluded or more stringently under surveillance) refugee settlement as I write and you read these lines. In the place we see on screen, people lived and were treated as a managed population; they were immunised as a group; they were transported in and as groups.

At a later stage, in one of these rooms full of tents, the cosmonauts happen upon a TV screen. It plays in a loop scenes from the period when this particular room was full of the life of the refugees living in it. This, we are meant to think, must have been a video of 'life in the camp' that was made in the past as documentary evidence or as surveillance; we watch children playing, women moving around in groups, people half-asleep in tents. It looks like a surveillance video. It also looks, eerily, like a post-modern video installation project. As this video is being replayed now, a screen within a screen, what is its function? And what is the function of the film we are watching? What is it surveying? What is it surveilling?

I am making much of these details in the rich archive of representation that Zois's film wants to conjure up, and I am deliberately holding up the possibility that these were actually 'fragments of the real', open but uninvestigated. I have deliberately not sought to do what would have been easier – to find out what exactly was there and what was not in the first place, what is real and what fictional – precisely because that would have defeated the purpose of the whole film, and it would have detracted significantly from its power. The power of what we watch derives a lot from the fact that it is made from within a biopolitical settlement, engaging with modes of representation available and developed within such settings, which over the years have become so familiar. We do know an intensified biopolitical site when we see one. We do live next to them, in constant fear that 'next to' might not always be the right preposition.

The film thus 'visits' an extended biopolitical settlement; it is about biopolitical settlements, but it is also about making a film *in* them, about trying to find a suitable genre to talk about (and to revisit) a biopolitical settlement. And, of course, it is aware that it talks (and is being produced and will be reproduced) within a larger economy that has in various ways influenced the state of what is being shown here. It is aware that it talks within a cultural economy that allows for referential fragments, to connect what is on screen with images of pain, seclusion and refugee settlements in this and other places in recent years. No matter how stylised it is, *Third Kind* seems also very much aware of (and to a certain extent exploits) the fact that audiences will relate what they see to the images of refugee camps (in Greece and elsewhere) which they have seen in non-fictional representation, in documentaries, on the news and in online commentary. The film knows. It also knows, for instance, that audiences may also push this contiguity further, to its allegorical extremes; it knows that, while watching the sci-fi treatment of an airport in Athens, audiences may also be thinking of Greece as a whole. This is an engagement with (and a search for) genre; a self-conscious take on the idea of dystopia; a reframing of what is left behind, as an archive of the future past that is playing a role in the present; a pacing and spacing that is also a thinking *with* what it means to be alive, to order life, to frame life, to respect (or not respect) life, to have life ordered, to set limits and borders and frames of reference, and to surpass them.

In my analysis of Zois's *Third Kind*, I have implied that the relation with the immediate socio-economic and political context of this very stylised work is both multi-layered and inescapable. Is the Athens Airport in this film a fantasy space separate/analogous or part of/contiguous with our own world? We might distinguish the modes of fantasy, as Jonathan Culler once reminded us, following Roman Jakobson's distinction between metaphor and metonymy: 'A metaphorical world is separate but analogous, a member of a paradigm of conceivable worlds, while a metonymical world is contiguous with or part of our own, unexplored but governed by the same laws' (Culler 2001: 60). Following this, how is the airport's site in Zois's film related to contemporary Greece? Are we in metonymyland or in metaphorland? *Third Kind*'s efficacy as a political commentary rests not on any polarity or incompatibility between the two, but precisely on the sliding between them. It works its relationship to the immediate socio-political context on the axis of metaphor *as well as* on the axis of metonymy. What we see is a dystopic place, an abandoned camp that can be taken as a reference to the plight of today's refugees, to the state of contemporary Greece and to the larger questions of biopolitical management in terms of analogy. Based on these analogies the site works as a metaphor. However, what we also see *are* the remains of a former camp, an abandoned national airport whose future use has been hotly debated for years and seen as a symbol of Greece's need for restructuring and development according to some, or of the country's mismanagement and neoliberal exploitation according to others (Arhitektones 2001). These references relate to each other in chains of contiguity, on the basis of their proximity in experience; we are here deep in the world of metonymy.

Zois's *Third Kind* presents its elaborate futuristic setting as a defamiliarising experience of the present. In the very interdependence of the metaphorical and the metonymical, it creates an allegory that is constantly haunted by reality and its forms of representation. In Chapter 4, revisiting what critics, after Mark Fisher, have called 'capitalist realism', I will explain why I am tempted to call the poetics in which a film like *Third Kind* participates not capitalist, but biopolitical, realism. As I will explain in Chapter 4, if a capitalist realist setting is often haunted by its allegorical potential, in biopolitical realism allegories are also haunted by the constant return (remnants, ghosts, fragments, ruins, archives) of biopolitical arrangements.

THE PERSISTENCE OF THE BIOPOLITICAL AND THE INESCAPABILITY OF CONTEXT

One aim of this chapter was to present some of the ways in which critics have used the concept of biopolitics in the analysis of cinema. This was complemented by my attempt to show why I need biopolitics as a category to comprehend the films that have shaped and kept reshaping the Weird Wave. I explained how Kotzamani's *Washingtonia* operates like a generic meta-commentary on the Weird Wave. Not only does it presuppose knowledge of that cinematic wave to a certain degree, but it also reworks the idea of weirdness as a conscious cinematographic style. Ill-fitting, ill-matching, weird – one is tempted to call thus the characters, the sequences and the storyline. And this is not coincidental. *Washingtonia* is rich in references to a contemporary cinematic context in which being weird is a way of saying, a way of being heard and a way of doing. *Washingtonia* makes a further important step, however. It suggests that what looks weird is the outcome of a conscious strategy (of the characters' as well as of the *mise-en-scène*) to underline the metonymical relations between scenes, characters, stories and situations. Based on unexpected editing, it foregrounds montage as a metonymical pole that has the tendency to expand outwards. As I showed in my analysis, the emphasis on such metonymical connections has a defamiliarising force that plays a key role in the overall production of weirdness and the possible effect of the film on the viewer. This production of unfamiliar metonymical chains thus assumes a political weight: It challenges the viewer to make connections in the film and to keep extending them outwards. Such a poetics of metonymy, unexpectedly perhaps, has the potential to become a poetics of engagement. We are *edited in*.

Interestingly, these chains of references in *Washingtonia* return, almost obsessively, to biological and biotechnological details, to maintaining health in animal and human populations, to sorting out and cataloguing, people, animals and plants. It is as if one cannot escape the biopolitical, not only as a general frame or analogy, but also in its small details and signs, its sites, institutions and genealogies. It is also as if one way to be more reflexive about one's position within a biopolitical present is by claiming and realigning those metonymical chains that keep stumbling upon biopolitical knots.

In my discussion of various critical views on biopolitics and cinema, I reminded that the contemporary political use of biopolitical reference is not historically unique – that is, biopolitics has been politically and culturally significant not only *now* – but that it is also a historicising gesture, a gesture that has a particular importance for the present moment. Zois's *Third Kind* was crucial in order to reiterate that point: Biopolitics has turned into the common denominator in the politics of the present moment, it has *become* contemporary politics. Greece, for at least a decade, became an internationally spectacular example illustrating this, and Zois seems to have found a perfect 'part for the whole' in the abandoned-to-be-redeveloped Athens Ellinikon International Airport. In the interview I have quoted, he explained how he and his team happened upon the abandoned camp in the old Athens airport – and in my analysis I showed how the film recreates that scene of discovery emphasising the camp/airport as a biopolitical site (managing, immunising, surveilling a population). This point is similar to that of *Washingtonia*: One happens upon the biopolitical in today's Greece. Accounting for that encounter becomes a political gesture, and this also means a search for genre, a mixing of metaphor and metonymy with an emphasis on the latter, a dialogue between realism and allegory, an archival impulse.

I will revisit these aspects in the following chapters. What I want to underline further here, however, is the specific relation to context that this type of biopolitical cinema introduces. While the metaphorical side could keep context present as a possible analogy, but quite in abeyance – as, for instance, the sci-fi setting and the intertextual references of *Third Kind*, which could make one momentarily forget contemporary Greece – the metonymic s(l)ide has the potential to keep bringing it back in, more experientially, insistently and intriguingly. One feels compelled to talk here of the inescapability of the biopolitical context. Like the screen playing in a loop that one encoutners in the middle of an old-style sci-fi film, bio/socio/political context throws itself into these films, often unexpectedly and in quite peculiar ways.

It is to this specific argument about the contours and inescapability of context that I want to turn in the next chapter, starting with the first commercially successful (and English-language) film of the Weird Wave, Yorgos Lanthimos's *The Lobster*.

NOTES

1. That part of *Washingtonia*'s subject-matter, with an emphasis on the visual iconography of the dying palm trees and a more obvious reference to the Greek Crisis, became the basis for Kotzamani's next film, the equally celebrated *Yellow Fieber* (2015).
2. Of course, the intertwinement of power/knowledge, the observation of movement and the production of life have affected cinema since the first experiments with the moving image, and the discussion of how this happens has always been the focus of Film Studies, even if the word 'biopolitics' is not mentioned. On Muybridge, from this perspective, see Prodger and Gunning 2003. On museums, power and regimes of visual knowledge, see Eleftheriotis 2010.
3. Not everyone would agree with this. Georges Didi-Huberman has devoted his whole life's work to an effort to argue exactly the opposite point. See, for example Didi-Huberman 2011; 2013.
4. The different directions that the concept of biopolitics takes, especially in Italian theory, have been the focus of major debates, both historicising (Gentili, Stimilli and Garelli 2018) and oppositional (for instance, Revel 2018). It is beyond the scope of this book to cover them in detail, but I mention them here in order to underline how diverse conceptualisations of the biopolitical can enhance (rather than subtract from) a political cultural expression within biopolitics.
5. As I am working on the final edits of this text, most countries around the world have imposed lockdowns in order to manage the spread of COVID-19. The whole world remains at a standstill, with populations listening, every day, to announcements about national and global health measures, making it difficult to deny that this *is* an intense biopolitical present *par excellence*. Having said that, I would argue that the biopolitical excess of the global Coronavirus crisis does not take anything away from the (slower and perhaps deeper) development of the governmentalities of the post-2008 (Greek and global) financial crisis. Indeed, obsessed with the focus of my study as I write and watch from my balcony the empty streets of Athens in March 2020, I am constantly reminded of the many Greek films that, since 2009, have been showing the individual locked indoors, or walking through deserted or semi-deserted urban landscapes: *Attenberg, Dogtooth, Alps, Park, L, Boy Eating the Bird's Food, Pity, Third Kind* and so on. All these films were not prefiguring anything, nor were they describing life during a total lockdown. What they were doing was trying to think through a prolonged period when the politics on/over/of life take precedence. They seem to have sensed that a way to visualise the intertwinement of politics and life, of the body of the individual and the population, is to show life ordered, and sometimes ordered (to be) elsewhere.
6. An indicative example is the Greek TV programme 'Sites of Life and Ideas: Biopolitics', containing interviews with Giorgio Agamben and Wendy Brown, whose transcripts were also eventually widely circulated online: *Topi zois, topi ideon,* 2011 ET3 https://www.youtube.com/watch?v=No1JTntYsJw. Agamben's November 2013 lecture in Athens, titled 'For a Theory of Destituent Power', was

also widely circulated (Agamben 2014).

7. The defunct Ellinikon International Airport has become the setting for works as different as Christophoros Papakaliatis's blockbuster *Worlds Apart* (2015), Loukia Alavanou's video installation *Pilot* (2017), Konstantinos Prepis's short film *Ellinikon* (2019), Naeem Mohaiemen's *Tripoli, Cancelled* (2017) and even Eleni Foureira's video for her international pop hit *Tómame* (2018). The gleaming Ellinikon Airport of the 1960s and 1970s had once been a very popular shooting location for the old commercial cinema of that time, a symbol of modernisation, mobility and Greece's international standing.

CHAPTER 3

'A Cinema About Being Governed'

DEAD INSIDE/OUTSIDE ALIVE:
THE LOBSTER'S INESCAPABLE CONTEXTS

Well into Yorgos Lanthimos's first transnational and English-speaking production, *The Lobster* (2015), people start moving in slow motion. Splatter, war
scenes and B-horror films all come to mind as a group of people goes into
the woods in order to hunt – other people. The group hunting consists of the
'guests' of a hotel, which is as austere as a totalitarian state summer camp and
as hilarious as an outdated tourist resort, both tinged with an element of fear.
The hunted group had previously been at the hotel, too, but they have run
away to live in a semi-organised guerrilla community in the woods.

   In the dystopian world of the film, people are required to check into
this particular facility if they have become single – for example, left by
their partner (as is the case with the protagonist David, played by Colin
Farrell), or widowed. They have only forty-five days to acquire a plausible
new partner among the other hotel guests in order to regain their freedom.
Otherwise, they will be medically/technologically transformed into an
animal of their choice. The hotel guests, however, do have one way to gain
time: They can go hunting in the woods, where a number of escapees from
the hotel are still lurking, as we learn. And here comes the main sequence
of hunting on which I am focusing. The group of hotel detainees are seen
first being assembled outside the hotel, given guns, loaded onto a bus and
getting ready to hunt – those last action scenes appear in slow motion. The
spectacular 'chase' that ensues is slowed down in an overtly self-conscious
mockery of classical cinema slow-motion scenes, and the full length of the
chase sequence is taken up by the duration of a whole song. As we see the
'hotel inmates' slowly moving and shooting their prey in the woods, their
faces in awkward grimaces, we listen in full to a 1925 song by the Greek
singer-songwriter Attik, titled 'Από μέσα πεθαμένος' ('Dead on the Inside'),
performed in Greek by the legendary singer Danae in a later recording.[1] I
do not know how many of its international viewers have looked or would
look for that piece of contextual information. In most international-release

versions of the film, the lyrics of the song are not provided in the subtitling panels. Indeed, most of my non-Greek friends who watched it had not even registered that the song was in Greek. Yet, for a Greek viewer, the initial dissonance between the actual song lyrics and what happens on screen cannot be bypassed. This is what the song says, as it is heard in its entirety in the film:

Τον καιρό που μ' αγαπούσες με ρωτάς ένα πρωί
στην κουβέντα μας επάνω τ' είναι άραγε η ζωή
τότε γύρισα και σού 'πα γι' άλλους είναι το κρασί
γι' άλλους δόξα γι' άλλους πλούτη μα για μένα είσαι εσύ

Τώρα που άλλαξε η καρδιά σου κι έναν άλλον αγαπάς
απορείς μου λεν ακόμη η δική μου πως χτυπά
μήπως τάχα σαν κι εμένα δεν είν' άνθρωποι πολλοί
από μέσα πεθαμένοι και απ'έξω ζωντανοί

At the time when you loved me
As you asked what makes life true
I turned and said it's what one wants to be:
Drunk, rich, famous – but for me, life is you.

Now that your heart has fully changed, and you love someone else
You wonder they tell me, how come my heart still beats.
But why? Aren't there many like me, those who survive,
Dead inside, outside still alive?

To include in the film's soundtrack a love song in Greek could simply be seen as an affective gesture from a Greek director in his first widely distributed international co-production in English. Yet, the song is not heard in any of the scenes in which there is talk about love in a straight-forward or comic setting. It is, on the contrary, heard during a chase, and against images that might remind viewers of George Romero's *Night of the Living Dead* (1968), *Dawn of the Dead* (1978) and the various scenes in these and similar films in which zombies are marauding (or being chased) in the woods. As the Greek song builds to its final line, the repetition of the phrase 'Dead inside, outside still alive' may make some viewers think of the very condition of the 'living dead' that so many commentators projected onto Greece and Greek society when talking about the Greek economy, state and people in the years after 2009. Modern economic politics thrive in their use of metaphor, and the 'living dead' was such an obvious one in the years of the culmination of the Greek Crisis. 'Greece, a Financial Zombie State' read the title of an editorial in the *New York Times* on 12 June 2015.[2]

Keeping this detail in mind, this film, which internationally was largely received as a comment on modern society's insistence on coupledom and normative sexual and affiliative relationships, can also be read as a critique of social experiments, over-eager profiling and suffocating control.[3]

Critic Kenan Behzat Sharpe (2016) further elaborates on a similar reading, even though based on other aspects of the film. In a persuasive political interpretation, he argues that *The Lobster* offers a radical allegory about the current politics of neoliberalism, not only in Greece, but in the world as a whole, thus becoming a true 'transnational allegory' of the global moment. Sharpe even berates international critics who 'would have us assume that [it] is exclusively concerned with romantic relationships'.[4] On the contrary, he maintains, 'the film is very much revealing of the current [political] situation in Greece'. He establishes this point by focusing on the 5 July 2015 Greek referendum. In that now notorious turn of events, Greeks were given the opportunity to decide whether they were in favour of a set of austerity measures then proposed by the EU, the IMF and Greece's international creditors. Answering 'no' to these austerity measures in an overwhelming vote, they were eventually offered an even worse set of austerity measures, which the SYRIZA radical left government signed and set out to implement in the following four years. For Sharpe, *The Lobster* is an eloquent allegory for the meaningless 'yes or no' questions that neoliberal governmentality creates on a global scale today and of how inescapable this system of 'two choices and no real alternative' is, how we all 'lack a coherent narrative for a rupture'. To illustrate his reading, Sharpe then offers a poster from the film's own American advertising campaign. It looks exactly like a referendum ballot asking which animal the viewers would like to become, should they be left single for a long time ('deer', 'peacock', 'bison'). The question is ironic precisely because it offers a meaningless choice, as there is no real choice of 'not becoming' an animal. Next to this promotional image of a fictitious questionnaire, Sharpe puts a Greek 2015 referendum ballot. They look remarkably similar.

The point is not that *The Lobster*, which premiered in Cannes just before the 2015 referendum, had foreseen what was coming. Obviously, the poster that Sharpe mentions is a clever advertising tactic, aiming to capitalise on the international headlines about the referendum that came in the meantime, before the film's wider international distribution. Sharpe's argument is different, however: What *The Lobster* was already engaged with was not specific events, but *the type* of current socio-political conundrums that we see manifested in events such as the Greek 2015 referendum.

It is difficult to underestimate how much *The Lobster* is about the biopolitical texture of (our) life, as is the case for all of Lanthimos's films, in fact. This extends from how the 'good life' is described and imposed on individuals – and how coupledom and what Melinda Cooper (2017) so aptly calls 'Family Values' is instrumentalised to that effect – to how bodies are policed, surveilled, surveyed *and* transformed, and how populations are governed 'more efficiently' as a result: as living, dead, or living dead. *The Lobster*'s story can work at the level of analogy; it can be considered an allegory of the contemporary regimes of control and life optimisation, as well as the necropolitics for those proscribed as unwanted. There is, however, also an undeniable level of contiguity: the fact that this film is close to a certain social and cultural reality. That level of engagement may be recalled much more playfully – by putting, for instance, a film's poster next to a ballot paper, or trying to decipher the lyrics of a seemingly unrelated song. The result is similar: As it allows context to make a sudden appearance, it opens its floodgates, and it makes one realise the different ways in which it has always been, *persistently*, close.

This chapter returns to the debate about the relation of Greek films to their immediate socio-political context after 2008. There is a literalist version of this debate, which questions whether specific films were 'really meaning to refer/reference' Greece's specific socio-political troubles in their text (cf. Chalkou 2012). There is also an allegorist version of this debate, wondering whether a certain national allegory is immanent to these films, or something 'placed upon them through the act of circulation across cultural difference' (Larkin 2009: 165). I tend to circumvent them both, by asking a different set of questions.

First, I want to see how both the films' texts and their critical reception engage with aspects of contemporary biopolitics, and how much this, as in the example of *The Lobster*, creates a common ground, a context *already shared*. What we saw happening with *The Lobster* in the previous pages is an anchoring to other cultural texts and to specific political debates, which bases its accuracy not on any knowledge of authorial intent, but on a suggestion about this shared common ground. These complementary strategies of contextualisation, the cultural and (bio)political anchoring, have been crucial for the national and international reception of the Greek Weird Wave as a cinema of (the Greek) crisis. My second aim is to see them not as something that 'happened to' films, but as a pluri-dimensional process in which films, artists and viewers participate, constantly reshaping them.

As Joanna Page, following Fredric Jameson, has so usefully described in the case of contemporary Argentina, cinema 'is very much part of the economic system, the social relations, and the cultural milieu it might be supposed to depict' (Page 2009: 4). 'Intrinsic' and 'extrinsic' meanings, 'superstructural and infrastructural codes', 'formal readings and just accounts of the economic and technological determinants of these cultural artefacts' might be diverse and even at odds with each other, yet they end up equally constituting the films as cultural texts (Jameson 1990: 144).

This is a dynamic that I outline further in the rest of this chapter. I do so by first turning to a special TV programme shown on French and German television in 2012, a very typical instance of the international expectations of 'a Greek cinema and culture of the Crisis'. In a most helpful fashion, this specific example also clearly shows how a particular economy of reception was (en)countered by the artists themselves. What emerges is a processual dynamic that is not external to the Weird Wave, but, crucially, has been a key aspect of its formation as a collective and genealogical project. In the last sections of the chapter, I will use the example of an Athenian film collective and their screening and social events, so as to show exactly what I mean by the term 'processual dynamic' in this context.

LANTHIMOS UNDER THE PARTHENON

The *Square* special programme on Greek art and crisis, which first aired on the French/German arts channel ARTE on 25 March 2012, starts as one would expect: with establishing shots, first of the Greek capital (the Parthenon, the Herod Atticus Odeon, the ancient Agora and Monastiraki Square) and then of the capital in Crisis (walls full of graffiti, more graffiti under a statue, with the slogan 'wake up and fight now'). Journalist Vincent Josse then introduces the programme:

> Γεια σας, Wilkommen, Bienvenue. Our guest today is a country whose civilisation makes us dream, but a country that no longer dreams. Eleven million Greeks, one million unemployed, one in two young people unemployed. We will meet a number of artists here, in Greece, in order to understand how their art is inflected by the Crisis [est traversé par la crise]. The first is a cinema director who has been lauded for his film *Dogtooth* in Cannes and with his film *Alps* in Venice. His name is Yorgos Lanthimos.

Even though Lanthimos's name is introduced almost matter-of-factly, it will soon become obvious that he is the main focus of this presentation, that the whole programme is structured around him and his work, since his films are taken as exemplary of this 'Crisis-traversed art' that the programme has set out to find in Greece. His personal interview will book-end the programme, and he will stay with the journalist/producer for most of its running time. But before we ever see the Greek director, we see a graphic with major events of Greek history: first a title (below in bold), followed by a gloss (below in brackets) against the background of an illustrative photograph. It goes like this:

- **3200** [Greek civilisation is born in the Mediterranean basin]
- **Papadopoulos** [1967, the Greek dictatorship of Georgios Papadopoulos]
- **Lanthimos** [1973, Yorgos Lanthimos is born in this context of the Junta]
- **Dimokratia** [the restitution of democracy in 1974]

- **Goldman Sachs** [2009, the subprime market collapse in the US, provoking, through contagion, a Greek debt crisis]
- **Kynodontas** [2009, same year, Lanthimos reveals his talent with his film *Dogtooth*, which takes the 'Un certain regard' prize in Cannes, before being nominated for the Best Foreign Film Oscar]
- **Krisis** [at the same time, for months in Greece demonstrations proliferate, denouncing the drastic austerity measures. The cradle of Democracy falls into chaos.]

In this narrative beginning with the dawn of Greek civilisation and ending with Krisis, the hellenised spelling of the last word underlines its singularity and local character. One is not sure whether the story of this director, his life and his films are subsumed under this Krisis-story of the nation, or whether the opposite happens. National allegory is here not simply presented as an all-encompassing modality, but also proposed as an ever-expansive map that eventually becomes co-terminous with the mapped.

As happens with most directors of the Weird Wave, Lanthimos expresses

Figures 3.1a–f *Lanthimos interviewed for* Square *on the channel ARTE; digital stills.*

his unease with this narrative, with its assumptions and linear chronologies, but to an important extent he also plays along with it. '[My generation and I] are interested not in the picture-postcard Greece. I prefer exploring other, more contemporary themes, which relate to more contemporary Greeks, more contemporary people', he replies when asked whether he thinks that his generation has broken away from 'that traditional way of making cinema in Greece'. But, the journalist retorts:

> Take an example from your cinema, *Dogtooth*. In that film you speak about a family and a patriarch, you tell the story of a man who has confined his family in the home so that they do not have any contact with the outside world; thus starts a film that reminds one a lot of the cinema of Michael Haneke. I would like to know whether that family, the family of *Dogtooth*, is a kind of metaphor for Greek society. Isn't that society also too enclosed on itself, too conservative, isn't it also a victim of patriarchy?
>
> Lanthimos: *Dogtooth* shows a patriarchal family, this is clear, but what we were interested in was not so much whether it was patriarchal or matriarchal, since both parents have an important role in the way in which relations within this family, this group, are formed and crystallised. What interested us were the ways in which *a family or a group*, no matter what the leader is, *is governed and what kind of impact this has on every member of the group, on their understanding of the world, on their education*. What interested us were the ways you can mould a human being's mind and body with extreme methods and the limits this situation can reach. In other words, *Dogtooth* was not a film on the Greek or the patriarchal family or society; we might have been inspired by it, but it relates to all kinds of similar groups.
>
> Vincent Josse (inverviewer): You know, the British newspaper *The Guardian*, has said that you participate in the Weird Wave of Greek Cinema . . .
>
> Lanthimos: I don't know how weird it is, actually. Of course, there are strange elements: in my films, in other people's films. What we do is what we believe flows naturally from the exploration of the issues we engage with. (Arte 2012; emphasis added)

I do not know whether Lanthimos has read work on governmentality and biopolitics, but these are exactly the terms in which he describes his most famous Greek-language film here. Even though he resists being pigeonholed, he still describes *Dogtooth* as a film about being governed, about how a group is managed, about how this is internalised and diffused in everyday praxis by every member of the group, how it becomes a mentality. 'Strange elements', Lanthimos then says, 'flow naturally' from engaging with such issues.

This is, perhaps predictably, the moment in which the programme cuts to images of demonstration and civil unrest, hooded youth writing anti-establishment slogans in graffiti, extracts from international news reels on the

Crisis and caricatures of 'lazy Greeks' published by international media, recognizable images of Greece-of-the-Crisis, before cutting back to Lanthimos (always in the shadow of the Acropolis). The director is then asked to explain how difficult it is to make cinema in the country under these conditions, to express his opinion on mounting unemployment and racism, the tension of everyday life in Greece and the people's loss of confidence in the state and the political system. In this context, he says at one point, 'this whole generation [to which I belong], has decided to make films any way they can. They realise they cannot expect anything from anyone'.

In the final scene of the *Square* TV programme on Lanthimos's Greece, after a number of additional interviews that I will describe later on, the journalist ends by acknowledging an awkward set-up: 'You were telling me that you are not very happy our interview is happening with the Parthenon as a background . . .' Lanthimos replies: 'Yes, I am generally concerned with the ways Greece is being represented in the media. We are trying to do something different; I am therefore feeling uncomfortable and uneasy (αμήχανα και άβολα) [being represented like this]. I am trying not to be yet another part of the picture postcard (να μην είμαι μέρος της καρτ ποστάλ)'.

The irony is that this programme has also ended up producing a 'picture postcard' view of Greece; even in the moment when Lanthimos utters these words, he is being filmed in the area of the Kerameikos, the ancient Athenian cemetery. Furthermore, one could argue that the contemporary version of Greece, the 'Greece of the Crisis', is also introduced as a picture postcard by such media texts as this programme. For instance, the graphic with the 'list of events' reproduced above was made to look like a postcard, its background a combination of classical Greek pottery and contemporary Greek demonstrators. Crisis Greece has, indeed, become a new picture postcard, and the Weird Wave fits into it and provides a necessary illustration. There is no protest against that aspect of the Weird Wave's international presentation, here and elsewhere. Yet, there is also that final moment, marked by the statement 'I feel uneasy and uncomfortable', that awkwardness. As was the case with Yorgos Zois in a similar interview analysed in the Introduction, as was the case of so many other directors of the Weird Wave in their interaction with film festival audiences, international and local media and critics, Lanthimos here is at the same time both familiar and dissonant; the weirdness, palpable in the air, is already an effort to answer back.[5]

'AND . . . HOW DO YOU PAY YOUR RENT?'

Its framing of national allegory notwithstanding, the TV programme *Square* aimed to show contemporary Greek culture as one that resists and survives underinvestment and social upheaval, mainly relying on artists' inventiveness, stubbornness, cruel optimism, spirit of collaboration and solidarity.

I have already explained why I think Lanthimos's interaction with this global framing is interesting and in no way simple. Further evidence of this is what he does some twenty minutes into the programme. Asked about his work's further relevance to Greece's current affairs, he does not bring more examples from his films. Instead, he mentions his network of cultural collaborators and peers. Thus, he introduces choreographer Dimitris Papaioannou, actor Giorgos Valais and musician/filmmaker Alexandros Voulgaris. As he explains, they represent a much wider network of artists and cultural producers active in contemporary Greece.[6] What I find worth pursuing here is that, when confronted with both of the types of contextualisation I have described in the previous section – the anchoring in cultural/historical detail and the political debate – Lanthimos responds with a possible third: He offers the idea of a cultural *community*, one that is always already engaged, *in context* already, and thus the most concrete framing of his films.

Papaioannou is a choreographer famous for his work for the 2004 Olympic ceremonies (in which Lanthimos, Tsangari and other artists eventually involved with the Weird Wave had worked). Valais is an actor and member of the physical theatre group Blitz, which he founded with Christos Passalis and Angeliki Papoulia, the protagonists of *Dogtooth*. Blitz started life as an artists' collective shortly after the 2004 Olympic Games , representing a new theatrical scene that was then gaining pace in Athens, significantly involving physical theatre, audience participation, site specificity and the undermining of a stable theatrical text (Arfara 2014). It has been widely seen as the theatrical equivalent of the Weird Wave (Papanikolaou 2017).

The last 'friend of Lanthimos' to be presented on the TV programme is Alexandros Voulgaris, a prolific musician, film director and video artist (to whose work I will return in the Epilogue of this book). Lanthimos and Josse visit him in his studio. The two Greeks start by explaining that their acquaintance and creative friendship goes a long way back ('he was once my assistant when I worked as a cameraman . . . '). The discussion very soon turns to the economic situation. 'Is the financial crisis a stimulant for your art?' asks Josse. 'To be honest, I have not thought how my films would be if I had money for a big production; but I am going to every length in order to find solutions and, after all, I always appreciated B-movies', replies Voulgaris, who is indeed known for the extreme shoestring budget on which he shoots his films. As the camera moves around his spartan studio, we hear him playing music, describing how he sources his equipment on the flea market, trying to make do with what is available. Then, following the journalist's quite insistent questioning, we hear how much money he makes as an artist. 'I am sorry to be posing this question, but, Alexandros, you live on how much money per month?' Embarrassed laughter in the room. 'Well . . . I haven't got a fixed revenue, there is a month I might make 100 euro, and another 1,000. Let's say I earn 500 euro per month'. 'And your rent, here, how do you pay it?' More laughter, more embarrassment. The discussion then moves on to Alexandros's music, and whether Lanthimos listens to it now that he has emigrated to London.[7]

The *Square* programme aims to show the cultural life of the country in full swing and to offer a commentary on the 'brain drain', on alternative forms of cultural production and the spirit of (cultural and social) solidarity. Yet, what further interests me is how all the Greek artists involved describe a context of cultural production that is not fully specified and mapped, as well as a tendency to relate to the events around them, which is particular even though it does not have recognizable characteristics. What they all point to, as Voulgaris puts it, is a strategy of *making do*: This is what links their creative gestures. There is a situation in which these artists have found themselves, one which is neither adopted nor opposed, but instead *responded to* – surely in metaphor, but more in metonymy, surely through analogy, but more through contiguity. As this is a form of engaging with a globalised setting – let us not forget that the Greek artists here are giving an interview to a European channel – Lanthimos's and the Greek artists' responses can help us rethink how the very context of globalisation has changed in the twenty-first century, especially after the major financial crisis of 2008, and how it has impacted our understanding of cultural circulation in this new globality.

In the following section I will take my cue from a critical framework that has been proposed precisely in order to analyse how national film cultures respond creatively to a new globalised cultural and financial market. More than twenty years ago, Mette Hjort set out to document and analyse the success of the New Danish Cinema in the global cultural market; along the way, she proposed the concept of the 'cinema of small nations'. This concept works brilliantly, I think, for my case-study: The Greek Weird Wave, much like the New Danish Cinema, is a model cinema of a small nation. Yet, the differences between the New Danish Cinema of the 1990s and the Greek Weird Wave of the 2010s can also be very telling. They show an intensification of certain modalities of response (and of doing national cinema) in the contemporary moment which, I believe, also speaks to the intensification of our sense of a biopolitical present, as well as to the dynamics it inadvertently sets in motion.

HOVERING, WALKING AROUND, IN PROCESS: ON THE SMALL-NATIONALITY OF THE WEIRD WAVE

The TV programme I have examined above does not offer a full analysis of any film of the Greek Weird Wave; neither can it be claimed to be a deep contextualisation of its poetics. However, it functions as a powerful (and indicative) tool of what anthropologist Greg Urban has called meta-culture, that framing of cultural texts that 'aids culture in its motion through space and time. It gives a boost to the culture that it is about, helping to propel it on its journey' (2001: 4). The films of the Greek Weird Wave were from the beginning helped by such meta-cultural responses. The ARTE programme follows a pattern that can also be found in countless similar media presentations, articles and festival curatorial texts.

As Mette Hjort explains in her influential *Small Nation, Global Cinema* (2005), such a meta-cultural framing is the most effective (and often the only) way for a cinema of a small nation to make it today in the global arena of cultural circulation, marketing, festival circuit and multimedia platforms. There has to be a discourse, specific anchoring points (such as the presence of a central director and some iconic films) and a continuous discussion about the national cultural specificity, but also the globality, of these films. If this happens, if a global momentum is created for the cinema of a small nation, every film recognized as part of it then works as an instigator of 'metacultural moments' (46). Every film becomes an opportunity to continue the global discussion that promotes, groups together, identifies and often politicises the films of the small nation – a discussion that explains to a global audience not only where they are coming from, but also why they matter. Such a discussion eventually becomes as much a part of every single film as their other main characteristics.

A cinema of a small nation, therefore, is one whose relationship to an international public is by no means a given, which has to find and develop its own politics of recognition, fighting against cultural and economic inequalities (Hjort 2005: 520). It can be seen as a 'minor cinema', if the term is understood in the way in which Gilles Deleuze and Félix Guattari see 'minor literature' – that is, as pointing 'to the existence of regimes of cultural power and to the need for strategic resourcefulness on the part of those who are unfavorably situated within the cultural landscape in question, be it a national context or a more properly global one' (Hjort 2005: 9). Globalisation and internationalisation can have a negative impact on some small national cinemas, but they can also offer opportunities to others to develop, in specific periods, 'positive definitions of world cinema', 'evidence of the diverse ways in which global forces affect local cinematic contexts, and conceptual models that acknowledge that cinema is caught up in a web of international relations and not merely in an ongoing drama with Hollywood' (Hjort and Petrie 2007: 18).

Researchers and cultural practitioners who have underlined the importance of this framework for the success of Greek Cinema in the late 2000s and 2010s have made useful comparisons with other national cinemas, such as the cinemas of Spain and Portugal during the same period, the New Argentine Cinema of the mid 1990s, or the Romanian New Wave (Basea 2014; Nikolaidou and Poupou 2017; Tzouflas 2018; Astrinaki 2015; Kourelou et al. 2014; Karkani 2016b). As had happened before with New Argentine or Romanian Cinema, it is the small-nationality of contemporary Greek Cinema that facilitated the Weird Wave's international success, while also supporting the tendency to view its films in the contemporary socio-political reality of Greece. Inescapable context, the recognition of a specific 'cinematic wave' and even 'weirdness' are intricately related, I would argue, to the position that Greek Cinema has as the cinema of a small nation at the present moment. They are the conceptual tools that help position Greek production within a global political and economic environment already affecting it. My persistence with the term 'Weird Wave' is itself a recognition of the importance of this framing and an account of the way in which global forces impact local cinematic developments.

A further note about this framing is in order. Hjort developed her ideas on the Cinema of Small Nations with the Danish Cinema of the 1990s and early 2000s in mind, and with the Dogme 95 generation as her major case-study. Much of her analysis fits with the analysis of the Weird Wave, too, and it obviously helps that the major Danish directors of Dogme, Lars von Trier and Thomas Winterberg, have been recognizable influences for many new Greek directors, especially Lanthimos, Avranas and Tzoumerkas (Koutsourakis 2012).[8] Of crucial importance for the Greek case has also been what Hjort identifies as 'the dynamics of a cinematic "gift culture" in which various forms of generosity and collectivism become the means of enhancing the opportunities available to filmmakers, their efficacy as filmmakers and their visibility, both nationally and globally' (Hjort et al. 2010: 9). However, there are also important differences between my contemporary Greek and Hjort's earlier case-study of Danish Cinema.

Hjort starts with a concrete group of Danish directors who had a very clear agenda for their cultural poetics and oppositional politics. Dogme published a manifesto on cultural politics and cinematic form. Even when its specific pronouncements were not followed to the letter, the manifesto nevertheless became a platform with which directors and films, and later other artists working in other fields could be identified. Dance theatre practitioners published their version of the Dogme manifesto. Theatre groups developed a similar aesthetics, and even advertising followed suit. Crucially, the idea of a national cinema, with its own national references, constantly informed the Danish directors' statements, and the Danish Film Institute often played a role in their efforts. Indeed, the Danish Film Institute remained strongly supportive of this new movement throughout and saw it as an opportunity to redefine itself. Building on these quite concrete foundations, the Danish Cinema of the 1990s clustered around Von Trier and the Dogme group and developed a new style of production whose clear aim was to negotiate the new terms of (cultural) globalisation and to create a wider public for itself.

The Greek directors of the 2000s cut a completely different picture. They may have made their first public appearance collectively and with the public announcement of the *Filmmakers in the FOG* (see Introduction). Yet, they did not ever constitute a closely-knit group in terms of their cinematic choices. They did not publish a manifesto on form and concrete cultural politics – even the first *FOG* announcements were not on how to make films, but on the need to keep making them. Finally, the majority of them had not studied together in a state film school (as the Danish filmmakers had done in the National Film School of Denmark, which plays a central role in Hjort's account), nor did they enjoy continuous and guaranteed state support.

For these reasons, I tend to locate the beginnings of the Greek Weird Wave in the moment when a group of younger Greek directors realised that they were facing a series of gaping holes: in the very existence of their state, in national cinematography, financial support and their own self-understanding as a group within a national (cultural) history. In other words, a series of categories that we recognize as crucial in the development of the cinema of a small nation and its emergence as culturally defining – categories such as 'cinematic culture', 'cinematic genealogy', nationality, national cinematography, film institutions, collectivity, specific context and the like – were in the process of being denied, being undermined or made absent in the case of the Greek Weird Wave. They were extant, still interacting with the films, but they stood somewhat emptied of their former power, as if they had already been removed. No wonder a critic has so aptly called this 'a cinema of abeyance' (Karalis 2012).

It is spectacular that these categories, in clear small-world-cinema fashion, ended up playing an important role in the Greek Weird Wave anyway. They kept returning, as haunting presences and as categories with which the films worked processually, developing them as they went along, not adopting them from the outset. Yorgos Lanthimos's celebrated *Dogtooth*, for instance, is a film that initially seems eager to provoke the impression that it is not related to a system of national representation. There are no references to recognizable Greek landscapes, no obvious reference to a Greek socio-political context (or, indeed, to any socio-political context) and, perhaps more crucially, no effort to attach itself to a national (cinematic) culture. Unlike in any film by Theo Angelopoulos, for example, there is neither literary reference to a recognizable national cultural/literary canon, nor a visual anchoring to a national iconography, nor thirst for a national archive. Nevertheless, as I explain at various points in this book, all these different anchorings do eventually come to play a role, even in their absence. They may reside in the small details of the *mise-en-scène*; in the star text of the actors, in the specific poetics of allegory; they eventually develop as references because of the discussions provoked in the reception of a particular film or the way in which it might be seen to be related to other films.

Contextualisation and political readings of a film can thus return and reassess specific details in the cinematic text or rearticulate others. It was often in this manner that a series of issues – including ethnicity and citizenship, Greek cinema history and pedagogy, social dynamics and the precarity of living in the conditions of the Crisis – made their presence felt in (and with) the films of the Greek Weird Wave, rarely following a strictly realist protocol or a direct 'reference in the story'. They sometimes developed as parallel discussions, as responses, as *'necessary contexts'*. The fact that they were not a given from the outset offered these films an additional shared characteristic that, with time, also went some way towards defining them as a group.

To speak of the Greek Weird Wave as a cinematic movement means that we can acknowledge its processual dynamic, viewing its collective poetics and contextual engagement as unfolding over time. It means that we can accept its way of engaging with Greek film history and genealogy as a continuous process (cf. Kazakopoulou 2017a). Last, but not least, it means that we can reflect on the complex ways in which it redefined the national cultural and film industry, often by relying for its production and promotion on transnational financial and cultural capital and how it saw, partly as a result of this, its transformation into a 'movement' with specific traits and patterns (Papadimitriou 2018a; 2018b).

As I watch Lanthimos walking around Athens in the ARTE special programme described in the previous section, trying to introduce a French journalist to a larger group of artists that circles around and informs the films he and his peers make, I see emerging from this interview the need to show how much a series of categories that we have learnt to recognize as central to a national cinema should be rethought in processual terms and with a larger cultural context in mind. As I watch actor Valais, choreographer Papaioannou and musician/filmmaker Voulgaris talk about their work in the company of Lanthimos, as I follow their attempt to explain how they try to make ends meet, but also to promote their projects abroad without any specific institutional support for doing so, I am reminded of the fact that even this international-media-framed walking shows the effort of these artists *to engage* (cf. Athanasiou 2016). What I see in this talk about a frameless movement is that it eventually creates a tangible, workable frame-in-process.

I will offer a telling example of what I consider as the processual poetics of the Greek Weird Wave in the next and the final section of this chapter.

Waving is Weaving: Exercises in Genealogy

The Astor, one of the oldest Greek cinema venues, has operated in Athens under its current management since March 2015.[9] As one of the oldest cinemas of Athens still in use, the Astor has been revamped under the new direction, focusing, according to its manager, on new *auteur* cinema. In its vicinity are other well-known Athenian art cinemas, including, some fifty metres away, Asty which also specialises in art films and is often the first and only to show Greek productions supported by the Greek Film Centre. Upon walking 200 metres in the opposite direction, one finds the remains of the neoclassical building that once housed the cinemas Apollon and Attikon, two of the most historical theatres in Athens and the place where the first sound movie was shown in October 1929 (ElCulture 2016). Moreover, these are the cinemas where most of the early Weird Wave films had their premiere in the late 2000s, before the biggest part of the building was burnt down during the mass demonstrations that shook Athens in February 2012.

The new, refurbished Astor cinema was not created in order to replace Apollon and Attikon. After all, it cannot compare with the grandiose environment of those earlier theatres. It no longer even features an entrance to a main street, as it is tucked deep inside the modern arcade starting on Korae Street. However, in recent years the Astor has become the hub for new Greek art cinema, showcasing not only new work, but also creating events around new Greek films on many occasions. The small distribution company that owns it is called 'Weird Wave', a title which it took, as its founder Babis Kontarakis says, from the internationally recognizable label of the Greek new wave films. Weird Wave is a distribution company which, apart from managing the Astor Cinema, also brings to Greece small world cinema productions – such as, in recent years, Argentinian Lucretia Marcel's *Zama* (2017) and Romanian Radu Jude's *Aferim* (2015). The underlying idea is that there exists a wider new wave developing internationally in world cinema, a wave that is as weird as the Greek Weird Wave, but that, most importantly, reacts to a similar socio-economic environment and has adopted a similar agenda of cultural response.

It was in the Astor that a group of directors, critics and Greek cinema afi-
cionados organised their monthly meetings between 2016 and 2018.[10] Their
project was called *Η χαμένη λεωφόρος του ελληνικού σινεμά*, in English *The Lost
Highway of Greek Cinema*. It consisted of themed screenings from an earlier
period of Greek Cinema, introduced by a younger generation of artists and
followed by public debate on the first Monday and Friday of each month,
as well as an after-hours party, often DJ'd by film directors and musicians.
To complement the screenings, the group behind the project organised new
posters and specially commissioned graphic designs for the film programmes
it curated. It also disseminated new critical texts on these older films in social
and conventional media, as well as other work, such as new trailers, podcasts
or mixtapes. The *Lost Highway* project is not the only such project organised
in Greece in recent decades; however, it does showcase a type of engagement
that defines the dynamism of the cinema of a small nation today, perhaps
more than the international success of specific films or directors.

There is an additional reason for focusing on this project as I bring this
chapter on weird contextualisations to a close. What struck me from the first
time I heard of this group of cinema practitioners and their successful events
was their effort to produce, performatively, new historical insights into Greek
cinema and their tendency to do so in a way that one could call not simply
historical or archival, but genealogical. As the title of their initiative implies,
there is an alternative way to go about the history of Greek Cinema. These
alternative visions need to be rethought in the context of a local history;
yet, they already also belong in a transnational context, as the nod to David
Lynch's 1997 film *The Lost Highway* implies. Indeed, they are not only small
roads, but highways – one just needs to search for the right openings in order
to locate them. These lost highways are there to be retraced, remapped,
traversed again, backward and forward. Organised and publicised mainly
through the internet and a Facebook account where members of the audience
could also post comments and suggestions, *The Lost Highway* programme had
all the characteristics of a specialists' night out. But it was more.

Even though the cornerstones of the project were cinephilia and archival
research, *The Lost Highway* meetings were organised on the basis of themes,
not historical periods or directors. 'Invisible Threat', 'Bitter Bread', 'Wasted
1980s' and 'Threatened Genres' were some of the inventive titles for those
first thematic weekly screenings, which showcased Greek films from the
1960s to the 1990s. In a series of special screenings in the first months of
2017 (repeated later in Thessaloniki in 2018), which became the reference
point for the whole project, a number of earlier films were proposed as 'The
Weird Back Then' or 'The Weird before the Weird Wave'. The films shown in
these events included, among others, *Eastern Territory* (Vasilis Vafeas, 1979),

Figure 3.2 The Weird Past, *poster by Nikos Pastras for one of* The Lost Highway *events, Athens,* 2018. *Copyright: Nikos Pastras and* The Lost Highway.

About Vassilis (Stavros Tsiolis, 1986), *Nike of Samothrace* (Dimos Avdeliodis, 1990) and *Oh Babylon* (Costas Ferris, 1989). When first produced, all these films had been considered uncategorisable, and some had remained for years unreleased or unwatched while also acquiring cult status.

Perhaps the most peculiar of them, Nico Papatakis's *The Shepherds of Disaster*, made and finished just before the advent of the Colonels' Dictatorship in 1967 and for years without an official release in Greece, still has the power to shock and unsettle the contemporary viewer. The level of violence, of crude, carnivalesque humour aimed against bourgeois normativity, the relentless way in which the symbolic weight of the Greek Family is torn down can remind contemporary viewers of films of the contemporary Weird Wave. In this discontinuously edited story that simultaneously brings to mind Felini's

La Strada and Georges Brassens's song *Le Gorille*, a shepherd who returns to his village falls in love and abducts the mayor's daughter, before running away with her and staging a grand spectacle in which they both direct all manners of conceivable obscenities and verbal abuse against the 'good society' of the villagers who have been chasing them. Crucially, all the actors speak in a defamiliarising off-tone delivery, as if they are reading out a script for the first time.

In the beginning of *The Shepherds*, the main character's mother, after being ridiculed and humiliated for wanting her son to marry the daughter of the village's foremost landowner, turns to the rich man's house and starts berating him and the social structures supporting his powers. She lifts her dress and, turning her privates towards the house, starts shouting: 'Take this from me, all of you . . . This is the only thing I have left'.

'Did you notice how this scene is copied, gesture after gesture and word for word, in Economides's *Matchbox*?' director Elina Psykou asked me during the screening of *The Shepherds* in the *Lost Highway* series.[11] 'You remember the scene towards the end of *Matchbox*, don't you? There, the mother of the family, played by Eleni Kokkidou, turns to her husband during their final altercation and performs exactly the same physical gesture you see in *The Shepherds* thirty-five years beforehand. And, did you know that the same Eleni Kokkidou was the first choice to play the mother in *Dogtooth* – the role that eventually went to Michelle Valley?'

For Psykou, there was an obvious line connecting *The Shepherds* and its violent critique of Greek social and filial structures, with *Matchbox* and then the more recent films of the Weird Wave. Moreover, for her, fleshing out this connecting line had the power not only to make a new audience appreciate that older film, but it also made the more brutal and obvious social critique of *The Shepherds* a key for our reading of the later films of the Weird Wave. The characters in Papatakis's film act in public, and all the verbal and bodily language is enacted as a challenge to propriety, in public. In *Matchbox* (whose impact on the Weird Wave I have described in Chapter 1), in the iconic *Dogtooth*, as well as in many later films of the Weird Wave, a similar tension is played out mostly in private – with many of the films shot almost entirely within the walls of the family home (see Chapter 5). Therefore, suggesting that these later Greek films belong in the same line as Papatakis's *Shepherds* has the potential to effectively allegorise their private spaces as references also standing for the public. It also has the potential to show their critique of family as a targeting of wider social structures, which belongs to a genealogy that runs deep within Greek Cinema.

The important point is not whether the similarities that may link the older film by Papatakis with films of the Weird Wave are deliberate references, whether they are as accurate as suggested, or, in the final analysis, whether they provide sufficient evidence for an intertextual reading on their basis. The details and the examples are not as crucial as is the critical, creative and participatory gesture they are called on to support, the *desire for genealogy*.

In a similar effort to create a genealogy, in a text read as the introduction to the film's *Lost Highway* special screening, director Syllas Tzoumerkas praised another earlier film, Kostas Manousakis's *Fear* (1966) – 'one of my three favourite Greek films'. *Fear*, so the younger director explains, had managed to show 'how this country hides its secrets in the lakes and in the swamps' (Tzoumerkas 2017). In Tzoumerkas's enthusiasm for this earlier film about incestuous desire, familial violence, abuse and silenced rape, it is easy to discern an effort by the younger director to contextualise his own movies *Homeland* (2010) and *A Blast* (2014) – they are, after all, films about similar themes.[12] Tzoumerkas does not hide this potential influence. Moreover, based on this specific example, he offers a more practical explanation of how this and other similar films have influenced 'a new generation of Greek Cinema'. This is what he says about *Fear*:

> Official selection for the 1966 Berlin Film Festival, the film (and its director) was completely erased by the advent of the cinematic nonsense promoted by the Dictatorship. It was similarly cast aside by the implosion of the heavy lefty Greek arthouse cinema of the 1970s, when everyone was too serious and otherwise engaged to deal with a film like *Fear*. The film, however, came back with a vengeance in the 1980s, first on the state TV channels, and later, in the 1990s, in the late night programmes of the new private TV channels, which showed it as soft porn. It was then that *Fear*'s legend was built, slowly. Because, by then, a new generation of Greek cinema [to come] was already sat in front of their TV screens, avidly watching. (Tzoumerkas 2017)

What hides behind this paragraph is another exercise in genealogy, this time decisively more collective. According to the picture that Tzoumerkas paints, films like *Fear* were too radical to survive the onslaught of cultural populism that the 1967–74 Dictatorship brought with it. At the same time, their poetics were not easily discernible as political by the leftist generation of the New Greek Cinema that followed the Dictatorship and participated in the cultural resistance against it. Therefore, those earlier films did not make it into the national film canon, and they were not part of a national cinematic tradition. But then, he reminds us, those earlier films were rediscovered by Greek TV in the 1990s, and it is there that they were seen again and again, circulated also on home video. Thus, they were able to have an impact, as 'a new generation of Greek cinema was already by that time watching (a lot of) television'.

A generation of filmmakers, those very same filmmakers now recognized as part of a 'distinct wave', are here described on the basis, not only of their cinematic references, but also their common media practices and experiences – outside of cinematic institutions and schools. What is produced, therefore, is the idea of a group of people who lived through the Greece of the 1980s and 1990s, worked in the country's media industry, often in advertising and TV productions, and developed their aesthetic as well as their critical objectives during that period. This is not a specifically defined group, but a broader space where people found themselves together and could work retrospectively towards a common genealogy.

These are only a few of the many similar genealogical gestures of the *Lost Highway* project, or other similar ventures. They were genealogical gestures that took the films of the Weird Wave as cues in an effort to work their/our gaze backwards, creating in the process not only a sense of collectivity and topicality for the Weird Wave, but also a richer cinematic contextualisation for its films.

A CINEMATIC MILIEU AND THE PRACTICE OF 'MAKING DO'

Following a linear and teleological periodisation that works in a similar way for many national cinemas, we tend to think of the history of Greek Cinema as evolving in four distinct periods: Early Greek Cinema (1920s to late 1940s), Old Greek Cinema (1950s and 1960s), New Greek Cinema (1970s and 1980s) and Contemporary Greek Cinema (1990s) (Athanasatou 2001; Kolovos 2002; Bakogiannopoulos 1993; cf. Demopoulos 1995; Constantinidis 2000; Karalis 2012). This historical narrative pivots around the emergence of New Greek Cinema (NGC) in the late 1960s. Hailed as the period of the Greek *auteur*, it was anticipated by figures such as Michael Cacoyannis and Nikos Koundouros and then spearheaded by filmmakers such as Theo Angelopoulos, Pantelis Voulgaris and Lakis Papastathis. It was characterised by the advent of new journals and cinema clubs and a certain reorganisation of the cinematic field in Greece around specific institutions and funding bodies (Chalkou 2008; Basea 2011). It is this recognition of New Greek Cinema's central importance by Greek film critics that make some Greek film histories look like no more than an effort to provide its background. The commercial and genre-centred 'Old Greek Cinema' is seen as NGC's opposite; the 'Early' period is seen as its prehistory, and 'Contemporary Greek Cinema' is taken to be an anti-climactic moment in the 1990s, supported by a new and expanding TV industry.[13] Evidently, when following this logic, one ends up with no further space for another 'period' to emerge. Early, old, new, contemporary – the list is so teleological that it looks as if there are no further chapters to come.

No wonder, then, that initially many Greek critics felt quite uneasy about including the Weird Wave as an additional period in the history of Greek

Cinema. Measured by the criteria of the previous categorisations, the Weird Wave was simply felt to be non-conforming and not sufficiently coherent. It was not so much an *auteur* cinema, as there was no clear intellectual discourse – no unifying style, agenda-setting publications or 'central' events – emanating from the directors and becoming the films' central characteristic. Nor was it 'Greek enough'. It worked with film genre, but no specific genres seemed to be giving it an identity. Its success could be seen as a product of specific agents – such as producers, film festival curators and journalists – but the dynamic it was producing seemed larger than that. It was given a specific name, but then again, this name did not cover all its films equally, and neither was it adopted unequivocally.

Had I been writing a book on Greek Cinema of the 1980s or 1990s, I would have started by researching the major institutional and state-funded players of that time, such as the Greek Film Centre or the Thessaloniki Film Festival, reading detailed catalogues and lists of state awards, and the official institutions' rationales for the funding of specific film projects each year. But by 2008, such institutional players and data, even though still in existence, had already lost their authority and priority in Greece. A more complex landscape of funding, network support, peer culture and alternative development of cinematic projects was already being established (Papadimitriou 2018a, 2018b; Meuer 2018). While the very medium of cinema was changing, allowing for more flexible productions and cheaper and more creative ways of filming, those people who found themselves at the centre of national cinema life were no longer a well-defined group concentrated around specific institutions and lining up for the same resources, as they had been in previous periods (especially in the 1980s and 1990s). That 'other generation of Greek Cinema' of which Syllas Tzoumerkas spoke in the previous section was also a generation that cut its teeth working in TV productions, advertising and journalism, as well as in multi-media event organisation and performance. It came together, as I have suggested in the previous pages, in ways that can best be described as processual, often creating its own quasi-insititutional frameworks, rather than relying on preexisting structures.

The Lost Highway shows exactly the type of collectivities, events and 'places' that come to play a crucial role in a culturescape like that of contemporary Greece. I hesitate to call them 'institutions'; even though they do institute new discourses and cultural works, they are not clearly instituted in that they do not have clear-cut roles, sources of funding, or roles for their key players. The group that eventually supported and made possible *The Lost Highway* tried to operate the events and their related outcomes (books, public for a and websites) in a horizontal manner, deciding collectively and, most of the time, debating their next steps in public. It was made up of directors, film critics, academics on precarious contract employment, journalists and cinema specialists sometimes working with the Greek cinemathèque and the Greek Film Centre. Most of them also participated in ESPEK, the Greek Film Directors and Producers Guild that had been reorganised after the 2009 *Filmmakers in the FOG* movement (see Chapter 1). Some had already finished their first or second film, while others had not yet managed to find funding for projects they had been developing for years. Most were working on different small projects and only employed part-time and with precarious contracts. Some of their most elaborate projects were supported by initiatives that had a similar structure, such as the websites *Flix* and *Popaganda*, the electronic journal *Filmicon*, or small publishing houses run by groups of their friends and colleagues.

A further point worth underlining when it comes to these groups and their initiatives is that they are highly intersectional, having neither a specific form of power dictating their priorities and choices, nor specific forms of funding shaping their efforts.[14] If in a previous period of Greek filmmaking most directors and producers would line up, often waiting for years, in order to receive funding from the state's Greek Film Centre, today's context of production has changed radically – funding may or may not come from different national, supranational, or private sources. In the meantime, the very definition of a project has also changed. Even though this new generation of cinema makers still consider a feature-length film the pinnacle of one's achievement, today the actual engagement with a more general *milieu* much more seems to be the aim. For many filmmakers active in contempoprary Greece, the aim is not necessarily to direct a finished feature-length film, but to participate in that milieu – even if it means that they keep producing shorter films, hand-made personal projects, unfinished material, or even narrating one's film projects in text and reading out that text in one of these weird evenings of drinking, projecting, organising and posting mixtapes online, dancing and talking.

I have mentioned the word 'milieu' above, and not coincidentally. Today's neoliberal biopolitical present is constantly governed through the reinforcement of milieus, spaces where the actions of people, their co-dependence and roles, as well as the overall 'balance' and the 'security' of the space, are safeguarded through governmentality, external and internalised functions of power, discourse and control. As a famous passage from Foucault's lectures defines it, '[t]he milieu is what is needed to account for action at a distance of one body on another. It is therefore the medium of an action and the element in which it circulates. It is therefore the problem of circulation and causality that is at stake in this notion of milieu' (Foucault 2007: 20–21; cf. Laval 2018: 76–81). Foucault himself, and many of his critics, insisted on the importance of the notion of milieu for natural space and its biopolitical governance (for instance, town-planning, or the ecosystem). However, within a theory of biopolitics at a time of neoliberalism, it is also worth pursuing the more meta-phorical (and more sociological, cf. Laval 2018) concept of the milieu as the workshop where specific cultural and social domains take shape, where co-dependence and social transformations are reworked, and together with them social categories such as class, ethnicity or group identity. On the one hand, it is by emphasising milieus that biopolitics works at the level of populations: Biopolitics produces constant narratives of functional, safe and sealed spaces that need to be defended at all costs – such as nation, family, national space, national culture, prosperity, futurity, monetised insurance, monetised educa-tion that guarantees future prosperity and so on. On the other hand, as new theories and theorists of gender, radical politics and sexual citizenship have been so successful in arguing, it is also by working *through* milieus as open-ended projects, by over-appropriating them and by a constant reworking of the condition of (dis)possession, that social and cultural transformation can be effected at the present moment (Butler and Athanasiou 2013; Athanasiou 2017).

It is this notion of the milieu as the workshop of cultural work and social categories that I want to recall here. If we see the concept of 'making national cinema' put forth by collectivities such as the one formed around *The Lost Highway* in Athens, we realise that it is based neither on a very concrete defini-tion of an artform, nor its products, nor their national characteristics and value (cinema, films, national culture). Neither is it the closely guarded idea of a profession, a solely cultural field, or even a narrow cultural practice. 'Making cinema' in this context comes to mean interacting with an open-ended milieu, adding one's presence and intellectual/social effort to it, and entering it as a space of cultural and social dialogue, transformation and production (without any of these aspects, or their final outcome, ever guaranteed). This is no longer a closely guarded cultural field with specific boundaries, decision-making bodies with absolute power and cultural agents (producers, film archives, festivals) able to make or break a whole movement; of course, these exist and retain a role, but one can play with them. In fact, a much larger interaction, a set of cultural practices that develops in different directions and that, as it develops, creates more processual definitions is what now comes to identify as 'the space of new Greek Cinema', as well as the new Greek culture more generally. For this conclusion I take *The Lost Highway* to be a significant part of a much larger cultural interaction which I have experienced in Greece of the last fifteen years. Here we have both a mockery of a neoliberalised milieu, as well as its exploitation and subversion, with the aim to organise strong, further and different contextualisations that are as political as they are genealogical.[15]

PROCESSING A CINEMA OF BIOPOLITICS

This book has started with a set of quite simple and often repeated questions about the Greek Weird Wave: What are the thematic and formal elements that bind the new Greek directors together? How are their works related to the specific context of the Greek Crisis? How (if at all) are they related to national culture? How do they become meaningful as national films? Last, but not least, what is their collective position as a distinct wave in the history of Greek filmmaking?

Instead of directly answering these questions, I have tried to show how they end up being by-passed in the continuous cultural interaction with the films and, in doing so, how they also end up being resignified. If the Greek Weird Wave is to be seen as a characteristic wave of the cinema of biopolitics, this is most crucially because it develops these categories (Greek, weird, biopolitical cinema) in such a processual way and, to an extent, helps to redefine them.

The examples in this chapter made evident how a certain relationship to the socio-political context and a traditional narrative of national film history are shaken up by the Weird Wave. Thus, national context is being revisited as an inescapable context; yet, it is also fluid and open and thus can always be seen as a metonymic site towards which the film either gravitates or from which it tries to move away.

Being reconsidered in this process is also the multi-layered function of national allegory: In the performative contexts in which a cinema like that of the Greek Weird Wave has circulated and been redistributed, national allegory always works as a platform for debate, even if it is at a later stage to be dismantled and found inadequate or irrelevant. Let us not forget that festivals, collectives and special screenings normally work with a concept of the national and the transnational in mind – for instance, *The Lost Highway of Greek Cinema* presupposed, even in its title, an allegory for a national cinema and its 'lost opportunities', nested within the transnational allegory of a weird moment. The 'Weird Wave' or the 'New Wave' appellations were themselves also forms of national-allegory-framing with a transnational effect. That audiences, critics, or films themselves can go on to dismantle these frames does not diminish their initial national-allegorical function.

For this reason, I purposefully intermingled a media discourse on the Weird Wave (as evident in ARTE's special programme *Square*, which I described) with efforts to create a meaningful collectivity around cinema in Greece in the present moment. The underlying argument posits that, if politics today is always already a biopolitics, then the Greek films' almost obsessive reference to how (not) to be governed presents not merely a political statement. Rather, it is an incitement towards a much more extensive and participatory questioning of the biopolitical arrangements that are both general and, often in unexpected and less obvious ways, culturally specific.

In the following chapter, starting with a 2018 film that seems to be narrating the end of the Greek Weird Wave, I will attempt to synthesise the conclusions of the previous three chapters and turn to a discussion of the Weird Wave's realism. It is certainly difficult to include a mention of realism in the case of the Weird Wave – after all, the over-abundance of the term 'weird' in the previous pages hardly prepares one for such a discussion. Yet, one could argue that it is precisely notions such as weirdness that force us to reconsider realism from new, (bio)political, perspectives.

This chapter has persistently discussed real conditions of life, cultural work, the circulation of cultural meaning and cultural politics that are not extrinsic, but become part of the filmic text and that make the films of the Weird Wave not an undermining, but potentially a reconsideration of realism. It is for this reason, and with the already mentioned questions in mind, that I will now turn to examine how contemporary capitalist realism is revisited by the Weird Wave as a *biopolitical realism*.

NOTES

1. For more information on this song, see https://www.musicpaper.gr/editorial/item/6987-apo-mesa-pethamenoi-kai-ap-okso-zontanoi (accessed 16 June 2020). The song becomes quite prominent in the film, as it takes three minutes of screen time, accompanying the prolongation of a sequence that many viewers might otherwise just see as a gimmick of secondary importance. It was also given additional semiotic weight, as it was used for most of *The Lobster*'s promotional trailers.

2. Available at https://www.nytimes.com/2015/06/12/opinion/greece-a-financial-zombie-state.html (last accessed 16 June 2020). This was one of the many similar references to the Greek economy, as well as to Greek society and politics, that characterised the period from 2009 to 2018. A brief internet search of the words 'Zombie' and 'Greece', in either Greek or English, gives results in the hundreds of thousands, showing how much the public discourse about Greece was dominated by the metaphor of the 'Zombie Nation'.

3. For a reading that expands on the film's themes of normativity and coupledom, see Cooper 2016. For a reading focusing on the human/animal metaphor and transfer, which also explains how *The Lobster* thematises biopolitical control, see Galt 2017. For a reading positioning it firmly at the centre of contemporary Greek political debates, see Peroulis 2015a.

4. *Variety*'s critic, for instance, had called the film a 'moving satire of couple-fixated society', available at https://variety.com/2015/film/festivals/the-lobster-review-colin-farrell-rachel-weisz-1201496633/ (accessed 16 June 2020).

5. Following an insightful comment by Thomas Elsaesser, one could say that the *Square* programme presents Lanthimos as a national *auteur*, but at a time when auteurism has changed function, to become a 'second-order category: not self-expression of a uniquely gifted individual or the moral conscience of a nation, but the auteur as a "specialist" within a set of conditions of possibility which s/he can also use as creative constraints' (Elsaesser 2018: 33). Elsaesser further argues that 'national cinema' has similarly become a second-order category today – something that slightly differs from what I go on to argue in this chapter.

6. Apart from the interviews I describe in this chapter, the programme also briefly featured interviews with the young gallerist Helena Papadopoulos and the photographer Spyros Staveris.

7. Indeed, the entire programme may have started on the occasion of the successful international run of Lanthimos's *Alps*; yet, it takes place after Lanthimos's move to London to focus, among other things, on his later English-language projects. An underlying narrative of the programme is that of Greece's brain drain to the West – and, equally, the success of its arts under the Crisis, exemplified by the films of the Weird Wave.

8. The case of Costas Zapas, idiosyncratic as it may be, is perhaps the most obvious example of a Greek director closely related to Dogma. Zapas, some of whose films were co-financed by Lars von Trier's production company Zentropa, directed four films in which non-normative desire acts as a catalyst for the explosion of traditional Greek kinship, social and political structures. Increasingly, Zapas cut a lonely figure within the Greek cinema world, and his immensely interesting films did not circulate widely (Karalis 2017: 233–38).

9. See http://www.astorcinema.gr/?page_id=158

10. Even though these meetings have continued after 2018, they do no longer have the structure and frequency of *The Lost Highway*. It should be noted that the initial idea for this project and the main curatorship came from directors Elina Psykou, Alexis Alexiou and Yannis Veslemes, director and graphic designer Nikos Pastras and critic Afroditi Nikolaidou. A large number of Greek cinema practitioners, however, helped along the way.

11. The observation is factually correct. Indeed, in a scene towards the end of *Matchbox*, the mother performs exactly the same gesture, showing her genitals to her husband and screaming: 'Look at this, look at it; our daughter is not your child'. This time the undermining of authority is against the patriarchal figurehead of the house, in a moment when the *oikos* has already exploded in the constant altercations between the members of this nuclear family.

12. Tzoumerkas third feature-length film, *The Miracle of the Sargasso Sea* (2019), is even more closely related to Manousakis's *Fear*, to the extent that some scenes look almost like a remake.

13. The centrality of 'New Greek Cinema' and the way in which it has influenced most historical narratives of modern Greek Cinema have recently been the target of very powerful critiques. See, for instance, one of the most accomplished in Mini 2018. An effort to give more prominence to earlier periods and different

questions has been made by Vrassidas Karalis (2017; 2018). For a reappreciation of the popular cinema of Greece in the 1960s, see Eleftheriotis 2001; of the 'contemporary cinema' of the 1990s, see Kazakopoulou 2017a.

14. As I write this, I am aware that the dynamic entry of strong private institutions with a national and transnational agenda has already been changing this landscape (see Mais 2020).

15. A good example is the publication *I hameni leoforos tou ellinikou cinema* [*The Lost Highway of Greek Cinema*] (Nikolaidou and Poupou 2017), where artists from different media contribute texts on the older films presented during the *Lost Highway* screenings. There is in these texts a shared sense of a contemporary moment that needs to look back and position itself genealogically, as well as a feeling that this can only be done as a collective project.

Part II

Keywords:
Realism / Family / Allegory /
Archive / Assemblage

CHAPTER 4

Biopolitical Realism

A Dog in the Middle of the Sea: *Oik(t)os*

From the very first scenes of Babis Makridis's *Pity* (2018, based on a script by Efthimis Filippou), it is striking to see how frequently all the characters appear in frames: not only framed by the rectangular film image, but also by architectonic and scenic elements in the *mise-en-scène*, an effect commonly referred to as a 'frame within a frame' (cf. Treske 2011). They stand in front of new, shiny buildings; they loiter next to spotlessly clean windows with views of the Athenian coast; they sit behind expensive rectangular furniture; they walk past recent additions to the coastline of Athens (from the early 2000s), including some major commercial and corporate landmarks. The buildings are largely empty, as is the coastline; yet, they offer enough vertical and horizontal lines to frame the characters moving around them even further.[1]

A father-and-son duo visit their wife and mother while she is in a prolonged coma in hospital, only to find themselves more elaborately framed: by hospital doors, stands, beds and medical equipment. Later, one sees a dog abandoned in the middle of the sea by its owner, from a drone shot, as a spot at the centre of the blue horizon. There is no point or character in the diegesis that could make us think of this as a point-of-view shot. Neither is this constant framing and 'measuring' of living beings accidental. From a certain moment onwards, it becomes so excessive that it becomes the film. You are meant to interpret it as something more than the idiosyncrasy of the *mise-en-scène*.

The fact that a frame can serve as a visually significant metaphor is apparently not unknown to the characters of the film, either – it forms a significant part of the overall joke: they pose, deliver their lines and move through space as if constantly aware of the way in which they themselves are being framed and of the visual metaphor in which they are participating. First and foremost in this process is the obsessive and distanced central character, who will remain unnamed for the duration of the film. He is a lawyer whose wife has for a long time been in a coma in hospital. He enjoys the pity that he and his son have been receiving, to such an extent that he decides to continue with

this story even after his wife makes an unexpected recovery. With the pros-
pect of continuing to elicit pity now challenged, the lawyer suddenly faces a
sense of unhomeliness, trying to cling on to the previous situation as much
as he can. Pity and compassion have suited him well – and some of the most
hilarious scenes occur as he tries to maintain this pitiable quality in front of
hundreds of suits hanging in a dry cleaner's shop. Given that a constant play-
fulness with words and concepts is very much encouraged by the *mise-en-scène*,
it is not far-fetched to contemplate the film's title in terms of another possible
wordplay: The Greek title translated into English as *Pity* is *Oiktos*, just one
letter away from '*oikos*', the word for house, which has given us concepts and
words such as 'ecology' and 'economy', among others.

The over-use and concomitant devaluation of visual metaphor continues
throughout, and the characters within the narrative participate in it. For
example, when we see the lawyer in his office, he sits framed by a painting
hanging behind him, a painting of a ship calmly sailing on the ocean. Towards
the end, he receives the delivery of a new painting. It depicts a shipwreck
during a storm. Unsurprisingly, this marks the moment when the lawyer starts
losing his composure. Only a few scenes later, he will turn this film about the
ennui of (not) being pitied enough into horror, as he kills all of his immediate relatives. Ravaged bodies and a shot of blood-spattered furniture, again
framed within a frame, bring the film to an end.

Awkwardly, *Pity* is punctuated from the very beginning by frequent
intertitles, which offer forensic or biological descriptions: of bodies and their
reactions in specific affective states (fear, loss, the agony of death); of the
specific details of a mental disposition; of the details of a crime scene. Again,
the characters seem to be in on the game, too: When the wife wakes from
her coma, she describes her ordeal in meticulous medical detail to friends, as
part of a dinner entertainment. Throughout the film, her husband has also
been rehearsing moments from his court depositions, where he describes in
forensic detail a crime scene and the psychological profile of the perpetrator.

These framings – the intertitles, the ironic visual metaphors and the odd
twists and turns of the story – lead to an excessive production of visual and
conceptual grounds for allegory. The film's main objective seems to be to
highlight how hyperbolical and excessive the process of allegorisation can
be. If initially *Oiktos/Pity* seems like a simplistic irony against the Weird
Wave, eventually one realises that, on another level, it offers a more complex
commentary on this type of filmmaking and the significance it accumulates
through its form.

Excessive allegories, biopolitical anxieties, trapped bodies: *Pity* seems eager
to give us this assortment as the main story of the cinema of the Greek Weird
Wave. To that extent, the film is a very self-conscious showcasing of a certain

Figure 4.1a–d *In multiple frames: waiting, pain, emotion and touch, from* Pity *(Babis Makridis, 2018); digital stills.*

Weird Wave poetics which has been used as a signature trait in the cinema of Lanthimos, Tsangari and Makridis, as well as of their frequent collaborator Efthimis Filippou, and to a degree also in the films by Sofia Exarchou (*Park*), Argyris Papadimitropoulos (*Suntan*), Elina Psykou (*The Eternal Return of Antonis Paraskevas*) and Giorgos Georgopoulos (*Not to Be Unpleasant But We Need to Have A Serious Talk*). *Pity* showcases characteristics that these directors' films share: the unexpected and often ironic shot selection; the way in which actors read their lines sometimes mechanically or with characteristic dissociation and long pauses; the focus on figures who are lonely, disturbed and jarringly misplaced in their social and physical environment; the scenes in empty urban landscapes; and the absurdity of the storyline. Even the intertitles are closely reminiscent of the prose texts that scriptwriter Filippou (responsible for, among many others, the scripts of *Dogtooth*, *Alps* and *The Lobster* by Lanthimos, *Attenberg* and *Chevalier* by Tsangari, and *L* and *Pity* by Makridis) has published in recent years, in a literary production that parallels his film work.

This poetics, as I have been arguing throughout, does not exhaust the Weird Wave. It does not represent all the films we might discuss within its ambit. It does, however, point to a recognizable cluster which, as *Pity* seems to be telling us, has reached a certain limit. Not only the references and self-conscious allusions to form, but also the central character who adopts a weird disposition throughout as a survival tactic, may lead the viewer to think of the film as a more general ironic comment on the whole Weird Wave as a movement (past its prime).

Allegorically through its storyline and performatively through its form, *Pity* is suggesting that Greek art cinema, in search of an (international) audience, has relied for too long on visual allegories, framed and often visually fragmented bodies, awkward storylines and a constant feeling of unease and malaise, often related to bodies being trained or in a hospital bed. As with the main character of *Pity* and the pitiable fiction he has invented for himself, the implication is that, by 2018, Greek Cinema had also reached saturation point, exactly because it had become a national oddity for international consumption, and had not yet decided where to go from there.

In the very last scene of the film, the protagonist's dog (which had been abandoned to die in the middle of the sea) is seen to be finally reaching shore, in the centre of the shot, framed equally by the sea and the beach. In the end, the dog we thought had drowned has survived and returned. It is as if all this effort towards overblown signification has ended with an empty joke; *or*, as if it has culminated with a scene of impossible persistence, a scene of cruel optimism shown by the dog, despite all its travails. I have placed emphasis on the word 'or' precisely because the decision about how to watch and make sense of such a scene (and of the film as a whole) very much relates to what is at stake with the type of cinema on which *Pity* seems to offer a meta-commentary.

To point to the 'emptiness' of this last scene means that we may want to watch the film as a statement on/of its realism, an ironic comment on the very emptiness of the capitalist everyday otherwise depicted in the film and orchestrated to support its absurd turns. Yet, something much more complex emerges when tracing further the systems of representation, the political arguments and the analytical concepts that, for instance, this last scene may conjure up. Other aspects emerge if one decides to read the last scene as a reflection on, say, cruel optimism and why it still matters *today*. When pondering the scenes in hospitals and the visual allegories of the empty yet 'good life' with which *Pity* seems to abound, much of its opposite – that is, the 'unlivable life' – seems to have been clinically purged from the picture. Another side emerges when considering the film, and especially its central concept of 'pity', as a statement on the economies of affect today (including pity and compassion in Greece and about contemporary Greece). Who can read this Greek, absurd, 'weird' film today without entering these long signifying chains? And is this not evidence of the film's connection to contemporary reality? How 'realist' is this cultural text?

HOW REALIST ARE YOU?

The question about the realism of Weird Wave films is worth pursuing precisely because it challenges our understanding of what cinematic realism should be (and is currently) doing, and how it could be positioned within a cultural economy of Crisis. It is also worth pursuing, as I will argue in this chapter, because it offers a chance to reappreciate the political potential of that aspect of contemporary Greek Cinema that is considered facile and simultaneously too intellectual. Following a rather traditional understanding of both realism and its social relevance, Greek journalists have at times complained that recent Greek art cinema does not show enough 'love' to its audience: 'We would like a film based preferably on classical narration, with carefully crafted aesthetics, as genuine dialogue as possible, where we could recognize our deeper sorrows and/or comic impulses, in a frame that would seem realistic and dispense with fashionable trends and half-baked politics' (Politakis 2019).

Such assessments try to measure recent Greek Cinema against a classical version of realism traditionally associated with Hollywood (classical narration, simple dialogue and continuity editing). This version is not absent in Greek film history and was particularly identified with the popular cinema of the 1950s and 1960s. Other versions of cinematic realism with a very influential presence in Greek film history could have equally been employed as the yardstick to measure the Weird Wave's 'realistic frame' – from the poetic realism of Koundouros (*The Ogre of Athens* [1956]) or Cacoyannis (*A Matter of Dignity* [1958]; *A Girl in Black* [1956]), to examples of Greek neorealism (Alexandrakis's *Neighbourhood The Dream* [1961]; Voulgaris's *The Matchmaking of Anna* [1972]) or docurealism (Kanellopoulos's *Macedonian Wedding* [1960]; Giannaris's *From the Edge of the City* [1998]). One also should not forget the immensely influential modernist realism of the cinema of Theo Angelopoulos. Angelopoulos adopted an aesthetics very much in tune with, if not directly influenced by, André Bazin's theorisation of realism (2004). In Angelopoulos's work, the filming of 'natural' space, urban and, more often, rural landscapes, the long takes, the camera's lateral and receding movement, as well as certain types of focus and shot (deep focus/depth of field) are all employed to create a dominant and powerful version of a Greek national-political cinematic realism (cf. Jameson 2015).

I have listed these different versions of (Greek) cinematic realism in order to allude to the fact that most films of the Weird Wave start by ostensibly adopting at least one of them. In each case, they eventually move to undo them, with the Bazinian realism of Angelopoulos being a particularly popular target. Therefore, a common pattern in the films of the Weird Wave is, on the one hand, their undermining of received notions of realism (classical or other) and, on the other hand, a persistent effort to engage with 'the world we live in' on different terms. They seem to be searching for a different and, under these circumstances, more powerful *type* of realism – a conceptual, rather than strictly cinematic realism.

The flat and its surroundings, as well as the environment that the main character inhabits in *Pity* (as is also the case with the house in *Dogtooth*, to use the most iconic example) are not only 'real', but they are also indexical in the sense of being deictic (Doane 2007), pointing to recognizable upper-middle-class contemporary urban living in Greece and to a specific moment of brief affluence in the recent history of the country. However, in *Pity* and so many other flagship Weird Wave films urban and occasionally rural spaces are filmed empty, almost devoid of social life, class interaction and antagonism or ethnonationalist characteristics. What we see instead is a different mode of realism: a realism of the built structure, of the archival, sometimes also of the depleted and the ruined. (The same happens, quite emblematically, in such diverse films as *Park*, *Standing Aside Watching* and *Boy Eating the Bird's Food*). This is a realism that accommodates weirdness, eeriness and defamiliarisation as strategies that actually make viewers more alert to the structural foundations of certain 'realities'.

Many of the films also employ a deep depth of field and long takes, devices classically associated with film realism as theorised in complementary ways by figures such as Bazin (2004) and Siegfried Kracauer (1997). *Pity* is a particularly good example of this – at times, the film exhibits a self-conscious enthusiasm for difficult travelling shots and deep focus (as in the scenes of the dog in the middle of the sea). Similar choices shape Tsangari's *Attenberg* or Elina Psykou's *The Eternal Return of Antonis Paraskevas*. Meanwhile, the same films treat the scale in which the human body is filmed in relation to the environment as a source of anxiety; they underline the deliberate framing of bodies and objects; they insist on the excessive performativity of the characters' actions (cf. Nikolaidou 2014); they keep cutting parts of their subjects (especially human and animal bodies) out of the frame. All these gestures end up undermining, dissolving and mocking their claims to realism, especially if one compares them to, for instance, the way in which individuals are filmed as harmoniously immersed in the landscape in Angelopoulos's modernist cinema.

As Roman Jakobson ([1922] 1987) has remarked in an early text, if there is a characteristic that defines the concept of 'realism', it is its extreme relativity, as well as our predisposition to conflate its two different tendencies: on the one hand, an academic, always already outdated understanding of what realism should be; and on the other hand, a belief in the radical potential of new realisms to foreground the limits of realist conventions. Most Weird Wave directors appear extremely cognizant of this dynamic. Thus, Lanthimos's 2011 film *Alps* can be seen as an elaborate questioning of the social uses and abuses of realism. As the director explained, the decision to cast non-professional alongside professional actors was made not in an effort to add authenticity to the story – as was arguably the aim in, for example, the films of Italian Neorealism – but in order to thematise such an expectation and to exceed it (cf. Brophy 2011).

Alps follows the story of a group of people who have formed a company of 'emotional release helpers' called Alps. Its members agree, for a fee, to take the role of a deceased person for a certain number of hours per week in order to help the family grieve. We follow them as these amateur mourners (sometimes played by amateur actors) are called and cast to play the deceased kin, to follow daily routines with the deceased's family members and to enter different situations, in improbable pairings. We watch them desperately trying to fit into the awkward scenarios desired by the relatives each time, wearing the clothes – and, as one scene takes pains to underline, the shoes! – of the deceased, which do not fit them. Predictably, they speak oddly, with a deadpan delivery that seems realistic precisely because it can be seen as the result of that peculiar situation: At the level of the story these are, after all, untrained actors who have been called on to take the place of other people's real life, just for a couple of hours a week; one *would* be stilted in such a scenario. At the level of the story, therefore, Alps can be seen as a company offering its clients a construction of realism in order to help them cope with loss and bereavement. In the manner (and detachment) of companies offering assisted suicide, Alps promises assisted mourning, or, rather, assisted realism, a realism that has to be negotiated, organised and stilted, in order to be as close to the real as possible. But then again, *that* negotiated and stilted realism spills over in excess. In most scenes, the actors continue talking artificially even outside the mourning scene, thus becoming more realistic when they are 'in character' for their role in assisted mourning, and less realistic when they are 'in person'. The awkwardness of the scenarios in which they are involved in their assisted mourning arrangements eventually seems to penetrate most of the interactions in their everyday life, too. Seen from that perspective, *Alps* becomes an extensive, quite hilarious comment on various realisms (including neorealism), their politics and their claims to reality.

Initially we watch the members of Alps concocting a scheme to earn extra money – let us recall here that the film was made in 2011, in a country with rapidly rising unemployment and austerity measures. The selling point of their secret company (almost a start up, one may claim) is a promise to manage economies of emotion and loss and to bank on a generalised commodification of affect. We eventually see them in extended, awkward scenes supported by slow camera movements and long takes, *managing* realism as a very constructed, self-consciously employed, negotiated and arranged economy. What Alps the company promotes is realism as an economy. And as it spills over, one realises that it is *that* version of (stilted, prescribed) realism that is shown to have (always?) been the underlying political economy for everything else in the world of *Alps*.[2]

In *Alps* we see how an economy of representation becomes realism, how it is used as such. Then, we observe how it spills over to claim its share of the real, to *become* reality. In an analogous way, even though starting from a different premise, many films considered in this book adopt an in-your-face depiction of violence and suffering, especially violence and suffering within the family. They begin with a strict adherence to traditional realist protocols, but end up constantly posing questions about the ethics and aesthetics of this violence and its larger structural position within (Greek) society, as happens paradigmatically in the films of Economides and Tzoumerkas (cf. Kaloudi 2014). The focus is on violence as an economy of representation and social interaction. Much like in *Alps*, but through vastly different means, this is an economy that spills outwards. The screening of excessive bodily, verbal and situational violence in these films aims to provoke a strong affective reaction in viewers. In this way, not only do the borders between film and filmwatching, image and spectators become blurred, but so do the limits of realism. We are in exactly the domain that one critic has so evocatively called a 'realism of the senses' (de Luca 2014).

To recapitulate, the films I consider in this book produce their 'weirdness' exactly from a relationship between accepted versions of realism (including cinematic realism) and their unsettling. They do so, as I have suggested in the preceding pages, by over-appropriating; by showing realism's limits; by playing, iterating and reifying it as a style and a system of reference; by showing its constructedness and its power as an economy. In these terms, the Weird Wave has to be seen as part of the much more general tendency of World Cinema to return to realism and renegotiate with its tradition (Nagib and Mello 2009; Nagib, Perriam and Dudrah 2011). When considering it as an open and agonistic category, as Thomas Elsaesser has done in a recent essay, then one can go so far as to argue that realism has been 'a defining element of world cinema of all times', a tendency which today, however, is 'bringing into question terms such as "evidence", "authenticity" and spectatorial presence' (Nagib and Mello 2009: xxi; Elsaesser 2009). On that basis, we may find in Lucia Nagib's more recent reappraisal of the 'ethics of realism' in world cinema a lot that could feed into a reappraisal (sometimes *pace* Nagib), not of the Weird Wave's realisms, but of their contribution to ethical, identitarian, conceptual and cultural-political agendas. The next chapters of my book consist of an effort to address some of these issues.[3]

In a recent volume to celebrate the fortieth anniversary of the Parisian festival *Cinéma du réel*, the editors point to the fact that it is not just realism, but also the concept of the real, that has today become a constantly shifting ground. It is . . .

... a conceptual conundrum [. . .] during this contemporary moment, in which falsehoods are propagated, where representations of the world are often no longer representative of the world, where the constant flow and sharing of images has further drained reality of its 'realness', where abuses of power signify alarming, widespread regression. (Picard 2018: 10)

To respond creatively to such a situation, they suggest, filmmakers need to 'acknowledge cinema's abilities to evoke, to express, to renew or to research what is real'. From the very beginning of this book, and in what follows, I have been trying to assess the extent to which the Weird Wave has come together as a result of precisely this realisation, by filmmakers, filmmaking communities and spectators.

Portuguese director Pedro Costa has memorably said that 'the primary function of cinema is to make us feel that something isn't right' (in Picard 2018: 11). There could not be, I think, a better overall motto for the films I discuss here. And it certainly is a perfect description of what Tsangari's *Attenberg* achieved so iconically in 2010. I turn to this film in order to explain the Weird Wave's realist and meta-realist strategies in more detail. *Attenberg* starts with the very uneasy spectacle of two young women over-appropriating and then etiolating modes of realism, in a deserted, heterotopic, modernist town. Something is not quite right with that setting; most crucially, something is spilling over, something is already in excess of the life contained and excessively framed therein.

WAITING, WAVING, WEIRDING: *ATTENBERG*'S REALISMS

Marina is with other people. But, essentially, she is alone. She walks and dances and moves in funny ways; but, really, she is standing still. Marina's favourite pastime is to imitate realism. But she is very much off key.

In the first instance, *Attenberg*, directed by Athina Rachel Tsangari based on a script co-written with Efthimis Filippou, tells the coming-of-age story of a young woman living with her dying father in an unnamed and almost empty coastal town. Her favourite pastime is to watch David Attenborough's natural history documentaries, alone or in the company of her father. She is used to mispronouncing Attenborough's name as Attenberg, and this is what gives the film its title. She also has a habit of imitating the movements of the animals she sees in the documentaries, pushing her body into strange postures, often resulting in funny and/or awkward mimicries, sometimes in the company of her father as a bonding ritual, at other times alone. One of these postures, with protagonist Arianne Labed's back curved to the extreme, became the main poster of the film. It is a picture of a body part that at first glance looks non-human.

Figure 4.2a–b *Guerillas in the bedroom: Marina (Ariane Labed) and her father (Vassilis Mourikis) in* Attenberg *(Athina Rachel Tsangari, 2010); digital stills.*

From the privacy of Marina's own bedroom, this mimicry of the 'natural kingdom' and its most recognizable 'real' representation then spills over into the public (yet deserted) space. This is because, as the viewer eventually recognizes, Marina's second-favourite pastime is to team up with her best friend Bella and create elaborate physical performances that may be loosely based on the movements first studied in those documentaries, or just a mockery of 'accepted' types of movement (a mockery of a walk, of a dance, of a parade). Alone in the empty streets and squares of the unnamed town, with the camera following them in long takes, Marina and Bella jump, leap, run, emit funny noises and make moves that bring to mind Monty Python's famous sketch *The Ministry of Silly Walks*: another funny ritual, one thinks, helping them to deflect their ennui and apparent loneliness (cf. Poupou 2014: 57).

There is an obsession here with 'the real' and its prominent modes of representation, as well as its etiolation, encapsulated by the initial fixation on Attenborough/Attenberg: His documentaries stand, after all, as the representational degree zero of 'the natural world', in a certain popular understanding of the term in the late twentieth and early twenty-first century. They depict 'life in nature', in the way that a specific culture has nominated as one of the most accurate, realistic and authentic.[4] Marina watches, from her small TV set, the British wildlife expert watching orangutans in a nature reserve, and as she keeps copying the animal's gestures, the scene ends up being extremely awkward – not because it does not relate to a possible scenario (indeed, a lonely girl could have been acting like this for fun), but because it is based so much on an over-appropriation of the conditions in which this scenario, this 'reality', is mediated. Marina's gestures make the viewer think of the way in which the animals are observed, of her making sense of that observation and drawing attention to her own body's constant internalised observation. She does not, ever, say that she feels as if she is in a zoo or wildlife reserve, but her body persistently shows something eerily close to this. This is not simply a character who is locked in what looks like an observatory; she is someone who feels it, who has interiorised it, who expresses this interiorisation even when (or, rather, especially when) she is trying to dislocate it.

The scenes shot in public and semi-public spaces are based on a similar structure. The camera lingers on buildings and the layout of town planning, as well as their interior design, with a *quasi*-ethnographic scrutiny and pensiveness. It becomes clear that this is a specially built industrial town, past its prime, but planned and constructed in a recognizable modernist architectural idiom. Parts of the film, with their long travelling shots around the town's structures and locations, even look as if they belonged to a documentary about that town. And then the characters enter these spaces, excessively framed by them, very often in frames within frames. They interact awkwardly with each other, speaking in a defamiliarising tone and, in the case of Marina, a heavy 'foreign' accent.[5] If the town works as an enclosure, the characters do not say so out loud, but they show how they have interiorised it; even when (or, rather, especially when) they look ill-fitting and sound out of tune.

Marina's father is an architect who was, it is implied, a member of the original team that designed the town. This could explain why his house/office is situated in a prime location, with views overlooking the entire town. It would also go some way to explain why, when this dying architect thinks about his town, its architectural project and the country in which it is located, he speaks in grand terms. This is what he says, for instance, in one scene where he is standing on his veranda with his daughter, binoculars in hand, looking over the town. He purposefully mixes a general reference to Greece with a deictic gesture to the town lying below:

> It was as if we were designing ruins... As if we were calculating with mathematical precision the formula of their destruction. What bourgeois arrogance! Especially for a country which had not gone through the Industrial Revolution. From the shepherds to the bulldozers and from the bulldozers to the mines, and from the mines directly to the petty-bourgeois paroxysm. We built an industrial colony on a sheep shed. And we thought what we were doing was a revolution.

In other words, what lies at the architect's feet, the now empty (ruined?) modernist town once made as part of Greece's belated and limited industrialisation could stand for a whole country. In a way reminiscent of Walter Benjamin's remark that 'allegories are in the realm of thoughts what ruins are in the realms of things' (Benjamin 1998: 177–78), the town's current state is laid out as a (metonymic) allegory for the country's history and current predicament, the visible part of a larger project of modernisation that has failed. Yet, it is also worth noting how in the father's monologue there is no taking into account the people's own wishes and potential reactions in that process; the 'we' of his discourse is not the people, but the arch-designers. The focus is on their misplaced 'design', bad 'calculation' and mismanaged population.

This scene alone would certainly offer a field day to anyone wishing to categorise the film as a national allegory.[6] Yet, my point is that Maria interiorises in the same way both the setting in which she lives and its obvious allegorisation. She deals with allegory (for instance, as presented to her by her father) as she inhabits this town: in dislocated bodily movements, in a voice that sounds off-key, in an effort to understand through making odd connections, in an accent that is out of place. If we often expect allegory to be based on distance, analogy and substitution, here it is inflected through the body; it makes it touch the thing it substitutes, it relies on the disjointed experience of trying to reconnect, to test the chains of reference and substitution developing metonymically. This is not simply a national allegory, but a multi-layered effort to take national allegory (to task) and give it a twist.[7]

Tsangari has variously pointed out that this is a film directly and indirectly related to Greece's recent socio-political history, as well as a nostalgic return to her own personal story. As she said in a TV interview, 'when I shot *Attenberg*, it was the beginning of the crisis, in a way the crushing of all the dreams of modernity; and I liked the idea that where I grew up was a very beautiful place, very multicultural, which was rare of Greece then, and the

Figure 4.3a–d *The town below and the frame within: Marina (Ariane Labed) and Bella (Evangelia Randou) observed and observing in the town of Antikyra, from* Attenberg (Athina Rachel Tsangari, 2010)*; digital stills.*

children grew up in the street, and thirty years later it is almost like a ghost town' (Tsangari interviewed in Arte 2016; see also Arte 2011).

Attenberg was indeed shot in the town of Aspra Spitia in the bay of Antikyra in Boeotia. As the father implies in the film, Aspra Spitia had been a well-known town-planning and architectural experiment, as much an economic as a social one. The town was designed and built by the renowned architect Constantinos Doxiadis in 1965, in order to house the industrial workers and personnel from the nearby aluminium plant, expanded and managed by the French giant Pechiney. Tsangari's nostalgic comment notwithstanding, various critics have pointed out that the town was built with little to no relation to the surrounding villages and local economy – that is, apart from its obvious relationship to the mine and factory (Eleftheriotis 2020; Poupou 2014).

There are, therefore, different types of 'reality' that intersect in the very ordering of life in *Attenberg*. The first we could call an economic reality. The town was built as part of a development project, attached to the nearby factory. Unable to dissociate from this connection, it has shared its fortunes. Discontinued investment in the nearby bauxite mines and the aluminium factory after the 1980s has meant discontinued investment in the town; the rise in unemployment has meant an emptier town. The metonymical/allegorical link with the larger story of a national economy that, by 2011, had gone awry and was in a downward spiral of disinvestment is not hard to make in *Attenberg* – neither for the viewer of the film, nor by the characters in the story. In the last sequence, in gloomy rainy weather, Marina and Bella scatter the cremated father's ashes in the bay of Antikyra, then take their car and motorbike and leave to the sound of the 1960s French pop hit *Le temps de l'amour* by Françoise Hardy. The camera, in a long take and extreme long shot with enough depth of field, stays still. Against the continuing song, we keep watching trucks come and go in and out of the mine area. Are these the last signs of industrial activity, or a sign of its regeneration?

If Marina's body lives in and moves through the ruins of a full economic project that has defaulted, what remains is a second, interrelated reality that she has grown to consider her world. This is a biopolitical reality, her being part of the population of this model town, as well as of the family of this domineering pater-architect. She is unable to let go of either. Everything in her life seems to have been predetermined, valued, prescribed and scripted. Everything is already set up. Yet, nothing seems in place. Everything looks empty, and she herself moves as if she does not fit. There are connections to make, but she is also at a loss about how to make them. Her silences and stillnesses seem to be a direct result of this, as is an awkward sense of humour that her responses sometimes show. There is an interiorisation that is palpable, a feeling of limits being played with, an awkwardness in the air. If we saw the comical potential of this awkwardness in films such as *Suntan* or *Pity*, in *Attenberg*, which came seven years prior, we had been treated to its more tragic side. As Marina sits, looks and is looked at, as the town overflows with her weird acts, as in the very end the trucks come and go into what may be a last exploitation or the construction of new ways of life, we viewers sit back and watch how economic realism has now slowly been mutating: Welcome to the desert of biopolitical realism.

'A CULTURAL PARADIGM IN IMPLOSION' AND ITS TRANSGRESSION

It is telling that the first attempts to read the Greek Weird Wave within a history of Greek cinematic realism have ended up employing much less strictly cinematic and much more conceptual categories in order to characterise its engagement with realism. Vrasidas Karalis in his *Realism in Greek Cinema* (2017), to take one prominent example, does exactly that. Throughout his monograph he maintains an interest in the ways in which landscape and social antagonism are depicted on screen and how specific historical signifiers come to play a central role in each film's plot or setting. Yet, when in his final chapter he moves on to offer an 'Optimistic Epilogue' on Greek realism, he shifts gears. Focusing now on the films of the Weird Wave, he employs a notion of realism that relies not so much on visual, but on conceptual and cultural politics. The Weird Wave, so Karalis maintains, is a 'cinema of transgression' precisely because it aims to transcend the very codes of reference of a national canon of cinematic realism, often by over-doing them. Crucially, . . .

> [t]he 'Weird Wave' or the Cinema of Transgression is not the product of the economic meltdown: on the contrary, it refracted the panicked reaction to the absurd conspicuous consumption, the reckless consumerism and the systemic abuse of power that were taking place before and after 2004. [. . .] During the crisis, Greek cinematographers have shown enviable resilience and tireless inventiveness; austerity of means, starkness of dialogue, unembellished settings, all created a form of anti-aesthetics purifying cinematic form of all superfluous and artificial illusionism. Although they never presented a manifesto, like the Dogma 95, they stopped posturing as the victims of history and detached themselves from the self-congratulatory melancholia of the past. [. . .] Young cinematographers used the economic collapse as an opportunity to explore the deep social implosion that has engulfed all levels of culture – especially the level of symbols, representations and cultural iconographies. (241)

These films, so Karalis argues, 'don't pretend to be outside [the] reality' of a late capitalist corporate culture and meaningless spectacle; instead, they thematise them: 'They depict a cultural paradigm in implosion and in conflict with itself' (238).

This is a perceptive, if at times problematic, analysis[8] that is shared by many commentators (cf. Varmazi 2019). What lies behind it is the following premise: The late capitalist expansion in Greece reached a peak in the preparations for the 2004 Olympics, which included a big construction bubble and a stock exchange frenzy. This climate provoked a frenzy of commercialisation and financialisation that expanded in all spheres, including that of culture. Eventually, it offered the prime material for a critical and subversive cultural representation, too. It is no coincidence, according to this view, that some of the main representatives of the Weird Wave (including Makridis, Lanthimos, Avranas, Papadimitropoulos and Filippou) worked for long spells in advertising and commercial video production in the early 2000s, and that in their films they often self-consciously imitate hyper-capitalist imagery and advertising or propaganda.

Babis Makridis's films offer perhaps the clearest examples of this tendency. Like *Pity*, his first feature-length film, *L* (2011), was shot in Athens and, according to one review, took 'the deadpan absurdism [of new Greek films] and stirred it into a dead end' (Weissberg 2012). It includes hilarious scenes in which characters turn directly to the camera and, addressing the lonely main character, describe the benefits of a particular product that they have bought, or the performance targets of an advertised job. These scenes effortlessly bring to mind similar examples, as well as the overall atmosphere in Peter Weir's *The Truman Show* (1998), where the protagonist grows up in a commercial 24/7 TV reality show. Advertising is included as part of Truman's overmediated everyday world. It is cleverly placed in his path by professional extras and experienced on a continuum with the various propagandistic mechanisms that the show's producers use in order to keep him in this (TV) set and to convince him that this is the only reality available. As a result, Truman grows up to be as deadpan in his conversations as those product announcements. Progressively, he demonstrates an acerbic humour as his only way to articulate a personal voice, which he keeps even after the show starts falling apart. *The Truman Show* may have been a direct intertext only for Makridis's *L*, but not explicitly so for other films of the Weird Wave. However, it offers a good visual example of a point made in most of these films – that is, the demonstration of *accepting while at the same time undermining* a particular form of imposed reality and its preferred modes of representation. There is a little Truman sh(ad)ow in almost all the films of the Greek Weird Wave, and for good reason.

A subtler elaboration of such a strategy of accepting while undermining the dominant mode of (capitalist) representation was offered by scriptwriter

Filippou's various texts for Greek magazines, literary publications and the theatre – published before and alongside his influential scriptwriting for the Weird Wave. One can see in these texts a self-conscious effort to over-appropriate the conventions of realism in each medium, to push them to their limits and to present, out of the very codes of a society of the spectacle, its subtle and humorous undermining (see Filippou 2009). For instance, in a series of 'interviews' that acquired an enormous following when they were published in the popular freepress *Lifo* between 2011 and 2014, Filippou presented stories of 'good life' and success from the Greek art world: actors, writers, singers and performers. Yet, the third-person-introduction to the interviews, as well as the answers, are outrageously aimed at capturing the insignificant detail, the fragment of experience, the very subjective viewpoint, the irrelevant metonymic association and the overtly fictitious.[9]

Characteristic of Filippou's overall style, which marries the absurd and the clinical, these interviews were also very well placed in the publication in which they first appeared. *Lifo* has been the one media outlet that more than any other exemplified the changes from the 1990s to the 2000s in Greece. Coming on the heels of a number of lifestyle magazines (such as *Nitro*, *Klik*, *01*, *Symbol* and *Athens Voice*) that enjoyed a rise in popularity during the economic boom of the late 1990s and early 2000s, *Lifo* was still a product of the enthusiasm and the increase in advertising expenditures in the period immediately after the Olympics. But, as it first appeared late in 2005, it was also one of the mainstream media that first started expressing the disillusion-ment which soon settled in as a general atmosphere. Its wide circulation and successful internet presence were from the outset supported by advertising alone. Its insights, significantly influential for a generation of Greeks, became legendary in the way in which they could balance between two opposite poles. On the one hand, they were a celebration of capitalist over-abundance, over-development and the defence of lifestyle cultures. On the other hand, they offered a subtle (and, at times, in-your-face) critique, the dismantling of grand narratives (including those of nationalism) and an ironic scepticism. Alongside the editorials of its main publisher, Stathis Tsangarousianos, the photographs of the French-educated photojournalist Spyros Staveris early on became iconic for bringing together a rich archive of images of the neocapi-talist 'high society' since the 1990s, captured from the most unexpected and often quite provocative angles.[10]

CAPITALIST REALISM RECONSIDERED

Above I have briefly veered off into this analysis of Makridis's *L*, Filippou's texts and the pages of *Lifo* magazine in order to show how, in the 1990s and 2000s in Greece, there undoubtedly was fertile ground for what Mark Fisher and others after him have so influentially described as *capitalist realism*. According to Fisher's well-known argument, neoliberal capitalism is so powerful and overarching today that it becomes 'evident' as the ubiquitous and ubiquitously (and painfully) obvious way of the world. Rather than *a* reality, capitalism has constructed its logi(sti)cs as *the ultimate* reality, an endpoint and a totality, 'a pervasive atmosphere, conditioning not only the production of culture but also the regulation of work and education' (Fisher 2009: 45; cf. Shonkwiler and La Berge 2014). This is always the function of realism, you could say: a modality, a specific historico-political consensus about what constitutes the real and its representation at any given time. Yet, what Fisher argued and maintained in the very interesting conversations that followed his initial intervention throughout the 2000s is that today's late capitalism co-opts realism to such an extent that even its denunciation in 'non-realist' art is always already co-opted as well. We are all in it, inescapably, and quite realistically so, as Fisher reiterated in an argument that developed over time in the first decade of the twenty-first century, in his blog, short commentary articles and public speaking.

Two crucial remarks about Fisher's intervention need to be taken into account here. First, part of Fisher's argument about capitalist realism relates to the diffuse and all-encompassing control that an economic system constructs for every aspect of life. In this respect, what he says about capitalism could also be valid for socialist realism. This point had already been elaborated upon by a group of artists (among them Gerhard Richter and Sigmar Polke) who had first used the term 'capitalist realism' to describe their work in the 1960s, in a tongue-in-cheek response to socialist realism (Evers et al. 2014). I am mentioning this because, to some, *Attenberg*'s town may not look too different from an abandoned Soviet purpose-built settlement (or, at least, the image we have of it). Yet, the issue is not which economic system built it, but that it was built on the basis of a specific economic/development project that aimed at managing life. This project did not simply promote a modern(ist) understanding of what a good life (in it) *could* be; it effected a modern apparatus to determine how life *should* be. Fisher's argument is that such a type of economic planning, especially as it develops and mutates, has generated an all-encompassing culture. It promotes its mode of self-representation, its *realism*, as the only *reality* available. As he points out, this ends up making people extremely passive, silent, depressed and unable to react – unless, that is, they turn to mimicry, satire and awkward gestures.[11]

The second point to be underlined is that the simple idea that everything is being enveloped within a type of capitalist realism started gaining momentum as the first decade of the twenty-first century progressed. The 2008 financial crisis and its aftermath, crucially, became capitalist realism's ideal case-study. As faltering financial organisations kept being bailed out so as to prevent a collapse of the overall system, the localisation of the crisis in various parts of the world (including Greece) started to show how very much political elites and grassroot movements alike were unable to propose a plausible alternative solution 'outside' the late capitalist worldview. They were dovetailed in the production, not so much of more capitalism, but of more realism, so that the economic, institutional and political progression of the neoliberal model and the extreme financialisation of all levels of life could continue their establishment as the 'only way of the world'.

Take as an example this description offered by the liberal Greek sociologist Panayis Panagiotopoulos: During the Crisis, he says, Greece very often came close to a 'departure from the realities of economics, of global correlations and obligations inherent in the adherence to the EU and the western value system' (2020: 59). This feared 'departure from the realities of economics' Panagiotopoulos repeatedly calls 'a disruption of (modern) normality' (54; 58; 60). The local debate referenced here is the one about *kanonikotita* – in English, normality, but in Greek a word that sometimes is used to denote not only the normal, but also the normative – which set the tone for Greek politics after 2009. An effort to think differently, outside the system of 'western values and the realities of economics', was simply denounced during that debate not only as unrealistic, but also as non-normal and anti-real. A 'return to normality' therefore became a slogan for both the Right and parts of the Left during the period under discussion. It peaked every time negotiations for new loans and packages meant that a short injection of cash was offered to the collapsing economy. It was also used as the reason for the population to accept new austerity measures as the necessary sacrifice for the said (and projected future) 'return to *kanonikotita*'. The discourse of 'normality', as well as the discourse of 'returning to normality', is precisely what Fisher called capitalist realism. An all-enveloping sphere, an episteme of the now, that makes everything look connected and warns everyone to keep labouring so that it can also keep posing as real.[12]

It is thus not surprising that, in a review article on Lanthimos's *Dogtooth*, published a year after his *Capitalist Realism* book, Fisher repeatedly alludes to the film's realism 'despite appearances':

> The camera lingers impassively, unobtrusively, as if it is performing a merely documentary function. There is neither a score nor any incidental music; all of the music is diegetically embedded. The actors are deadpan, undemonstrative. (At times, there is almost a feeling of reality TV – and after all, in their isolation, in their submission to a cruel and arbitrary regime, what do the children resemble if not Big Brother contestants) [. . .] The element of

> absurd theatricality should not, however, distract us from the extent to which *Dogtooth* presents, in an extreme form the ordinary gestures and habits, the storytelling and tricks of discipline, of so-called normal family life. (Fisher 2011: 23–24; 27)

What I find fascinating in this review is not its welcome observations about *Dogtooth*'s realist gestures, but the eventual use to which they are put. In *Dogtooth*, Fisher is attracted not by the fact that what is being realistically depicted is an enclosure within which the three children cannot think of the outside. Nor does he analyse the realist filming of the very neocapitalist setting of this house, which could lead one to read the whole film as an allegory of capitalism and its enclosure. Instead, he directs our attention to the small gestures, the discourses and the repeated acts that make the subjects of this enclosure interiorise control and shape their bodies and pleasures according to a specific governance of life. He is interested in how, in such a system, first, knowledge circulates as part of an economy of representation and, secondly, instances of undermining appear from within. In *Capitalist Realism*, Fisher had been at pains to point out that a subversion of the all-encompassing realism can only come from a fissure, a rupture, a sudden flooding of the Real, understood here in its Lacanian connotations. In his review of *Dogtooth*, however, as he focuses on what clearly is a biopolitical setting and reminds us of other popular audiovisual biopolitical settings (such as reality TV's *Big Brother*), Fisher underlines awkwardness, absurd turns, 'pathetic' bodies and 'the constant feeling of unease that *Dogtooth* generates' (22), as ways of both reacting to and of making do with what is (realistically) depicted on screen. In my reading, this is a text that reminds us of how *Dogtooth* has been a thematisation both of capitalist realism's ubiquity and of how it is already moving in a new direction.

Barking from Within

Capitalist realism cannot be thought outside the continuing rise of the neoliberal 'subject-as-enterprise' (Brown 2015) and the growing understanding of the 'representationality' of economic movements, financial products and financial crises. The understanding that the world economy is more and more based on speculation and its forms of representation – namely, that it is in itself a form of capitalist realism – has now become not only commonplace, but also the basis for most of the effective critiques of late capitalism from within, with the recent Greek Crisis becoming a key site for the articulation of such a critique. While global, late capitalism has continuously produced spectacular localities, one of the most notable cases is the Greece of the Crisis.

In such spectacular economicopolitical localities, what I have already described as an 'intense biopolitical present' provides a new context and framework for the ever-present and ever-mutating capitalist realism. What becomes obvious in them is that the production of capitalist realism is unavoidably intertwined with the policies of life and death, as well as the economies of managing bodies and populations, so much so that it seems to be moving in a new, very tangible direction. Capitalist realism, in the same way that it still 'conditions' the production of culture, work, education and financial (re)production, is now allowing us to view how the body of the individual and the population is documented, categorised and disciplined in thick webs of interdependence; how contemporary neoliberal governmentality means a constant taxonomy of which lives matter (and how much they matter) and which groups of people are left to die (and the technologies in which this is asserted); how for the first time so intensely the concepts of human and social 'rights' and 'achievements' are fully marketised and constantly under review; how the very concept of crisis rests on the success of the fear that specific disciplinary and biopolitical techniques of 'the good life' will be withdrawn, as well as on the disciplined iteration that there is no alternative (the so-called TINA doctrine).

Optical technologies and the various economies of vision and visibility – from screening techniques and drone cameras, to instagram narratives of the good life and the ubiquity of 'amateur' video – participate in this process, in a world of proliferating 'biopolitical screens', to recall Pasi Väliaho's term (2014a). Today, individuals are constantly aware that they are more and more 'screened' in everyday life, while at the same time becoming all the more what Laura Mulvey (2006) has termed 'possessive spectators': holders of the material and technical means to influence viewing, able to review, to edit, to reframe and reuse images, from the amateur video to the cinematic image. Constantly screened and screening, being a possessive spectator today does not describe a position of power and full agency, as Mulvey had suggested, but indicates participation (more often than not, self-conscious participation) in the larger network of politics, representation and signification that I have just outlined.

My argument is that, in those spectacular biopolitical sites – such as the Greece of the last decade – and with cultural genres such as the Greek Weird Wave, one is faced with the sense that capitalist realism does not suffice as a conceptual framework to describe what is happening. In those sites and with such examples, one sees the need to talk about a new phase – a phase I would propose to call not just capitalist, but biopolitical realism.

In the previous section, my reading of Tsangari's *Attenberg* was very much based on this idea of an all-encompassing economic realism mutating into a biopolitical realism. I showed how the understanding of this slow mutation is shared by the characters of the film and how the protagonists' body movements can be seen as not only showing a malaise and passive acceptance, but also a form of critically engaging with this mutating, yet still all-encompassing realism.[13] Surveillance and the prearrangement of people's lives are now interiorised, and the interaction with them is much more self-conscious, multi-layered, idiosyncratic and subtle. At one level, I am thus reading *Attenberg* as an allegory of the entry into biopolitical realism (that is, I am the allegorist of this reading). But at another level, I am proposing that the characters and their reaction are conscious of this mutation and participating in it; therefore, they themselves can be seen as the allegorists in this case. They co-produce allegory, not just by participating in it, but, much like the reader/viewer, by 'reading' allegorically, too.

Biopolitical realism is exactly that type of capitalist realism that ponders, remains and rests on the biopolitical structures that produce the contemporary moment, *as* they produce it. As I set out to write about biopolitical realism, I every so often feel like the dog in *Pity*, swimming in the middle of the sea, the camera angle suddenly changing and shooting from above, the analytical viewpoint (*my* analytical viewpoint) thus becoming part of the overall setting, visual signification and tool of governance. We are all in it; we are all in biopolitical realism. You may not be able to do much about this, but you may as well start barking from within.

THE WEIRD WAVE AS BIOPOLITICAL REALISM

Biopolitical realism is not a common term. One of the rare mentions I have found is by the artist and theorist Hito Steyerl (2003) who has used the concept for completely different ends, in an essay about contemporary documentary practices. For Steyerl, biopolitical realism aligns with a certain type of documentary film popular in the early 2000s, which tried to depict a 'reality' ethnographically, often prioritising resistance, the survival of subcultures (or 'other cultures'), or forms of contemporary life untouched by late capitalism.[14] Those films, Steyerl maintained, seemed too often oblivious of their own *documentality* – the governmentality to which they belonged, the fact that, even when denouncing them, they themselves participated in and strengthened a certain form of power, marginalisation and financial and environmental exploitation. They were complicit in a biopolitical organisation; they were not simply realist, but biopolitically realist. Their subjects could not break out of the biopolitical frame in which they found themselves, and neither could the documentaries that purported to be giving them voice and public representation. By being so ethnographic and by not exposing their own agency in the complex game of representation, these documentary techniques ended up contributing to the biopolitical management of their subjects, rather than exposing or critiquing it.

To counter that, so Steyerl argued, artists had to explore new forms of exposition and exhibition of material, new styles of participatory art and ways to engage the audience, making spectators more self-conscious about tactics of representation and the normalising power of the films' claims to realism and reality, especially since it was exactly the organisation of that reality that the films were purportedly critiquing.

This oppositional tendency would be a much more self-reflective turn to a type of film that 'perceives its own devices as socially constructed episte-mological tools'. These works, then, would become much more inventive in terms of how they theorise questions of viewpoint and often undermine or break down filmic continuity; they would question the politics of screening and production, the various economies of viewing, as well as their own visual and discursive intertextuality and the genealogy of media/optical technolo-gies. Last, but not least, they would be decisively archival, contemplating the archive not only as a depository of data and historical information, but also in its institutional, ethical and aesthetic functions: 'In these works there is no intention at all of depicting the authentic truth of the political, but rather of changing the "politics of truth" on which its representation is based' (Steyerl 2003).[15]

What intrigues me in this and similar essays from the same period is that the central dichotomy which they propose between 'biopolitical realism' and 'reflexive documentality' has been fully superseded a decade and a half later. As we conclude the second decade of the twenty-first century with a pro-longed financial and political crisis engulfing the whole world while continu-ing to produce spectacular localities (for instance, in the Greece of the Greek Crisis), who remains oblivious of the biopolitical realms in which we all live, which we interiorise and constantly reframe?[16]

In recent years these more self-conscious and participatory exhibition and production techniques (which for Steyerl should come in response to biopolitical realism) – these ways of making use of material in a self-conscious manner and of exposing its biopolitical employment while also trying to find ways to disrupt it, these efforts to make biopolitical noise while being *within* a biopolitical frame – have certainly entered the cinematic text *and* the ways in which communities of viewers, as possessive and biopolitical spectators, interact with it. They do so, however, not as an answer to capitalist realism, but as its development, or, rather, its mutation.

Even in contemporary ethnographic documentary film, to stay with Steyerl's initial example, we witness common understandings of cinematic

realism combining with archival questioning and a more self-conscious production of visual metaphors meant to incite critical arguments and analytical
debates. The exposition of alternative archives, the concern with embodied
affect and with how it frames perception, also become a questioning of the
forms of power that have fashioned representation and cultural production
(including ethnographic depiction) so far. Biopolitical realism has become a
tool in documentary film, especially because it relates to the larger culture of
biopolitics and responds to an intense biopolitical present.[17] Crucially, audiences are becoming more and more self-conscious about their participation
in such a culture of biopolitics, as this is manifestly ubiquitous and matter-
of-factly ingrained in the thick structures of the everyday (Rawes et al. 2016).

Take as example the documentary series *Mikropoleis/Microcities* (briefly
mentioned in Chapter 2), produced in 2010–11 and broadcast in Greece
repeatedly during the period under study here. It can be seen as an exemplary
work of biopolitical realism, in this new, defamiliarising understanding of
the term I wish to propose. Its initial scope was to provide 'the [new] map of
the city that keeps changing every day'; its expectation, from the very beginning, was that this was a documentary on the Greek Crisis as it is being lived
and narrated in the urban centre of Greece. In each of its fourteen thirty-
minute instalments, the audience was invited to visit one specific Athenian
neighbourhood or site: Omonoia, Kypseli, Kolonaki, Apropirgos, Ekali,
Kaisariani, Perama, the Olympic Village and so on. The idiosyncratic viewpoint is made evident even from this list, which mingles the central Athenian
square and the Olympic village with working, middle-class and high-class
neighbourhoods. On the one hand, the city is shown as fragmented, as an
agglomeration of micro-cities, each one's 'story' told based on one micro-
characteristic – Kolonaki, for instance, the upper-class central neighbourhood, is narrated in relation to the theme of 'Stairs'; Kypseli 'the Basement',
Perama 'the Rooftop' and Kaisariani 'the Doorstep'. On the other hand, the
city's social tapestry (and especially the social differences often framed in the
same shot) become the material for both endless visual irony and a pensive
reflection, especially as the subject of 'Crisis' comes up all the time. Awkward,
'weird' scenes abound: Suddenly a young man talking about Kolonaki is seen
wearing a dog's mask and playing with his dog, while at the same time analysing the social structure of the neighborhood; an elderly woman is narrating,
completely out of context, the story of her father's favourite bird; a poet is
shouting 'this is realism, and you see, I am not interested in realism'; a lonely
musician says that he will never leave the old house of his refugee grandparents because 'when it rains, the water that falls from the rooftop is the blood
of my dead grandparents'.

The scenes in every episode reminded viewers of both the inescapable

context in which the series was being made, as well as its role – its documentality, as Steyerl would have it. A continuous emphasis on the episodes'
own visual poetics, the allegorical potential of certain shots, the function of
pauses, of stillness, of waiting and certainly of framing (and of cutting the
frame in unexpected ways) went hand-in-hand with an emphasis on economies of production and distribution, on the waves of urban investment and
disinvestment, on citizenship and belonging and, crucially, on the fact that
people who were presented in the documentary appeared constantly aware
and conversant with both sides of this process. They were conversant with
both the economies of the image and the potential of their own framing
within it, as well as with the new financial and biopolitical regimes that
governed their life. At crucial moments, they were also happy to make that
connection even more powerfully evident for the camera. They talked about
it, assumed roles, sometimes resorted to deadpan delivery and/or funny and/
or overdramatic postures in order to underline the constructedness of the
setting in which they put themselves; it was all the more real(ist) for that.
Mikropoleis/Microcities, often at the instigation of their subjects, did not present
the neocapitalist everyday as inescapable; instead, they showed a mapping of
efforts to make do, a palimpsest of cruel insistence which, precisely because it
relies so heavily on the capitalist realism of the everyday, starts to look much
less 'real' and much more like an escape.

As I explained in Chapter 2, one of the most celebrated medium-length
films of the period under discussion, Konstantina Kotzamani's *Watshingtonia*,
potentially creates a visual conversation with *Mikropoleis*, while almost becoming a manifesto for the poetics of the Weird Wave. Is *Washingtonia*, with its
extremely challenging (to the level of non-existing) continuity, realist or not?
Is its visual proximity to *Mikropoleis* an effort to go against such documentaries' realist poetics, or, conversely, a gesture underlining and expanding their
most prominent characteristic – that is, their biopolitical realism? To believe
that it was the latter rather than the former has not been a peripheral question
for this book; on the contrary, therein rests its central argument.

My research on the Greek Weird Wave as a cinema of biopolitics has
been alert to such signifying chains that its biopolitical realism establishes.
On the one hand, I have traced these films' reflection on how systems of
power manage groups of people (from a family to a population) and the
bodies of individuals, as well as the films' attention to forms of resistance: to
noise, unease and subversion. On the other hand, I have supplemented this
analysis with a revisiting of my own and others' interaction with these films,
in the variable contemporary frames within which this interaction can and
does happen. A formal and content analysis that takes into account affective
investments and reactions can thus interrelate with an analysis of concepts

and their metonymical relation to specific events, political pronouncements, social movements, production and promotion tactics, as well as accounts of the communities of viewers that have received these films and the use they have made of them.

Biopolitical realism thrives on collation, seriality, contiguity, metonymical thinking, posturing, framing, performatively gesturing, moving and filming. This inadvertently influences its relationship to allegory. More 'traditional' (metaphorical) allegory – as a mode based on substitution of something with something outside of its system of reference and narrative (something extradiegetic, outside the 'text') – is almost impossible in the biopolitical realist totality. A metonymical type of allegory thus appears as a mode of holding on, of making do, of making sense. This is the argument I foregrounded in my analysis of *Attenberg*, where I noted that for its central character the national allegory in which she participates is something she considers as part of her own everyday biopolitical setting and present. Her awkward reactions, her efforts to create links by gesturing, by touching, look weird as they themselves are also metonymical: based not on what can be inferred as analogous and exterior, but on what is near. The viewer is invited to join in; to make connections and disrupt the metaphoric potential of this ('coming of age') film, by metonymical references to economies of contemporary life, realisms, diverse genealogies of town planning and underinvestment, contemporary 'realities'. We are all in it; weirdly all in it.

In this way, I propose biopolitical realism not only as something that the films *do*, but also as the climate in which these films are watched, circulated and debated. To put it in simpler terms, capitalist realism is not enough of a frame for me to describe what happens when films such as *Dogtooth* and *Strella* enter a social reality and a cultural economy like the one they entered in 2009 (cf. Karalis 2017; see Chapter 1). Unless I talk about a biopolitical realism, I cannot fully explain how these two films ended up reading each other. I cannot explain how the new queer realism of *Strella*, which for the first time in Greek Cinema presented a transgender character and actress demanding a presence and position in the public sphere and the film industry, intertwined with the allegorical expansiveness of *Dogtooth*, haunting it and being haunted by it in return (see Chapters 5 and 7). As I show in the following chapters, biopolitical realism starts exactly when one realises that a film like *Strella* has also taken on allegorical weight in the years that followed it, that it became a platform for queer politics within the crisis (as I show in Chapter 7) and that it achieved the status of a text that talks about how bodies are managed, governed and/or proscribed at a national and transnational level. Biopolitical realism is the frame in which a film like *Dogtooth* has become totemic, the way for a national cinema to acquire international circulation and recognition, its scenes cut by users and circulated in order to illustrate (sometimes *contra* the film's abstracting poetics) specific politics and to discuss specific social formations such as the state of the Greek family or the Greek political system.

Biopolitical realism is exactly what emerges once you follow the thematics of the Greek-family-in-trouble that preoccupied so many of these Greek directors in the first decades of the twenty-first century and reflect on the reasons why it became such an overarching theme. I will move on to explain this in the next chapter. With narrative cinema as the most influential artform, Greek artists and spectators started revisiting the Greek family more widely in theatre, performance and literature in the twenty-first century. They did so in unexpected ways, combining a realist critique with complex arguments about disciplinary control, nationalist rituals and iconography, official and unofficial archives of belonging and, last, but not least, the biopolitics of the (national) family at a time of Crisis.

In the following chapters I will continue revisiting some of the better-known films of the Weird Wave, which have formed a canon of sorts over the last decade. My main aim is not to return to a familiar analysis – especially where this has been done so comprehensively in the past – but to use them in order to keep revising the Weird Wave's vocabulary. As with the terms 'weird', 'allegory' and 'metonymy' in the previous chapters, now discipline, family, archive, identity and assemblage become the pathways into the Weird Wave's biopolitical realism.

Notes

1. Many, but crucially not all, of these shots are also examples of what David Bordwell (2017) has called a 'planimetric shot'. The same happens in the next film I analyse in this chapter, *Attenberg*. For a good analysis of the latter's planimetric shots, see Poupou 2014. I do not make further use of this shot categorisation. It is, I believe, secondary in importance to the 'frame within a frame' tendency, which is more extensive in the films I discuss and which could contain planimetric shots typically employing shallow focus, as well as other shots where the focus is deep, but the individuals are shot suggestively framed by the built or natural environment. I should acknowledge, nevertheless, that some possible effects of the planimetric shot as Bordwell describes them – expression of enclosure and anxiety; a weird 'realist' effect as, for instance, in Takeshi Kitano's films; and, simply, the surveillance effect of a mugshot photo – can be found in many examples from the Weird Wave, too.

2. On Lanthimos's realism, Moisés Feliciano's video essay is spot-on (Feliciano 2019; see also St. Clair 2018). It is worth noting that, once Lanthimos moved to making films outside Greece, he also started using the playful and self-referential antirealist formal devices that became characteristic of his later cinema. In *The*

Lobster, *The Killing of a Sacred Deer* and *The Favourite*, the narration is punctuated by the extensive use of distorted camera lenses and slow motion, devices almost absent from the earlier Greek films.

3. As film practitioners and critics in Greece have variously pointed out, a stricter 'film realist' approach is bound to distinguish eventually between two broad categories of post-2009 Greek art fiction films: those that follow a 'more realist' trajectory, and others, the 'weird wave proper', that consistently undermine cinematic realism (see Papadimitriou 2014; Nikolaidou and Poupou 2017). Yet, this is exactly where problems emerge. For one, the distinction cannot hold for long before collapsing under its own weight – where would one position films such as Psykou's *The Eternal Return of Antonis Paraskevas*, Alexiou's *Wednesday 04.45*, Kekatos's *The Distance Between Us and the Sky*, or Papadimitropoulos's *Suntan* (see Introduction, Chapter 1 and Epilogue)? Most importantly, as I explained in the previous chapters, such distinctions between a 'realist' and an 'anti-realist' new wave of Greek cinema run the risk of missing the real story here: the films' address of specific realities, their effort 'to evoke, to research, to renew or to research what is real' (Picard 2018: 10).

4. Of course, nature documentaries of the type that Attenborough presents belong less to what Bill Nichols (2010) calls the 'observational mode' (which is supposedly more 'authentic' and with a greater truth-claim as the filmmaker's interference is shown as minimal) and much more to the 'expository mode'. In the latter, there is a clear authoritative function (voice-over and so on) and a point of view: An anthropocentric narrative is being imposed on the animal world in order to make it more understandable, less weird or estranging. These, to be sure, are conventions that *Attenberg* undercuts and reverses, by weirding the human instead of 'domesticating' the animal through observation, but also by collating the two as contiguous practices.

5. Again, this follows a realist protocol: According to the implied lifestory, Marina's mother must have been French, something which fits with the fact that Pechiney employed many French nationals in their plant and that many lived in the town. It also follows a real production detail: Arianne Labed, who plays the role, even though having for long spells lived and worked in Greece, is French. The main role was originally written for Mary Tsoni, the dancer/actress who played the younger daughter in *Dogtooth* (for her impact on the Greek Weird Wave, see also the Epilogue). Labed was initially offered the role of Marina's best friend Bella, which eventually went to dancer and actress Evangelia Rantou, also known for hser role in Lanthimos's early film *Kinetta*.

6. I do not imply that a character speaking in allegorical terms in a film suffices to make it a national allegory. But the father in this scene surveys the empty modernist town and talks about the (un)building of modern Greece. This is what allows the viewer to see this film's story and its main location as an allegory of the nation.

7. The obvious allegorical impulse of the film has made commentators present diverse readings: from those that stay close to a reading of national allegory,

even down to specific scenes (e.g. Psaras 2016, who reads in the awkward walks performed by Marina and Bella in the empty town spaces an allegory of national parades; see also Comanducci 2017), to feminist analysis of how sexual difference inhabits the built environment and readings that extrapolate towards larger themes, such as the anxiety about the environment and the human/animal continuum (Galt 2017). An insightful reading of Tsangari's films based on the development of an auteurist style has been articulated by Anna Poupou (2014), while a rebuttal of the tendency to read national allegory in them has been offered by Sophie Coavoux (2018). Meanwhile, Dimitris Eleftheriotis (2020) in a very persuasive essay argues for a literal reading of *Attenberg*, as an example of what he calls 'introvert cosmopolitanism'. The film, he posits, turns inwards, to the national and the local, in order to offer a direct critique of Greek attitudes towards the family and closed kinship networks. For Eleftheriotis, *Attenberg* is un-homely, precisely because it is so much directed against the oppressive versions of the Greek *oikos* still found in contemporary Greece. For another impressive reading of *Attenberg* as representative of a new film 'aesthetics of recession', see Karkani 2016b.

8. The insights of this analysis notwithstanding, Karalis seems to be adopting the problematic narrative that Greek governments (which he takes as single, unified actors) kept offering money that was non-existent and thus created an implosion of the state. See also Papadimitriou 2017.

9. *Lifo* has republished these interviews collected online at https://www.lifo.gr/topics/view/4, calling them 'short theatrical pieces'. This confirms the view that they were more of a social commentary and an absurdist extension of the magazine's own style of describing Greek cultural and social life. These interviews have had an enormous readership over the years, creating a style that has been widely imitated. There still exists speculation that the conversations they purport to relay never actually took place.

10. In 2017, Filippou published some of his 'interviews' and other texts in book form, in dialogue with a series of photographs by Staveris (Filippou 2017).

11. In the second part of his 2009 book, Fisher bemoans contemporary students' apparent passivity and inability to react. In later works, however, including his collection *Ghosts of My Life* (2014) and the posthumously published *The Weird and the Eerie* (2017), he showcased the unhomely, the ironic, the awkward and the eerie as modes of critical reaction. I turn to these arguments in the Epilogue.

12. One may contrast David Harvey's similar thought on neoliberalism from the beginning of his *A Brief History of Neoliberalism*: 'Neoliberalism [. . .] has pervasive effects on ways of thought to the point where it has become incorporated into the common-sense way many of us interpret, live in, and understand the world' (Harvey 2007: 3). There are reasons, however, that Fisher, even though in much of his writing he has the logics of neoliberalism in mind, ends up talking about a Capitalist (and not Neoliberal) Realism. Apart from secondary reasons – capitalist realism makes a reference to socialist realism, and at the same time has echoes of previous artistic movements, such as the one under the same name

once spearheaded by Richter – Fisher most importantly describes a wide cultural logic that presupposes capitalism, capitalism's history and capitalism's cultural history. Earlier capitalism thus contributes to the smooth development of its new phases as the only reality. Neoliberal economy and neocapitalism are not the same as capitalist realism; they support it as their 'evident' cultural logic, and in turn it supports them as a fact of 'natural' evolution. See Baumbach, Young and Yue 2016; Stiegler 2019.

13. One is here reminded of Maria Boletsi's ingenious reading: Taking not only tense and voice, but also larger modal categories of expression as grammatical, she argues that cultural responses to the Crisis (and neoliberal politics more generally) tend to be expressed neither in an active nor passive voice, but in the middle voice. Boletsi's influentrial example was the common slogan appearing on Greek walls for years after 2011, stating just one word, 'βασανίζομαι', a word in the middle voice that has to be read as standing semantically between 'I am being tortured' and 'I torture myself' (Boletsi 2016; 2020).

14. Refreshingly, Steyerl does not follow more established categorisations of documentaries. Nevertheless, were we to combine her arguments with one of the categories proposed by Bill Nicholls, one could say that Steyerl seems to be both critiquing what Nicholls describes as 'performative documentary mode' and asking for more radical versions of it (see Nicholls 2010).

15. See also essays by Boris Groys (2008) and Okwui Enwezor (2008). Like Steyerl's essay, they, too, were written in the context of Documenta XI, as a reflection on the artwold's turn to biopolitics and documentarism that the exhibition itself performatively thematised.

16. Hito Steyerl acknowledges this in her later essay 'The Cut', first published in *e-flux* in 2011 and later as the last chapter of her collection *The Wretched of the Screen* (2012). She starts with the tentative argument that the editing cut in cinema, as well as the cutting out of the picture in framing, could be seen as related to the politics of austerity – she does not elaborate; yet, how appealing an argument for the framing politics of the Weird Wave . . . Towards the end of the essay, she further argues that the power of contemporary spectators to cut and rejoin visual material (analogous to what I here describe as acts of 'possessive spectatorship') can become a weapon against the imposition of specific forms and formats of representation.

17. I elaborate further on this argument in Papanikolaou 2019a, focusing on the later documentary practice of Patricio Guzman and the auto-ethnographies of Agnès Varda and Vincent Dieutre.

CHAPTER 5

The Biopolitical Family: (Miss) Violence, Discipline, Allegory, Dogteeth

A GIRL AT A CELEBRATION: *MISS VIOLENCE*

First you see a door opening, the door frame just fitting inside the camera frame. We enter the middle-class sitting room of an Athenian family. Confetti, dancing, the celebration of a birthday and of intergenerational kin cohabitation, as you often find it in Greece: a daughter confiding to her mother that she is pregnant; a father and/or grandfather dancing with his young grandchildren and/or children (exactly in this 'and/or', as the viewer will soon realise, lies not only the interpretative anxiety that the film provokes, but also the violence structuring the life arrangements of this family group). There is a close-up of the eleven-year-old girl whose birthday they are celebrating. She balances on the window to the soundtrack of Leonard Cohen's *Dance Me to the End of Love*. She falls.

The camera then follows her out of the window. We realise that the flat in the previous scenes has been on the fifth floor or so. As the camera pans to a vertical crane shot, the dead body of the young girl now lying on the ground seems like it is being inspected, surveyed – the square-tile pattern now looks more and more like a graph measuring her dead body, blood slowly pouring from it.

In the first three minutes of Alexandros Avranas's *Miss Violence* (2013), we have gone from an opening that alerts to its allegorical potential, to a realist depiction of a family celebration and a suicide, to a body filmed lying still and framed as a sign of something larger. For the two hours that follow in this gripping, harrowing film, which is often extremely difficult to watch, we will be constantly moving between several levels. There is the story of abuse, exploitation, child sex-trafficking and incest during the Greek crisis; a *pater familias* inflicts all of the above on the members of his family, in order to 'make ends meet during a difficult period'. Another level involves an allegory of Greek society seen in the microcosm of this family flat, behind its closed doors (the doors open in the first shot of the film and close in its last one). At least one other allegorical level concerns the vicious circles of power and control and the inability to break them: In the last scenes the father is killed; yet, control is regained by the mother of the family. Last, but not least, the

Figure 5.1a–d *A family celebration, and a body's fall measured from above; from the opening sequence of* Miss Violence *(Alexandros Avranas, 2013); digital stills.*

film presents a self-conscious micro-exploration of how bodies are trained through discipline, sexuality, welfare, affect and kinship.

The family lives under the absolute control of the father/grandfather, unnamed throughout, who in the first scenes gives us the impression of being a caring figure. Themis Panou's performance in this role was commended for the way in which he was able to communicate the surface characteristics of absolute care, implying only by way of small gestures or merely a look the horror he inflicts on the members of his family, and the violence and sexual abuse he has placed at its centre. At that surface, caring, level, we see an extended family that circumstances have forced to live under the same roof of a middle-class, well-proportioned but crammed apartment. The group is composed of an older couple in their late fifties, joined by a woman in her late twenties, who is presumably their older daughter, and her own young children, as well as two more girls, aged fifteen and eleven. At first glance, the family appears to consist of a couple, their daughters and the children of their first daughter. Indeed, this is the story that the father will register with the police and welfare services who investigate the eleven-year-old girl's suicide. Only later, as we witness the father manipulating the children, raping them, forcing at least one of them into sex work and abusing them all as a group does it dawn on the viewer that abuse and incest have been the main glue holding this family together; that the younger children may be the offspring of the father and his older daughter, or that they may have been her unwanted pregnancies as a result of the sex work forced on her by the father. It dawns on the viewer that Angeliki, the younger girl whom we have seen jumping out of the window at the beginning of the film, must have done so because she knew that it was usually after their eleventh birthday that the father/grandfather would start to abuse his children and force them into sex work. What makes the film even more harrowing is the fact that its everyday life rituals – the family table, the stern but caring father, the stoical mother – seem so familiar, especially from past cultural representations of the 'typical Greek family' narrative.

As it progresses, the film is not sparing with its scenes of violence, sexual or otherwise; however, its power also rests on insinuation and the adoption of violence, not as an event, but as a framework. As Marios Psaras has astutely pointed out, . . .

> [*Miss Violence*] is raw, impassive, but still violent, especially with its audience. It is a film that communicates in ellipses and insinuation, as the haunting images of empty corridors and closed doors deny the audience – at least, for its greater part – any visual access to the horrific events that form the temporal rupture of the familiar familial narrative [. . .] Violence is ubiquitous; sometimes unprovoked, often sudden and unexpected, but always deglamorised. (Psaras 2015)

The indirect referencing or the direct screening of violence are such that affective reactions are not simply evoked: They are provoked, forced and manipulated all at the same time. From the outset – and even from its very title, which also in its Greek release consisted of the English phrase – *Miss Violence* associates itself with the cinematic trend that has been described by European film critics as 'New Extremism' (Horeck and Kendall 2011). As in the films of Gaspar Noé or Catherine Breillat, violence in *Miss Violence* is not simply a part in a system of representation, but used as a conduit for representation to provoke affective reactions in the viewer and make those reactions an integral aspect of representation.[1] Following many other films of New Extremism, violence here does not simply represent, inviting you to decipher context; it drags you into the events. Watching the film, I keep shivering; I also keep repeating to myself: *This is not my family experience, this has never been an experience I have ever been close to, this violence cannot touch me.* And then I keep wondering – why on earth did I feel the need to say that? What is it that makes that specific subject-matter affect me in this way? What is it that makes me want to shelter myself from the porosity of its violence?

WHAT IS WRONG WITH THE GREEK FAMILY?

After *Miss Violence* was first presented at the Venice Film Festival in 2013, where it won the Silver Lion for Best Director and Themis Panou received the Volpi Cup for Best Actor, the film's director Alexandros Avranas was quick to reassure audiences that this was not a film specifically made about the Greek Crisis, or even about Greece. For that matter, he kept insisting on the fact that he had taken his prime material from a real story that took place in Germany; he had read about it in a newspaper. Predictably, he had trouble persuading a gathering of international critics eager to hear the opposite and ready to elaborate on the Crisis. By that time, Lanthimos's *Dogtooth* (2009) had already become *the* cinematic narrative of the Crisis (once again, sometimes against the objections of its director about such a contextualisation). In that earlier film's central scene, just as in the opening of *Miss Violence*, we were presented with an oppressed family engaged in a similarly awkward celebration, with the girl at the centre of the celebration, in a desperate act, trying to react to and break the family's vicious circle.

Suddenly, there was something about these families that kept haunting contemporary Greek films, something violent, explosive and contagious, making an allegorical reading – alongside the realism of domestic violence and abuse that dominated the storylines – almost impossible to resist.[2] Hence emerged one of the ideas that would become central to the reception of post-2009 Greek Cinema for years afterwards: the family in tatters, in violence, in explosion, in disarray was now firmly seen as a form of national allegory for the nation in crisis. No matter how much Avranas protested (and, potentially, his protest might have created even more discussion about these issues), *Miss Violence* was firmly categorised as a product of (and/or an allegory for) the Greek Crisis:

> Cruelty [in this film] could be blamed on the economic crisis. You would have to believe that the Greek economy has ended up leading to either derision through the absurd (in line with Yorgos Lanthimos's cinema) or, in a more worrying way, to monsters like this pater familias [of *Miss Violence*], the real master of the house who imposes discipline by enslaving his children (La Porta 2013).[3]

In what follows, I will try to address these recent portrayals of Greek families and return to some of the debates sparked by them. The international success of films such as *Dogtooth* or *Miss Violence* notwithstanding, in order to review this trend, one also needs to take into account a series of other, less internationally circulated Greek cultural texts – from cinema, but also theatre, literature and performance art. I will then turn to the question of why, in a deeper and more theoretically productive way, the family might be a vantage point for cinema and culture at a time of biopolitics. In the last part of this chapter, I will return to *Miss Violence* and *Dogtooth*, exploring their biopolitical realism further, in a comparison with the Mexican film *El Castillo de la pureza* (directed by Arturo Ripstein, 1973), which has been suggested as a source of inspiration. In the Greek films, discipline, sexuality and allegory become mechanisms of subjectivation, but unlike the early Mexican film, their cinematic representation underlines more firmly the biopolitical power structures that today shape kinship, national belonging and crisis citizenship.

As I have already explained in Chapter 1, the thematic pattern 'Greek family in crisis', strictly speaking, predated the period of the Greek Crisis. It was also present before Lanthimos's *Dogtooth* – significantly, for instance, in Economides's *Matchbox* (2002) – and certainly was not limited to the field of cinema. An exploration of kinship and family dynamics, either as national metaphor (the family as the symbolic core of the nation) and/or as national metonymy (the family as the signifying part of the whole) certainly is not an exclusively Greek concern. One could go so far as to argue that such use of family narratives, apart from being constitutive of a cultural understanding of belonging for centuries across the globe, has seen a particularly dynamic comeback in the last decades, especially in cinema. The cinema of Michael Haneke and Lars von Trier, as well as very specifically Thomas Vinterberg's film *Festen* (1988), have been mentioned as specific influences on Lanthimos and other Greek directors who turned to the family as a site of hidden traumas and their spectacular eruptions. The older Mexican film *El Castillo de la pureza* (1972) also constitutes an important influence. In that film, a *pater familias* keeps his family of five trapped in their house, obsessed with maintaining them uncontaminated by the outside world and making them create pesticides against vermin, in a paranoid family economy project that will explode in the end. When following this linear critical narrative, one can certainly see *Dogtooth* and *Miss Violence* as an update on the imagery of the troubled Greek family based on those world cinema predecessors – *El Castillo de la pureza* meets *Festen* in a Greek setting and as a contemporary answer to the demand for complex narratives of 'troubled families from a troubled country'.

The reason I have called this a 'linear critical narrative' is that it fails to take on board a number of parallel and equally important developments. As I have already mentioned, the family-in-tatters became an identifiable and much wider theme in Greece in the first decades of the twenty-first century, so much so that critics in the country even started treating it as a distinct cultural genre.[4] This genre not only involved diverse films, but also novels and short story collections that appeared after 2000, as well as theatre and other art forms (including, for instance, photography).[5] It was treated as the tip of an iceberg, with critics wondering: 'Is the family the seed of evil in Greek society? Is it a machine for the reproduction of rage, which accumulates from generation to generation?' (Katsounaki 2010; cf. Xydakis 2011).

For film critic Evgenia Giannouri, who also surveyed the wider critical debate, 'whether depicted clinically or in a baroque and exuberant manner, the [Greek] family stands for the allegorical analogon of national schizophrenia and corruption, the root cause of individual and collective paroxysms' (2014: 158). Usefully, Giannouri reminds us that, apart from an insistence on the family, this thematic turn also means an insistence on the house, the idea of home, the *oikos*. This 'oikographic drive' is not new in Greek culture, far from it; it has for long periods propelled Greek literature, theatre, popular and art cinema, as well as public discourse. What is new is not the cultural pervasiveness of the *oikos*, but its toxicity: 'What contemporary films add to the equation is a substantial dose of cynicism and introspection with regards to social toxicity and its moralities. They suggest a kind of social pathology performed in the rescaled field of the domestic' (2014: 161).

THE NOXIOUS OIKOS/FAILED COUNTRY: FAMILY ECONOMIES OF INCEST, ABUSE AND CRISIS SURVIVAL

Faced with this thematic turn to the family-in-tatters, film scholars and critics reacted in two different and at first glance seemingly irreconcilable ways: One type of reading sees the focus on the troubled family as a way to create an allegory – of Greek social institutions, of paternalistic behaviour in Greek society, and so on (Karalis 2012; Celik 2013; Papadimitriou 2014; Lykidis 2015; Brinkema 2012). The other tends to see in the actual issues highlighted by the films, especially domestic violence and abuse, important discussions of the Greek family itself and then, synecdochically, of Greek society more generally (Metzidakis 2014; Barotsi 2016; Aleksic 2016; Kazakopoulou 2016; cf. Eleftheriotis 2020).

For instance, in Ipek Celik's reading, which is representative of the first tendency, the family is seen as an allegory of 'internal and external borders'. She reads the focus on families which are secluded, locked down and largely sealed off from the outside world (for instance, in *Dogtooth*, *Attenberg*, or *Miss Violence*) as an allegory that speaks about Fortress Europe, European racial and ethnic profiling, and the obsession with a 'clean and bordered' nation. She reminds us that, if in the 1990s and the mid-2000s, Greek Cinema's dominant theme had been migration (and thus a focus on crossing borders and people moving), after a certain point the direction changed and turned inwards. Instead of migrants, co-ethnics, and narratives of identity and belonging, the focus now turned to the inner and impenetrable circle of the Greek family, as a unit of surveillance, (imagined) purity and discipline. Beforehand, borders were seen as external and crossed; with the new obsession with enclosed family narratives, they were shown to be mostly internalised and uncrossable. The family in these more recent films stood for the pure, gated, financially pressured (and abused) European nation at the time of Fortress Europe.

Other critics, however, have shown the potential for a literal reading of this same material. According to Dimitris Eleftheriotis, . . .

> the privileging of allegorical readings of the family in the Weird Wave films constitutes a form of critical denial of the deeply problematic and specifically Greek ways in which the family (dys)functions. [. . .] [These films] can and must also be read literally, as bearing witness to a very real issue (Eleftheriotis 2020: 4).

As Eleftheriotis also points out, the problem with the way in which this debate is conducted is that it too often gets schematised as 'family allegory vs. family realism' or 'family as national allegory vs. family as realist social critique'. This, I would argue, underestimates the persistent focus of the films (and other similar cultural texts) on forms of governing and types of power, on how power takes hold of the body, organises life and manages a group. One realises that the specific and the general, the real(ist) and the allegorical, the familial and the social, the familiar and the weird intersect in these texts in ways that are both unexpected and productive. When considering this turn-to-family-trouble that Greek cultural texts took in the first decades of the twenty-first century as a whole, one realises that it was all along their aim to explore these specific intersections (real/allegorical; familial/social; familiar/ weird).

Let us once again take *Miss Violence* as an example. At first glance, the film looks as if it was made to respond to a call for 'more social realism' during a difficult period.[6] It is enclosed in the four walls of a family home, but it also veers outside; it is a film about suffocating, incestuous, violent kinship, but it is also about failed markets and social institutions. Based on a script co-written by Avranas and Kostas Peroulis (an author known for his social realist short stories), *Miss Violence* is at pains to show that the family violence at its centre is socio-culturally endemic, directly related to and supported by the (failures of the) social and financial system in which it flourishes.

The father is unemployed, and the film makes it clear that he has recently lost his job; he joins queues to apply for state support for the children of the family; more than once does he make the claim that the reason why he prostitutes members of his family is 'so that we can enjoy all these good things and be happy'. Crucially, a long sequence of rebellion and punishment directly involves money. The fifteen-year-old daughter, who earlier on had been the subject of the most harrowing abuse scene in the film, is caught in her school tearing a fifty-Euro note to pieces. The teacher calls her father in to discuss the issue – 'we are supposed to value money' – and hears from him: 'You have my word; this will not happen again'. Of course, what he means at that point might not be exactly what the teacher has in mind, and the disciplinary actions that the *pater familias* will eventually take against the prodigal daughter would certainly not be supported by the school system. But, as this scene labours to make clear, the two disciplinary institutions, school and family, even when misplacing each other's advice, seem to be reaching an understanding. Disciplinary control will be regained, and money will be revalued. In classic capitalist realist mode, money, its circulation and 'the respect for it' is shown as the purloined letter, the signifier around which positions of subjectivation are arranged. Only, in this case, the positions arranged are not simply positions of power and agency; they are also positions of kinship, of citizenship, of education and of sexualisation, while also (quite disturbingly) tactics of austerity survival.

Miss Violence at the same time makes clear that abuse, incest and most notably child prostitution had been taking place much earlier on in this family. Interestingly, this provokes a complex vision of the specific economies at play, not only of violence, but also of morality and care. The economy of violence and sexual abuse expands beyond the current financial pressures that the family is experiencing. As financial gain and money exchange seem to be continuously (and seamlessly) connected to abuse and incest, so the latter are connected to family stability and the idea of happiness.

Figure 5.2 a–b *The father (Themis Panou) photographs children, victims, viewers, from* Miss Violence; *(Alexandros Avranas, 2013) digital stills.*

Similarly, the father is too knowingly portrayed as the monster at the centre of this arrangement. In terms that very much recall Gillian Harkins's analysis of the incestuous father as the useful monster of neoliberalism (2009), the father in *Miss Violence* personifies absolute evil. Yet, his strategies, all those practices at which he becomes adept, are painstakingly shown to be much more generalised and common in the society in which he lives. When he procures one of his daughters for a group of men, they treat him as a friend, offering him drinks, sharing jokes, eventually sharing their sexual victim, too, in a harrowing sequence of scenes that underlines the contiguity of (spaces of) homosociality, sexual abuse and incest. When he takes his older daughter to another man, who seems to have been a long-standing client, the atmosphere has something of a family reunion, as all three bond over a drink, sitting on a family sofa and taking polaroid photographs. We have seen the father taking a polaroid in exactly the same way during the family birthday celebration with which the film opened – are these photographs just tools of affective reassurance, or do they end up also being used in the market that the father has set up?

This is a story of abuse and procurement that portrays itself as the governance of a happy family. The examples of a larger social circle being the silent (and thus complicit) onlookers proliferate. A neighbour looks on with a pensive gaze, as the father greets her – how much does she know? The same happens with the sister of another of the father's 'friends' who is asked to help with money for an abortion – is he a friend or just another member of the client network? Is he being asked to offer help, or is he being blackmailed? She then also looks on with a similar gaze, eventually leaving the scene where the financial transaction is taking place – how much does *she* know? How much has *she* been abused?

Of course, in all these cases, onlookers might not know the exact nature of the father's relationship with his children and the exact level of incest and violence that binds the family together. But these onlookers do participate in practices (from homosocial bonding to child prostitution rings, and from gender violence to family secrecy and propriety) that allow incest and abuse to take place unnoticed. The fact that incest is also often recalled as the utmost abomination within some or all of these practices belies its structural compatibility with them; it is there as a limit supposedly not to be crossed, but, as the film takes pains to show, it lies at the very core of this system of abuse. In other words, the father's incestuous abuse of the members of his family is presented as potentially the key factor in the reproduction of practices such as exploitation, gender violence, familial abuse, secrecy, patriarchal authority *and* the constant marketisation of individuals, in the same way as it has also guaranteed the reproduction of this particular family itself. Perhaps the film's most potent critique is that it shows this type of incestuous and abusive family to have been run like a new-style financial project, where individuals are marketised through and through and the domestic is run like an enterprise – an enterprise that, quite successfully, has been growing, expanding and remaining afloat.

Miss Violence ends with the mother ritualistically preparing and then committing the killing of the father. She kills him, it seems, not so much because of what he has done, but because he has lost control of *that* family project. In the last scene, after the patricide,[7] as she sternly commands the children to stand in a line, there is no ambiguity about the fact that she is now assuming the governance of a similar family structure. The film ends with a close-up shot of the apartment's outside door closing and being locked. What has started as a social realist dissection of an extremely abusive family unit at a time of crisis ends with reminding the viewer how much it has also been a kinship allegory of enclosure, sealed borders and structural violence. It is a disturbing allegory, precisely because of its metonymic placement; it is placed, literally, next door.

This is how *Miss Violence* and most of the films of the Weird Wave end up retaining room for both the allegorical and the 'literal': by insisting, often through the focus on the family, on systems and structures, and on economies of power. The larger cultural turn to 'family trouble' that Greece saw after 2004 has to be considered precisely within this dynamic. A whole economy of power mechanisms and impositions was the focus of these films and other cultural texts: It ranged from surveillance, to disciplinary and more largely biopolitical control. A traditional understanding of allegory simply as an extended metaphor does not suffice if one wants to see these cultural texts as allegorical.

Paul Preciado has aptly reminded us that 'the politics of the border [. . .] are now reproduced in the interior of the national territory, spread out on the total population, reinscribed on individual bodies' (Preciado 2020, n. p.). This is exactly how an intense biopolitical present works, reinforcing external and interiorised borders, their constant reinscription onto one another showing how contiguous and continuous the body, the population and the territory are. To say, for instance, that in the films of the Weird Wave, the internal (family) borders and controls stand as a metaphorical allegory of external (national) borders cannot fully explain the complexity of the contemporary moment. It does not sufficiently address the fact that these 'external' borders are nowadays more and more continuous, reachable, tangible and internalised. If, however, we conceive of allegory as a trope that can also be based on an extended and extensive metonymy, these family stories about abuse, power and external/internal control fit the description exactly. Their allegories are nothing other than extended metonymies.

In the previous chapter, I have talked about biopolitical realism as a diffuse cultural modality in which all the films of the Weird Wave participate. In my understanding of biopolitical realism, allegory is neither the opposite of realism, nor is it absent from the domain of the 'real'. Moreover, the more the allegorical is connected to the metonymic, the more it operates on the same axis as the 'real' and the filmically constructed. Allegory, in that case, does not start by introducing another axis of reference, but by participating as an instrument in the very governance of the real, within the film and as it reaches outwards.

As I have shown with the example of *Miss Violence* (and that of *Attenberg* in the previous chapter), there is a visual, narrative, affective, embodied exploration of the dynamics of power and of life management in these films, one that is very specific and instrumental, while also creating a powerful metonymic allegory of larger biopolitical governance. I will explain this further in the following section, where I focus on the biopolitical aspects of the family and how these were reflected in the Weird Wave.

Yet, it is also crucial to remember that biopolitics as a form of politics over life and biopolitical realism as a cultural modality work in similar ways. They bring together the specific and the generalisable, the relatable and the related, the minutely analysed and the pattern, the body/the group/the population. They bring all of them into serial contiguities, and they combine them. In these terms, when thinking back to the central idea of the 'anatomopolitics of the human body *and* the biopolitics of the population' (Foucault [1976] 1998), one realises how inherently metonymical biopolitical thinking has been from the outset. If cultural discourse also tends to work with the body as an allegory for the population, this does not diminish their intensified proximity in a biopolitical arrangement. It is for this reason that allegory within biopolitical realism tends to put such emphasis on metonymy, so much so that a type of metonymic allegory often becomes the very cultural logic of an intense biopolitical present. This will be the underlying argument of the last two sections of this chapter, which will develop a reading of Lanthimos's *Dogtooth* and its biopolitical, allegorical and metonymic poetics.

THE BIOPOLITICAL FAMILY

The family can be seen as a drama of sovereignty. Structures of sovereignty order the role (and the name) of the father and the parents, as well as the organisation of power and kinship relations. The family, nevertheless, also develops as a space where discipline is exercised, working as a functioning part of the disciplinary society at large (Foucault 2008; Donzelot 2005). If sovereignty and discipline are traditionally acknowledged as main poles of family life in modernity, the family becomes in a more pronounced way also the site for the employment of that third modality of power, biopolitical power. Apart from its psychosymbolic and disciplinary roles, the family works now more intensely on the bodies of its members with a view to their biosocial function – that is, the organisation of the biological dimension of life, as it is constantly being reframed by socio-political forces. The family is supposed to concern itself with its members' health and has the responsibility to secure their future health with the help of scientific reason and medicine, from vaccinations to the charting of children's bodily growth. It undertakes surveillance over their 'natural' gender and their 'normal' development. It imposes borders between normal and abnormal. It organises the way in which bodies interact with each other and with the (projected idea of the) population.

We often forget that role; yet, if it did not exist, if the family were functioning solely on the basis of the traditional system of kinship and its relation to discipline, it would have been difficult for it to underpin modern developments such as the construction and evolution of the modern nation-state.

The biopolitical side of the family provides the route to its constant modernisation.[8] Precisely because biopolitics becomes so central in the modern family, the institution of the family, while remaining seemingly untouched as a symbolic structure, is also engaged in a constant development and diversification, always in response to new needs and intricately related to new (biotechnological, bio-educational and generally biopolitical) opportunities (Taylor 2012; Bell 2012). Moreover, in the era of the nation-state, the family does not simply participate in the symbolic, disciplinary and biopolitical aspects of national life; as a safeguarded molecule of the national body, it becomes a primary location for their much needed intertwinement.

With this in mind, I want to return to the reason why in recent years Greeks have focused so much, at least at the level of cultural representation, on the subject of the family. My analysis of *Miss Violence* in the preceding pages prompts the following idea: The Greek turn to the thematics of family-trouble seems to be characterised by an impressive structural reversal. If we are used to the nation (and at least in modernity, the state) being presented as a big family (a connection largely based on metaphor), *Miss Violence*, and with it a long series of Greek cultural texts in the twenty-first century, shows a deep interest in the opposite. A focus *not* on how the state should be run as a family, as Margaret Thatcher allegedly would have it, but on how the family (can be) governed as a state; how within the family the lives of its members are organised, their positions, skills and gendered roles distributed; how the family becomes precisely the space where room for manoeuvre and ways to act are offered or denied; how the family vows to secure or to expel, to embrace and protect, or to abandon and close off; how it treats the education and health of its members as a form of investment for the future and how, on that basis, all future prosperity plans are laid out; and, finally, how the family can turn itself into a nucleus for the reproduction of neoconservatism, intolerance and racism, or their opposite, a site for bodies that try to resist this framing by moving differently (Cooper 2017). This is a family presented at the same time as a symbolic, disciplinary and biopolitical organism.

Films like *Miss Violence* or *Dogtooth* point towards this overlap of different modalities of power; they are not only narratives of (a loss of) sovereignty, nor are they solely extreme scenarios of the imposition of discipline. Their effectiveness and topicality stem from the fact that they show with clinical precision and intensity how sovereignty intertwines with discipline, and how this intertwinement relies on and expands with the biopolitical modalities of power. They also astutely make the point that sovereign, disciplinary and biopolitical power, especially as they intertwine, create an economy that can be seen, both on an allegorical and a literal level, as compatible with contemporary financial and political developments.

Seeing the family only as a network of affective relations always runs the risk of overshadowing its deep involvement in the politics of life and death, its resolutely biopolitical role. Yet, within a larger tendency towards biopolitical realism, the family became just such an embattled cultural source in the Greece of the twenty-first century, precisely because it mingles life, economy and politics. It develops ways that tie the bodies of people to the idea of the population, the personal lives and the psychological pressure and violence upon them with the violence of plans, of models and of the grander narratives of survival and prosperity (Athanasiou 2012; Butler and Athanasiou 2013). From that perspective, one realises that the almost clichéd persistence of the theme of sexuality-within-the-family in those Greek cultural texts was not coincidental either. As Michel Foucault reminds us, sexuality (its surveillance, the organisation of taboos around it and the phantasmatic yet constant invocation of incest) underpins precisely this intertwinement of symbolic (patriarchal), disciplinary and biopolitical organisation of power, with an emphasis on the latter.

Moreover, sexuality becomes one of the most prominent conduits between family and society, even if this role is traditionally depicted as one-sided. Society might often be presented as the space where sexuality is liberated from family-imposed boundaries. As a popular understanding of psychoanalysis would have it, facing up to and analysing the threads of desire within the family may be seen as the subject's entrance into the phase of (sexual and social) maturity. Yet, upon reviewing these aspects one realises that the opposite is also true. Society also seems to be continuing the work of the family, instrumentalising familial sexuality, as it maximises the use of sexuality in disciplinary and biopolitical ordering: taboos, the limits of the desired and the proscribed, the said and the unsaid, normal and abnormal, the generalisation of a system of power/sexuality/knowledge, the classification and exploitation of sexual and gender difference, the organisation of sex work in biopolitical and necropolitical terms, and the instrumentalisation of racism within the redemptive narratives for the survival and reproduction of (our) society. All these, to be sure, have not been fully elaborated or finalised within the family. They nevertheless are based on what, for most people, once started there.

THE CASTLE OF SEXUALITY

Let us return to *El Castillo de la pureza*, the Mexican film of the 1970s, directed by Arturo Ripstein. A certain theatrical realism that characterises the film, especially in terms of acting, stage set and lighting, might seem to the contemporary viewer somewhat dated. Nevertheless, what has safeguarded the place of *El Castillo* in the history of world cinema is to a large extent the way in which it has been deciphered as a transparent allegory of the historical moment and geopolitical place in which it was made (Sisk 2019).

In *Castillo*, the father is a tyrannical figure who controls in minute detail the life of his family of five members – his wife, two daughters and a son. They live in a large house with a yard, and the children, named Porvenir (Future), Utopía (Utopia) and Voluntad (Willingness), are never allowed outside, with the youngest two even born and raised within the confines of the house. They have to follow the orders of the patriarch and help him safeguard the family economy that is meant to rely on two aspects: on the one hand, enclosure and, on the other hand, the production of poison and traps for vermin, which are then sold on the market and proposed to state institutions by the father, who writes letters to the governor demanding the wide-scale eradication of vermin in society.

Sounds familiar? It certainly did to many reviewers who, upon the international success of Lanthimos's *Dogtooth* after 2009, noted the resemblance between the two films, going so far as to argue that the Greek film was an unacknowledged remake of its Mexican predecessor.[9] It is true that various moments in the narrative, even some of the most awkward ones, point to a close affinity between the two films – for instance, the children playing blind man's bluff in the garden; the parents engaging in mechanical sex; the two daughters in the bathroom, playing on their own; or the insistence, by both fathers, on the family's seclusion from the outside world in order to retain its purity. *Castillo* portrays the family as a closed camp, with its members as inmates, insisting on the productivity of this closed-off system and relying on the house as an economy and a production machine. It also gives to the mother the role of an accomplice in the end: She assumes responsibility for the remaining members of the family in a way that reminds the viewer of the father's practices. In this respect, it can equally be considered a predecessor of *Miss Violence*, whose last scene almost seems to be paying tribute. What interests me here, however, are not the similarities between these films, but a very crucial difference.

The turning point that signals the dismantlement of the father's absolute power in *Castillo* comes as the three children begin to explore their bodies and sexual desires. The very idea that he cannot order or contain that desire is what makes him lose control and, eventually, power over the whole family and enclosure arrangement. He repeatedly punishes his children when he discovers any hint of sexual (and, as all members of the family are entrapped within the family house, incestuous) desire.

Compare this to *Dogtooth* in which, in all similar scenes (and there are many), the father ends up doing the opposite, not avoiding but caring for the development and instrumentalisation of sexuality. He notes signs of sexual maturity, tries to anticipate expressions of desire and then proceeds to organise further the children's sexualisation. After a discussion with his wife, he decides to enlist the services of a worker in the factory that he manages and who, apparently, accepts to offer sex work. And when this plan fails, he arranges for the boy to decide which of his sisters he wants to sleep with. In *Miss Violence*, as we have already seen, the father goes even further: Now it is sexuality, monitored and framed by the father, that becomes the centre of the house's economic model and, to an extent, its self-marketising response to austerity measures.

The difference is crucial. Even though all three films focus on sealed-off families and on this basis provide an allegory for the governance of people, it seems that, in the thirty years that have passed between them, our understanding of (and cultural obsession with) the type of governing that groups people together and is often predicated on the representations of the family has changed.[10] If the Mexican film focuses on how power is administered, the later Greek films primarily focus on how subjects internalise the elements of power/knowledge, the tenets of government, and the mentality of constantly 'being in check'. If in the former sexuality was presented as disruption, a nuisance for the system of power ordering the family, in the latter it has become its major component.

The *Castillo* family arrangement is clearly not one in which biopolitics is absent. The insistence on health, purity and the surveillance of the children's bodies points to that aspect of family life, too – and in the story overall, the father's insistence on providing his family as an example for the biopolitical arrangement and the health and safety of the whole state works exactly as a

Figure 5.3   *The three children (Angeliki Papoulia, Christos Passalis, Mary Tsoni) assessing their bodies in the bathroom, demonstrating the biopolitics of familial sexuality in* Dogtooth *(Yorgos Lanthimos, 2009); digital still.*

parable of how families work together *with* the state in order to frame biopolitical (as well as disciplinary) arrangements.

Different in the later Greek films, however, is their further exploration of the dynamics of the biopolitical. If in the Mexican film the emphasis was on the power of the sovereign, his decisions and his disciplinary measures, in the Greek ones, especially due to their insistence on sexuality, the focus becomes the internalisation of control, the production and expansion of mentalities, and the instrumental role that the healthy and sexualised body of the individual and of the group play within this arrangement and often clinical environment. *Miss Violence*, *Dogtooth* and a long series of Greek films and cultural texts of the same period, especially those dealing with family arrangements and enclosure, are not indifferent to the sovereign and disciplinary forms of power; on the contrary, they thematise their dynamics only too clearly. Yet, at the same time, they expose the crucial role of the biopolitical modality of power, its contemporaneously organising importance and intensification.

Does this emphasis on the biopolitical make films like *Dogtooth* or *Miss Violence* less allegorical than *Castillo*? The question arises because all three films have, from the outset, been involved in debates about cinematic allegory. If *Castillo* builds a family allegory with an obvious national and political meaning, *Dogtooth* updates this allegorical poetics (and, as I will explain in the next section, allows its allegorical impulse to frame all levels of the *mise-en-scène*), while *Miss Violence* responds to a Greek call for less allegory, thus infusing the story with an extreme realism that seems, in the first instance, to be resisting the allegorical. Yet, my discussion so far, in this and the previous chapters, has aimed to show that the real tension here is not between realism and allegory; after all, even the very realist opening scene of *Miss Violence* can be interpreted as an allegorical gesture towards life in a biopolitical order and the measuring of death, and Ripstein, just like Avranas, kept insisting on the life-story that became the basis for *Castillo*'s script.[11] Rather more important is the tension emanating from the ways in which aspects of these films relate to life decisions, formations, experiences and life-political positions that spectators face in their everyday reality, the very matter of their experience of the real. This tension expands, as it touches not simply on similar experiences of the spectator, but on the structure, the systematicity, of any similar experience.

My argument, therefore, is that their emphasis on the biopolitical does not stop *Miss Violence* and *Dogtooth* from functioning as allegories – whether political, national, or otherwise. It means, however, that they appear much more conscious of their politics of allegory and their complicated relation to realism. I would further argue that, especially as they become proponents of biopolitical realism, the films of the Weird Wave have a more pronounced role for the metonymical elements within their potential allegorical address. Their structural use of sexuality is a particularly good example.

In almost all of the films that I have analysed so far, scenes involving sexual conduct can rarely be called erotic. They affect the viewer, but it is not eroticism that emanates from these scenes to create the viewer's affective response. Something else comes close to our senses in these moments, something else touches us. Because we are sexualised subjects watching these films, the systemics of sexuality we see on screen do not simply strike us as examples of sexualisation; they also participate in a domain in which, perhaps placed far apart from but tied with a continuous thread, we find the elements of our own sexualisation. It is itself also a product of images, incitements, impositions, affective resonances and dissonances, and a myriad touchings. Sexuality, in relation to what we see on screen, has similarly been part of the larger biopolitical setting into which our bodies have been introduced. This does not mean that our body has had the exact experience that we see on screen, perhaps not even a comparable one; but it means that awkwardness, or violence, or the imposition of limits or norms, or internalised discipline and its frictions have been experiences that our body has had when entering the biopolitical world. It does not mean that the body exactly recognizes. It all means that the body suddenly remembers.

Here, I am approaching an analysis that perhaps reminds of recent theorisations of affective and embodied spectatorship. In recent years, critics have focused on the affective energy released by cinema and, as it were, shared with the spectator, in complex ways that surpass (or at least complicate) the emotions provoked by the storyline and the elements of the *mise-en-scène* (Aaron 2004; Boljkovac 2013; Lübecker 2015). The turn to affective and post-affective analysis of how in cinema (viewers') bodies are impacted (Sobchack 2000; Shaviro 1993; Marks 1999; Barker 2009), even though based on a different agenda and epistemological basis, allows me to push my argument into a bolder direction. What I want to point out is an affective intensity that is based less on analogy and commonality and much more on contiguity; it does not arise by the steering of emotions, but is recalled or summoned as biopolitical micro-sites are explored on screen. My additional argument is that this type of contiguous/contagious intensity is related to and has an impact on the poetics of allegory emanating from the filmic text and surrounding its reception (and this includes its reception by/on our bodies).

In the following section, my aim will be to explore these terms more fully and to take them a step further. Based on an analysis of Lanthimos's *Dogtooth*, I will argue that allegory itself can be employed as a biopolitical tool. Crucially, this type of biopolitical allegory does indeed tend to rely more on metonymies, especially the ones that can hurt.

DOGTOOTH AND THE BIOPOLITICS OF ALLEGORY

What is a biopolitical allegory, and how is it applied? Can it become a tool for discipline? As such, would it only be a matter of the mind, or does it also, can it also, affect the body? How, then, is allegory applied to the body?

The unnamed father of the enclosed family of five in *Dogtooth* looks as if he knows the answers to these questions. With the complicity and help of his wife, he has gone to great lengths to make these issues part of the family's everyday practice. Even the central story repeated to his teenage children in order to keep them inside their comfortable suburban house/enclosure, the very story that will eventually grow to envelop the whole film and its title, is an elaborate allegory. The children are told that they will be able to leave the house only when their dogtooth falls out. In Greek, κυνόδοντας, also the Greek title of the film, is more often translated into English as 'canine tooth'. The word 'dogtooth' was apparently chosen for the Anglophone release of the film to retain a reference to the concepts of 'dog' and 'tooth' which audiences would immediately understand.[12] This is because dogs, people being trained as dogs and a tooth become elements with a crucial role in the story.

The children are told that they will only be allowed to leave the enclosure of this house 'once their dogtooth falls out [. . .] and grows back again'. The first time we hear this, it is delivered in the third person, as an uncontested truth together with a sense of order and obligation ('kids are meant to . . . '). Dogtooth is a signifier: of immaturity, at the initial level of the story, and of enclosure and subordination at the level of the film as a whole. But 'dogtooth' also develops as a cautionary tale with a temporal and spatial arrangement. The children are told that they will be allowed out (*out of* a permanent *here*) once their dogtooth falls out. This introduces a future anterior and an 'elsewhere' anterior, which, incidentally, are very characteristic of biopolitical rhetoric, especially in what Elizabeth Povinelli (2011) calls late liberalism: There is somewhere a moment when dogteeth (and any 'special measures') will have fallen; there will then be a place to which the children will have been released. This *future perfect* and *heterotopic perfect*, the tense and placement that flood in phantasmatically with the dogtooth tale, slowly build the central signifier into a fully-blown allegory. This is because allegory essentially needs a narrative, even if it is meant to remain only phantasmatically present. The canine tooth that will *eventually* fall and allow the children to go outside thus becomes a story about the benefits of being obedient. The dogtooth story is there no longer to shape the expectations of the children, but to organise their docility, their internment and their state of being. This is exactly the reason why, once the older daughter starts wondering persistently *when* her dogtooth *will* fall out, once she starts *touching* her canine tooth and plotting to remove it, that things start to fall apart.

Cautionary tales, as well as the series of punishments, limits and pedagogic tools used within a family setting, are normally understood as instruments of discipline. They form boundaries and instruct caution through magnified threats. It is worth observing in *Dogtooth* how much measures of punishment and outright prohibition come to work alongside (and sometimes together with) allegorical structures in this story of enclosure, family abuse, control and education. We watch as the cautionary tale of dogtooth *becomes* an allegory of enclosure. As it orders the children, trains the children and organises the development of their body, it alerts viewers to how a host of other allegories function in the film as a whole. They hover in and around the house of *Dogtooth*, as viewers (inside and outside the film) watch how they are also *woven into* and *woven through* the time, space and emotional arrangements of the familial. The Dogtooth tale gives a great example of how allegory becomes a biopolitical tool, located exactly at the intersection of discipline and this more novel technology of power that Foucault calls biopower.

As Foucault (2003) explained in his lecture series '*Society Must be Defended*', biopower constitutes . . .

> . . . a new technology of power, but this time it is not disciplinary. This tech-nology of power does not exclude the former, does not exclude disciplinary technology, but it does dovetail into it, integrate it, modify it to some extent, and above all, use it by sort of infiltrating it, embedding itself in existing dis-ciplinary techniques. (242)

I have already mentioned at various points in this book that, since its first appearance, *Dogtooth* was seen as an allegory by viewers and critics, even though there was not always a consensus about the aim of the allegory. Suggestions ranged from seeing it as an allegory of the Greek Crisis or of paternalistic Greek society, to assessing it as a broader allegory of totali-tarianism, fascism, capitalism, communism, neoliberalism and so on.[13] As an online review titled '*Dogtooth*'s Infinite Allegories' put it, 'You've heard of the Choose Your Own Adventure books? This is Choose Your Own Allegory' (Stewart 2010). What has been noticed less often, however, was the extent to which allegory is a trope that operates within the film, too. The *Dogtooth* family itself is presented as an enormous allegory machine.[14]

In *Dogtooth*, instead of simply subjecting people to strict control, allegory is there as docile bodies are not only being produced, but also as they exceed that production. Viewers are invited to watch as allegory *introduces* its own vocabulary, its rituals, its temporal and spatial frame, its grammar, and, last, but not least, a way of seeing. The intensity provoked by engaging with this type of allegory, both *in* the film and in its address to the viewer, is felt through the body. And it is through the body that a critical, antagonistic effort to unsettle biopolitical mandates emerges as possible. There is, in other words, a triangulation of allegory/family/body which operates throughout *Dogtooth*: to settle things, to produce docility and to release an unsettling energy.

In the very first and one of the most commented upon scenes of *Dogtooth*, we see in close-up an old tape recorder playing an old-style language lesson. We will eventually realise that it is the voice of the mother who is heard repeating the meaning of words. Differently. 'The sea', the voice says, is a leather armchair 'like the one we have in the sitting room'. The motorway is a very strong wind. Excursion is a way of manufacturing surfaces with a resistant material. Rifle is a type of bird. These are all words related to the 'outside world', of course, replaced by denotations whose referent can be perceived from within the borders of this family's house enclosure. Later on, words referring to body parts and ones that can relate to sexual acts will be dealt with in a similar way.[15] If allegory is about *allos agoreuein*, about 'speaking otherwise', as the origin of the Greek words indicates, what we hear in this vocabulary lesson is a list of materials with which allegory is being built in this home's everyday. Crucially, as the vocabulary lesson is being heard in the first sequence of the film, we see the children in their white underwear in the bathroom, listening somewhat anxiously, their back to the wall and the mirror, their figures contrasting with the lines of the white tiles; these new words are there not only organising their world, but equally framing their body.

How long can this vocabulary reassignment go on without falling into inconsistencies? The viewer cannot help but noticing the artificiality, as well as the fragmentation and precarity of this vocabulary lesson. The point of the exercise, however, is not consistency, but to provide mechanisms of internalised control. As the children are asked to learn the redrawn meaning of new words, what is being conveyed are not specific ways of understanding the world (let alone communicating with it), but technologies of internalising orders and arranging the notion of the 'good life' in terms of a well-managed space, place and frame of experience. By allegorising words related to movement, borders, the body and sexuality, this whole arrangement early on thematises its biopolitical claims; biopolitics, after all, starts with the imposition of social and sexual transcripts. Notice also how this rearrangement of vocabulary enforces codes that are shared as well as related to the near-world. As much as possible, notions are meant to relate to the contiguous, to the world that is close. Allegory here is based on proximity and contiguity, on knowability, on touch. This is an allegory, in other words, that keeps relying on metonymical proximity to develop.

Once you start looking for them, allegories seem to be found everywhere in *Dogtooth*. They present themselves at different levels and move in different directions – becoming more, not less, powerful as a result. We can see how allegory develops in the various cautionary tales with which the children are presented (including the central one of the falling dogtooth). Yet, they are also visible in the games they play, the surroundings of the house and the discussion about those surroundings, the father's soliloquies about the external enemies and the new children 'about to be bred' by the mother, the retraining of the family dog (simultaneously with the training of the children and their efforts at un-training), the children barking, the sparseness of the landscape (interior and exterior) and the way in which this sparseness is filmed, the camera lingering on doors, mirrors and the family table.

I am here purposely mingling together allegorical levels that, one could argue, work in distinct ways in the film and that are meant to be decoded as allegorical from different viewpoints and subject positions. Obviously, the house and garden, and the way in which they are filmed, are building an allegory of enclosure and governmentality aimed at (and to be deciphered by) the viewer of the film, not the characters in the film. The training of the dog and the discussions around that process have a similar function (and the viewer might see the training as an allegory for the training of the docile children). Yet, notice how the proximity of the dog's training with the actual training of the children also makes the allegory all too palpable within the film's narrative. This is true at least for the father, who in one scene talks about the best types of training for his own dog and in the next is seen training the children, only a little later to be shown, along with the children and the mother, imitating a dog barking at the apparent attack by 'the outsider enemy' in the shape of a cat. Exactly in this moment, when the children are put to barking in the garden, it is as if different levels of allegory have started leaking into each other. The dog's training is not only an allegory of what is happening to the children (an allegory that would have worked for the viewer). It also becomes, for the father, the blueprint for this training (the allegory now working, within the film, as an originator of ideas about producing discipline and docility), before actually working on the bodies of the children themselves, leading to actual effects. The children are not trained *like* dogs, they are trained to take on the dog's function, or at least to play the role of dogs in an allegorical film whose title is *Dogtooth*, and within a family script that repeats to them that children are only allowed to go out when *their dog*tooth falls out.

At another point, as an airplane flies above the garden, the father rushes to throw a small model airplane into the garden – the model of the airplane does not *stand for* a real airplane anymore, since the father explains that this small object is the real airplane that has fallen into the garden, and he incites the children to search for it and collect it. First, the entire scene works as an

Figure 5.4a–d   *Talking about training dogs, observing trained dogs, training the children as dogs,*
from Dogtooth (Yorgos Lanthimos, 2009); *digital stills.*

allegory on two levels. On the one hand, this is an allegory of the outside/ inside dynamic, just like the taped vocabulary lesson: In this garden of enclosure, as in all states of control, anything that is seen outside is crudely (and from the outsider's perspective, quite hilariously) manipulated inside. On the other hand, this could also be read as an allegory of manipulating perspective and representation, as an allegory of the cinematic medium itself. But, at the level of the story, what this father is labouring to do is to guarantee the docility of his children by teaching them that anything that is outside can be allegorised by something else that eventually falls inside, something that can be searched for, touched, or repositioned.

As it unfolds, *Dogtooth* makes clear that its aim is to explore those in-between spaces, those grey areas where allegories are being built, operate, are managed and mismanaged, transported and repositioned, where they leak into 'reality', where they short-circuit and are put to use again, often in a different direction. Crucially, all this allegorical mobility relies much more on contiguity and transposition, and much less on analogy and transfer. In other words, allegory in this context tilts progressively more towards the axis of metonymy, rather than the axis of metaphor.

The father realises that, in order for allegory to work biopolitically, he has to emphasise the metonymical side of its structure. For the airplane to keep working not simply as a sign of the outside(r), but as an allegory of 'staying in the house in order to be safe', a metonymic extension of the airplane needs to be offered to the children (and to the film) to search for, to find, to touch, to place. For all this to work as a biopolitical allegory, the model airplane needs to be connected to the airplane just seen flying in the sky not in terms of analogy. Instead, it should be connected in terms of temporal proximity and perspectivally doctored spatial contiguity. This is not too far from what the film itself attempts at the level of *mise-en-scène*. Organising a distinctive style of shot and framing that would be theorised more than any other Weird Wave filming technique, Lanthimos persistently shoots his subjects from unexpected angles, framed within frames, and very noticeably often cuts and divides up the human body by containing only parts of it in the shot (for instance, the lower parts of bodies during a conversation). This has been seen as an effort to underline a feeling of claustrophobia and enclosure (Karkani 2016a). But it is also a *de facto* training of viewers in the metonymical poetics of proximity, seriality and contiguity.[16]

A GIRL AT A CELEBRATION . . . ONCE AGAIN

In *Dogtooth*, the metonymical side of allegory is maintained as a tool for its disciplinary and biopolitical effectiveness; but from a certain moment onwards, it unfolds equally as a platform for its potential destabilisation. Nowhere is this more obvious than in the disruption caused to this enclosure by the unexpected smuggling in of videotapes from the outside world. These come as a gift for the older of the daughters from Christina, the factory security worker whom the father has enlisted to offer sex work services to his son. Christina secretly brings in three homevideo tapes: pirated copies of *Jaws* (1975), *Rocky* (1976) and *Flashdance* (1983). As has been noted, all three are well-known Hollywood narratives that can be seen as allegories of the individual hero struggling and overcoming powerful adversity, enemies and competition (Celik 2013; Kapsaskis 2017). Predictably, the daughter's cine-visual world, up to that point confined to the short-circuiting activity of watching only videos of her family's previous gatherings, is now shattered. And she revolts.

However, her revolt is not based on the metaphorical dimension of those Hollywood allegories; it is instead based on reacting to them metonymically and disrupting the confines of her enclosure in a similar fashion. She does not respond to the films as narratives of freedom, release and the heroic overcoming of adversity; instead, she mimics fragments, phrases and gestures from them. In a climactic moment, after she is asked to perform alongside her sister and brother in a specially organised celebration to mark the parents' anniversary, she starts embellishing her expected performance with clumsily imitated moves from the famous dance climax of *Flashdance*. The result is unsettling and, quite literally, un-homely. These new gestures come from outside the house and, although they show the daughter performing her role in the celebration even more eagerly than the parental order, they essentially also destabilise it. The upset mother rushes in to stop her with the words 'That's enough!'

The girl does not deny the rules of the performance; she does not storm out, but she starts participating normally and then overdoes it, infusing her dance with an embodied quotation from another (cinematic) set of dance moves. In other words, she does not disrupt the celebration as a paradigm; she distorts the ceremony organised by the parents at the level of syntax. She has understood (and she uses) the Hollywood allegories more as metonymies, and through them she metonymically disrupts the allegory of wellbeing imposed on her own life.

No wonder, then, that the father turns to these same films in order to organise his punishment and revenge. And he uses them metonymically, too. First, taking part for the whole and container for the contained, he tapes the videotape to his hand and with it hits his daughter on the head.[17] Then, he turns up in Christina's flat unannounced and hits her over the head with her own VHS player. He, too, has seen these Hollywood videos as allegories working metonymically. And he labours to create out of them metonymies that can punish, discipline and hurt.[18]

It might certainly be argued that all these allegorical readings can only happen outside the frame of the story of the film: While *we* see the allegory of it all, the children only live in a 'distorted' reality, imposed on them as a feature of governmentality. But are these borders, the outside and the inside of allegory (and hence, of the film), so tightly sealed? My argument so far has been that they are not. The film hovers around this idea almost manically. On the one hand, we see the constant effort by the parents to produce allegory – an effort which, in its persistent unveiling of its own constructedness, creates complicity: in us, the viewers, but from a certain moment onwards in the children, too. The allegorist's viewpoint is already deeply lodged in the film's narrative, while also being demanded from the film's viewer. We watch allegories as they are being made; but the characters in the film watch that process, too. Sometimes they also trigger it. At other times, they contribute to its misfiring.

These are the moments when the stakes of the allegories in 'reality' become tested. Either by those (mainly the father) who try to reaffirm them and maintain their constructedness, or by the children who, while following them to the letter, end up supporting (or exposing) their reality game with violence. Watching the children interacting with the allegories shaping their lives, it is difficult not to think of Walter Benjamin's idea that the allegorist's gaze is characterised by irony and melancholia (2006). And in crucial moments, allegories by which they are meant to live are pushed to their (metonymical) limits. The most memorable such instance comes from the older daughter who, in the penultimate sequence of the film, decides to remove her dogtooth by knocking it out in front of the bathroom mirror, which is spattered with her blood, before attempting to flee the family house by hiding in the trunk of her father's car. As when she staged her disruption of the celebration scene, here again it is with her body – her body in excess, in anxiety, in agony, in pain – that she attempts to explore the limits of biopolitical allegory. And it is there, in those moments when allegory's stakes are tested with and on the body, that the triangulation family/allegory/body that *Dogtooth* has so well put in motion, is tested – as I would argue, both within and outside the film.

It is significant that, in the end, the film shies away from providing a happy ending of 'release'. We are left, instead, with the image of the girl locked in the car trunk. The girl has substituted one enclosure for another (she only knows, after all, how to make do with *what is near*). In the very final shot we see the car, presumably with the girl still inside the trunk, parked outside the main factory building, framed by its imposing building structures. A final ironic wink to the viewer: What we watch is an allegory of the larger enclosure which the film is about, a part of the whole. It is also a real enclosure with dramatic effect in the story, as it leaves it in suspense. We see yet another allegory, concluding an allegorical film about allegories, and, crucially, this last one originates from

Figure 5.5a–b *The daughter overstretching the family ritual and its biopolitical allegory: Angeliki Papoulia rebels in* Dogtooth *(Yorgos Lanthimos, 2009); digital stills.*

the actions of one of the subjects who was at the receiving end of allegories all along. Allegory is perpetuating itself even when people are trying to break free from it: There is no way out of this family-allegory-machine. Or, is there?

Even if we follow the allegory of the film in its exterior function – that is, its address outwards to the viewer – this family's story is offered to us as a platform for critical understanding of a culture in crisis, of power dynamics, of repression, of (bio)political control and so on. But then, from its centre comes a body itself conditioned by the power of allegories and which, in its excess, decides momentarily to undermine control, mock allegory's organisation and disturb its narrative coherence from within. In doing so, it exploits and expands on affective commonalities and contiguities – when the girl's body erupts from within the family celebration or in front of the mirror crushing her canine tooth, everyone (and everyone's body) is affected.

As I have explained, allegory works with and imposes a narrative, a space, a grammar and syntax; allegory invites, enables and engages a way of seeing.

These are processes that could provoke anxiety: both to measure up to allegory's mandates and to undermine them; but also an anxiety to create frames, to contain allegory. This *anxiety of allegory* is a pervasive state, a contagious merging of affect. It provokes an assemblage 'viewer/viewed' that is based, as I explained in the previous section with the example of sexuality, on the contiguities and commonalities created within biopolitical realism.

As anxiety takes over, biopolitical allegory starts leaking: Is what I am watching in *Dogtooth* a safely packaged allegory of totalitarianism, or is it an allegory of the Greek family? Or could it even be a snippet in the life of *a certain* Greek family (perhaps *my* Greek family), an archive of abuse potentially happening on bodies as I am watching this? Where is this happening? How close?

What about the affective reaction I have in the moment when I am watching these scenes in *Dogtooth*? What does it have to do with my own connection to the family-allegory-machine and to the biopolitical state in which I find myself? How has my body been conditioned? When and how will it react?

The ethical and potentially political dimension that opens up here relates to an emerging affective commonality, if not community, a connecting line that, in its intensities, cuts through the film and creates assemblages inside and outside its frame. How does one take responsibility for the affective over-reaction of the body – one's body and the body of the other? How can one capitalise on this affective reaction? How can one turn it into a platform from which to understand and work through the biopolitical dynamics that condition subjectivity at a given moment? How can one make affect the key to dealing with different layers, levels and types of allegory? What is the syntax of affect when it meets the syntax of allegory? And how does one dismantle the grammar and syntax of allegory as a biopolitical tool?

The answer to these questions extends to the realms of ethics and politics and, for this reason more than anything else, places *Dogtooth* at the very centre of that progressive cultural production that has come out of the Greek Crisis, part of which consists of the Weird Wave. In the following two chapters, I will move from allegory to archive and then to assemblage, as I analyse other types of biopolitical organisation in which the body and the population intertwine, as well as other types of metonymical reaction to them.

But before doing so, let me return to that celebration scene and say this: As I watch this girl's disturbing dance, I feel that I get to inhabit an affective present which dismantles the hold that biopolitical tense and placement have over me. The future perfect and the heterotopic perfect introduced by the cautionary tale of the Dogtooth have momentarily now been dislocated. As I watch this girl dance, I feel present/becoming/contiguous/continuous.

Notes

1. A number of critics have been ambivalent about the actual politics of the film, rightly pointing out that the lines between audience manipulation, exploitation and critique are not easy to discern.
2. At least one critic pointed out that allegory is much more present in the films of Lanthimos than in *Miss Violence* (La Porta 2013). Having said that, reviewed as a whole, the critical response to *Miss Violence* did not shy away from reading a national allegory into this film, too.
3. See also, among many others, Varikos 2013 and Aftab 2013, as well as the discussions in Aleksic 2016 and Psaras 2015.
4. I was one of those critics, recapitulating the discussion on the cultural poetics of 'Greek-family-trouble' in a 2018 monograph in Greek (Papanikolaou 2018a).
5. To take just a few examples, one could mention the stories and public performances of Lena Kitsopoulou; the novels of Auguste Corteau and Angela Dimitrakakis; the public writings and autobiography of Soti Triantaphyllou; the theatre of Maria Efstathiadi, Vassilis Noulas and Yannis Mavritsakis; the poetry of Vassilis Amanatidis; the photography of Periklis Alkidis; and, last, but not least, the new interest in the theatre of Dimitris Dimitriadis, whose larger influence on the Weird Wave (especially on Lanthimos) is considerable.
6. In many ways, *Miss Violence* directly responds to a very pointed critique 'against allegory' that gained purchase in Greek debates after 2010 – with *Dogtooth* being the most obvious target. Kostas Peroulis, who co-wrote the script of *Miss Violence*, is also the author of one of the most accomplished social realist collections of stories from the Greek Crisis (Peroulis 2015b). He was a member of the collective that published the political fanzine *Leuga* (2011–14), where this 'anti-allegory' critique found some of its prominent articulations. In an influential polemic published in the first issue of *Leuga*, another member of the collective, Kostas Spatharakis, set the tone by describing how, for the new Greek films about the family, 'the world "out there" seems too far away, threatening, dangerous, an uncharted territory. The characters in these films, therefore, remain at best "imaginary rebels" within the family, while the real revolt in the social sphere looks like a lost opportunity to them, a "wasteland" [. . .] When political critique remains, in this way, absent, then what prevails is a plenitude, a simplification: a distanced observation of social decay or a very general, and for that matter painless, denunciation of oppression and violence' (Spatharakis 2011: 28–29; for a similar argument, see Karalis 2012: 280–81).
7. In actual terms, this is a mariticide, as the killing has most probably been carried out by the spouse. However, it is the father and his authority that are slain in the last scenes, which strive to underline their allegorical potential and possible reference to ancient tragedy.
8. My discussion here is influenced by Foucault's analysis of the role of biopolitics in the family, as evinced in the fourth part ('The Use of Sexuality') of the *Will to Knowledge* (1998 [1976]) and elaborated further in his lectures in the Collège de

France between 1973–78. See Taylor 2012, and the illuminating articles collected by Duschinsky and Rocha (2012); see also Feder 2007.

9. The link between *El Castillo de la pureza* and *Dogtooth* has been the topic of numerous critical and fan-page discussions – for instance, it is mentioned in the IMDb and Rotten Tomatoes entry for Ripstein's film, whereas in the MUBI discussion list one user offers a testimonial from Ripstein: When he heard that *Dogtooth* had been nominated for an Oscar, he thought about sending Lanthimos a message saying 'I heard about the nomination! I hope we win' (see https://mubi.com/films/castle-of-purity). Even though Lanthimos never acknowledged Risptein's film as a potential source, the latter was theatrically released (for the first time!) in Greece in March 2011, the distribution company explicitly relating this move to the success of *Dogtooth*.

10. Of course, I am not arguing that sexuality as a form of power and a modality of governance has been absent from the history of cinema – after all, *El Castillo de la pureza* comes only four years after Pier Paolo Pasolini's *Teorema* (1968) and three years before *Salò* (1975). My aim is to underline the fact that such an insistence on the functional role of sexuality in the governance of family as a closed system characterises too many films of the Greek Weird Wave, and that this can be contextualised on the basis of the socio-politics of new capitalism and neoliberalism. It is no coincidence that, in Pasolini's *Teorema*, sexuality comes to break apart the bourgeois family. In *Dogtooth* it is instrumentalised in order to keep the family together.

11. On the events that inspired *El Castillo de la pureza*'s script, see Ripstein's own description in Guttiérez and Gottberg 2019: 45–47. For a reading of *Castillo* that resists national allegory, see Noble 2005: 95–122.

12. In French, for instance, the title was *Canine*. On the particular choice of the word 'dogtooth' for the Anglophone and international circulation of the film, see Lanthimos's own comments in Zalenko 2010 and a critical reading different from mine in Eleftheriotis 2020: 18–19. I will keep referring to the canine tooth as dogtooth throughout, in order to keep the immediate reference to the film's English title.

13. The official Greek communist party newspaper *Rizospastis* denounced the film as a propagandistic allegory against communism (Giovani 2011). For a recent reading of *Dogtooth* as an allegory of fascism, see Mazierska 2015: 249; and Lambie 2018.

14. In her brilliant – I think, unparalleled – analysis of *Dogtooth*, Eugenie Brinkema (2012) makes a similar statement, even though eventually developing it into a different direction: '*Dogtooth* constitutes itself around this primary allegorical disjunction: any person, any object, any relationship can mean absolutely anything else. Any sister can become a lover; any lick can be redirected from its initial target of a keyboard to different sites on the body; any word can be deployed to mean any other word. This fecund allegorical "any" becomes the principle of formal possibility of the film, and becomes its logic of violence as well' (n. p.).

15. We realise in other scenes where words are used out of context that shoes have

been defined as eyelashes, the telephone as a form of salt-shaker, and that the vagina is called a keyboard. When one daughter sees the word 'pussy' on the tag of the parents' hidden porn tapes and asks for its meaning, the answer is: 'Pussy is a big lamp'. And when the son asks about the meaning of the word 'zombie', he receives the answer that a zombie is a small yellow flower. In a later scene he is shown on all fours searching the grass and shouting: 'I have found two zombies here'. Brinkema (2012) focuses on the meaning of this constant allegorising beginning with this scene, as does Mademli (2015), who argues for the wider importance of weird 'language games in contemporary films'. See also Dionysios Kapsaskis's compelling argument about *Dogtooth* and the politics of (mis)translation (2017).

16. In the one scene where we catch a glimpse of the home videos that this family has been stocking and watching as their only form of entertainment, the videos are also awkwardly framing the human body, often fragmenting it, presumably because of the clumsy way in which the camera is held in these familial settings.

17. We see him prepare the punishment in front of his daughter and, in full revenge-metonymy mode, he underlines the word tape (ταινία), as he asks for it so that he can tape the videotape onto his hand.

18. In a recent, still developing, work, Tonia Kazakopoulou has taken issue with the fact that in most cases the violence in the films of Lanthimos is exerted on women and their bodies. See Kazakopoulou 2020.

CHAPTER 6

Archive Trouble:
Homeland, *National Poetics, Family Albums*

CITY/STATE/PERFORMANCE/ARCHIVE

In November 2010, the Onassis Cultural Centre in Athens hosted a major conference entitled *Athens Dialogues*.[1] With leading academics invited as guest speakers, simultaneous translation in three languages and cutting-edge technology allowing it to be streamed across the globe, the conference aimed to showcase the historical importance of 'Greek thought' to the world: what the Greeks had done and the reason why it still matters. Only, in this case, most of the participants and certainly the larger part of the audience understood this to mean 'Ancient Greeks'. Modern Greece, including its handful of powerful private institutions and their well-handled cultural globality, was once again seen as the quintessential archive of a perennial past. According to this logic, Athens was the perfect place to have this 'international dialogue' about the undisturbed relationship between the present and its past.

Less than five months later, in the same Onassis Cultural Centre, spectators were able to see an experimental play by the theatre group Kanigunda. The performance started with one of the actors in the role of 'Myrtis,' a girl who died of the typhoid plague that hit Athens in 430 and then again in 427/6 BC, in the middle of the Peloponnesean War.[2] The Ancient Greeks, once again! Yet, the process now was somewhat reversed because this time, with the voice and face of 'an ancient inhabitant of the Athenian city state' who had died during the ghastly biopolitical crisis of a plague, the audience was introduced to a postmodern political satire about the concurrently unfolding Greek Crisis.

Cunningly entitled *The City State*, this play was one in a series of works to take the Greek Crisis explicitly as its subject-matter. The very discursive tapestry of the socio-economic crisis as it had already started registering in the Greek everyday – in words, phrases, images, videos, names, well-known and rehearsed arguments – was broken to pieces and reassembled in this performance extravaganza, which also included Greek twentieth-century popular revue songs, archival material on the building of Ancient and Modern Athens, on the German Occupation, the Greek Civil War and other moments of modern Greek political history, all spliced together and interspersed with a long array of literary quotations about rootedness and uprooting, about the state of fear and its pervasive effects, and about waiting for the end of the world. A performance that had started with the reassurance that the Ancient Greeks are still with us – the Myrtis impersonator in a low voice whispering: 'Good evening, I am alive! I am very happy to be meeting you' – ended with another actor impersonating Prime Minister George Papandreou and exclaiming (in a parody of Papandreou's announcement of the IMF loan in 2010 in Kastelorizo): 'I am your prime minister. The perennial doctor. And I've got something to tell you. I want to tell you that we have just ceded part of our national sovereignty'.

The effort to produce a political 'art of the Crisis' was not, from the outset, an unproblematic development in the Greek cultural landscape after 2008. From the very beginning, artists, directors and authors were uneasy when asked, more and more frequently, 'how the arts have responded to the Crisis'. I still remember a prominent Greek author telling an eager audience in London early in 2011 that 'we are in the middle of an earthquake; there is no time to pause and think how we scream about it' (Galanaki 2011). And in many ways, performances such as *The City State* were influential, not because they signalled their readiness to make political art out of the Crisis, but because of their investment in specific devices and gestures of form and genre, their insistence that what was at stake was not the question of 'what to say' in the present moment, but to find a way to reflect on 'how' to speak.

In doing so, the performance of *The City State* also pointed to something else: a larger effort to critique, undermine and performatively disturb the very logics through which the story of Greece – the narrative of its national, political and socio-cultural cohesion – had been told up to then. In its collage of images, archival footage, historical and political texts and contemporary opinion-makers' slogans, the play first rehearsed well-known arguments about the past's burden on the present. It talked about the historical responsibilities of the ruling classes and of generations of politicians and corrupt entrepreneurs for the current failures. But in its mixing of forms, in its disturbing of the linearity and generational logics of the question of blame, in its excess, this troubled and performed archive ended up reframing the question of responsibility altogether. This was not just a story about ancient democracy, the ancient polis, gone awry in its modern retelling. It was instead a radical questioning that started from the current state of precariousness in order to critique the reading of the past and ask: Who has been doing this reading on our behalf, in what ways and to what effect? Furthermore, it asked how not only modern political elites – 'the perennial doctors' – but even the images of antiquity have been biopolitical agents and tools for ordering and framing which lives matter.[3]

As the cultural logics of continuity and traditional modes of thinking about political agency and blame were being undermined, responsibility was now becoming a genealogical question, or rather the imperative for a critical genealogy. Suddenly, for instance, in what essentially became a revue performance, the MC started calling herself 'the sponsor of the event', before 'confessing' at the end of her act that, in fact, s/he was the former head of Siemens Hellas, the company accused of repeatedly bribing Greek politicians for at least twenty years before the eruption of the Greek Crisis. The point was made forcefully: What the audience was watching was a performance that could not dissociate itself from a (narrative and material) economy that included corrupt neo-colonial financing as its very core.

Therefore, instead of 'who will take the blame for having pushed us to this point?' the question now became 'how can one tell the story of the now in relation to the past?' – what does it mean to act while also positioning oneself within a genealogy that has reached a critical point? It was also becoming a tale of how (not) to govern, and how (not) to be governed. Listening to catchy old popular revue songs, while watching archival footage of archaeological sites being excavated, modern Athens being built, popular images from political events of the past, photographs of political families posing in generations – father, son, grandson, politics as a patriarchal family arrangement – people dying in battle and people demonstrating in groups, snippets of history and fragments of lives arranged as an anarchic visual surface in the background, the audience was called to reflect on its own position in this archive. Making sense of it all would perhaps open up a new space for critique: an incitement to act, therefore, just like in epic theatre. Yet, unlike epic theatre, an incitement to act from within, not from a vantage point (with)out.

Watching the short extracts that have survived online from this performance today,[4] with the actors dancing out of control in front of a claustrophobic parade of archival images projected behind them, one might even think of the celebration in *Dogtooth*, as described in the previous chapter. The archival images on the stage backdrop create a sense of enclosure that feels like *that* family home; and as the actors speak out of tune and dance, they look like those children, awkwardly having to perform in the frame, and then growing out of it.[5] To be sure, it is easy to say that now; the connection was less obvious at the time, because critics tended to see two very distinct thematic responses to the Crisis in the Greek artworld. The thematic obsession with the (Greek) family-in-trouble, as I examined in the previous chapter, was developing as one. A turn to history and the historical archive – in theatre, literature, performance and the visual arts – was seen as another, very different trend. If in the first case the theme was a disturbed family, in the second audiences were faced with a disturbed archive. A possible connection between the two tendencies lay initially unexplored.

But late in 2010 there emerged one film that made clear why we needed to see these two elements, the family turn and the archival turn, as complementing each other. It focused exactly on the connection between family, biopolitics and the (historical) archive and provided that missing link with unexpected force and staying power. Syllas Tzoumerkas's *Homeland* (in Greek *Χώρα προέλευσης*, literally 'Country of Origin') left an indelible mark not only on other films, but also on the way in which we could now review and understand the archival within the larger preoccupations of the Greek Cinema of the period. It is to an analysis of this film that I now turn. Looking closely at elements of its *mise-en-scène* and specific gestures of film form allows one to discern more clearly the wider cultural significance of a certain type of archival poetics for Greece in the period under discussion.

In *Homeland*, the story of a repressive, incestuous Greek family pushed to its limits is interspersed with archival footage of past political demonstrations, photographs of major historical moments, the private archive of this family, reconstructions of the December 2008 riots in Athens and a teacher's lecture on the Greek national anthem. When it was first shown in Greece, the film actively asked its audiences to trace the connection between all these events. The visual archive fragments it edited into its narrative were not offered as a settled historical record, but as material to be rearranged and replotted.

Representation, family, desire, and official and unofficial archives are blasted (and blasting) together in *Homeland*; this is where the story starts.

'DECEIVED, BETRAYED, TERRORISED': TEACHING THE GREEK NATIONAL ANTHEM

From the very first scene of *Homeland*, people trip over each other in their small, cramped family houses. They gesture and touch one another in an almost erotic and altogether neurotic way. Cut to young children reciting their morning prayer and shortly afterwards starting a lesson on Dionysios Solomos' *Hymn to Liberty*, the long romantic poem that became the Greek national anthem, published in 1823 during the Greek War of Independence, with the express aim to galvanise Greek national sentiment and promote the Greek cause of independence. As the film continues, scenes from this (interactive, intensive, but also oppressive) class will keep interrupting the main diegesis. Next, we see the film's protagonist, Stergios (Thanos Samaras), shot from behind, kneeling on his bed in his room, nude as if just out of a Robert Mapplethorpe photograph. His legs are spread apart as he masturbates in front of a photo of his cousin, until his mother suddenly enters the room to wish him, in a loud and high-pitched voice that sounds completely out of context, 'Happy Birthday'. The day that this film's main narrative time will cover is indeed Stergios's birthday, and throughout many members of his extended family will keep reminding each other that they 'must wish Stergios a happy birthday'. Among these strands, facilitated by editing that certainly undermines classic cinematic continuity and could be called palimpsestic, we see scenes from large demonstrations, images of Athens burning and protestors dancing. As the schoolteacher recites a verse from *Hymn to Liberty* – 'I recall you from the face that surveys the land with haste' – a crane shot shows a scene from a demonstration which has at its centre a girl dressed in white, dancing.

Homeland premiered in the International Critics' Week of the Sixty-Seventh Venice Film festival, as the third Greek film of the year to be presented in that edition of the festival, alongside what are now Weird Wave classics, Athina Rachel Tsangari's *Attenberg* and Yorgos Zois's short *Casus Belli*.[6] It was first released in Greek cinemas in October 2010 – a year after *Dogtooth* and *Strella*, and at the same time as *Attenberg*. Even though it was not greeted with unanimous acclaim by the Greek critics, almost all the articles that discussed it on its release related its subject-matter to the spate of recent cultural works that had focused on the Greek family-in-trouble and the Greek Crisis.

As had been the case with other films of the Weird Wave, the debunking of the Greek family in *Homeland* was taken to be a direct critique of the Greek social formation. As a model, a metaphor for society at large and its important nucleus, the Greek family was seen as 'the seed of the ruin' of a society that was now becoming aware of some of its fundamental problems (Papanikolaou 2010a; Galanou 2011). The agonised tone of such media responses was echoed at various points by Tzoumerkas himself. What brings together all the disparate films of the Weird Wave and creates a movement out of them, he argued in a text published in Italy on the eve of *Homeland*'s premiere there, is that they are all 'revenge tragedies' (Tzoumerkas 2016). They are the stories of children who want to take revenge on their parents for the position in which they find themselves in history. '*Homeland* is a film born of rage; rage against both family and country' (Marzec 2015).

However, these observations only go some way towards addressing *Homeland*'s most daring suggestion. The film interweaves the familial with the social and the personal with the collective in unexpected ways. But it does not stop there. It also suggests that there is a rich archive that has been shaping feelings, bodies and national history; that this archive is constantly reperformed and rearranged; and that in its contemporary reiteration, it is performed as trouble during an unfolding socio-political crisis. As I have

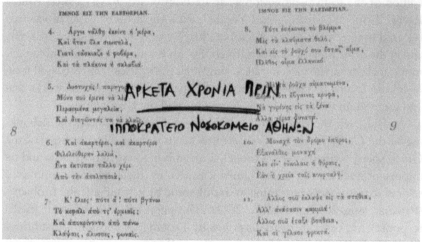

Figure 6.1a–b   *A teacher (Amalia Moutousi) teaches the Greek national anthem; the film's scenes are then divided in chapters and shown archived with labels written on the poem's typescript, from* Homeland *(Syllas Tzoumerkas, 2010); digital stills.*

suggested already, more than simply being a film about intergenerational conflict, 'revenge tragedy', kinship trouble and historical conflict, this is a type of cinema whose central political point owes a lot to the disturbed archive it integrates on screen and the thick cultural context at which this disturbed archive poetics points.

Homeland's plot starts from its very first scenes to link together a family and a nation in trouble. A family, like a kettle left to boil, explodes in Thessaloniki; all their dirty laundry is washed in public, and everything that has been repressed suddenly returns to the surface of words, voices and bodies. At the same time, violent demonstrations are taking place in Athens. The film thus begins to narrate parts of what is presented as a typical Greek family's story, through flashbacks that counterpoint the present-day scenes of familial crisis. Past scenes of this family's life start to intertwine with the present. Simultaneously, images from contemporary demonstrations in Athens are juxtaposed with photographs from the archive of Greek history: the 1944 Civil War altercations known as 'the December Events', the 1965 pro-democracy demonstrations known as the July Events, the celebrations for the return to democracy after the fall of the military Junta in 1974 and the socialist party PASOK's electoral victory in 1981. The rapid and unrelenting editing, however 'chaotic' or didactic as it may seem, ultimately weaves together, or rather artfully muddles up, the past (of the family, but also of Greece), the short-circuited present and the undermined future. '*Homeland* is the most functional organisation of chaos ever to grace the Greek screen', wrote the critic Dimitris Bouras. He continues:

> The 1950s and the 1960s emerge stripped of nostalgia. The post-Junta years appear without the well-known narrative tropes of the generation of the anti-Junta student uprisings; and this is because the burden now is shifted entirely onto a familial trauma. The present sounds like an atonal sonic background for the existential cry of today's twenty- and thirty-year olds, and at the same time it is mistaken for a realistic chronicle of their political and social drama: this is, once again, the howl we heard in December 2008. (Bouras 2010)

The mention of the December 2008 riots that shook Athens and other Greek cities after the shooting of teenager Alexis Grigoropoulos by a police officer on 6 December 2008 is not just a reference to a recent social upheaval that was initially seen as an expression of intergenerational conflict. Instead, what this critic insightfully explains is that intergenerational conflict and the 'trauma of the family' have now become ways to retell national history and to relay much deeper social rifts. Moreover, they have prompted a retelling of history that happens in urgent new forms and styles: '[This is not the old-style way of remembering our history]; this is [a] howl'.

On the film's poster and other promotional materials, three words are repeated: 'Deceived. Betrayed. Terrorised'. According to the director's interviews, the grammatical subject of these verbs – 'deceived, betrayed, terrorised' – was not one of the characters, as one might have expected. It was the Greek family, as an institution. In *Homeland*, the extended kin network decides to fortify its borders, as it organises how a child will be adopted by close relatives in order to 'remain in the family'. But as the story develops and as we see these people having grown up, we realise that what has also remained in said family is rage, violence, desire and affect. People, their acts and their emotions are moving constantly inside, while also bumping against the walls of the enclosed container that this extended family has become.[7]

At the heart of the film lies an adoption dating back to the 1980s. When the imposing *pater familias* and grandfather of the family (whose name we never learn) suddenly falls ill, the relatives decide he can no longer look after his daughter, the single mother Gina and her two children, who have lived with him until then. As a result, they arrange for one of Gina's sons, Thanos, to be adopted by her brother's family, comprised of Nikitas, a university professor of art history, and his wife, Stella, the teacher we see at the beginning of the film teaching the national anthem, about twenty years after the adoption. Their daughter, Anna, has now grown up as Thanos's sister, with Thanos only recently learning of his past adoption and the identity of his biological mother. Gina's other son, Stergios, continues to live with his mentally unstable mother in a disorderly house in a working-class neighbourhood of Thessaloniki. 'I am never going back to *that* mess again', says Anna at some point, and it is obvious that what she refers to is not only the physical disorder of the house.

As has been the case with Thanos, the emotional ecosystem of all of these characters, with their feelings ranging from rejection all the way to self-destructive pleasure, seems trapped within the familial framework. The moment when the film starts, the family is at boiling point; expressions of emotion have started to overflow, becoming awkward and indeed 'weird'. The mother and the daughter whisper to each other 'I want to see you tonight' in a manner full of erotic innuendo. A little later, Stella calls her brother-in-law, and again the way in which she speaks to him sounds erotic. Stergios patiently stalks his cousin Anna, and at one point we realise that they are having an affair. The same kind of relationship has been going on, it transpires, between Anna and the other son, Thanos, who until recently believed that he was her brother. Furthermore, we never learn who the father of the two boys is, although we do learn that their mother was pathologically attached to the grandfather. Whether the relationship between the grandfather and his daughter was sexual is one more potential suspicion that lingers under the film's (and this family's) surface. Emotion and desire are not simply confused in this family; *Homeland* does not simply reach, and sometimes transgress, the bounds of what is acceptable for kinship relations. The film's point is that the setting of boundaries and their potential transgression are not two opposite practices, but that they run parallel to each other, constituting the very matter from which the extended family *is made*. Both the grammatical (the incest taboo, adoptions and so on) as well as the ungrammatical (incest) expression of kinship are, in other words, part of a system that conditions emotion, logic, the wellbeing of the group and the embodied incitement to 'remain with us'. *Within* the family.

Of course, while all this is going on, the world is burning around this particular family. How are these characters related to everything that is going on around them? In the first instance, one might feel that there is no connection whatsoever. Thanos and his uncle find themselves in Athens trying to catch the train to Thessaloniki. They pass by demonstrations, avenues packed with stationary cars, tear gas used on demonstrators and piles of rubbish on fire. None of this seems to pique their interest: They talk only about the family and constantly pick up their phones to call different family members. Anna, the object of both of her cousins' desire, works for the state television channel in Thessaloniki and, as the demonstration in Athens unfolds, she organises how it will be reported in the news bulletin. She is not concerned with the wider significance of the events: The only thing that seems to occupy her intellectually, psychologically and bodily (insofar as these three categories are not that easy to distinguish) is the web in which she seems to be trapped, the net of the extended family.

Some of the scenes showing the characters' disarticulation from the social commotion happening around them are significantly the same ones that keep emphasising metonymical connections through the organisation of frame and editing. For instance, as Anna works at the open desk of her news office, we can see from the screen of her computer the demonstration unfolding and turning violent in front of the parliament in Athens. At one moment the camera pans from a close-up on a computer screen playing live footage of the demonstration to her face; she picks up the phone to discuss with her editor how the final editing of these demonstration scenes will be handled for the main news bulletin. 'We check them shot by shot, sir; we will not leave anything [we don't want to show] in [δεν θα φανεί τίποτα]; I will bring over to you all the relevant footage to choose; no, we will not put in whatever we want'. At that point we cut back to the school classroom and the lesson on the national anthem unfolding on the same day. The handheld camera offers similar close-ups on the teacher and the pupils. The similarity of these shots and now the shot/reverse-shot sequence somehow produce a reassurance of continuity to the otherwise sudden edit. At the same time, the sound from the different scenes overflows from one scene to the next and is additionally mixed together with a continuous electronic soundtrack acting not only as an alternative bridge between scenes, but also as a device increasing tension because of this bridging. In the class, teacher and pupils are now talking about

Figure 6.2a–d *From a typical sequence from* Homeland: *footage of demonstrations, a close-up of the teacher (Amalia Moutousi) in her classroom, Anna (Gioula Boudali) in the newsroom where similar footage is being edited and the edited footage now in the sequence; digital stills.*

violence, enemies being pushed far away and the persisting force of slavery. Cut to the actual footage of the demonstration (one realises that it must be real footage from a recent demonstration and, thus, by the time the film is being made, already archived material): wide establishing shots and then the TV camera zooming in on a group of demonstrators setting fire to a police van. With the voice of the teacher remaining as a voice-over and the noise of the demonstration mixed together with the electronic soundtrack, we cut back to the newsroom, again with a shot that pans from the computer screens (showing the previous footage) to Anna's face. Another telephone call: 'No, I will bring the footage myself; we will work as fast as we can'. Anna here talks about editing. But, in more than one way, she is the one who is being edited in.[8]

The sequence is paradigmatic of the style of editing throughout the film. Scenes from the remote and the recent past of the family, as well as historical footage and photographs, are collated together in this way, undermining traditional expectations of continuity and underlining an ongoing process of connecting, contextualising and archiving. To be sure, some of these connections are initially based on a basic parallelism, a starting analogy. But all these scenes, as they are edited together unexpectedly and tightly, forming an unrelenting continuous series, are now proposed as standing too close to each other. Concepts, words, bodies, postures and framings touch each other and keep linking. It happens so intensely that, when a little later during these back-and-forth cuts from the TV newsroom, to the classroom and the demonstration, the teacher in the classroom moves to focus on the next core word of the poem, it sounds almost as if she is proposing a key for the film as a whole. She picks the word 'chains' and repeats it – 'chains . . . yes, chains . . .' – as she touches the heads of her students. One is not sure whether she has just emphasised a symbol for incarceration or helped the film make yet another self-conscious reference to its own poetics of metonymic montage.

The main characters may thus initially look as if they have been cut off from their historical and social setting; yet, the viewer is constantly pushed to establish the links with what is happening around them (events related to the socio-economic crisis, the demonstrations, the fires), as well as the historical archive and the family's past. To the extent that the family's past is opened as a family album aiming to historicise this kinship network and to explicate its logistics, the historical archive and the archive of the contemporary crisis also demand a place in the story – and *vice versa*.

How does the story of this family, and the dramatic condition in which it finds itself, relate to the historical archive of the Greek twentieth century, or even to its own archive – the archive of family photographs which often appear in the film, but also the archive of its members' feelings, acts and traumas? How does all this relate to Greece's socio-political situation in 2010? A first response is to view the film as a moment of generalised crisis during which whatever is buried – intergenerational guilt, trauma and disavowed historical moments – suddenly comes to the surface: It explodes. Another preliminary response could be to see this film as a realist narrative of decline, based on cause and effect: What we are seeing, according to this response, is the pathology of a Greek family which has been caused by a national environment enthusiastically approving of autocracy, debtocracy, violence and concealment. Or, alternatively, one could see it as an allegory for the weakening of the symbolic centre of a whole society, or as a classic national allegory. Indeed, the film lends itself to such a reading, especially when we note that the national anthem is discussed and questioned from beginning to end.

Gradually the figure of the grandfather begins to take on a distinctively symbolic weight. When all the characters are searching for him in one of the flashbacks to the family's past, the camera gives us a close-up shot of their faces desperately calling out 'father' or 'grandfather'. Here the visual allegory seems so obvious that it almost takes on a life of its own. As they run around, followed by a hand-held camera eager to take shaky close-ups of each of them, the characters seem not to be searching for the father whom they are calling, but to be uttering a performative statement about the loss of the centre of signification. Towards the end of the film, the grandfather's reappearance at Stergios's funeral, an event which is orchestrated to mark the climax of the family saga, seems almost unreal: What returns is the former symbolic centre which is now both present and absent, a symbolic centre in abeyance. At this point, *Homeland* self-consciously asserts itself as neither a simple realist narration, nor a classical (national) allegory. On the contrary, it invites the viewer to think about the limits and the poetics of realism and allegory, their effects and their political use. This is the point where the archive – as a concept, a metaphor, a strategy, a metonymic organisation and a repository of shaping images – comes to play a crucial role.

Family Frames, Historical Footage, Latent Trauma

In *Homeland*, the Greek family yells and is yelled at, rewrites itself and breaks down into its constituent parts. It crucially also becomes the framework for an iconoclastic revisiting of the archive of the past. Once the black-and-white images from the past are interpolated into the modern story of violence and non-normative desire, and into the 'family album' of this extended Greek family, *Homeland* presents its viewers with a challenge: to resist their initial urge to either allegorise the past (as another form of the present), or to see in it the causes of the present. While these are certainly possible readings of the film, one is also made to feel uneasy about any 'cause and effect' linear understanding, any narrative that could go like this: 'Greeks have a violent political history, which is mirrored in the violence in this family's history'. Or alternatively: 'Where did all the old revolutionary enthusiasm, resistance, the post-Junta transition and the socialism of 1981 end up? In an image of the family that violently cannibalises itself'. The more you watch, the more these questions feel inadequate.

The reason for this is the handling of the film's archival poetics. It makes these images fragments of a very tangible past and an integral *part* of a present marked by violence, stagnation and short-circuiting. The challenge with which the film presents its viewers, therefore, is to see the archive of the past, not as an explanation of a contemporary social crisis, but as one more of the factors that play a role within it, one more problem that needs to be resolved, another trauma that needs to be em-bodied, the very moment in which the genre, the form and the poetics of a new cultural/social intervention emerge as objects of a painful conjuncture. What is at stake here is a complicated gesture that, while offering the outline of an explanation, ultimately transcends any simple explanation of the present through the past. Without the didacticism of cause and effect, it instead suggests the radical energy that a simultaneous exposition of the present and the past can have, positioning family, society, genealogy and their deconstruction inside the same throbbing frame.

It is worth examining in more detail how *Homeland* establishes its archival poetics, prompting the viewer to reconsider their centrality. To begin with, the film is divided into narrative 'chapters', thus further underlying the metonymic function of the narration. Each chapter is introduced by using a static shot of a printed extract from the text of Dionysios Solomos' *Hymn to Liberty*, on which are added handwritten notes giving the titles of the upcoming chapters marked in pen. The titles often relate to the stages of construction/deconstruction of this film's extended family. They include: 'The Athens Ippokrateio Hospital, Some Years Before', 'Antonis, Nikitas and Gina Care For Their Father', 'Everything's Fucked Up', 'Adoption', 'Epanomi, Thessaloniki, Some Years Before', 'Grandfather Recovers and Everyone Comes to Terms with Their Actions'. Do these letters scribbled on the script of the national anthem not resemble the notes that archivists would take as they organise documents into an archive? Does this gesture not make the national anthem part of the archival material, too, alongside the parts of the film which are also becoming archive? Yet, we should not forget that, at the same time, the film is framed by the intensive school lesson on the national anthem that Stella's character has been teaching to her students. 'Family', 'kin' and national networks, as well as the return to the archive, are framed by a recitation of Solomos' *Hymn to Liberty*, which stresses its present potency and relevance. We cut time and time again back to this classroom, the camera held in the middle of the room, panning from one pupil to the other and to their teacher, often with extreme close-ups of their faces or bodies as they make an effort to speak. Thus, the nationally canonical text becomes an opening: an interpretative opening, an educational opening, a space where people can question and share codes of belonging, while also experiencing worry, shame, pressure and the touch of each other's body. National allegory is not an answer; it is texts and bodies in trouble, in an unfolding archive, in a bursting collage.

The way in which the camera is handled in the school scenes is crucial: While the teacher asks her students to pay attention and understand the text she is teaching to them, the framing suggests that they have to respond in an analytical and intellectual way, as well as emotionally, corporeally and affectively. Also moving incessantly, the teacher herself enters the centre of the frame as the handheld camera zooms in on her facial features or the edges of her body. The liberating, enlightening discourse of Solomos's text is here invoked beyond fixed national mythologies, as the shots assemble bodies that try not only to comprehend, but also to intuit something. Indeed, towards the end of the lesson, the discussion ends up once again focusing on the body and its precarity. As both lesson and film end, Stella goes beyond the text of *Hymn to Liberty*, while keeping her comments in context. She explains to her pupils, using an assortment of their own words: 'Liberty is a gaze that judges, a gaze that frees . . . liberty wears clothes bloodied, her own body is bloodied, she's in tears, alone, asking for help . . . she has a body . . . that's why we see her in tears, bloodied, asking for help, alone, betrayed . . . that is Liberty'. This class teaches that, in order to understand national allegory, especially in times of crisis, you need to turn to the metonymies that keep (re)constituting it in the national everyday; you need to assemble images, words, verses and titles, but also a myriad moments of touch. At the level of the film as a whole, something similar has happened with their lesson. It is cut and collated, assembled from private and public scenes of the national everyday in the present and the past.

The national anthem in *Homeland* is a text summoned from the dense cultural archive of a country in crisis. In the moment when a class of school children, alongside the peculiar archival poetics of a film, brings up this text from the archive of national culture and underlines the metonymics of such a gesture, reality bursts in from all sides.

However, reality also appears archived. The images of demonstrations and the general tension in Athens constitute material that is already archived, and at least at two different moments within the film they are discussed as such. The first occurs when Anna is at her computer, looking at the footage of the Athens protests and speaking to her editor-in-chief. The discussion is fundamentally about the representation (and media construction) of reality. It can also be interpreted as a moment where a decision has to be made about what remains in the archive, about what will be archived and how. As she is being pressured by her editor and as she experiences a personally tense day, she starts having trouble breathing. The scene with her in the toilet gasping for air is inter-cut with footage from the demonstration, the very footage she was editing a moment ago: Showing the air full of tear gas, these are also images of people similarly fighting to breathe.

The relation between the two images of people struggling for breath starts, one might say, as an analogy. But the archival poetics of the film has laboured to show how Anna is also edited in these other images, much like the story of her family is edited in the story of the nation as an unfolding archive in trouble. In this unfolding archive, the relationship between these scenes of bodies gasping for air is no longer one of analogy; it has become one of contiguity.

Very soon after this scene, when Anna has exited the building, because the TV station has received a bomb threat and the building has to be evacuated, she speaks on the phone to Thanos and tells him that she loves him, while behind her, without her realising, her other cousin Stergios approaches and touches her. As this happens, a photographer on a rooftop takes photographs of the whole scene and the couple. (One of these is the photograph that would eventually become the cover of the film's DVD release). These intra-diegetic photographs are introduced in the final edit, through the classic device of a freeze-frame accompanied by the sound of a shutter. They therefore transform the image we see on the screen momentarily into a photograph, turning the diegetic photographer – the photographer who is near the scene – into a hetero-diegetic one, a possessive spectator *closer to us*. These sudden photographs of Anna and Stergios could be a comment about a society of surveillance: Our movements are recorded, filmed and photographed so much in everyday life, with recording (or, rather, being in the recording) now a synonym of being, of being in life, of being alive. As a cinematic device, this has a long history, especially in film noir. However, at the point at which it emerges in this particular film, the photographing of very personal moments between close family members asks us to wonder where these photographs will end up, if and where they will be archived, who is taking them and why, and how and with what ulterior motive they will be used. Surveillance is everywhere, but also constantly dispersed. Will these photographs become part of yet another family album, like those old family photographs which interrupt and comment on the film's narrative at different moments? Or are they part of a wider policing strategy now in place in this crisis-ridden country, destined to be archived in one of the novel surveillance repositories? The freeze frames, coming immediately after the scenes of protest in Athens and the discussion in the TV station about how to present them, occupy a conceptual and physical space in the archive of the socio-economic crisis. And *Homeland* at this point offers its most explicit visual comment on the triangulation of the embodied, the familial and the archival, which has been operating in the film all along. The social ramifications of this triangulation are left open. We will never find out what these photographic moments stand for. We do not know their precise archive, but we do know that they are archival, and we know the metonymical chains this sets in motion.

The almost continuous electronic soundtrack, a long composition by the electronic group Drog A Tek, smooths out such moments, as it also does elsewhere with the jumps between past and present, or between a closed family circle and wider social events. This incites the viewer to look for alternative continuity throughout the film.

The viewer becomes thus intensely conscious that what mostly determines editing in *Homeland* is not temporal sequence and classic continuity, as the film undermines this entirely, but the structure, position and form of bodies, and the expression of emotions. Very often scenes seem to have been edited one after the other simply because, as scenes, they closely resemble each other. Hence, the image of Maria, Antonis's wife, in the present is collated with the image of Maria in the past during a family reunion. The position of the protester's body within the frame in the footage from a demonstration is followed by a similar image of the teacher's body conducting her lesson on the national anthem. And the embodied despair and frustration that Anna expresses in the scene I have just analysed is edited into the sequences of footage with protesters struggling to breathe because of the tear gas.

To recapitulate, what this editing technique ultimately expresses is a disposition towards making new connections. This is how cinematic continuity becomes contiguity; it is not ruled by the axis of chronology, but by the axis of space and the archive, the sorting of the image as material. Similarly, the resulting national allegory is not ruled by the axis of metaphor, but by the axis of metonymy. In other words, the images come together not according to our narrative expectations of how they relate in a chronological, cause-and-effect, or metaphorical sequence. They are bound together because they happen to fit as images, because they have been, or they can be, contiguous as material. Here we arrive at the centre of this film's archival poetics, where the basic strategy is mixing and matching, where the tendency is to find new pathways through the material traces of the past and present, to find new methods of genealogical criticism rather than means for simple evaluation. This entails a genealogical criticism in which the body, rhythm and feeling participate, much more than what traditional understandings of the historical archive would allow. What we see is not a traditional patrilineal and national genealogy, but a novel assemblage that articulates a genealogical critique.

ARCHIVE TROUBLE: A CULTURAL POETICS

As I have explained already at the beginning of this chapter, *Homeland* came to participate in an archival poetics that was gathering momentum in Greece after 2008, with the express aim to problematise and question the relation with the past in the contemporary context of Crisis. What emerges as crucial from Tzoumerkas's film is the emphasis it puts on the body in jeopardy, in crisis, *in/as trouble*, alongside a *technics of the archive*, a way of connecting archival threads incessantly, without necessarily finding answers. This was a cultural strategy that acquired wider ramifications in the Greece of the Crisis. In an early review of *Homeland* and its cultural context, I was led to call this 'archive trouble', an obvious pun on Derrida's *Archive Fever* (1995), Judith Butler's *Gender Trouble* (1990) and the rich analytical frameworks that they both represent (Papanikolaou 2010a; cf. 2011; 2017).

'Archive trouble' was meant to denote a poetics in which crisis became visible on the body, in which the body's foundational precarity and the iconoclastic return to an archive of cultural and historical material were proposed as interconnected narrative gestures that could link past and present in a radical mixing. Such a poetics could transform the analytical return to the past into a more complex process which cannot resolve itself but is contained and embodied within the present. Archive trouble's poetics could transform the current state of precarity and its often violent images into a form of criticism that does not simply record the stagnant past, but also rewrites it genealogically, historicises it, embodies it and at the same time demonstrates the political dimension of such an act.

The poetics of archive trouble that I am trying to frame is, of course, by no means a completely new trend in Greek culture. Postmodern thinkers and artists have been performatively undermining Greek national narratives in such a way for a number of years. One famous and extremely influential theatrical production of this kind, Michail Marmarinos's *National Anthem* (2001–2), may indeed be a common intertext behind a performance such as Kanigunda's *The City State*, a film like Tzoumerkas's *Homeland* and a video art installation like Stefanos Tsivopoulos's *History Zero*, which represented Greece at the 2013 Venice Biennale.[9] Furthermore, Greece's turbulent twentieth-century history has time and again been revisited through a reinvigorated interest in unofficial and non-normative archives and a critique of official archival logics. My argument, therefore, does not focus on the originality of this archival poetics, but on its density in Greece after 2008 and the use to which it was put. Archive trouble became a dominant political and cultural critique in the Greece of the Crisis, a full-blown genealogical attack that took the current state not as a symptom of things that had gone wrong in the past, but as the very point from which the past should be reviewed, revisited, recollated, reassembled and reassessed, in both political and identitarian terms.

This type of archival poetics and such a political recontextualisation of archive-based art are not unknown in the international context of cultural history, either. Since the late twentieth century, progressive artists have shared an extensive and far-reaching 'archival impulse', to borrow Hal Foster's apt term. As Foster put it, archival artworks 'make historical information, often lost or displaced, physically present. To this end they elaborate on the found image, object, and text' (Foster 2004: 4). Critics have, accordingly, read the archival turn in the visual arts as a result of new developments in museum and exhibition practices, as well as the widespread 'personal archiving' craze enabled by new media. The archival turn has been theorised not only as a turn towards participatory and democratic art, capitalising on the iconoclastic, palimpsestic and playful practices reemployed by postmodernism, but also as a conduit for new identity politics at a time of globalisation and information mobility. It has been received as a recontextualisation of older avant-garde movements such as the Dadaism of the 1920s or pop art, but also as a radical revisiting of issues such as memory, post-memory and ideology (Van Alphen

2014). All this 'archive frenzy' has created a particular tradition of works and installations and a growing bibliography on similar trends in the worlds of theatre, literature, theory and art cinema. In the words of Okwui Enzewor, from a very influential curatorial introduction, . . .

> The variety and range of archival methods and artistic forms, the mediatory structures that underpin the artists' mnemonic strategies in their use of the archive, and the conceptual, curatorial, and temporal principles that each undertakes, point to the resilience of the archive as both form and medium in contemporary art. In the works, we are confronted with relationships between archive and memory, archive and public information, archive and trauma, archive and ethnography, archive and identity, archive and time. [. . .]
> [A]rchival documents, information gathering, data-driven visual analysis, the contradictions of master narratives, the invention of counter-archives and thus counter-narratives, the projection of the social imagination into sites of testimony, witnessing, and much more inform and infuse the practices of contemporary artists. (Enwezor 2008: 22)

My argument is that this more international trend in the first decade of the twenty-first century became related to a very urgent and direct need for political expression in Greece. After 2008, archive trouble is what very much characterised the work of many theatre groups, collectives and artists. These include the theatrical productions of the groups Blitz and Kanigunda, Angela Brouskou and her Theatro Domatiou, Vassilis Noulas and Nova Melancholia, Argyro Chioti and Vasistas, Michail Marmarinos, Dimitris Karatzas and Konstantinos Dellas; the theatrical writing of Lena Kitsopoulou, Giannis Mavritsakis and Efthimis Filippou; the performances of Mary Zygouri and Georgia Sagri; the dance and music performances of Kostas Tsioukas and Mary Tsoni; the writing of such diverse authors as Christos Chrissopoulos, Glykeria Basdeki, Angela Dimitrakaki, Giannis Makridakis, Dimosthenis Papamarkos, Thomas Korovinis, Vicky Tselepidou and Vassilis Amanatidis. Archive trouble could also be seen as the organising principle behind many large art projects, including Kunsthalle Athens, all of the Athens Biennials since 2009 and a number of smaller exhibitions and art initiatives organised by Elpida Karampa, Angela Dimitrakaki, Syrago Tsiara, Stefanos Tsivopoulos, Yorgos Tzitzilakis and Theofilos Tramboulis. Last, but not least, concepts similar to 'archive trouble' became the main narrative framing the 2017 Documenta exhibition, especially the part organised in Athens, as well as its publishing venture, the special issues of the journal *South*.[10]

Contemplating the cultural poetics of archive trouble in all these (and many other) works, as well as in the cinema of the Weird Wave that engaged directly with this context, it is important to underline two further issues. The first is that, as it intertwines thinking about (an image and the deployment of) the body in crisis, with (a mourning for and a messing with) archives of culture, of belonging and of social life, archive trouble articulates a biopolitical critique. As I have shown in relation to *Homeland* and the performance *The City State*, archive trouble contemplates how the body not only historicises, but also internalises; how certain discourses work so that power takes hold and operates surreptitiously; last, but not least, as was so evident in *City State*, archive trouble takes central biopolitical questions currently prominent in the public sphere and insists on their interconnectedness with complex questions of national politics and belonging. In this way, archive trouble is a central element in the composition of biopolical realism.

My second point is that, as archive trouble becomes a central modality for biopolitical realism, archival and allegorical modes of expression start working together, echoing one another, feeding off one another. I will briefly explain these two points before bringing this chapter to a close.

ARCHIVE/ALLEGORY

Hal Foster published his famous article 'An Archival Impulse' in the journal *October* in 2004. In it, he talked about the turn to archive as a . . .

> desire to turn belatedness into becomingness, to recoup failed visions in art, literature, philosophy, and everyday life into possible scenarios of alternative kinds of social relations, to transform the no-place of the archive into the no-place of a utopia [. . . a] move to turn 'excavation sites' into 'construction sites' [which] is welcome in another way too: it suggests a shift away from a melancholic culture that views the historical as little more than the traumatic. (Foster 2004: 22)

'Archival impulse' may be considered a major intervention in theories of art in the twenty-first century, and rightly so; yet, what is less often remembered is its intellectual genealogy. As a matter of fact, Foster's piece was written less as a debunking and more as a response, an updating of Craig Owens's earlier influential article titled 'An Allegorical Impulse', published on the pages of the same journal in 1980.

In an effort to offer 'a theory of postmodernism' in art, Owens had pointed to the discontinuous, idiosyncratic and iconoclastic use of images in postmodern conceptual art. The past is given to postmodern artists, he maintained, as an onslaught of images, which are copied and referenced with an allegorical intensity, but without the artist's effort to create an overall narrative, to cover the gaps and to provide links. The past is made of images and fragments of a catastrophe. And the links between them are not provided – it is the role of the reader, the viewer, to provide those instead. Hence, the allegorical impulse in postmodern art is characterised by 'appropriation, site specificity, impermanence, accumulation, discursivity, hybridisation', modalities aiming to install a more active audience response at their centre (Owens 1980: 75).

The allegorical impulse, as an idea, is important, not only because it recapitulated the larger thinking on postmodernism and art that developed during the 1970s, but because it announced (and in a way shaped) what was still to come, as a major cultural tendency. 'Allegories are, for the world of thoughts, what ruins are for the world of things', wrote Walter Benjamin in the famous phrase from his *The Origin of German Drama*, which I have already quoted in Chapter 4. The phrase was the centre of Owens's 'Allegorical Impulse' and would frame the discussion on allegory, history and writing that would blossom after 1980.[11]

Foster's 'Archival Impulse' enters this specific tradition in an effort not to oppose, but to redirect Owen's idea. From the perspective of 2004, Foster proposes the archival impulse not as contrary to the allegorical impulse, but as its developing and more politicised extension. Archival artists have been working in a world where fragmentariness, the gap between signifier and signified, discontinuity and contingency are a given. And they make do; they try to 'recoup failed visions of art' and (re)articulate a politics of affect, participation and critique, out of what used to be just an aporia of reference and a subversion of totality.

> In [Owen's] account the allegorical is a fragmentary mode, one pitted against the symbolic, which aims for integration (this is a traditional opposition) [. . .]. The dispute with symbolic totalities of this sort is not as important to archival artists, for whom the fragmentary is a given state of affairs. By the same token the archival impulse is also not 'anomic' [. . .] This is not the fight of archival artists: as with the fragmentary, the anomic is assumed as a condition, one to work through where possible. To this end they sometimes propose new orders of affective association, however partial and provisional, even as they also register the difficulty, at times the absurdity, of doing so. (Foster 2015 [2004]: 59–60)

Bringing these two texts closer together reminds us of the deeply symbiotic relation developed between the allegorical and the archival, and how it is often disavowed by those who maintain that the archival is about organised fragments *of* the real, whereas the allegorical only works with metaphors *about* the real. I have already problematised this distinction in the previous chapter, where I argued that the allegorical is not only a way to talk about the unfolding of reality, but also a force shaping it, something that in an intense biopolitical environment often becomes more palpable, more evident, more visible. In my reading, Foster allows us to think of archival works as continuing the political work of postmodern allegory. In doing so, he also allows us to reconsider allegorical modes as equally haunted by an archival impulse to come.

It is fascinating to follow the analogy and the interaction between the allegorical impulse and the archival impulse today, if we go back to revisit films such as *Homeland* and *Dogtooth*, different as they may be, but also circulating together within the new wave of Greek Cinema after 2010. As I have explained in this chapter, *Homeland* produces a triangulation of archive/family/body. It is based on this triangulation that it develops its biopolitical critique: Bodies are shaped equally by the archive and the family dynamic, and it is in these contiguous frames that they erupt. Interestingly, *Dogtooth* works, one realises, with a similar schema, only that in this case the place of archive is taken by allegory. Allegory/family/body is the operative triangulation in *Dogtooth*, which I explored and theorised in the previous chapter. Thus, just as in the dialogue between Owens and Foster, while the two films at first seem antithetical in terms of their relationship to their historical moment – with *Dogtooth* being allegorically detached from its historical context, and *Homeland* recollecting and revisiting that context forcefully through an archival poetics – one realises that they actually work in a very analogous way. In both films, the triangulations allegory/family/body and archive/family/body essentially map out the domain of the biopolitical. They show how bodies are governed, how they (do not) react, how they make do with what is already assumed as a generalised condition. What I have described as the anxiety of allegory in the previous chapter and as archive trouble in this one, therefore, are ways to make noise within the biopolitical arrangements that have already framed reality. They are both played out on the body and can trigger a deeply critical revisiting of categories such as the national, the familial, the historical and the affective. Following archive trouble and the anxiety of allegory in tandem also showcases their interconnectedness within the domain that I have described as biopolitical realism.

I explained in the previous chapter how *Dogtooth* was read together with many other films on the family (indeed, on the Greek family) that came out during that period, including *Attenberg*, *Homeland* or *Miss Violence* (see Chapter 5). I have also mentioned how out of this allegory on governance sprang a very topical, situated and at times very archival discussion about Greek systems of kinship: their representation, their effectivenes and their affectiveness. The point here is not to argue for the possible archival poetics of a film like *Dogtooth*, something which can certainly be pursued, but to show how *Dogtooth*'s allegories are haunted by the archival and the historical, often in unexpected ways (see, for instance, the role played by a *cinematic* archive in the eventual crisis within the house enclosure, in Chapter 5). At the same time, as I have implied throughout this chapter, *Homeland* is a film in which the archival comes to disrupt settled national allegories; it excels in doing so, like *Dogtooth*, by consistently treating allegories as metonymical terrains. The Greek family with its allegory of balance and symbolic central-ity is approached as a set of documents to be torn apart and reassembled, much in the same way as is Greece's national anthem and its central allegory of Liberty:[12] As the film unfolds, it becomes simultaneously palpable, con-textual and textual. In *Homeland*'s archives the allegorical is always only one step away, a difficult balance that director Syllas Tzoumerkas would continue to work on in his later films, *A Blast* (2014) and *The Miracle of the Sargasso Sea* (2019).

This interpenetration of the allegorical and the archival, alongside the embodied, the affective and the historicopolitical, is exactly what orders the domain of biopolitical realism. It occurs to such an extent that it ends up more and more powerfully recontextualising films that may not have been received in this way in the first place. This is exactly the case with the two films that become the focus of the next chapter, the short *Mum, I'm back* by Dimitris Katsimiris (2017) and the celebrated trans political work *Strella* by Panos Koutras (2009). In the former, a trans woman is lynched for her effort to participate in her mother's funeral procession. In the latter, a transgender sex worker (ab)uses the Oedipal myth and pokes fun at the official tourist slogan 'Live your myth in Greece'. Seen in hindsight, contemporary Athens emerges in *Strella* as both an identity matrix palpitating with personal archives and itineraries, and a crisis space that allows archival logics (including that of the nuclear family) to be radically reframed. In the last few chapters, we have revisited biopolitical realism in metonymies that hurt and in archives in trouble. What comes next are assemblages, ways not only of collating, but of holding together disparate visions, ideas, images, things, bodies, gestures and positions. They are not the solution, but out of losses, falls, fissures and cuts they create potential openings.

Notes

1. The Onassis Cultural Centre (just like the Niarchos Cultural Centre, which would open several years later) came to play a central role in Greek cultural politics during the period on which this book focuses, often taking a role that state institutions had fulfilled until then. For an overview of the impact and role of private institutions during the Crisis, see Mais 2020.

2. Myrtis was the name given by scientists to the image of a girl whom they claimed they were able to reconstruct from skeletal remains, an announcement that made

headlines in Greece in 2010 and a reconstruction that instigated a number of articles about modern Greek's 'ancient DNA' and the like.

3. For a decade or more, this would be a central research question in the work of archaeologist Dimitris Plantzos. See Plantzos 2012; 2017b; 2018; 2019a. In 2017, Plantzos rounded off this research with a monograph in Greek, analysing in detail the uses of archaeology during the Crisis, under the title *The Recent Future: Classical Archaeology as a Biopolitical Tool* (2017a).

4. See, for instance, this seven-minute-long video: https://www.youtube.com/watch?v=w_yFpUaVbb4 (accessed 16 June 2020).

5. A performance following the same logic as Kanigunda's *The City State* was *Late Night* by the theatre group Blitz. It premiered in 2012 and then toured extensively around the world, received as a representative of a very specific Crisis culture (see Papanikolaou 2017). Angeliki Papoulia and Christos Passalis, the actors playing two of the *Dogtooth* children, were central in this performance, making the link between *Dogtooth's* family trouble and the archival challenge of performances like *Late Night* or *The City State* even more irresistible.

6. In the Sixty-Seventh Venice Film Festival, *Attenberg* was awarded the best actress prize to Arianne Labed and the Lina Mangiacapre Award to director Tsangari; a year later, at the same festival, Lanthimos would take the best screenplay award for *Alps*.

7. Casting helps contextualise *Homeland* in the line of films immediately before it, which had focused on similar family critiques. The role of one of Gina's brothers was taken by Errikos Litsis, the iconic father of *Matchbox* (see Chapter 1). The role of Thanos, Gina's boy given up for adoption, was given to Christos Passalis, the iconic son of *Dogtooth* (see Chapter 5).

8. According to the story, Anna's cousin Thanos and their uncle are in Athens and pass through the demonstration, even though avoiding any interaction with it – there are a few scenes with them in the same shot with a demonstration in the background. Attentive viewers will notice that these scenes cannot have been shot with a staged demonstration, especially in a relatively low-budget film such as this. They must have been shot 'in real context', on the fringes of one of the many demonstrations happening in Athens while *Homeland* was being made in 2008–9. More attentive viewers might also notice that the two actors who are thus similarly 'edited into' a real event, are those whose casting references previous films – Litsis (from *Matchbox*) and Passalis (from *Dogtooth*) (see note above). Watching these scenes today, they both look as if they have come out from the claustrophobic home-environments of the previous films, directly into the middle of the social upheaval of the Greek Crisis.

9. I have mentioned here only three of the many similar archive-trouble works that kept appearing during that period (cf. Tsiara 2018; Zaroulia 2015; Zaroulia and Hager 2015; Hager 2016).

10. I am by-passing here an extensive discussion of the Documenta 17 exhibition which in many ways also touched on the issues discussed in this book. However tactfully one wants to put it, Documenta 17, for the first time staged partly

outside Kassel, went to Athens in search of weirdness and indeed produced a very weird interaction. See Tramboulis and Tzirtzilakis 2018; Batycka 2017; Demos 2017; Smith 2017.

11. This part from Benjamin's *Origin of German Drama* is equally at the centre of J. Hillis Miller's analysis of allegory in his famous article 'The Two Allegories' (1981).

12. As Foster maintains, the distinction between symbolic totalities and allegorical fragmentariness is not too important for the archival impulse. Accordingly, Dionysios Solomos's version of Liberty may be read as a Romantic symbolic totality in the original poem, but is certainly used in *Homeland* as a fragmented and very metonymical allegory.

CHAPTER 7

Assemblage, Identity, Citizenship:
Strella's Queer Chronotopes

HOW LIVES MATTER:
MOM, I'M BACK AND THE KILLING OF ZAK KOSTOPOULOS

The camera in Dimitris Katsimiris's *Mom, I'm back* (2017) closely follows a woman's figure from behind as she walks first outside and then into a cemetery in order to attend a funeral procession. She moves closer to the assembled group of people. They start coming towards her, with some of the men in the group eventually attacking her and beating her to the ground. She falls, her wig drops to the ground, and her shaven head can now be seen, covered in blood. The shot is still from behind, but as the woman falls, the camera falls with her, too – maintaining the single take through which we have been watching the entire scene. Beating and spitting continue for some time, the spectator now sharing the viewpoint of the victim.

At some point the men stop – and this will be the only cut in this four-minute film which, therefore, is comprised of only two shots. When the viewpoint changes, we cut to a medium-long shot of the whole of the funeral assembly, standing opposite their wounded and bloodied victim. She stands up with some effort, while some of the men are holding back the one man who has been beating her most aggressively, looks at all of them, then turns and goes away. She is the son, now a trans woman, who has come back to attend her mother's funeral; they are the extended family and the community who have shown her how they respond to difference, with the brother who wants to impose his moral code most visibly being the most violent. Finally, this is a short film mediated by a camera which has already made a point on empathy. Falling, sharing the violence and the meaning of these blows, and witnessing the victim stand up again, the camera has assumed an ethical position: It has taken sides.

As with most Greek directors of his generation, Katsimiris works in various part-time jobs related to the entertainment industry to make ends meet and raises the (minimal) budget for his films through crowdfunding or special grants. After an initial run in festivals, these young directors eventually make their work freely available on the internet. This is where I saw *Mom, I'm*

Figure 7.1a–c *A trans woman (Eva Koumarianou) facing her family, from* Mum, I'm Back *(Dimitris Katsimiris, 2017); digital stills.*

back first, on the afternoon of 22 September 2018, when users started posting the link as a response to the sudden and shocking news that Zak Kostopoulos was dead.

Kostopoulos was a gender and HIV activist with a very public profile, also known by his drag persona Zackie Oh. He had died an agonising death the day before. He had been brutally beaten and kicked by shop owners on Gladstonos Street in central Athens and then heavily restrained by police, on the (as it turned out, false) pretense that he had entered a jewelry shop in order to commit a robbery. All this happened in broad daylight, on a central pedestrian street near Omonoia Square in Athens, in front of eye-witnesses and people who were filming the event with their mobile phones. Some of them later sold their material to news outlets or posted it online.

The videos of Kostopoulos's beating started circulating widely very soon after the event, and before the identity of the victim became known. They show two men kicking a younger man who has fallen to the ground and is unable to defend himself. Onlookers become involved in the incident, while some can also be seen holding up their mobile phones and recording it. What is still shocking in these scenes is a silent acceptance that such a thing *could* happen in central Athens, that the person on the ground could be treated in that way, that he was, in a way, already marked for such treatment.

It is not difficult to see why social media users decided to upload Katsimiris's short film the next day, as a comment on what had happened on Gladstonos Street, especially after the public finally learnt the identity of the victim in these already viral scenes. A first obvious reason was the gender identity of the victim in each case: Apart from being a well-known HIV and gender activist and commentator, Kostopoulos had a career as a drag artist, and in the year before his death his drag persona, Zackie Oh, had already made a name as a radical social commentator on new media. The main character of *Mum, I'm back* is played by Eva Koumarianou, a trans activist, sex worker and drag performer, also well-known for her media appearances. Both Koumarianou and Kostopoulos had in the past commented on violence targeting queer and trans bodies.[1] Yet, the link that brought the short film and the real-life event together was not so much gender and sexual identity, or the way in which the victim in each scene was treated; it was the *structure* of violence that could make such a scene possible. Not so much gender/sexuality, but (its) biopolitics, were in evidence here. This was the point made by those who posted Katsimiris's film as a comment on the deadly violence on Gladstonos Street.

In *Mom, I'm back*, familial heteronormativity is shown as the motivating factor for an extreme and collective physical assault happening in the very location where kinship is meant to make its presence felt as an affective and mnemonic network: in a cemetery. The ideology of 'proper' kinship is giving the assailants, so they believe, the right to attack, as is also leaving the rest of the gathering with the impression that they should remain inactive (as familial matters 'need to be resolved' by family members). In the beating scene on

Gladstonos Street, the shop-owners were from the outset presented in the media as good family men and adherents to law and order.[2] They were seen unleashing an attack on someone they conceived of as being outside the frame of 'law and order' which they felt they represented. With the victim described as a drug addict and petty thief in those first media reports, it was now 'law and order' that was presented as the motivating and enabling factor behind the attack against him. Much like the short film by Katsimiris, in the incident on Gladstonos Street the person who is considered to be outside the network of acknowledgment and value is treated as someone who should not have been there in the first place, who ought to be eliminated, a disposable person. What we see at work in each case is not just a matter of transphobia, homophobia and addictophobia; it is not just normativity. What we see is their biopolitical/necropolitical deployment and its results.

The enormous national and international mobilisation that followed in the wake of Kostopoulos's death lasted for a long period after September 2018 and was certainly triggered by what his public persona had been. Even if gender/sexuality had not been the initial reason behind the fatal attack against him, a demand for 'queer politics/public memory' ultimately became central in the wider response to his death.[3] In his short life, Kostopoulos had represented a new example of socially engaged and very vocal public figure whose demands for new types of sexual citizenship had resonated with a broad audience in the Greece of the Crisis. His gender, HIV and social activism, his public politics, his videos, posted online over a long period now returned to the spotlight. His written and recorded performances had talked about his experience as the son of immigrants, an HIV-positive man struggling with austerity and health system underfunding, a drag performer, a precarious worker, an anti-fascist campaigner and a victim of homophobic and racist violence in the past. Watched again after his death, with greater emphasis on their political agenda, they were this time appreciated as manifestos on intersectional politics in a time of crisis, on the value of parrhesia and the demand for visibility, on the structural tendency of Greek society to disavow gender and sexual violence (Lavelle 2019; Alexakis 2018; Preciado 2018b; Anagnostou 2018; Poulis 2018; Athanasiou et al. 2018; Papanikolaou 2019a).[4]

At the same time, the way in which Kostopoulos's death had occurred, the lynching scene on Gladstonos Street, recorded and circulated so many times immediately after the event, entered a long metonymical chain of similar events. It was seen as connected to the series of attacks that since 2008 had happened in broad daylight, against people in vulnerable positions or those defending them: not only migrants, drug addicts and sex workers, but also unionists on strike, refugee workers and social activists defending refugee sit-ins and so on. More often than not, the perpetrators belonged to organised groups with links to the neofascist organisation/party Golden Dawn (Ellinas 2013; Kotouza 2019; Kampagiannis 2020). It was not only the phantom of gender and homophobic violence, but also that of racist and fascist attacks, which was once again conjured up by the circulation of these scenes on Gladstonos Street after 21 September 2018. Images were not treated as evidence of one incident but seen as a link in a chain of events and significations.

Moreover, if one needed reminding of the biopolitical/necropolitical undertones of what had just happened, several days after the event a small group of neofascist protesters staged a gathering that was meant to convey exactly that message. Putting together a public protest that lasted only a few minutes, but was recorded and posted online, the small group of neofascist protesters can be seen standing in front of the place where Kostopoulos had been killed, unfolding a banner that read: 'Πρεζάκια και γκέϊ/δεν είστε αναγκαίοι' – in English, 'Addicts, gays and the lot/necessary you're not'.[5]

The movement that followed Kostopoulos's death brought together queer, feminist, antifascist and anti-austerity activists for more than a year in 2018–19, for the first time in such spectacular synergy in the Greek public space. And it took it upon itself to answer back to exactly that increasingly confident proclamation, that indictment 'you are not necessary'. This public anti-fascist mobilisation understood Kostopoulos's killing as a necropolitical act, and it responded with an assemblage of public demands, articulated by an assemblage of voices. 'Οι ζωές μας έχουν αξία' – 'Our lives have value/our lives matter': This was the title of a public announcement, signed by activist organisations that participated in one of the demonstrations in memory of Zak Kostopoulos two months after the incident.[6] They protested about the ways in which . . .

> . . . social barbarism, institutional racism and police brutality [. . .] take it upon themselves to sort out our bodies as meaningless bodies, bodies that do not matter, and our lives as lives unlivable. [. . .] They insult, they demean, they attack, they kill, and they clear themselves from any responsibility afterwards. They build, every day that goes by, a dystopian condition of sexism, homophobia, transphobia, toxicophobia, racism. Every day they build the substratum of fascism in society, they construct unidimensional and walled cities. They render our lives precarious. [. . .] We demand respect for our being. We want a society that will have space for all [. . .] our lives have value; our lives matter.[7]

Kostopoulos's killing and its aftermath were not the first occasions on which the debate about specific forms of biopolitics and necropolitics became more urgent and politicised in the Greece of the Crisis. This central question, *which lives matter*, had resonated widely as a slogan before in the country – for instance, in the many media reports on the deaths of refugees trying to reach Greece after 2009, or in the camps in which they were held after their arrival. Similarly, and interconnectedly, the same question and its repercussions dominated public discussion after events such as the killing of refugee Sahzat Luqman in January 2013, by members of the Golden Dawn neofascist party; the fatal stabbing of rap singer and social activist Pavlos Fyssas by Giorgos Roupakias, a member of Golden Dawn, in September 2013; the acid attack against the immigrant unionist Konstantinka Kouneva by an unknown assailant in December 2008; and the assault on four Egyptian workers in Perama by members of Golden Dawn in June 2012. All these were acts of violence performed against people whose citizenship was in question, in suspension, or held in outright contempt, and whose very lives were considered disposable, punishable, or a combination of both. These were all events that had happened during the period of auster- ity and crisis, often striving to gain their legitimacy from that socio-economic context. Each time, the mobilisation following these events also aimed to detect similarities between them, underlining what I have already called a metonymical chain connecting them. Each time, the agonising question 'which lives matter?' recurred as a main political platform and gesture, also linking each mobilisation to series of similar movements around the world. It was not simply a question that would preoccupy the Greek public sphere at critical moments. Rather, it became the very way to reclaim the public sphere and to propose its radical reconstruction at a time when bodies, population(s) and how (not) to be governed were felt to be categories of experience in constant dialogue with one another. Rather than a question underlying intersectional political demands, 'which lives matter' or 'how do our lives gain or lose their value today' became a form of constant interrogation of an intense biopolitical present.

GENDER, ASSEMBLAGE AND THEIR BIOPOLITICAL REALISM

In its modern trajectory as a concept, biopolitics has been analysed as a form of power paradigmatically seen in relation to gender and sexuality. The most spectacular turn in Foucault's first volume of the *History of Sexuality* is his assertion that the modern construction of a gendered/sexualised body with specific limits, properties and 'internal', 'deep', 'secret' sexual desires also meant the intertwinement of the body with the population, as well as the administration of new forms of governance that aimed to be internalised, disciplinary and expansive. Foucault is interested in how projects such as the normativisation of sexuality and family in a (nation) state, eugenics and racial profiling and segregation, national health and security, or new forms of biopower, biotechnology and population management were combined in the later period of modernity, crucially also bringing together more closely the anatomopolitics of the human body and the biopolitics of a population.

A simple reading of the events I have described so far would therefore be to reiterate that, if gender is a privileged site for the articulation of biopolitics, it will at the same time offer a way to answer back, to reform, to reposition oneself *vis-à-vis* biopolitical power. However, as the story of what transpired in Athens in September 2018 very well shows, if any of these 'answering back' moments happen, they do so in a different mode: Gender and sexual identity are not simply revisited as object(ive)s of biopolitics and/or positions of resistance. Instead, they participate as positionalities in the complex sites of biopolitical and necropolitical ordering today.

Biopolitics and necropolitics are not something that happens to the gendered body. They are related to a complex assemblage of gestures, impositions, capitulations and reconsiderations that are already there when one assumes a gendered and sexual body, orienting that assumption, while also being reoriented by it (Repo 2015; Quinan and Thiele 2020; Preciado 2018a).

I am echoing here a long trajectory of recent theoretical discussions that have reviewed the position of gender and sexuality in the biopolitical/ necropolitical order, by also taking into account the concept of assemblage, as suggested by Gilles Deleuze and Félix Guattari in various places, most prominently in *Kafka* (1986), *Anti-Oedipus* (1972) and *Mille Plateaux* (1980). Translating the French *agencement* as assemblage (another translation could have been 'assortment, arrangement') has arguably given the term a further dynamic in English theoretical discourse (Phillips 2006). On the one hand, this is because it became the centre of various post-Deleuzian philosophical programmes, most notably that of Manuel DeLanda (2016) and, to a certain extent, of Brian Massumi. On the other hand, this is because it was also reinforced, as a term, by its long employment in art history to describe art based on ready-mades and collage.[8] For Renate Lorenz, who has written an influential book on queer drag based on this double tradition of the concept, drag art and performance is a quintessential example of assemblage, as it . . .

> . . . may refer to the productive connections of natural and artificial, animate and inanimate, to clothes, radios, hair, legs, all that which tends more to produce connections to others and other things than to represent them. What becomes visible in this drag is not people, individuals, subjects, or identities, but rather assemblages; indeed those that do not work at any 'doing gender/sexuality/race', but instead at an 'undoing'. [. . .] In so (un)doing, drag proposes images in which the future can be lived. (Lorenz 2012: 21)

As Tobias Rees adds, 'to speak of an assemblage is to relate to the present [. . .] as if it were a form-in-motion composed of a set of different elements (these can be concepts, practices, institutions, machines, technologies or people and other things)' (Rees 2018: 84). The concept of assemblage thus points to a new way of thinking about how ideas, ideologies, gestures, bodies, positions and movements are co-articulated, embodied, emplaced, situated and biopolitically/necropolitically enunciated, put in check and experienced, in time, in a present continuous. This is, for instance, how Jasbir Puar (2007) presents assemblage as her key concept in the paradigm shifting *Terrorist Assemblages: Homonationalism in Queer Times*, starting with Deleuze and Guattari's definition:

> On a first, horizontal, axis, an assemblage comprises two segments, one of content, the other of expression. On the one hand it is a machinic assemblage of bodies reacting to one another; on the other hand it is a collective assemblage of enunciation, of acts and statements, of incorporeal transformations attributed to bodies. Then on a vertical axis, the assemblage has both territorial sides, or reterritorialized sides, which stabilize it, and cutting edges of deterritorialization, which carry it away. (Deleuze and Guattari 2004: 97–98; in Puar 2007: 193)

With the biopolitical and the necropolitical becoming such crucial agonistic grounds today, it is evident that they also point to extensive assemblages, a co-presence of different parts, acts and demands, and sites of emergence, rather than the work of a specific hierarchy of agents with precise roles. In its territorial sides, the assemblage is the object of biopolitical/necropolitical control; at its deterritorialising edges, it is part of the biopolitical at the same time as of its destabilisation. Optical technologies and the modality of the possessive spectator are becoming part of these assemblages. They offer ways to react – for instance, to start sharing images in order to mobilise against surveillance and violence – but also to be reactionary (that is, to capture a scene, for instance, and sell it for money to a media outlet). They are thematised as enabling, but they do *not* offer a way out. Instead, if anything, they offer a way *in*, at best a way to negotiate from within.

Puar, again:

> I propose the assemblage as a pertinent political and theoretical frame within societies of control. [. . .] This foregrounding of assemblage enables attention to ontology in tandem with epistemology, affect in conjunction with representational economies, within which bodies interpenetrate, swirl together, and transmit affects and effect to each other. (2007: 205)

The reason why I find the concept of assemblage useful here is because, first, it allows us to expand the discussion from Puar's rather unidirectional 'societies of control' to what I have described an intense biopolitical present. Thinking about the biopolitical and the necropolitical as grounds of/for assemblage brings us back to what I have elsewhere in this book pointed to as an economy of biopolitical realism. Biopolitical realism is more than a territorialising mode of expression for contemporary assemblages. It is, rather, a milieu where both their territorialising utterance and their cutting edges of deterritorialisation can co-exist. It foregrounds not only histories, agents and origins, but also forms in motion, questions of frame, of speed, of relation, of density.

It is within such an economy of biopolitical realism that the videos of Kostopoulos's beating and their circulation in September 2018, the photographs from the ensuing social mobilisation or the sites devoted to his memory and to organising public actions to defend it, the affective and representational explosions of those public demonstrations, as well as a film like *Mum, I'm back* could all equally participate. It is within biopolitical realism that they create metonymical chains; that they read each other; that they show assemblages; that they become part of assemblages; that they contribute to, as they have been emerging within, biopolitical realism; that they point to what Puar calls 'ontology in tandem with epistemology', to bodies that swirl and emerge, but are also shown and conceptualised *together*; that they point to emotions reframed by and reframing representational economies, as well as to representational economies becoming the context for (but also called upon to contest) the neoliberal economies of precarity, state of emergency and crisis.

Seeing, for instance, how Katsimiris's short was recalled within this flow of images that evening of September 2018, I could not help but notice how the scene of family and gender violence in this earlier short film was taking on a different political meaning and entering a new economy of readings and contextualisations. The shot of the extended family, in gender-hierarchical assortment, appeared more clearly now as a site of transphobia and homophobia, and also as a biopolitical and necropolitical nexus assuming an expansive allegorical quality. At the same time, the movement of the camera at the end of Katsimiris's short film made me want to review the scenes of the beating of Zak Kostopoulos circulating online the evening after his death. In *Mum, I'm back*, the camera first follows, then lingers on, but in the end falls with the attacked protagonist. When I watched the film as a visual comment responding to the footage of the event, I realised that this gesture had not been attempted by the cameras recording the beating and death of Zak Kostopoulos. The mobile phone cameras recording what happened on Gladstonos Street had kept their safe distance, as did most of the onlookers.

The camera in *Mum, I'm back* performs an ethical move as it falls – not only drawing with it the eye of the spectators, but also provoking their affective reaction – following the body of Eva Koumarianou, who acts in the scene.[9]

The trans performer, author and sex worker has to endure once again in that fictional setting the type of transphobic violence often described in her published memoirs (2012). In other words, if there is an assemblage character/ real person already in the short film, this is doubled up with an assemblage character/*mise-en-scène*/spectator through the handling of the *near*-subjective shot and the semiotic and affective weight that it achieves. Crucially, if the cameras recording the death of Zak Kostopoulos did not make that move, if they were not ready to share his fall, new and powerful assemblages came to take their position: the expansive public mobilisation that came afterwards, the use of videos from the scene in order to call for a political mobilisation, the optical commentaries by anonymous users and later by activist groups focusing on forensic video research (Forensic Architecture 2019). Also the public archive of Kostopoulos himself, his performances in drag and on video, his public presence and negotiated visual trace now shared, now redoubled, now repeated, emotionally charged and expanded as a platform for action, became a new articulation of political argument, public speech and a demand for a reorganised public sphere. It was pure biopolitical realism, and we all were in it, we all were weird in it. As Paul Preciado wrote, after describing Zak's videos circulating online in the days after the attack that had cost him his life, . . .

> Zak was one of us. Let's manage our anger, let's mobilize now that it's still possible. Let's stand up like Zackie, the whore; let's illegalize the parties of the far right. Let's depatriarchize the police. Let's decolonize the law. Zackie's soft voice comes out of his/her digital grave again: 'I think the people who attack other people, the fascists, enjoy seeing us terrorized.' Zak goes to the bathroom, takes off his/her shirt, shaves his/her armpits and eyebrows and prepares to be the Zackie Oh of Athens forever. (Preciado 2018b)

What I have called weird in the previous paragraph is not the way in which gender/sexuality became the centre of a wider public discussion on biopolitics and a social mobilisation. It is their tendency to point to the role of assemblage in biopolitical realism – gender (and) performance as assemblage, movement as assemblage, social mobilisation as based on assemblage, bodies as parts of assemblages demanding presence. What this constant repositioning and expansion of assemblage bring about is also a certain understanding of the act of giving an account of oneself as based on assemblage, of the archive as assemblage, of the self in archive trouble as the result of participating in a poetics of assemblage. Often queer film – itself a cinematic tradition very much based on the assemblage of styles, icons and politics and a cinematic style that also insists on foregrounding the poetics of assemblage of its own subjects – makes an evident example of how a poetics of assemblage can become the basis for a politics of demanding historical position, pace, space and public place (Schoonover and Galt 2016).

It is with this in mind that I want to return to a queer film that, as I have explained in Chapter 1, has since 2009 become iconic. *Strella: A Woman's Way* (2009, directed by Panos Koutras) is a new queer melodrama that engaged audiences and critics from its first release. *Strella* has been considered a central Greek Weird Wave film, often to the protests of many a critic who kept underlining its social realism as a crucial difference from the films of Lanthimos or Tsangari. *Strella* tells the story of a trans woman sexworker who first decides to avenge and then falls in love with the father who once killed her own lover. From the outset, it created a debate on trans/queer representation in Greece and has become a strong cultural reference point, thanks to its ability to elicit complex political and gender insights (Butler and Athanasiou 2013; Psaras 2016; Coavoux 2013).

In the following pages, I want to read *Strella* through an experience of what came after the film. What I realise now, and would like to underscore in the analysis that follows, is that *Strella* acquired such a central position in the Greek Weird Wave precisely because it foregrounded its new queer poetics as a politics of assemblage. At various points in Panos Koutras's film, we see the queer self performing assemblages, participating in them, understanding the self as assemblage, showing identity and kinship as assemblage, and prefiguring the importance that a politics of assemblage would take for the Greece of the Crisis. *Strella* is *not* weird because it focuses (just before the onslaught of the Greek Crisis) on a trans woman, the trauma of family violence and an incestuous relationship. It is weird because it does and transcends all this through a politics of assemblage that orients viewers to treat in a similar way the film's Greek/queer cinematic and more widely cultural genealogies, as well as the film's queer futures.

In the rest of this chapter I will analyse the film's new queer vocabulary, before contextualising it more in terms of Greek culture – more specifically, Greek queer culture. In the last part of the chapter, focusing on the film's two final scenes, I will return to the arguments I have already made about the public sphere and the assemblage poetics of social mobilisation in an intense biopolitical present.

STRELLA AND THE POLITICS OF NEW QUEER MELODRAMA

Somewhere in the middle of Strella's story, after a long, revelatory monologue delivered with her gaze lowered and fixed on a plate of snacks, a monologue that is part tragedy and part soap opera ... somewhere there, then, at the film's halfway point and at the moment it reveals a shocking secret, viewers are invited to consider what they have already seen happen previously on screen in two different, entirely erotic scenes. At this point the film *Strella: A Woman's Way* – which, like its protagonist, has introduced itself with a childish smile – now bares its teeth. One understands at this point that the film has not simply pushed the limits of what can be shown on the screen of a melodrama, but that it has already become an exploration of the limits that fabricate our embodied and sexual selves: the limits of the possible, of the permissible and of the representable.

Giorgos, the forty-five-year-old who is released from prison after serving a fifteen-year sentence for murder, meets Strella – 'My name is Stella, but my friends call me Strella, cos I'm a little crazy'[10] – the twenty-five-year-old trans sex worker, a *bricoleuse extraordinaire* who also works as a part-time electrician. We watch as their deadlocked affair unfolds. In terms of Greek Cinema, the film already from its title recalls Michael Cacoyannis's 1954 film *Stella*, the story of an emancipated taverna singer and her doomed fight with the patriarchal rigidity of Greek society, starring Melina Mercouri in the role that catapulted her to fame. Another intertext could be one of the legendary Greek melodramas of the 1970s, Alexis Damianos's *Evdokia* (1971), which followed the relationship between a sex worker and a soldier on day leave from his barracks.

Yet, the relationship between the two protagonists in Koutras's film, as the viewer soon realises, is a little more complicated. *Strella*, the sex worker who falls in love with the beautiful older convict whom she has met by chance in a cheap hotel, turns out to have been his son/now daughter, as well as a past victim of the familial violence that has sent her father to jail. She is the one who has now plotted their new meeting as a form of revenge.

Strella is seen at various times carrying a tote bag with the motto 'Live your myth in Greece', a phrase promoted after 2004 by the Greek tourist organisation as its main campaign slogan. This slogan had remained on posters and in international advertising (and ubiquitous tote bags) in the first years of the Greek Crisis. And live her myth in Greece Strella certainly does. She goes on a spree, a tragic (and at times tragicomic) postmodern revisiting of Oedipal wrong-doing, primal scenes and transgressive attraction. References to Sophocles abound, as do their queer realignments. Characters pass by a 'Sophocles Street', and in one scene we find out that Strella had hurt her foot a while back and, like Oedipus, is still scarred. Outsiders come with news that would give away Strella's real identity, revealing to the unsuspecting father the incestuous nature of the relationship he has been pursuing. When the revelation of the past connection between Strella and Giorgos occurs, the character of the older trans woman who has been like a mother to Strella protests by calling it hubris. As Judith Butler notes in her discussion of this scene, 'this queen paradoxically becomes a kind of Teiresias who sees the past in the present and the future catastrophe that will follow from not heeding the lessons of the past. We are here, of course, prepared for "tragedy"' (Butler and Athanasiou 2013: 60). A tragedy does, indeed, unfold before our eyes. Yet, it turns out to be a consciously pursued, camp tragedy.

Strella takes a tragic story of abuse, desire and revenge, and retells it with a camp aesthetics and idiosyncratic humour. As a style, it is firmly positioned in a world queer cinema canon, aligning itself with post-1990s *new queer cinema*, though, even in 2009, this was still quite a rarity in the Greek context.[11] New queer cinema, named after a very influential essay by Ruby Rich and a special issue of *Sight and Sound*, describes a turn in queer film-making identifiable after the 1990s (Rich 2013; Aaron 2004). Genre exploration and mixity, small-budget films and idiosyncratic *mise-en-scène*, a tendency to present characters with non-normative sexuality who have positive *and* negative characteristics, and, last but not least, a focus not on gay identity but on queer desire – these were its main characteristics as a world cinematic trend. Figures such as Derek Jarman and Pedro Almodóvar were seen as its queer forefathers, and directors such as Todd Haynes, Jenny Livingstone, François Ozon, Gregg Araki, Gus Van Sant and Isaac Julien became its initially most identifiable representatives. Present in that original group were the Greek director Constantine Giannaris (at the time moving from Britain, where he had produced his first films, to Greece, where he made his major feature-length films) and the Greek Australian director Ana Kokkinos (Papanikolaou 2009; Jennings and Lomine 2004).

Strella directly references that new queer cinema tradition and is especially in dialogue with its later and world-cinema representatives. A final scene, for instance, with a large queer family eating together, almost directly echoes the ending of *Le Fate Ignoranti*, the 2001 film by Turkish/Italian director Ferzan Özpetek. Strella's bedroom reminds us of Toula's room in Ana Kokkinos's *Head On* (1998). The figure of the 'mother of the house', Mary, leads us to Jenny Livingston's *Paris is Burning* (1990). Sébastien Lifshitz's *Wild Side* (2004) is also a possible intertext; much like in *Strella*, in *Wild Side* a trans woman sex worker is revisiting her old family home, her youth, her past desires and family abuse, through (and with the support of) the presence of her new queer family (cf. Rees-Roberts 2007). But even those who may not notice such references will certainly be able to recognize the undeniable influence of Pedro Almodóvar on Koutras – from the way in which the tragic is interwoven with hilarious comedy, to the bright colours, the makeshift costumes, the setting and even the way in which a drag show and a gay bar are filmed. Most importantly, as in many of the Spanish director's films (*Law of Desire* [1987], *Bad Education* [2004]), in *Strella* the heavy matter of memory, and especially the memory of abuse and non-normative desire, is prototypically represented, embodied, reified and redefined by (and on the surface of) a trans body.

Strella is Panos Koutras's third feature film and intricately connected to the filmmaker's previous works. His first feature-length film, the notorious *The Attack of the Giant Moussaka* (1999), was a laugh-out-loud parody of disaster B-movies, specifically referencing a John Waters aesthetic as it tells the story of a Divine lookalike, a trans woman by the name of Tara (Giannis Angelakis), who falls in love with an astronomist Alexis Alexiou (Christos Mantakas) and in the process saves Athens from the attack of the title. (The Giant Moussaka is a huge alien life-form from another universe whose plan is to attack and destroy the Acropolis.) *True Life* (2004), which passed very much unnoticed by Greek and international audiences, took a soap opera aesthetics as its starting point in order to narrate a melodramatic story of incest and devotion, once again with the Acropolis permanently in the background. Non-normative sexuality, queer aesthetics (and its cinematic genealogy), as well as genre pastiche are the devices that Koutras uses to undermine official cultural symbols and identities. Heteronormativity, as well as the normative foundations of a national culture, become his favourite targets.

In *Strella,* which has echoes of Koutras's previous films, it is heteronormativity, the (Greek) family, as well as the concept of a national melodrama, that are in the firing line. As Butler and Athanasiou discuss at length, 'the only heterosexuality in this film is queer, and the only kinship in this film is built upon the decimation of the nuclear family and its rules of self-constitution' (2013: 62). Understandably, these and other international critics were quick to focus on the film's radical potential for rethinking kinship in queer terms (Gourgouris 2019; cf. Žižek 2013). What I want to underline further here is the critical potential of assessing how the film repositions world cinema's new queer lexicon in a national terrain of family stories and melodrama at this crucial historical juncture. With its title, storyline, location and setting, *Strella* clearly aims to queer not only kinship and belonging, but also a national canon. The result could have been disavowed, objected to or remained unnoticed, as has often been the case with cultural works in the Greek queer canon of the twentieth and twenty-first centuries (Kyriakos 2017). As a matter of fact, the film itself makes implicit and more direct references to a series of radical Greek queer texts from the past, reintroducing them to a large audience and showing how much they had been marginalised in relation to the cultural canon (Papanikolaou 2010b).

Seen from this angle, it is even more interesting that in the winter of 2009–10, *Strella* became the director's most successful commercial film in Greece, and the one most favourably received by critics. This was not, I now realise, because Greece had suddenly decided to warm to queer film or queer identity. This was not the case of public culture suddenly welcoming a 'new queer Greece', as I had myself hoped in an earlier article (Papanikolaou 2009). Instead, I would argue that central to the film's reception was the way in which its new queer poetics became, at that crucial moment, the key to address pressing political issues. They included, but also extended beyond, its queer subject-matter, generating a dynamic political reception and new and more (bio)political recontextualisations in the years after the film's premiere. In retrospect, *Strella*'s new queer undermining of kinship and belonging seems to have been in much closer conversation with the more allegorical and 'systemic' attacks that the other films of the Weird Wave were already unleashing against Greek family and society in that period.

The main character's trans identity and the public presence of the charismatic transgender actress Mina Orfanou who portrays her were used from the very beginning to open up a wider discussion about sexuality, the politics of recognition and the history of Greek queer and trans people as an example of a disavowed community history. The bar *Koukles* in Syngrou, where many of the film's scenes were shot, became a well-frequented part of Athens after the film was first shown, and the film has arguably reignited an interest in drag performance and its politics that expanded and reached politically-minded audiences beyond those conversant with queer culture.[12] Almost ten years after *Strella*, drag culture in Athens was so expansive and politicised that it was becoming the focus of documentary and activist projects narrating precisely how the queer scene became more political, diverse and intersectional during the Crisis.[13] One such intermedial project, between documentary, video and performance, was still developing in September 2018; it featured Zak Kostopoulos/Zackie Oh as one of its protagonists: *Faster than Light*, directed by Kentaro Kumanomido and Thomas Anthony Owen. After Zackie Oh's death, however, this project turned into a more open process, with the directors inviting more community members to share their experience of activism, trauma and mourning, with the existing material already filmed becoming the basis of numerous debates, live performances, assemblies, remembrance events, mobilisation platforms and then a completely new film that also documented the mobilisation after Zackie Oh's death. The final cut of *Faster than Light* – still in progress as I write these lines, but shown at various versions at activist events throughout Greece – has been conceived as a piece on gender violence, transphobia and homophobia during the Crisis, both a mourning project on Kostopoulos and an exercise in highlighting queer power and h(er)stories.[14]

Reviewed in this later context, the profound relationship that a film like *Strella* had with the period in Greece starting around 2008 cannot be underestimated. The radical politicisation of the work grew with the years, as the film opened its dialogue with a culture of an expansive biopolitical realism and the role that gender/queer performance played within it. Returning to *Strella* today, with the knowledge of what came after it, one cannot help but notice how the film itself also insists – it has always insisted – on the radical assemblages of kinship, citizenship, queer political mobilisation and national belonging. *Strella* exemplifies what Eliza Steinbock has so astutely called the ability of 'trans [to] become a new assemblage that is capable of bringing disparate contemporary struggles into alliance' (in Schoonover and Galt 2016: 53–54). The ground that *Strella* has covered over the years, from a new queer film to a biopolitical realist example of radical assemblage, has inspired the argument unfolding in the rest of this chapter.

GIVING AN ACCOUNT OF THE QUEER SELF AS ASSEMBLAGE

In one of *Strella*'s most powerful scenes, Giorgos gathers various materials he finds in Strella's house and is handcrafting a lamp of different colours. When he is finished, he turns it on, and in its multi-coloured light he undresses Strella and stands in front of her, while the camera begins to search over their bodies in a series of close-ups. This scene, with its low multi-coloured lighting, would certainly bring to mind countless erotic scenes from the history of cinema; it may also be a more direct reference to *Hedwig and the Angry Inch* (2001, directed by John Cameron Mitchell). Its initial banality is the scene's main point: There is nothing original when it comes to technologies of the erotic; we construct the erotic, as well as the sexual self, with surface materials already on offer, already given, provided and now reassembled. What we consider the spontaneous expressions of our deeper desiring self are in fact based on iteration and iterativity. Even the multi-coloured lamp that Giorgos so movingly builds for Strella seems to be something he may already have constructed as a courting ritual in the past; in fact, in an earlier scene in which we see his previous sexual partner's bedside table in their shared prison cell, we can spot a similar lamp. As *Strella* reiterates in sequence after sequence, the sexual self's radicalness is not grounded in its originality, but in this constant 'making', in this act of assembling material already there, the do-it-yourself work that one is constantly compelled to perform. We watch Strella's erotic, kaleidoscopic body, lit by the moving colours of the makeshift spotlight. It emerges here both as the result of her own erotic, sexual and body technologies (from posture to biotechnology and pharmakopolitics) and as a result of this body's intertwinement with other (and others') technologies, from her lover's lighting to the scene's construction. Strella's erotic, sexual and biopolitical body is not original, but rather based on iteration and assemblage, an 'ontology in tandem with epistemology'. This scene encapsulates what the

Figure 7.2 *Whose assemblage is this? Strella (Mina Orfanou), her lover (Giannis Kokiasmenos) and their technologies, from* Strella *(Panos Koutras, 2009); digital still.*

film has to say about love, the technics of the human and the (biopolitical) way of the world.

In *Strella,* queer cinema's cunning ability to reassemble and reorganise helps the film to at once cite, represent *and* reframe a transqueer subculture and its cultural lineage. In one scene, we see a rehearsal for a drag show in the real-life bar *Koukles* in the Athenian district of Syggrou, where Mania Dellou, a well-known trans performer at drag shows and bars, imitates Melina Mercouri playing the role of Stella,[15] right when Strella is trying to spotlight her properly – 'hey, dude, where's my light!' This ironic citation of the first scene from Michael Cacoyannis's *Stella* (1955), where a waiter is spotlighting the Stella of Melina Mercouri, is not just a subtle nod to those in the know. Later on, in a violent altercation after the big revelatory scene, Giorgos starts to shout and move like the character of Stella's lover in that older film, and even Strella begins to speak, *mutatis mutandis,* like Mercouri – 'I'm a little too old to have a controlling father for a boyfriend'. In another scene to which I have already made reference, Strella is having a discussion with Mary, the aged trans woman who assumes the role of the matriarch in the film (uniquely played by Betty Vakalidou, the legendary activist sex worker and author of the 1970s and 1980s, to whom I will return in the last pages of this chapter). Listening to Strella talk about her relationship with Giorgos, Mary starts to shout, as if rehearsing ancient drama: 'That's hubris, my dear. Hubris, girl, the ancients said it, too. The ancients . . . lady Sophocles, lady Euripides . . . It's taboo, my dear, do you not understand?' The old feminist melodrama of *Stella* is here assembled with *Oedipus Rex*, as they both belong to the drag vocabulary, and the wardrobe, of these women. They perform in irony as they keep reminding you that they also know a thing or two about the tragic.

Precisely because of this game of mimicry and camp parody, while the film makes one consider it in relation to other model examples, it also undermines these comparisons. If Cacoyannis's *Stella* was about female entrapment within the traditional system of gender and Stella's need to revolt, Koutras's *Strella* does not exactly bring that history into the present day, and its subject-matter is not exactly that of trans liberation. Even if Sophocles's Oedipus is a tragic hero who struggles to escape his fate, but ultimately falls within its clutches, *Strella*'s plot, while it comments on Oedipus with the dynamism of a voguing contest, nevertheless slips away from the concepts of hubris, the incest taboo and insurmountable trauma. This film's queer aesthetic of assemblage pushes it towards doing exactly what a trans woman would do when she says 'those ancient girls, lady Sophocles, lady Euripides': They both maintain the sense of the tragic, but also avoid normatively receiving it as an absolute truth. They bring the gesture of the self to the surface, to a poetics of performativity and, in doing so, they relativise and historicise the ideology of emotional depth, of the unconscious and patriarchal self, of insurmountable hubris. This does not mean that they do not perceive the impasse, the tragedy; they just see it as a system of relations and suspect that these relations can be performatively rearranged or reassembled.

Koutras and Evangelidis handle the gradual unveiling of the big secret of their script in such a way that, when the final denouement happens, it is something most viewers have probably suspected anyway. Nevertheless, the viewer's surprise in *Strella* is not exhausted when we suddenly realise that Giorgos, the lover with whom she has already slept *before our very eyes*, is her father who was imprisoned for the murder of a nephew he once found sleeping with his son. And that she *knew* who he was from the very beginning of their relationship! The surprise comes not so much from these revelations, as from the way in which their agents decide to address them: through investigating the possibility of another type of ethics of the self, familial relations and togetherness.

'Thank you for making me love you in all the ways that a father can love his son', Giorgos says towards the end of the film – a line that can sound simultaneously comic, outrageous and moving, an effect on which the film probably banks (cf. Gourgouris 2019). This is the last phrase which Giorgos addresses to Strella, in what seems like their last meeting, in an Athenian hotel.

Strella storms out. She walks alone through the city – it is Christmas already; she keeps walking, the camera following her, alternating between close-up and medium shots. This is the conclusion of the film, followed by a black screen for ten seconds. The 'real' story may have ended here, one thinks, and what comes after that visual gap may be seen as a post-script, as an imaginary or alternative ending. And there, in that post-script of a scene, we see Strella and Giorgos together again, with their friends, under one roof. It is now New Year's Eve – of the same year? Or of another year? They all are preparing for the celebration. Here we have Giorgos's former roommate from jail, Strella's best friend with his/her baby sister and a Russian man named Yuri. As these five adults speak to each other, one no longer really knows what the relations between each of them are. This, first and foremost, applies to the relationship between Strella and Giorgos. As they interact in this scene, it is unclear whether Giorgos and Strella are still having a sexual relationship; what is clear is that they now, both, *know*.

This does not mean that the film bypasses the question of incest, of inter-familial violence, oppression and revenge; it does not mean that it puts all of these behind it, with this scene of ultimate familial celebration. Quite the contrary. This Oedipus-in-drag has proven the whole psychoanalytic culture of the Oedipus complex to be, though not un-insightful, quite rearrangable and potentially obsolete. The extended queer family with which the film ends provokes a similar destabilisation: It has value not as an example, and of course not as an exercise in forgetfulness, but as a strategy. It demonstrates that, if there are ways to conceive of the constitution of the self *differently* in relation to self/and/others, there must exist novel ways to move beyond the subject's past and the violence of others. The film thus concludes after Strella and Giorgos have had a final (final?) goodbye and offers an alternative possibility: a New Year's Eve celebration in Strella's house, a baby girl sleeping in the bedroom and five adults around the table. All five of them could now have any type of relationship – erotic, friendly, familial. Their interactions seem to be exploring the porous boundary that these three types of relationship can have in this setting. Family are those with whom we *decide* to bind our feelings; family can only be the family we choose. Reassembling the self around those we choose is a way to refract the heavy memory of the past, of 'nature' and of 'descent', to allow them to be reperformed in new, less traumatic assemblages.

In the last shot, Giorgos walks towards the window and opens it. The city is celebrating the new year countdown: There is the sound of fireworks, and one expects the camera to turn and show the Acropolis covered in confetti. However, it remains stuck here, still showing Giorgos-post-hubris framed by the window and his new queer family. Then, for the first time, the music becomes more intense, different from the rest of the soundtrack, almost hard rock. *Strella*, which began without family and in the mood for popular melo-drama, now ends *with family*, but also, blissfully, in genre trouble.

FILMING, REARRANGING, CONSTRUCTING A GENEALOGY: (OUR) EXTREME SELF

During one of the many interviews she gave at the time when *Strella* was first screened, transgender protagonist Mina Orfanou was asked: 'What is the most extreme thing you have ever done?' 'My self !' she replied – a phrase that Athena Athanasiou and Judith Butler analyse in detail in their book *Dispossession: The Performative in the Political*. As Athanasiou says, . . .

> In this performative proclamation of a self that has been undone and redone, the self is not created from scratch in the way of an alternative liberalist 'anything goes', but rather [. . .] troubles and repoliticizes the liberal typol-ogy of the self-owned 'I', as it responds to, and is bound by, the injurious, teratological implication ('the most extreme thing you have ever done') of the question-interpellation 'who are you?' or, more accurately, 'what are you?' In redistributing the norms defining the terms of a recognizable self (and a livable life), *this* 'self-authoring' self [. . .] institutes a different sociality. The normative discourse of abjected and adjudicated exception is performatively recast into exceptional self-poietics (Butler and Athanasiou 2013: 65).

Processes of community, kinship and cultural norm exist to frame and to form. They preempt the shaping of a self outside their ambit as a weird, extreme moment. They equally categorise certain bodies as unacceptable, unlivable and extreme. But, then, they happen: extreme moments, excep-tional selves. The image of a Greek trans woman in the first decade of the twenty-first century recalls such an exceptional story of patience, persistence and resistance. Mina Orphanou's story, like that of Strella, recalls (and spec-trally brings with it) a heavy past, other moments of exposure and discursive exploration, a large archive of feelings and of political assertion, as well as frustration and disavowal. It also brings forth a story of identity, a demand for public space and gender, a demand that is constantly in the making, constantly the result of a spectacularised, yet persistent and creative, bricolage. It is not a coincidence that *Strella* insists in so many scenes on its main character's habit of collecting, of picking up things and creating something else with them, on her talents at bricolage and electric circuiting. Similarly, in the years after the film, Mina Orfanou insisted on showing her own artworks, an idiosyncratic mixture of painting and collage, in community spaces in Athens.

Making oneself into a Greek trans woman with public visibility and dis-course in Greece, *circa* 2010, meant and still means today that one is haunted:

by a past full of trauma; by a discontinuous and inconsistent history that, nevertheless, keeps defining one's body and self; and last, but not least, by an ongoing, constantly present and uninterrupted condition of precarity, of making do, of reassembling and reperforming. Becoming trans and demanding public visibility as such involves a very specific history, spatio-temporally and culturally determined and significant, which at the same time, and precisely for this reason, acquires a timely allegorical potential. In other words, it becomes a paradigmatic story of the intense persistence which is called the self, as well as a story of emptying, deprivation, defeat, which is also a condition of self. It becomes a story and a history that are also a model for what it means for one to take responsibility for what (self) one has made, to bridge the public and the private, to forge links between selves and bodies, and to articulate a sense of self that comes from putting things together, from a making do; a sense of self that comes, emerges, as an assemblage, and that is no less demanding for that reason. This is, I believe, encapsulated in the film's climactic scene, to which I now turn as I bring this chapter to a close.

If *Strella* ends with the image of a new queer family and a non/*pater familias* looking us in the eye, it also makes clear that its emotional, melodramatic climax *has already happened* some minutes earlier, in that penultimate sequence in which Strella is seen leaving her lover in a fully lit Athenian hotel. The Acropolis (heavily featured in previous scenes) is now behind her; tragedy has been both her undoing and her making, and something new is happening while this trans woman is starting her long night walk in the centre of contemporary Athens. The camera focuses on Strella, with medium shots that track the city as they follow her steps, while Maria Callas dominates the soundtrack. Even though in many ways a scene of liberation, this is also a scene of a complex haunting. At the level of narrative, *Strella* is haunted by the difficult pattern that kinship, abuse, desire and the archives of the past make in their intermingling. But in the larger context of the film, this scene, in which a transgender sex worker (played by a transgender artist) walks through the centre of Athens and onto the screens of national representation, cannot avoid to also be haunted by the many other scenes of trans people forced into and/or erased from the public sphere in the past. Within the film narrative, as well as with its potential to break out of it, this can be seen as exactly what Lauren Berlant has called diva citizenship: an exodus into the public space, a demand made in the public sphere.

Diva citizenship, so Berlant explains, is precisely the moment of spectacular emergence of a gender/sexual subaltern, who demands to be taken seriously. And scanning the past for moments of subaltern emergence becomes a deeply critical historical project in that it shows, *in the present*, the ease with which sexual subalterns' 'bodies, their social labour and their sexuality are

Figures 7.3 a–b   *Strella on her final walk in Athens, from* Strella; *digital stills.*

exploited, violated and saturated by normalising law, capitalist prerogative and official national culture' (Berlant 1997: 222).

　　Diva citizenship therefore becomes . . .

> . . . a moment of emergence that marks unrealized potentials for subaltern political activity. Diva citizenship occurs when a person stages a dramatic coup in a public sphere in which she does not have privilege. Flashing up and startling the public, she puts the dominant story into suspended animation; as though recording an estranging voice-over to a film we have all already seen, she renarrates the dominant story as one that the abjected people have once lived sotto voce, but no more; and she challenges her audience to identify

with the enormity of the suffering she has narrated and the courage she has had to produce, calling on people to change the social and institutional practices of citizenship to which they currently consent. (223)

The cinematic metaphor is extremely fitting here: What if citizenship and belonging, as a political demand, were a question of suspended animation and of new voice-overs? What if they were a demand for new mixes, a completely new edit? What if the self, as an always weird demand in public space, is nothing but an open reassemblage of material? What if this assemblage brings with it new potentials, as well as retrieving other similar reimaginings of the public space, other previous moments of diva citizenship that may have lost momentum, gone astray, or been forgotten at earlier historical contingencies? What if this montage, this reassemblage, is no less than a signature moment of claiming political space in (the times of) biopolitical realism?

I am interested in this aspect of the film because it lies at the heart of its focus on reassemblage, biopolitics and transqueer emergence. Strella's diva citizenship claim, in its multiple queer time reversals, is able to remix past and future as political demands. As she stages her exodus to the public, Strella moves at the same time towards the past and towards the future, two directions I will now briefly outline.

Strella's Queer Temporalities

Telling a story of emergence and parrhesia, of a trans woman wanting to stand up for her own history of subjugation, suffering and patience, *Strella* insists on the site where this story unfolds and the dynamics it can bring with it. It is, after all, a tale of the private turning inside out as public, and in its last scenes the painstaking filming of the Athenian metropolis underscores this very development. The film was shot right before (yet screened a year after) the large-scale demonstrations of December 2008 in Athens, which many critics have pinpointed as the beginning of the Greek Crisis. Watching Strella coming out in(to) the public space in the film's final scenes, therefore, took on additional meaning in the years after 2010. Suddenly this melodramatic story of identity, trauma and loss acquired a further allegorical quality. It could now recall and be haunted by the multi-layered outings in public space that followed during the Crisis – the demonstrations, the sit-ins, the mass-gatherings of the Squares movement in 2011, the mobilisation against the shaming of HIV-positive women accused of 'illegal sex work' in 2012, the public protests staged by migrants, the celebrations after the 2015 referendum and the demonstrations after Zak Kostopoulos's death (cf. Douzinas 2013a, 2013b; Mavroudi 2013; Simiti 2014; Giovanopoulos and Mitropoulos 2011;

Papapavlou 2015). The impulse to stage an exodus into the public sphere, often from a space of secrecy, shame, disavowal and invisibility, is what ties most of these and other contemporary events together and mobilises their archives today as interconnected. To be sure, I am mixing together gender-centred and less gender-centred expressions of disobedience, mobilisation and protest; yet, as I see *Strella* haunted by their future arrival, I also see them as haunted by that previous image of Strella. This is how I want to reclaim them, to reconsider how much they were (and can continuously still be) instances of 'crossing police barricades and the civilising standards of public life, [in which] Diva Citizenship takes on as a national project the need to redefine the scale, the volume, and the erotics of "what you can do for your country"' (Berlant 1997: 224). Considering their diva citizenship characteristics means that these public mobilisations are not seen as defeated, forgotten or final; they remain, instead, always there to be redrafted, in a processual political economy that resists closure. Diva citizenship, let us not forget, is a persistent call not simply for citizenship, but also for realising the entitlements of existing citizens and the continuing disavowal of others. To that extent it is also, at the same time, a productive destabilisation of citizenship, as well as a reassemblage of citizen-ship, in the way imagined by Anna Carastathis: An effort 'to recognise and to whatever extent possible relinquish [our] entitlements as citizens in forging resistant attachments and transformative intimacies that carry possibilities for other ways of feeling, belonging and surviving together' (Carastathis 2015: 91).

In 2009, critics may have celebrated the success of *Strella* as the victory of a progressive, modern, new queer Greece over what was perhaps then seen as a long-gone traditionalist, patriarchal and homophobic past. Yet, it was to happen very soon and in the urban setting in which Strella walks at the end of her film that the rising power of the neo-fascist Golden Dawn party made itself felt in violent attacks against migrants, queers and unionist activists (Ellinas 2013); or that neonationalist movements expressed their anger against austerity in a neo-macho rhetoric that did not hide its hatred for anything falling outside the idea of traditional family values (Carastathis 2015; Kotouza 2019); or that Zak Kostopoulos would be fatally beaten in front of onlookers and their cameras. Watching the film today, one cannot underestimate how, in a queer-time reversal, *Strella* is imprinted with the phantom of this uneasy political future: As its protagonist comes out and walks outdoors in the final scenes of the film, the intersectionality and the thick archive of her demands previously implied within the film's narrative becomes more pronounced and more related to the public space that she traverses. These images of Strella walking in Athens in 2008, as they are watched and rewatched today, are imbued with what came afterwards, assemblage upon assemblage, in an economy of biopolitical realism now all the more strongly felt.

The Retrieval of Past Divas

In classic diva citizenship mode, *Strella* dragged along not only its agonistic future, but also a similarly demanding past, a difficult genealogy, voices from the queer and trans past that had made its own present possible. Lecturing on the new queer aesthetics of the film since 2010, I was confronted with these other, past stories, in the form of audience questions or, often, of people wanting to speak out, share old histories and take a stance. An archive of the past was assembling again, calling on us to retrieve possibilities, probabilities and potentials. The scenes from *Strella* were used as a catalyst in order to remember, for instance, a group of trans women sex workers who had appeared in Athens in the 1970s and 1980s and had tried for the first time to claim public space, voicing radical, but eventually disavowed demands about sexual citizenship. A classic 'gay history of Greece' would catalogue those instances as relics from the past, a prehistory of today's successful transqueer movements. However, the context I describe urged us to reconsider them as diva citizenship events – and to focus on how they had endured, how they faltered, how they could eventually be remembered and revisited as political performances in contemporary Greece, picked up by different agents and claims. We were, thus, forced to take into account diverse temporalities and contours, survivals and capitulations, moments of emergence and histories of resilience. *Strella*'s assemblage poetics, in other words, stood as a demanding genealogical gesture.

With that image of Strella in mind, one felt the need to go back and reconsider, for instance, the story of Paola Revenioti, the trans anarchist activist who was publishing her own fanzine, *Kraximo* (in English, shouting out/shaming) in the early 1980s. It was often to Paola's own queer archive that people returned after 2010 in order to reconfigure contemporary demands, or in order to use queer ephemera from a different era (see Papanikolaou 2018b). Paola herself came into public view in that same period, giving lectures, putting together hand-made documentaries, renarrating her life in new media (Karayanni 2018) and offering her own queer past as undone, redone, but also there to be politically reenergised. Something similar happened to Betty Vakalidou, another legendary trans activist from the 1970s – who was cast in the role of the trans mother figure in *Strella*. After 2010, she, too, once again became a public figure, participating in debates while also talking about her own past (see, for instance, Vakalidou 2011).

In one of the most intriguing aspects of her recent public engagement, Vakalidou was also cast by avant-garde theatre group Bijoux de Kant in 2016 in their performance *Amaranta* (Amaranths/Evergreen) as Antona, a gender-bending figure who stands up, in the middle of the performance of a different play, and recalls a story of abuse ending in her own death. A couple of scenes later, Antona would stand up again and interject another monologue, detailing another story of abuse, ending in yet another grotesque death; and then another, and another. The result is unsettling, not simply because of the violence described, but for the complex archival challenge it provokes. The name itself, Antona, is a reference to an old transqueer figure of the Athenian underworld, memoralised in Paola's photographic archives, an illustration often used to denote past queer suffering. In *Amaranta*, the fictional Antona stands up and delivers monologues penned by the contemporary author Glykeria Basdeki, written to be interjected into the performance of the one-act play *To Ftero* (*The Feather*) by Pavlos Matessis (1984), an older author known for his largely forgotten queer and gender-bending novels and plays.

Amaranta – a word that can also be freely translated as 'the Undead Ones' – was asking audiences to see disavowed gender-political histories as constantly haunted by queer affect and anti-queer violence, and *vice versa*, queer affect and the violence it confronts as haunted by its untold political histories. Thus, the performance produced its own archive trouble as an assemblage of queer, gay, Greek, contemporary, past moments of speech-capturing and asked the audience to actively take a similar stance, to continue assembling, historicising and repoliticising (cf. Sampatakakis 2017).

QUEER ASSEMBLAGES

In many central scenes of *Faster than Light* (as well as in more traditional documentaries such as *Drag Nights in Athens* [2018, directed by Thodoris Prodromidis]), we see Zak Kostopoulos/Zackie Oh walking in Athens, while giving in voice-over narration his/her thoughts on citizenship and Greece, austerity politics, homophobia, the plight of refugees in the country and the rise of neofascism on the Greek streets. The camera follows Zak/Zackie on the streets of Athens; it does the same with the other transqueer young activists appearing in the film. It also often films them when gathering, protesting, or while they are putting on their make up, getting ready to go out. These scenes are not simply motivated by an aesthetics of assemblage and an intertextual reference to this type of assemblage – for instance, to similar images in *Paris is Burning*, or to the famous walk of Strella herself in *Strella* a decade earlier. What makes them culturally and politically visible, readable and significant for the contemporary moment is an understanding of assemblage as a necessary political tactic. Assemblage is not presented here as just a visual metaphor for being-in-an-intense-biopolitical-present. It is shown as a way of making do; and the film itself, with its complicated history of production, is shown to be a product of assemblage, a processual effort to make something that was meaningful, mournful, affective and collective, before it ever became a finished project. I keep watching the walk of Zackie Oh in the snippets of *Faster than Light* released online after her death, with her voice-overs on society, violence and ways of surviving necropolitical tactics.[16] In my own assemblage of examples, in this chapter, this walk recalls both *Strella* and Katsimiris's *Mum, I'm back* as its necessary past. It also eerily, tragically, predates Kostopoulos's own death in Gladstonos's Street in 2018, in the days when s/he was still shooting for *Faster than Light* and other projects (Zak/ Zackie Oh 2019).

In the months after this untimely death, and as I participated in acts of remembrance for Zak Kostopoulos/Zackie Oh, I asked many activists the (I now realise, naive) question why they felt Kostopoulos's drag persona was equally celebrated, why s/he was mourned mostly as a trans and a transqueer activist, even though s/he had lived most of his/her life as a cis gay man.[17] 'But, don't you see', one activist told me one evening . . :

> Kostopoulos's double position in the public sphere, as both Zak Kostopoulos and Zackie Oh, underlines exactly what we have to say, makes us able to speak and to speak out: to claim identity in the making, as always in the making, but also as always demanding presence, rights, visibility, and liveability. Who are you to ask this question? Kostopoulos/Zackie Oh was one of the first activists who so publicly focused the discussion on his/her identity not as a finished position, but as an emerging part in a whole not yet (and not ever to be) concluded. In the current climate this was even more empowering, because it kept inventing space to speak from: it still does, after her/his death.

Somewhat later, as the 2019 Gay Pride in Athens finished 'exactly as it had done a year before', with pieces of Zackie Oh's final act of the 2018 event projected on the video walls around us – a gesture of mourning, as much as a statement of resilience performed in queer time – I saw another example of what my friend had meant. Gender, sexuality, performance and video walls were now becoming the assemblages for a new public emergence. What if a queer assemblage like this is neither the answer to biopolitics, nor a way out of biopolitical realism, but the unending destabilisation of their sites and forms? '*It allowed us to speak out, and to keep speaking*'.

I started this chapter with a short film and the mediatisation of a tragic killing in central Athens, before analysing and contextualising one of the most influential films of the Greek Weird Wave, the 2009 *Strella: A Woman's Way*. My aim has been twofold: on the one hand, to show how gender and sexuality participate in the assemblages emerging in the centre of today's biopolitical and necropolitical regimes. The image of a trans woman and/or a drag performer walking out and demanding public space and acknowledgment (a

Figure 7.4 a–c   *Reclaiming public space, once again: Zak Kostopoulos/Zackie Oh, in*
Faster than Light *(Kentaro Kumanomido and Thomas Anthony Owen, 2018–19); digital stills
from the project's website.*

central scene in *Mum, I'm back, Faster than light* and, of course, *Strella*) is weird not because it may be seen by some as strange, unexpected, or unhomely. It is weird because it starts from a position of ill-fitting, from a position out-of-frame, and it issues a demand for (sexual) citizenship within the frame of an intense biopolitical present. These walks are gestures of diva citizenship, unfolding in biopolitical realism and self-referentially acknowledging it – hence, their productive weirdness. My second aim was to show that it is exactly this productive relationship with biopolitical realism that might allow a film like *Strella* and *that* final walk around Athens to acquire the allegorical, the archival and queer-historical potential that it eventually would.

Diva citizenship, seen through these examples, is an assemblage of such moments of intersection between past, present and future, which demand to be respected as a genealogical exercise. In practice, this means a demand for a history of the present, one that foregrounds our intersectionality as present continuous; our need for historicisation as present archival; our citizenship claims as present processual; and our multi-layered precarity as present biopolitical.

I conclude this study with such a recontextualisation of diva citizenship in a Greek context, using a central Greek film of the Weird Wave as my main example, in order to return to a claim about weirdness that has underscored this entire book. In defiance of studies or reviews that have seen the Greek Weird Wave at best as an international opening for Greek film without much substance, and at worst as a completely disconnected intellectual/critical joke, I have preferred to over-appropriate it as a political possibility and to see the claiming of that possibility as a potentially collective assemblage. *Strella*, in that lexicon, provides a key: What if all these weird films were a way to 'live our myth in Greece', in an effort that seems as idiosyncratic, incomplete and out of frame, as it is processual, heuristic, metonymical and demanding? What if these films of the 'weird wave' were an effort to retell our story (including the story of *that* Crisis) to a new voice-over, a soundtrack that, as Berlant has it with diva citizenship's 'reprojection of one's life', would this time be completely our own? Even if that promise could not hold (and, actually, it never could), even if 'offering a new voice-over' for a social reality often meant making only a point about dissonance and out-of-tune-ness, it did produce a retelling that was also equally real, political and realistically biopolitical.

With this in mind, in these chapters I have attempted to bring the Greek Weird Wave films closer to the real (and followed others who have moved in the same direction). I have done so because the real returns anyway; sometimes as our affective metonymical relation to the extreme and the allegorical (*Dogtooth, Alps*); at other times as the shadow of power structures and disciplinary machines (*Miss Violence*), a fragmentary and now archival past/present (*Homeland*), an emptied site (*Third Kind; Attenberg*), as a collage of stories (*Washingtonia*), or as a constant irony of the effort to make it and to make do (*Suntan; Pity*). The real often also erupts in those spaces, facing those frames and forms that were trying to make sense of it in the first place, reiterating, provoking, reversing the sequence of images, thus underlining their metonymical co-existence. As I tried to show in this chapter, with the example of *Strella* being reflected in the mirror of the death of Zak Kostopoulos, it is not the films that are weird. It is their unending confrontation with the real.

Notes

1. As of May 2020 – that is, before the court case has even started – it is unclear whether Kostopoulos's sexual identity and gender fluidity played a role in the attack against him; most probably, on that occasion, it did not. On Kostopoulos's comments about the violence he had been subjected to in the past, see Palioura 2018; on similar comments by Koumarianou, see Koumarianou 2012.

2. They were presented in the media as '*noikokyraioi*', or 'family men', a term that became the target of the queer mobilisation that followed the events, along with all its hetero- and ethno-normative connotations.

3. Throughout 2019–20, a series of events were organised under the title Queer Politics/Public Memory, in memory of Zak Kostopoulos/Zackie Oh, convened by Athena Athanasiou and Dimitris Papanikolaou, with the support of Grigoris Gousousis. See https://rosalux.gr/el/event/queer-politiki-dimosia-mnimi (last accessed 20 June 2020).

4. Among the many detailed accounts of the hours and days after Kostopoulos's death, Dimitris Alexakis's tribute (2018), first posted in French on the website *Vacarme* and then translated for *e-flux*, is exemplary in its analysis of the initial popular media reaction to Kostopoulos's death, the different pieces of footage and cameras used, the phobic comments made by journalists and representatives of the police, and then the public mobilisation against them and in memory of Kostopoulos. In various parts of his text, he describes Kostopoulos's multi-media and pluri-performative public presence, as well as his intersectional activism that included being a member of refugee support groups, an HIV, LGBTQI and anti-fascist activist, as well as a vocal anti-austerity campaigner. Interestingly, in Alexakis's account all these are presented, not as unrelated actions and events, but as linked parts of an assemblage of acts, people, performances, conducts and counter-conducts.

5. Even though it was widely reported at the time and initially kept online by those who posted it, the video was eventually taken down. It remains, however, fully described in many articles that posted and commented on it. See http://www.katiousa.gr/epikairotita/prezakia-kai-gay-den-eiste-anagkaioi-oi-chrysavgites-

prokaloun-ki-eleeinologoun-sto-simeio-tis-dolofonias-tou-zak/ and https://
tvxs.gr/news/ellada/akrodeksioi-ston-topo-thanatoy-toy-zak-kostopoyloy-
prezakia-kai-gkei-den-eiste-anagkaioi, which also contain screenshots from the
video (last accessed 16 june 2020).

6. The open dialogue with movements such as Black Lives Matter is evident here,
as is the willingness of the participants to locate their mobilisation as an extension, a localisation, a reconsideration and an intersectional reappropriation of
other movements and their demands.

7. From the announcement published by fourteen activist organisations on 19
November 2018, available at https://www.facebook.com/justice4ZakZackie/
posts/463688260824192 (last accessed 16 June 2020).

8. It is interesting that, precisely as a result of its background in art history, the term
'assemblage' is nowadays often back-translated as *assemblage* (and not *agencement*)
in French discussions of precisely that Deleuze-oriented usage in gender theory
and art, as well as in anthropology. See, for instance, the French translation of
Anna Tsing's *The Mushroom at the End of the World* (2015; French transl. 2017) and
of Lorenz's *Queer Art* (2012; French transl. 2018).

9. On the aesthetics and queer ethical suggestions of the following shot, see Hanson
2014 and the insightful film essay by Schonig 2018.

10. In Greek, this phrase plays on the pun between the name Stella and the word
τρέλα (*trela*, madness).

11. The films of Constantine Giannaris are an exception, especially *From the Edge of
the City* (1997) and *Dekapentavgoustos* (2001), both quite popular with Greek audiences; see Papanikolaou 2009.

12. One cannot underestimate here the concurrent transnational influence of TV
and streaming platform programmes such as *Ru Paul's Drag Race* which, at least
since its second season (2010), has had a dedicated fanbase in Greece.

13. See, for instance, Maria Louka's 2018 Vice documentary *Drag Nights in
Athens* (directed by Thodoris Prodromidis), focusing among others on Zak
Kostopoulos: https://video.vice.com/gr/video/drag-nights-in-athens/5a4cbb
a1177dd45cf11e7fe2 (last accessed 19 June 2020).

14. On *Faster than Light*, see http://www.emare.eu/artist/kentaro-kumanomido-
thomas-anthony-owen; on the post-crisis drag scene in Athens, see Sampatakakis
2018.

15. Dellou, dressed up as Mercouri in *Stella* in this scene, is nevertheless heard singing *The Misunderstanding*, a song from *Never on Sunday*, the other well-known film
starring Mercouri. An invaluable visual and anthropological archive on the bar
Koukles is offered by Kostas Panapakides in his unpublished doctoral thesis
Drag Narratives: Staged Gender, Embodiment and Competition (2012).

16. See, for instance, the trailer video released on the project's website: https://fas-
terthanlight.wixsite.com/about and on https://vimeo.com/317329246?fbclid=
IwAR3N-7CO2jI86dRSiGdh4LJrhKy8U9nSyVOv1rua5vkJ37mQYjI6UakiZac
(last accessed 20 June 2020).

17. Even though in the last year of his life he maintained a parallel public persona

as Zackie Oh, Kostopoulos had a sustained public presence as a cis gay man since at least 2010. Of course, I realise that even posing this question of 'whom to mourn' of his public faces misses the point and is perhaps offensive for some people, as I explain in detail.

CHAPTER 8

Epilogue

WEERIE WINONA, OR THE FILM THAT ANGELOPOULOS NEVER MADE

At the 2019 Paris Book Fair, Alain Salles, the *Le Monde* journalist who has covered Greek culture and politics for years, chaired a panel on literature and the Greek Crisis.[1] 'The question of how the Greek Crisis has entered culture' was, said Salles at one point, one of phantoms, of projects undeveloped or unfinished – 'just like the phantom of the film that Theo Angelopoulos would have made, that film he was making when he died'. This is a statement that, perhaps in its willingness to find the Crisis *chef d'œuvre*, gets things so wrong that it ends up getting some of them right.

Greek cultural collectives, artists and producers have been so active during the Crisis that it may sound somewhat dismissive to suggest that the defining cultural text of that period is actually an unfinished and lost work: the film that the master of a different era would have made, had he survived a fatal accident that occured on the set of his last production. Based on how Angelopoulos had reacted to the most recent Greek and international social developments in his last films – for instance, the critically panned and now forgotten *The Dust of Time* (2008), released in Greek cinemas the same year as *Dogtooth* and *Strella* – it is very probable that *I alli thalassa/The Other Sea*, the film during whose production he died in 2012, would not have been such a game-changer anyway.

In many ways, the development described in this book, as well as the global discussion of the Weird Wave, is very much the product of this realisation. A modernist national poetics, represented so well in cinema by Angelopoulos, was itself inadequate to confront (and participate in) the complexity of a new situation. Not always referencing historical context directly, Lanthimos, Koutras, Kotzamani, Tsangari, Tzoumerkas, Economides and so many other directors often addressed issues that Angelopoulos had tackled in previous periods – such as exclusion, marginalisation, loneliness and abuse – but they did so in markedly different ways.

What Salles' statement, unexpectedly, does get right is the impulse to talk about ghosts, ghosting and haunted presences. One could, indeed, argue that the Crisis has haunted Greek cultural production in the decade after 2008 and that the cinematic Weird Wave is hauntologically related to this period and its narrativisation as 'the Greek Crisis'. For instance, how ghosted by this socio-cultural context are those empty spaces and interior (un)homely spaces in the films of the Weird Wave that I have analysed?[2]

Empty spaces and ruins, as Mark Fisher remarks, produce an eerie effect precisely because they make you think that an agent invisible and external to this scene of abandonment is really pulling the strings. And this, so Fisher claims, is very much what happens with capital, too. 'Capital is at every level an eerie entity: conjured out of nothing, capital nevertheless exerts more influence than any allegedly substantial entity' (2017: 11). Biopolitical ordering, I hasten to add, works in a similar fashion: In contrast to sovereignty, which governs through visible sanction, biopolitical governmentality rules through stimulus, through profiling and the creation of realisms. It is, therefore, largely realised by its effects and interiorisations, not by locating the moment or agent of its employment. Like capital, biopolitics is ghosting the scene, always and already.

This is exactly what I explain in Chapter 3, with the example of a scene from Lanthimos's *The Lobster*. The economic crisis and its biopolitical aspects have ghosted the Weird Wave in the same way as a (seemingly unconnected) song about undead love comes to haunt the scenes of hunting in this film, simultaneously reminding us how a narrative of the 'Zombie nation' had supported the new profiling of a population in the very same period.

However tactfully (or, in this case, untactfully) one puts it, the issue of people's lives, of lives lived or lost, of lives and deaths counted, and biopolitics and necropolitics experienced was never far away from the production/reception cycle of the cultural works that I have discussed in this book. It contributes to their lasting relevance.[3]

The context that is woven into the Weird Wave, the context within which these films have evolved and with which they have engaged was the same as the one in which people had seen their lives be at stake, discussed in new ways, reconceptualised, resignified as worthy or unworthy of protection. If the Weird Wave initially seemed to be presenting something that was out of place, that looked wrong or sounded out of tune and quite un-real, its aim was also to make us review the production of the densely biopolitical arrangements that we have ended up acknowledging as (the only) reality. Here is Mark Fisher, again, on weirdness as a concept:

> What is the weird? When we say that something is weird, what kind of feeling are we pointing to? [. . .] [T]he weird is a particular kind of perturbation. It involves a sensation of wrongness: a weird entity or object is so strange that it makes us feel that it should not exist, or at least it should not exist here.

Yet if the entity or object is here, then the categories which we have up until now used to make sense of the world cannot be valid. The weird thing is not wrong, after all: it is our conceptions that must be inadequate. (Fisher 2017: 15)

It is for this reason that I took the very term *weird* not as a description of a specific cinematic characteristic, or a film genre, but treated it as a challenge to further cultural analysis and debate. I allowed this term, alongside my intertwined analysis of biopolitics, to take me away from the framework of its initial use.

THE BIOPOLITICAL TIME OF THE WEIRD . . .

One of the unexpected protagonists of this book has been the cultural critic Mark Fisher. In Chapter 4, I explained the impact that his *Capitalist Realism* (as well as his review of *Dogtooth*) has had on my own thinking about biopolitical realism.

As I have noted in a brief footnote in Chapter 4, in his last collections of essays Fisher turned towards the unhomely, the ironic, the awkward and the eerie as modes of critical reaction to capitalist realism. Fisher's untimely death happened as his last book was going into print: Its title was *The Weird and the Eerie* (2017). There is so much in this book that would work well with my present case-studies. Films such as *Washingtonia* or *Pity* could have been read from Fisher's perspective on the weird, and *Attenberg* and *Third Kind* could serve as prime examples of his understanding of the contemporary eerie.

Moreover, the philologist in me wonders whether the very attachment of the word 'weird' to the new wave of Greek Cinema after 2009 by Anglophone critics may have something to do with the parallel rise of the interest in the literature of H. P. Lovecraft, especially among a circle of politically minded cultural critics, prominent among whom was Fisher himself. By 2010, when it started circulating as a term for Greek Cinema, the word 'weird' had, through Lovecraft's delayed impact, reentered the political lexicon. Weirdness was already thought of as a creative, affective and deconstructive response to a depleted overcapitalist world (cf. Sederholm and Weinstock 2016; Harman 2012).

At the same time, there was something that did not feel quite right with Fisher's account. The turn he proposes to a more experienced, more embodied and radical version of the unhomely usefully conveys the sense of an ending for capitalist realism.[4] Yet, it does not explain why this happens. Fisher's *The Weird and the Eerie* provides glimpses of the future, a future that looks like the setting of *Attenberg* or *Third Kind*, but it does not say how we ended up there.

It is exactly that missing itinerary that the Greek Weird Wave as a larger movement was pushing me to investigate further, with its emphasis on metonymy and its plurimodal response to an intense biopolitical present. These films contained weird and eerie affects in the sense in which Fisher describes them. But at the same time, they were participating in a much more complicated cultural and social environment, in which developing a new turn in the cinema of a small nation was also crucial. Equally crucial were the need to antagonise (expectations for) national allegory, (the instrumentalisation of) cinematic defamiliarisation, the expression of a sense of social unease and disarray and the development of a 'cinema about (not) being governed'. What brought all this together and also reinforced the films' weird and eerie moments was an expansive poetics of metonymy. I have tried to underline this in every chapter, most notably perhaps when discussing the importance of metonymic allegories in the Weird Wave.

As I have mentioned time and again, the poetics of metonymy became so crucial in biopolitical realism precisely because there is an underlying structural homology between the two. In many ways, the biopolitical is a metonymic modality of power. Unlike the metaphorics of sovereignty, the metonymics of biopolitics work by binding people together, by marking bodies synecdochically as members (or non-members) of a population, by crafting milieus as containers of life that matters (and using them as interchangeable with that form of life), by organising protocols of belonging and of proscription with the help of archival institutions, by emphasising the expansiveness and interiorisation of the biopolitical on the basis of endless metonymic chains. In chapter after chapter, I have shown how the Weird Wave engaged in diverse ways with the metonymic while it was developing as a cinema of biopolitics. In this context, the Weird Wave's metonymic poetics inquired about biopolitical sites (*Third Kind*), cultural arrangements and a sense of ennui (*Washingtonia, Attenberg*), national context, citizenship, kinship, discipline and affect within biopolitics. Last, but not least, the metonymic poetics of the Weird Wave helped me illustrate larger creative counter-currents such as the ones I have described in the final chapters as archive trouble and assemblage. The weird and the eerie, as Fisher describes them, are affects, yet, I argued, they are affects that result from all these processes, intricately connected to their contexts – which they also help to analytically reconsider.

This has been the more complex aim of my book: to highlight how intertwined the affective, the analytical and the political potentials of the weird were in a particular (biopolitical) context and cinematic production. One might note here how evident this intertwinement was, for instance, in my account of the collective *The Lost Highway of Greek Cinema*. As I stated in Chapter 3, even the title of this collective promotes an incitement to a different history of Greek Cinema, an alternative genealogical gesture, as well as a transnational reference to films such as David Lynch's *The Lost Highway* and the compelling and resting power of their weird affect.

> There is certainly something that the weird, the eerie and the *unheimlich* share. They are all affects, but they are also modes: modes of film and fiction, modes of perception, ultimately, you might even say, modes of being. Even so, they are not quite genres. (Fisher 2017: 9)

If one continues to survey Greek Cinema in the light of what I have argued in this book, one might claim that in recent years we are seeing a more decisive turn towards the weird as affect, mode of perception and mode of being. Examples abound: the recent films by Konstantina Kotzamani (*Limbo* [2016] and *Electric Swann* [2019]), Jacqueline Lentzou (*Hector Malot, the Last Day of the Year*, 2017), Evangelia Kranioti (*Obscuro Barroco*, 2018) or Elina Psykou's *Son of Sofia* (2017) and Angelos Frantzis's *Still River* (2018); equally so a turn to a Lovecraftian weird that exploits the neogothic (Yannis Veslemes's *Norway* [2014]) and political fantasy (Alexandros Voulgaris's *Thread* [2016]). As I write the closing lines of this book, I am deeply aware that the directions that these later films take have already opened up a new chapter for the Weird Wave – one that could be less obsessed with power structures and governmentality, and more focused on affect and cruel optimism.

However, if one looks closer, one realises that – even with these films – we are still firmly within the poetics of metonymic allegory, of archive trouble and of assemblage. This is to say that weird affect in these films still demands to be historicised within and through their biopolitical realism, something that certainly complicates Fisher's optic and politicises it more concretely.

See, for instance Vasilis Kekatos's *The Distance Between Us and the Sky*, the short film that was awarded the Palme d'Or in its category at the Cannes Film Festival of 2019 – ten years after Lanthimos's *Dogtooth* had started its long international career with a win at the same festival. Once again there is an emptied space, a character stranded, awkward dialogue, only that now the deadlock is temporary, there seems to be a way out and it is more confidently sought: as a matter of perception, of affect, of being – in that order.

In an empty gas station in a rural void, two young men meet and start speaking in whispers. They exchange half-saids and awkward metaphors, as they negotiate distance, movement and place(ment). This is a cruising ritual in an eerie setting; it is equally the story of someone stranded in the middle of the night, desperately trying to raise money for a ticket to Athens. The built structure of the gas station which we see with a single establishing shot only halfway into the film, the night lighting and the way in which individual bodies are framed and shaped by the frames recall paintings by Edward Hopper, as much as an already recognizable Weird tradition.

The first man asks the second, a passing motorist in leather gear, if he can help him raise the money he needs. He could offer something in return, he says, in slow exchanges, as the hand-held camera pursues them in extreme close-ups. He could offer, for instance, an opened pack of cigarettes; weed; two origami birds he holds in his hands; or he could even offer the moon, since the origami birds could cover the distance and reach it.

Reader, you have seen this before: In order to make do in that evening of poverty, loneliness and displacement, what this man negotiates is a take on metonymy. As the title of the short film and the *mise-en-scène* keep stressing, the effort here is to turn the most vertical metaphor of romance (moonlight) into an economy of contiguity, into metonymy ('the *distance between* here and the sky').

While they gaze at the distance between them and the sky, the two men equally negotiate the horizontal distance between themselves, in slow steps, the camera's extreme close-ups slightly shaking as it also tries to focus on the decreasing space between. This is a choreography that slowly settles their

Figure 8.1a–d *Negotiating distance and touch, from* The Distance Between Us and the Sky (Vasilis Kekatos, 2019)*; digital stills.*

touch, their embrace and the – indeed, awkward – hugging of their bodies, as they finally ride the motorbike to travel to Athens together. The last shot, panning together with the motorcycle as it speeds along the coastal road to the metropolis, focuses on this weird embrace and ends there, with that assemblage of bodies, wheels, night lights and dawn. The eerie and the weird are now a constellation of affects that have found their place, but the point of the film is not its confidence in having them rearticulated. It is, rather, its insistent reliance on the long and complicated (social, economic, sexual, aesthetic, cinematic) history ghosting this assemblage, even when (or especially when) it is not directly referenced in the picture.

. . . AND THE RESTING RITUALS OF THE EERIE

The most moving scene in Alexandros Voulgaris's 2019 feature film *Winona* comes, as one might expect, towards the end; yet, it comes, rather unexpectedly, from what is presented as a discussion about copyright. The four protagonists who have been spending their day frolicking alone on an empty beach dive back into the water, the camera following them, screening their bodies, as they start touching, supporting each other, caressing, kissing, singing, crying. It is already seventy minutes into this very weird film, and it is only now that one begins to realise that this whole day of girlish leisure was always meant – within the story, but also in terms of the gesture that the film makes – as a mourning ritual.

The four have spent the day laughing and playing all sorts of games (including 'remember all the films by Woody Allen in a sequence – titles in English' and 'which Spielberg film would we be, if we were one') and repeating the nicknames they take from well-known Hollywood and world cinema canon actresses – 'Meryl', 'Julietta', 'Jennifer Jason', 'Eiko'. But now, as the day is ending, the four young women have started to cry for their younger sister who has, we now suddenly hear, committed suicide – a fifth sister who 'would have become a great dancer' and went by the nickname of 'Winona'. This empty beach where they are is fully haunted by her absence; it was her favourite place. Or maybe it was not, as the viewer is never fully certain whether the girls are mourning for a real or an imaginary lost sibling – or whether they are even performing yet another cinema-inflected joke, based on Sofia Coppola's *The Virgin Suicides* (1999). Either way, as they hold on to each other, half in the water, their bodies a chain of meaning, mourning, quotation and affect, even then they keep switching roles and genres, referring to other films, rehearsing imaginary scripts and muddling temporal continuities.

One of the sisters says: 'If we were an American film with a happy ending, we would now hear Madonna's *True Blue* [which was Winona's favourite tune]; the credits would roll on, and that would be it, end of film'. 'But, of course, we would never have the money to pay for the copyright', another replies. 'So, we would lip sync it without making any sound'.

This is when, in imitation of what the imaginary film would be, of the resourceful devices of the very film in which they are, but also in honour of the sister who has gone, they start lip-syncing. Without making any sound. Madonna's *True Blue*.

The scene's emotional charge is a direct result of it being haunted by what it cannot fully say, what it cannot fully sing, what it cannot fully locate, what it cannot confront. The scene is framed not only by the knowledge of what and who is not there, but also by the shared effort to console.

I cannot possibly quote *True Blue* here either – academic rule number one: never quote internationally copyrighted lyrics. Or else I would have to spend months and grants trying to clear copyright, only to be able to reiterate what true love is and where happiness lies. But even if I cannot quote, I can certainly mimic on the page those girls' soundless singing of Madonna's early hit, in the hope of replicating some of its eeriness.

... ...
... ...
... ...
... .
... ...

'We find the eerie more readily in landscapes partially emptied of the human', says Fisher (2017: 11). Or, we go to the emptied and the ruined in order to experience the eerie, in order to think why it does not sound right; in order to fantasise about who is responsible for this depletion, these ruins, this disappearance; in order to make out of it a ritual of reassembling, of mourning, of returning and of remembering.

An alternative history of the Greek Weird Wave – one of the many versions I was not able to rehearse in this book – could have started with *Winona*'s director, Alexandros Voulgaris. A proponent of D-I-Y avant-garde filmmaking and a prolific musician and DJ with a devoted audience (see Chapter 3), Voulgaris's film- and music-making unfold in parallel, very much as an auto-fiction in multimedia chapters. Since the early 2000s, Voulgaris has been making low-budget – literally home-made – films that could be considered the unsung precursors and continuing proponents of a deeply engaged Weird Wave. Most of these films are not only made in a world apart, but they also operate as such: Enclosure and disjuncture is consciously proposed as an existential, a political, an aesthetic and a low-budget positioning.

Thus we have *Winona*, shot with a Kodak 16 mm camera on an empty

Figure 8.2   *Four girls and a dog during a day on the beach, from* Winona *(Alexandros Voulgaris, 2019); digital still.*

Figure 8.3a–d   *A chain of bodies reflecting, reflected, laughing, dancing, crying and mourning, from* Winona *(Alexandros Voulgaris, 2019); digital stills.*

beach of the island of Andros in May 2018, starring four of the most recognizable actresses of the generation of artists that grew out of the decade and the cultural texts on which this book focuses: Sofia Kokkali, Iro Bezou, Dafni Patakia and Anthi Efstratiadou. As with many of Voulgaris's projects, in

Winona the effect of the (un)homely is not simply achieved through extrinsic formal choices, such as the type of camera used, calculated here to bring a home-video aesthetics from a previous era. It is also the result of the fact that a closely-knit community labours to produce the film through gift economy and co-belonging, and thus makes its autobiographical references take on a deeper collective meaning in both content and form.

Genre aporia, intertextual conundrum, film essay on the structure of feeling and the purpose of commonality, but more than that, emotion on the edge: *Winona* is a bubble filled so much with affect that you constantly feel it is about to burst. I saw it first in February 2020 in Athens in the Astor, whose role in the promotion and expansion of the Weird Wave I discussed in Chapter 3. 'Weird Wave', the small independent company that owns Astor, had taken the film's distribution rights and was turning its first screenings into small celebratory events.

Was this phrase, 'weird wave', now a confident banner at the beginning of the film's credits, what made us think of *Winona* as announcing the incomplete ending of an entire era? The discussions after the screening revolved around the idea that the film somehow reflects on the experience of a thick decade and works on a melancholy that is here to stay, even if official political discourse persists in declaring the Crisis 'over'. (Ironically, we were watching this film just one month before Greece and the world went into complete lockdown in 2020.) The discussion also turned to Mary Tsoni – the charismatic dancer, actress, singer, avant-garde performer and lightning stage presence who had tragically died in May 2017, at the age of thirty. There was a time, before Athens became the cool art-crisis-capital of Europe, when the most subterranean thing you could do in the city was to catch a concert by Mary and the Boy, the creative duo Tsoni had formed with Alexandros Voulgaris (a.k.a. The Boy). Little survives on the net – but it is still enough to show exactly why assemblage is so crucial a concept in order to understand the socio-cultural importance of such performances.[5] Tsoni's short life has marked the thick decade that I have attempted to describe in this book, in ways that cannot possibly be contained in the international obituaries that announced her death in reference only to her role as the younger daughter in *Dogtooth*, under the banner 'Dogtooth Star Dies at 30'.[6] For many, *Winona* was Voulgaris's attempt to stage a belated wake, for all that thick past, for all that is difficult to narrate in a linear way and for her.

As I rewatched the film from this perspective, I kept thinking of those told and untold stories that have made and keep returning to remake the Weird Wave; of all those other paths that this book could have taken; the different narratives of the first decade of the Crisis, which will keep cropping up in the archival presents still unfolding; the unfinished projects; the talent and the possibilities, the options and the collectives, the affective energy spent and squandered; the hand-made heterotopic assemblages that tried to stand and to make do in a dystopic biopolitical present.

You can pinpoint the official beginnings of the Greek Weird Wave as you wish – a family behind four walls screaming, a trans woman claiming public space in a damaged social sphere, a girl knocking out her canine tooth in front of a mirror, or a long review in an international newspaper naming and framing a small local film production. But for me at this moment, and for this book, there is the sense of a circle closing. It ends with four young women and a hand-held camera mourning those (projects, contexts, genres, archives, sovereignties, lives, persons, bodies, touches – and words) that cannot be there, but still stand close by. The four women sing silently for those who can be felt, who can be inferred, who can still be held, who are asked to remain, even if this present absence still rings weird. This silent song is what overflows from lives that demand to have mattered, no matter the place they are assigned in biopolitical sorting; this silent song is the staying, continuing, ritual of the eerie at a time of biopolitical realism.

Because, as the girls start opening their mouths for Madonna's *True Blue* and no voice comes out, you still know that they are singing; you still know that there is singing; that there are words; that there is a gaping presence and then more.

There is that inescapable, biopolitical body. And then, there is the eerie shadow of the equally persistent question, that unending assemblage of *what-happens-to-the-heart*. Look . . . how weirdly . . . it turns up to claim its part.

Notes

1. The event was titled 'Radiographie littéraire d'une crise: Écrivains face à une quête d'identité nouvelle et collective'. I reconstruct the quotation from the notes I took at the time; the translation is mine.
2. Some key films of the Weird Wave make this their central point. Thus, for instance, Sofia Exarchou's *Park* (2016) and Ektoras Lygizos's *Boy Eating the Bird's Food* (2012).
3. The new relevance that recent Greek Cinema was felt to have during the COVID-19 emergency illustrates this well. See, for instance, the number of Greek short films that prominently featured at the online festival *My Darling Quarantine*, put together in March 2020 by programmers from the biggest international festivals, with the express aim to showcase films relevant to the 2020 global biopolitical emergency. https://www.talkingshorts.com/festivals/my-darling-quarantine-short-film-festival (last accessed 16 June 2020).
4. Fisher bases his analysis of the weird and the eerie on both earlier and contemporary

cultural texts, but it is clear that he proposes the two terms as crucial for the period and the environment in which he writes.

5. See, for instance, https://www.youtube.com/watch?v=ORhWJSfANyU
6. https://www.indiewire.com/2017/05/dogtooth-mary-tsoni-dies-at-30-yorgos-lanthimos-1201814405/

Bibliography

Aaron, M. (ed.) (2004) *New Queer Cinema: A Critical Reader*. Edinburgh: Edinburgh University Press.

Aftab, K. (2013) '*Miss Violence* Examines the Malaise in Greek Society', *Arts & Culture*, 10 December <https://www.thenational.ae/arts-culture/miss-violence-examines-the-malaise-in-greek-society-1.286211> (last accessed 8 June 2020).

Agamben, G. (2014) 'For a Theory of Destituent Power', *Chronos/Time*, <http://www.chronosmag.eu/index.php/g-agamben-for-a-theory-of-destituent-power.html> (last accessed 8 June 2020).

Agamben, G. (2011) 'Nymphs', in J. Khalip and R. Mitchell (eds), *Releasing the Image: From Literature to New Media*. Stanford: Stanford University Press. pp. 60–80.

Agamben, G. (2000) *Means without End: Notes on Politics*. Minneapolis, MN: University of Minnesota Press.

Agamben, G. (1998) *Image et mémoire*. Paris: Hoëbeke.

Ahmad, A. (1987) 'Jameson's Rhetoric of Otherness and the "National Allegory"', *Social Text*, 17, pp. 3–25.

Aleksic, T. (2016) 'Sex, Violence, Dogs and the Impossibility of Escape: Why Contemporary Greek Film is so Focused on Family', *Journal of Greek Media & Culture*, 2 (2), pp. 155–71.

Alexakis, D. (2018) '"Like a Prayer": In Memory of Zak Kostopoulos', *E-flux Conversations*, 2 November <https://conversations.e-flux.com/t/like-a-prayer-in-memory-of-zak-kostopoulos/8516> (last accessed 8 June 2020).

Alexandrakis, O. (2016) 'Incidental Activism: Graffiti and Political Possibility in Athens, Greece', *Cultural Anthropology*, 31 (2), pp. 272–96.

Anagnostou, Y. (2018) 'Nation, Diaspora, Homeland, TRANS', *Ergon: Greek/American Arts and Letters* <https://ergon.scienzine.com/article/essays/zak-kostopoulos> (last accessed 8 June 2020).

Andrew, D. (1984) *Concepts in Film Theory*. Oxford: Oxford University Press.

Antiohos, G. (2009) 'Kinimatografistes stin omihli. To elliniko cinema authadiazei' (Filmmakers in the Mist: Greek Cinema Speaks Back). *Athinorama*, 5 November 2009 <https://www.athinorama.gr/cinema/article/kinfistes_stin_omixli_-7762.html> (last accessed 8 June 2020).

Arfara, K. (2014) 'Reframing the Real: The Blitz Theatre Group and the Awareness of Time', *Gramma: Journal of Theory and Criticism*, 22 (2), pp. 147–61.

Arhitektones (2001) 'Aerodromio tou ellinikou' ('Ellinikon Airport', special folder) *Arhitektones* 28, pp. 78–105.

Arte (2016) 'Tracks: La nouvelle vague du cinéma grec'. TV Programme first shown on ARTE channel (France/Germany), 5 March 2016. Available at: <https://www.youtube.com/watch?v=53MsgZz5ipw> (last accessed 8 June 2020).

Arte (2012) *Square: Special Grèce*. ARTE, first shown 25 March 2012. Dir. Alexis Favitski.

Arte (2011) 'Grèce: Crise et cinéma'. *ARTE journal*, ARTE, first shown 15 November 2011.

Astrinaki, E. (2015) Film series, *Fight the Power: Films from the P.I.G.S.* <https://as.nyu.edu/content/nyu-as/as/departments/hellenic/events/2015/film-series-fight-the-power-films-from-the-pigs.html> (last accessed 8 June 2020).

Athanasatou, A. (2001) *Ellinikos Kinimatografos (1950–1967): Laiki Mnimi kai Ideologia (Greek Cinema [1950–1967]: Popular Memory and Ideology)*. Athens: Finatec Publications.

Athanasiou A, V. Kolocotroni and D. Papanikolaou (2018), 'On the Politics of Queer Resistance and Survival: Athena Athanasiou in Conversation with Vassiliki Kolocotroni and Dimitris Papanikolaou', *Journal of Greek Media and Culture*, 4 (2), pp. 269–80.

Athanasiou, A. (2017) *Agonistic Mourning: Political Dissidence and the Women in Black*. Edinburgh: Edinburgh University Press.

Athanasiou, A. (2016) 'Becoming Engaged, Surprising Oneself', *Philosophy & Society*, 27 (2), pp. 453–58.

Athanasiou, A. (2012) *I Krisi os "Katastasi Ektaktis Anagkis": Kritikes kai Antistaseis (Crisis as 'State of Emergency': Critiques and Resistances)*. Athens: Savalas.

Attridge, D. (2004) *J. M. Coetzee and the Ethics of Reading*. Chicago and London: The University of Chicago Press.

Atwood, M. (1985) *The Handmaid's Tale*. Toronto: McClelland & Stewart.

Audier, S. (2015) *Penser le "néoliberalisme": Le Moment néolibéral, Foucault et la crise du socialisme*. Lormont: Le bord de l'eau.

Bakogiannopoulos, G. (1993) 'I iposchesi enos nearou kinimatografou: Ena sintomo chroniko mias diskolis porias' ('The Promise of a Young Cinema: A Brief Chronicle of a Difficult Trajectory'), in G. Bakogiannopoulos (ed.), *Cinemythology: Retrospective Presentation of Greek Cinema*. Athens: Greek Film Centre, pp. 13–35.

Ball, K., K. Haggerty and D. Lyon (eds) (2012), *Routledge Handbook of Surveillance Studies*. London: Routledge.

Barker, J. (2009) *The Tactile Eye: Touch and the Cinematic Experience*. Berkeley, CA: University of California Press.

Barotsi, R. (2016) 'Whose Crisis? *Dogtooth* and the Invisible Middle Class', *Journal of Greek Media and Culture*, 2 (2), pp. 173–86.

Basea, E. (2016) 'The "Greek Crisis" through the Cinematic and Photographic Lens: From "Weirdness" and Decay to Social Protest and Civic Responsibility', *Visual Anthropology Review*, 32 (1), pp. 61–72.

Basea, E. (2014) 'Poverty Porn: Performing the National and Mapping the Cosmopolitical in Contemporary New Wave Films'. Paper delivered at Columbia University, New York <https://hellenic.columbia.edu/files/hellenic/content/040114%20Basea.pdf> (last accessed 8 June 2020).

Basea, E. (2011) *Literature and the Greek Auteur: Film Adaptations in the Greek Cinema d'Auteur*. PhD thesis, University of Oxford.

Batycka, D. (2017) 'Cultural Diplomacy and Artwashing at Documenta in Athens', *Hyperallergic*, 12 June <https://hyperallergic.com/384199/cultural-diplomacy-and-artwashing-at-documenta-in-athens/> (last accessed 8 June 2020).

Baumbach, N., D. R. Young and G. Yue (2016) 'Introduction: For a Political Critique of Culture', *Social Text*, 34 (2), pp. 1–20.

Bazin, A. (2004) *What Is Cinema? Vol. 2. Essays selected and translated by Hugh Gray. Forewords by François Truffaut and Dudley Andrew*. Berkeley: University of California Press.

Behrent, M. C. (2016) 'Liberalism and Humanism: Michel Foucault and the Free-Market Creed, 1976–1979', in D. Zamora and M. C. Behrent (eds), *Foucault and Neoliberalism*, Cambridge: Polity Press, pp. 24–63.

Bell, V. (2012) 'Foucault's Familial Scenes: Kangaroos, Crystals, Continence and Oracles', in R. Duschinsky and L. A. Rocha (eds), *Foucault, the Family and Politics*. New York: Palgrave Macmillan, pp. 39–62.

Benjamin, W. (2006) *The Writer of Modern Life: Essays on Charles Baudelaire*. Cambridge: Belknap Press.

Benjamin, W. (1998) *The Origin of German Tragic Drama*, reprint trans. by John Osborne. London: Verso.

Berlant, L. (2011) *Cruel Optimism*. Durham: Duke University Press.

Berlant, L. (1997) *The Queen of America Goes to Washington City: Essays on Sex and Citizenship*. Durham: Duke University Press.

Beugnet, M. (2011) 'The Wounded Screen', in T. Horeck and T. Kendall (eds), *The New Extremism in Cinema: From France to Europe*. Edinburgh: Edinburgh University Press, pp. 18–38.

Boletsi, M. and I. Celik-Rappas (2020) 'Introduction: Ruins in Contemporary Greek Literature, Art, Cinema, and Public space', *Journal of Modern Greek Studies* 38 (2), pp. vii–xxv.

Boletsi, M. (2020) 'Rethinking Stasis and Utopianism: Empty Placards and Imaginative Boredom in the Greek Crisis-scape', in M. Boletsi, J. Houwen and L. Minnaard (eds), *Languages of Resistance, Transformation, and Futurity in Mediterranean Crisis-Scapes: From Crisis to Critique*. London: Palgrave Macmillan, pp. 267–90.

Boletsi, M. (2018) 'Faith, Irony, Salt, and Possible Impossibilities: J. M. Coetzee's *The Childhood of Jesus* in Conversation with Zbigniew Herbert's "From Mythology"', in T. Mehigan and Christian Moser (eds), *The Intellectual Landscape in the Work of J.M. Coetzee*. Suffolk: Camden House, pp. 133–57.

Boletsi, M. (2016) 'From the Subject of the Crisis to the Subject in Crisis: Middle Voice on Greek Walls', *Journal of Greek Media & Culture*, 2 (1), pp. 3–28.

Boljkovac, N. (2013) *Untimely Affect: Gilles Deleuze and the Ethics of Cinema*. Edinburgh: Edinburgh University Press.

Bordwell, D. (2017) 'Shot-Consciousness', 16 January <http://www.davidbordwell.net/blog/2007/01/16/shot-consciousness/> (last accessed 8 June 2020).

Bordwell, D. and Thompson, K. (2003) *Film History: An Introduction*, 2nd edition. New York & London: McGraw Hill Higher Education.

Bouras, D. (2010) 'Thravsmata, epanalipseis kai mia megali kravgi' ('Fragments, Repetitions and a Big Scream'), *Kathimerini*, 3 October <https://www.kathimerini.gr/406687/article/politismos/arxeio-politismoy/8raysmata-epanalhyeis-kai-mia-megalh-kraygh> (last accessed 8 June 2020).

Brinkema, E. (2012) 'On Dogtooth' <www.worldpicturejournal.com/WP_7/Brinkema.html> (last accessed 8 July 2020).

Brody, R. (2016) 'The Petty Laments of Yorgos Lanthimos's "*The Lobster*"', *The New Yorker*, 23 May <https://www.newyorker.com/culture/richard-brody/the-petty-laments-of-yorgos-lanthimoss-the-lobster> (last accessed 8 June 2020).

Brophy, P. (2011) 'The Prisonhouse of Language: Yorgos Lanthimos's *Dogtooth* Makes Greek Mythology Modern', *Film Comment*, 26 (2), p. 16.

Brown, W. (2015) *Undoing the Demos: Neoliberalism's Stealth Revolution*. Cambridge: MIT Press.

Butler, J. (1990) *Gender Trouble: Feminism and the Subversion of Identity*. New York: Routledge.

Butler, J., Z. Gambetti and L. Sabsay, L. (eds) (2016) *Vulnerability in Resistance*. Durham: Duke University Press.

Butler, J. (2015) *Notes Towards a Performative Theory of Assembly*. Cambridge: Harvard University Press.

Butler, J. and Athanasiou, A. (2013) *Dispossession: The Performative in the Political*. Cambridge: Polity Press.

Calotychos V., L. Papadimitriou and Y. Tzioumakis (2016) 'On Solidarity, Collaboration and Independence: Athina Rachel Tsangari Discusses Her Films and Greek Cinema', *Journal of Greek Media and Culture*, 2 (2), pp. 237–53.

Campbell, T. (2017) *The Techne of Giving: Cinema and the Generous Forms of Life*. New York: Fordham University Press.

Carastathis, A. (2016) *Intersectionality: Origins, Contestations, Horizons*. Lincoln & London: University of Nebraska Press.

Carastathis, A. (2015) 'The Politics of Austerity and the Affective Economy of Hostility: Racialised and Gendered Violence and Crises of Belonging in Greece', *Feminist Review*, 109 (1), pp. 73–95.

Celik, Ipek A. (2013) 'Family as Internal Border in *Dogtooth*', in R. Merivirta, K. Ahonen, H. Mulari and R. Mahka (eds), *Frontiers of Screen History: Imagining European Borders in Cinema, 1945–2010*. Bristol and Chicago: Intellect, pp. 217–33.

Chalkou, M. (2012) 'A New Cinema of Emancipation: Tendencies of Independence in Greek Cinema of 2000s', *Interactions: Studies in Communications and Culture*, 3 (2), pp. 243–61.

Chalkou, M. (2008) *Towards the Creation of "Quality" Greek National Cinema in the 1960s*. PhD thesis, University of Glasgow.

Coavoux, S. (2018) 'Beyond Masculinity, the Female Gaze, and the Greek Crisis: Exploring Athina Rachel Tsangaris's *Chevalier* and its Particularizing Reception', *Journal of Research in Gender Studies* 8 (2), pp. 144–68.

Coavoux, Sophie (2013), '*Strella* (film de Panos Koutras, 2009), une version queer du mythe d'Œdipe', *transtext(e)s, transcultures*, 8 <https://journals.openedition.org/transtexts/487> (last accessed 8 June 2020).

Comanducci, C. (2017) 'Empty Gestures: Mimesis and Subjection in the Cinema of Yorgos Lanthimos', *APPARATUS: Film, Media and Digital Cultures in Central and Eastern Europe*, 5 (1) <http://www.apparatusjournal.net/index.php/apparatus/article/view/56/128> (last accessed 8 June 2020).

Constantinidis, S. E. (2000) 'Greek Film and the National Interest: A Brief Preface', *Journal of Modern Greek Studies*, 18 (1), pp. 1–12.

Cooper, M. (2017) *Family Values: Between Neoliberalism and the New Social Conservatism*. London: Zone Books.

Cooper, S. (2016) 'Narcissus and *The Lobster*', *Studies in European Cinema*, 13 (2), pp. 163–76.

Culler, J. (2001) *The Pursuit of Signs: Semiotics, Literature, Deconstruction*. Ithaca: Cornell University Press.

Dalakoglou, D. and G. Agelopoulos (eds) (2018) *Critical Times in Greece: Anthropological Engagements with the Crisis*. London: Routledge.

Dalakoglou, D. and A. Vradis, A. (eds.) (2011) *Revolt and Crisis in Greece: Between a Present Yet to Pass and a Future Still to Come*. Oakland: AK Press.

Dardot, P. and Laval, C. (2017) *The New Way of the World: On Neoliberal Society*, trans. by Gregory Elliott. London: Verso.

Davies, T., A. Isakjee and S. Dhesi (2017) 'Violent Inaction: The Necropolitical Experience of Refugees in Europe', *Antipode: A Radical Journal of Geography*, 49 (5), pp. 1263–84.

de Boever, V. (2013) *Narrative Care: Biopolitics and the Novel*. New York: Bloomsbury.

de Lagasnerie, G. (2012) *La Dernière lecon de Michel Foucault: Sur le néolibéralisme, la théorie et la politique*. Paris: Fayard.

DeLanda, M. (2016) *Assemblage Theory*. Edinburgh: Edinburgh University Press.

Deleuze, G. and F. Guattari (2004) [1972] *Anti-Oedipus*, trans. by Robert Hurley, Mark Seem and Helen R. Lane. London and New York: Continuum.

Deleuze, G. and F. Guattari (2004) [1980] *A Thousand Plateaus*, trans. by Brian Massumi. London and New York: Continuum.

Deleuze, G. and F. Guattari (1986) [1975] *Kafka: Toward a Minor Literature*, trans. by Dana Polan. Minneapolis and London: University of Minnesota.

De Luca, T. (2014) *Realism of the Senses in World Cinema: The Experience of Physical Reality*. London: I.B. Tauris.

del Valle Alcalá, R. (2019) 'Servile Life: Subjectivity, Biopolitics, and the Labor of the Individual in Kazuo Ishiguro's *Never Let Me Go*', *Cultural Critique*, 102, pp. 37–60.

Demopoulos, M. (ed.) (1995) *Le Cinéma Grec*. Paris: Centre Georges Pompidou.

Demos, T. J. (2017) 'Learning from Documenta 14: Athens, Post-democracy, and Decolonisation', *Third Text: Critical Perspectives on Contemporary Art and Culture* <thirdtext. org/demos-documenta> (last accessed 8 June 2020).

Derrida, J. (1996) *Archive Fever: A Freudian Impression*. Chicago: University of Chicago Press.

Didi-Huberman, G. and N. Giannari (2017) *Passer, quoi qu'il en coûte*. Paris: Les Éditions de Minuit.

Didi-Huberman, G. (ed.) (2016) *Soulèvements*. Paris: Gallimard/Jeu de Paume.

Didi-Huberman, G. (2013) *Phalènes: Essais sur l'apparition, 2*. Paris: Éditions de Minuit.

Didi-Huberman, G. (2011) *Atlas ou le gai savoir inquiet: L'Oeil de l'Histoire, 3*. Paris: Éditions de Minuit.

Dimadi, I. (2013) 'The Weird Wave of Greek Theatre', *Athinorama*, 2 December, <https:// www.athinorama.gr/theatre/article/the_weird_wave_of_greek_theatre-1001581.html> (last accessed 8 June 2020)

Dirven, R. and Pörings, R. (eds) (2002) *Metaphor and Metonymy in Comparison and Contrast*. Berlin: De Gruyter Mouton.

Doane, M. A. (2007) 'Indexicality: Trace and Sign: Introduction', *differences: a journal of feminist cultural studies*, 18 (1), pp. 1–6.

Domingo, A. (2018) 'Analyzing Zombie Dystopia as Neoliberal Scenario: An Exercise in Emancipatory Catastrophism', *Frontiers in Sociology*, 3 (1), pp. 1–9.

Donzelot, J. (2005) *La Police des familles*. Paris: Éditions de Minuit.

Douzinas, C. (2013a) 'Athens Rising', *European Urban and Regional Studies*, 20 (1), pp. 134–38.

Douzinas, C. (2013b) *Philosophy and Resistance in the Crisis*. Cambridge: Polity Press.

Duschinsky, R. and Rocha, L. A. (eds) (2012) *Foucault, the Family and Politics*. New York: Palgrave Macmillan.

ElCulture, (2016) 'Atikon kai Apollon, dyo simantikoi, istorikoi kinimatografoi tis Athinas kai i syntomi istoria tous ('Atikon and Apollon, Two Important, Historical Cinemas of Athens and Their Brief History') <https://www.elculture.gr/blog/article/αττικόν-και-απόλλων/> (last accessed 8 June 2020).

Eleftheriadis, K. (2015) 'Queer Responses to Austerity: Insights from the Greece of Crisis', *ACME: An International e-Journal for Critical Geographies*, 14 (4), pp. 1032–57.

Eleftheriotis, D. (2020) 'Introspective Cosmopolitanism: The Family in the Greek Weird Wave', *Journal of Greek Media & Culture*, 6 (1), pp. 3–27.

Eleftheriotis, D. (2010) *Cinematic Journeys: Film and Movement*. Edinburgh: Edinburgh University Press.

Eleftheriotis, D. (2001) *Popular Cinemas of Europe: Studies of Texts, Contexts and Frameworks*. London: Continuum.

Ellinas, A. A. (2013) 'The Rise of Golden Dawn: The New Face of the Far Right in Greece', *South European Society and Politics*, 18 (4), pp. 543–65.

Elsaesser, T. (2018) 'National, Transnational, and Intermedial Perspectives in Post-2008 European Cinema', in B. Kaklamanidou and A. Corbalán (eds), *Contemporary European Cinema: Crisis Narratives and Narratives in Crisis*. London: Routledge, pp. 20–36.

Elsaesser T. (2009) 'World Cinema: Realism, Evidence, Presence', in L. Nagib and C. Mello (eds), *Realism and the Audiovisual Media*. London: Palgrave Macmillan, pp. 3–19.

Enwezor, O. (2015) 'Documentary/Vérité: Bio-Politics, Human Rights and the Figure of "Truth" in Contemporary Art', *Australian and New Zealand Journal of Art*, 5 (1), pp. 11–42.

Enwezor, O. (2008) *Archive Fever: Uses of the Document in Contemporary Art*. New York: International Centre of Photography.

Evers, E., M. Holzhey and G. Jansen (eds) (2014) *Living with Pop: A Reproduction of Capitalist Realism*. Köln: Walther König.

Exarchou, S. (2010) 'Interview' with *35 mm.gr* <https://vimeo.com/11064307> (last accessed 8s June 2020).

Feder, E. K. (2007) *Family Bonds: Genealogies of Race and Gender*. Oxford: Oxford University Press.

Feliciano, M. (2019) *Yorgos Lanthimos and Realism*, video essay <https://www.youtube.com/watch?v=3Av-iXJoufs> (last accessed 8 June 2020).

Filippou, E. (2017) *Otan Otan* ('When When'). Athens: MNP.

Filippou, E. (2009) *Kapoios Milaei Monos tou Kratontas Ena Potiri Gala* ('Somebody Talks to Himself Holding a Glass of Milk'). Athens: MNP.

Fisher, M. (2017) *The Weird and the Eerie*. London: Repeater.

Fisher M. (2014) *Ghosts of My Life: Writings on Depression, Hauntology and Lost Futures*. Winchester: Zero Books.

Fisher, M. (2011) 'Dogtooth: The Family Syndrome', *Film Quarterly* 64 (4), pp. 22–27.

Fisher, M. (2009) *Capitalist Realism: Is There No Alternative?* Winchester: Zero Books.

Flix Team (2018) 'Agapi nai (kai polli) gia to ellhniko cinema, alla epitelous kai mia ethniki politiki' (Lots of Love for Greek Cinema, Yet, at Last, a National Plan of Support), *Flix*, 26 November 2018 <https://flix.gr/news/a-little-love-to-greek-cinema-meeting.html> (last accessed 8 June 2020).

Forensic Architecture (2019) 'The Killing of Zak Kostopoulos' <https://forensic-architecture.org/investigation/the-killing-of-zak-kostopoulos> (last accessed 8 June 2020).

Foster, H. (2015) *Bad New Days: Art, Criticism, Emergency*. London: Verso.

Foster, H. (2004) 'An Archival Impulse', *October*, 110, pp. 3–22.

Foucault, M. (2010) *The Birth of Biopolitics: Lectures at the College de France, 1978–79*, trans. by Graham Burchell. Basingstoke: Palgrave Macmillan.

Foucault, M. (2008) *Psychiatric Power: Lectures at the Collège de France, 1973–1974*, trans. by Graham Burchell. New York: Picador.

Foucault, M. (2007) *Security, Territory, Population: Lectures at the Collège de France, 1977–78*, trans. by Graham Burchell. Basingstoke: Palgrave Macmillan.

Foucault, M. (2003) *"Society Must Be Defended"*: *Lectures at the Collège de France, 1975–1976*, trans. by David Macey. New York: Picador.

Foucault, M. (1991) 'Governmentality', in G. Burchell, C. Gordon and P. Miller (eds), *The*

Foucault Effect: Studies in Governmentality. Hemel Hempstead: Harvester/Wheatsheaf, pp. 87–104.

Foucault, M. (1986) 'Of Other Spaces', trans. by J. Miscowiec, *Diacritics*, 16 (1), pp. 22–27.

Foucault, M. ([1976] 1998) *The History of Sexuality Volume 1: An Introduction*, trans. By Robert Hurley. London: Allen Lane.

Foucault, M. ([1975] 1991) *Discipline and Punish: The Birth of the Prison*, trans. by Alan Sheridan. London: Penguin.

Frauley J. (2010) 'Biopolitics and the Governance of Genetic Capital in GATTACA', in J. Frauley (ed.), *Criminology, Deviance, and the Silver Screen: The Fictional Reality and the Criminological Imagination*. New York: Palgrave Macmillan, pp. 195–216.

Galanaki, R. (2011), Oral presentation on the panel 'The Historical Novel in Contemporary Greek Fiction', Hellenic Centre, London, 14 October.

Galanou, L. (2011) 'Chora proelefsis' ['Country of Origin'], *FLIX*, 15 March <https://flix.gr/cinema/xwra-proeleyshs-1.html> (last accessed 8 June 2020).

Galt, R. (2017) 'The Animal Logic of Contemporary Greek Cinema', *Framework: The Journal of Cinema and Media*, 58 (1–2), pp. 7–29.

Galt, R. (2013) 'Default Cinema: Queering Economic Crisis in Argentina and Beyond', *Screen*, 54 (1), pp. 62–81.

Gedgaudaite, K. (2018) *Smyrna in Your Pocket: Memory of Asia Minor in Contemporary Greek Culture*, PhD thesis, University of Oxford <https://ora.ox.ac.uk/objects/uuid:864a8d4f-0e50-4241-8552-50bef1077f95> (last accessed 8 June 2020).

Genette, G. (1972) *Figures III*. Paris: Éditions du Seuil.

Gentili, D., E. Stimilli and G. Garelli (eds) (2018) *Italian Critical Thought: Genealogies and Categories*. London: Rowman & Littlefield.

Georgakas, D. (2002) 'Greek Cinema for Beginners: A Thumbnail History', *Film Criticism*, 27 (2), pp. 2–8.

Giannakopoulos, G. (2016) 'Depicting the Pain of Others: Photographic Representations of Refugees in the Aegean Shores', *Journal of Greek Media and Culture*, 2 (1), pp. 103–13.

Giannouri, E. (2014) '*Matchbox, Knifer* and the "Oikographic" Hypothesis', *Filmicon: Journal of Greek Film Studies*, 2 (1), pp. 156–75.

Giovani, J. (2011) 'O *Kynodontas* kai i metamonterna aisthitiki tis parakmis' ('*Dogtooth* and the Post-modern Aesthetics of Decadence'), *Rizospastis*, 17 March <https://www.rizospastis.gr/story.do?id=6154599> (last accessed 8 June 2020).

Giovanopoulos, C. and D. Mitropoulos (eds) (2011) *Apo tous Dromous stis Plateies: Dimokratia Under Construction* ('*From the Streets to the Squares: Democracy Under Construction*'). Athens: A/synecheia.

Gourgouris, S. (2019) 'Xenia: Debt at Home, Debt is Always Foreign', *Social Science Information*, 58 (3), pp. 521–35.

Gourgouris, S. (2011) 'Indignant Politics in Athens: Democracy Out of Rage', *Greek Left Review*, 17 June <https://greekleftreview.wordpress.com/2011/07/17/indignant-politics-in-athens—democracy-out-of-rage/> (last accessed 8 June 2020).

Greenfield, S. N. (1998) *The Ends of Allegory*. Newark: University of Delaware Press.

Gronstad, A. and H. Gustafsson (eds) (2014) *Cinema and Agamben: Ethics, Biopolitics and the Moving Image*. New York: Bloomsbury.

Groys, B. (2008) 'Art in the Age of Biopolitics: From Artwork to Art Documentation', in *Art Power*. Cambridge: MIT Press, pp 53–65.

Gržinić, M. and A. Stojnić (eds) (2018) *Shifting Corporealities in Contemporary Performance: Danger, Im/mobility and Politics*. Basingstoke: Palgrave Macmillan.

Gutiérrez Silva, M. and L. Duno Gottberg (eds) (2019) *The Films of Arturo Ripstein: The Sinister Gaze of the World*. Cham: Palgrave Macmillan.

Hager, P. (2016) 'Acropolis Remapped: On a Democratic Politics of Resistance', *Synthesis: An Anglophone Journal of Comparative Literary Studies*, 9, pp. 76–93 <https://ejournals. epublishing.ekt.gr/index.php/synthesis/article/view/16226/14493> (last accessed 8 June 2020).

Hager, P. and M. Fragkou (2017) 'Dramaturgies of Change: Greek Theatre Now', *Journal of Greek Media & Culture*, 3 (2), pp. 139–44.

Hamilakis, Y. (2016) 'Some Debts Can Never Be Repaid: The Archaeo-Politics of the Crisis', *Journal of Modern Greek Studies*, 34 (2), pp. 227–64.

Hanson, E. (2014) 'Cinema *a Tergo*: Shooting in *Elephant*', in M. Tuhkanen (ed.), *Leo Bersani: Queer Theory and Beyond*. Albany: State University of New York Press, pp. 83–104.

Harkins, G. (2009) *Everybody's Family Romance: Reading Incest in Neoliberal America*. Minneapolis: University of Minnesota Press.

Harman, G. (2012) *Weird Realism: Lovecraft and Philosophy*. London: Zero Books.

Harvey, D. (2007) *A Brief History of Neoliberalism*. Oxford: Oxford University Press.

Hesselberth, P. (2012) *Cinematic Chronotopes: Affective Encounters in Space-Time*, PhD thesis, Amsterdam School for Cultural Analysis <https://dare.uva.nl/search?identifier=9579e711-8fba-472c-ab2d-3b8375dbc056> (last accessed 8 June 2020).

Hjort, M, E. Jorholt and E. Novrup Redvall (eds) (2010) *The Danish Directors 2: Dialogues on the New Danish Fiction Cinema*. Bristol: Intellect.

Hjort, M. and D. Petrie (eds) (2007) *The Cinema of Small Nations*. Edinburgh: Edinburgh University Press.

Hjort, M. (2005) *Small Nation, Global Cinema: The New Danish Cinema*. Minneapolis: University of Minnesota Press.

Horeck, C. T. and T. Kendall (eds) (2011) *The New Extremism in Cinema: From France to Europe*. Edinburgh: Edinburgh University Press.

Hulot, M. (2014) 'Ta deka kalytera feteina album tou weird wave' ('The Ten Best Albums of the Weird Wave'), *Greka* <https://www.grekamag.gr/whats_new/ta-10-kalitera-fetina-almpoum-tou-greek-weird-wave/> (last accessed 8 June 2020).

Jakobson, R. ([1922] 1987), 'Realism in Art', in *Language in Literature*. Cambridge: Harvard University Press, pp. 19-27.

Jakobson, R. (1971), 'Two Aspects of Language and Two Types of Aphasic Disturbances', in R. Jakobson (ed.), *Roman Jakobson: Selected Writings*. The Hague and Paris: Mouton, pp. 239–59.

Jakobson, R. and M. Halle (eds) (1956) *Fundamentals of Language*. The Hague: Mouton.

Jameson, F. (2019) *Allegory and Ideology*. London: Verso.

Jameson, F. (2015) 'Angelopoulos and Collective Narrative', in A. Koutsourakis and M. Stevens (eds), *The Cinema of Theo Angelopoulos*. Edinburgh: Edinburgh University Press, pp. 99–113.

Jameson, F. (1990) *Signatures of the Visible*. London: Routledge.

Jameson, F. (1986) 'Third-World Literature in the Era of Multinational Capitalism', *Social Text*, 15, pp. 65–88.

Jameson, F. (1984) 'Postmodernism or the Cultural Logic of Late Capitalism', *New Left Review*, 146, pp. 53–92.

Jameson, F. (1982) 'Progress Versus Utopia; Or, Can We Imagine the Future?', *Science Fiction Studies*, 9 (2), pp. 147–58.

Jennings, R. and L. Lomine (2004) 'Nationality and New Queer Cinema: Australian Film', in

M. Aaron (ed.), *New Queer Cinema: A Critical Reader*. Edinburgh: Edinburgh University Press, pp. 144–54.

Jervis, B. (2018) *Assemblage Thought and Archaeology*. London: Routledge.

Johnson, B. (2014) 'Metaphor, Metonymy, and Voice in *Their Eyes Were Watching God*', in M. Feurstein et al. (eds), *The Barbara Johnson Reader: The Surprise of Otherness*. Durham: Duke University Press, pp. 108–25.

Kalantzis, K. (2016) 'Introduction-Uncertain Visions: Crisis, Ambiguity, and Visual Culture in Greece', *Visual Anthropology Review*, 32 (1), pp. 5–11.

Kaloudi, K. (2014) 'La Violence du quotidien dans le cinéma Grec contemporain: L'Exemple du cineaste Giannis Oikonomidis', in F. Thérond (ed.), *La Violence du quotidien: Formes et figures contemporaines de la violence au théâtre et au cinéma*. Laverin: L'Entretemps, pp. 83–92.

Kampagiannis, A. (2020) *Me tis Melisses I me tous Lykous? ('On the Side of the Bees or the Wolves?')*. Athens: Antipodes.

Kapsaskis, D. (2017) 'Translation as a Critical Tool in Film Analysis: Watching Yorgos Lanthimos' *Dogtooth* through a Translation Prism', *Translation Studies*, 10 (3), pp. 247–62.

Karalis, V. (2018) 'Greek Cinema as a Modern Historical Project: Some Methodological Questions', *Modern Greek Studies (Australia and New Zealand)*, 19, pp. 35–68.

Karalis, V. (2017) *Realism in Greek Cinema: From the Post-War Period to the Present*. London: I. B. Tauris.

Karalis, V. (2012) *A History of Greek Cinema*. London: Continuum.

Karayanni, S. (2018) 'Anamnesis and Queer Poe(/li)tics: Dissident Sexualities and the Erotics of Transgression in Cyprus', *Journal of Greek Media and Culture*, 4 (2), pp. 239–54.

Karkani, I. (2016a) 'Framing the Weird Body in Contemporary European Cinema', *The Funambulist* <https://thefunambulist.net/cinema/the-funambulist-papers-56-framing-the-weird-body-in-contemporary-european-cinema-by-ina-karkani> (last accessed 8 June 2020).

Karkani, I. (2016b) 'Aesthetics of Recession: Urban Space and Identity in *Attenberg* and *Beautiful Youth*', *Journal of Greek Media & Culture*, 2 (2), pp. 201–16.

Katsounaki, M. (2010) 'Me i horis oikogeneia' ('With or Without Family'), *Kathimerini*, 29 August, <https://www.kathimerini.gr/4dcgi/_w_articles_kathpolitics_1_29/08/2010_1292449> (last accessed 8 June 2020).

Katsounaki, M. (2003) 'To navagio tis ellinikis oikogeneias' ('The Shipwreck of the Greek Family'), *Kathimerini*, 30 March.

Kazakopoulou, T. (2020) 'Young Women's Deadly Rebellions: Cultural Complacency in the Films of Yorgos Lanthimos', *The Oxford Research Centre in the Humanities* <https://www.torch.ox.ac.uk/article/young-womens-deadly-rebellions-cultural-complacency-in-the-films-of-yorgos-lanthimos> (last accessed 8 June 2020).

Kazakopoulou, T. (2017a) 'Introduction', in T. Kazakopoulou and M. Fotiou (eds), *Contemporary Greek Film Cultures from 1990 to the Present*. Bern: Peter Lang, pp. xiii–xxxii.

Kazakopoulou, T. (2017b) 'In the Name of the Father: Rituals of Gender and Democracy in Olga Malea's *First Time Godfather*', in T. Kazakopoulou and M. Fotiou (eds), *Contemporary Greek Film Cultures from 1990 to the Present*. Bern: Peter Lang, pp. 151–78.

Kazakopoulou, T. (2016) 'The Mother Accomplice: Questions of Representation in *Dogtooth* and *Miss Violence*', *Journal of Greek Media & Culture*, 2 (2), pp. 187–200.

Kioupkiolis, A and G. Katsambekis (eds) (2014) *Radical Democracy and Collective Movements Today: The Biopolitics of the Multitude versus the Hegemony of the People*. London: Routledge.

Kokkini, M. (2019) 'Vasilis Kekatos: "Einai olofanero oti mas ehoun sto ftisimo"' ('Vasilis

Kekatos: "It is Evident They Think We Are Nothing"'), *Lifo*, 3 October <https://www. lifo.gr/articles/cinema_articles/253893/vasilis-kekatos-einai-olofanero-oti-mas-exoyn-sto-ftysimo> (last accessed 8 June 2020).

Kolovos, N. (2002) 'Enas kinimatografos tou dimiourgou' ('An *Auteur* Cinema'), in D. Leventakos (ed.), *Opseis tou Neou Ellinikou Kinimatografou ('Aspects of New Greek Cinema')*. Athens: Center for Audiovisual Studies, pp. 55–64.

Kontakos, V. (2009) 'Filmmakers of Greece Unite to Improve Film Regulations and Funding', *European Documentary Network*, <edn.network/news/news-story/article/filmmakers-of-greece-unite-to-improve-film-regulations-and-funding/?tx_ttnews%5BbackPid%5D=219 &cHash=2d15be279e1a6998998977457a653ba2> (last accessed 8 June 2020).

Kotouza, D. (2019) *Surplus Citizens: Struggle and Nationalism in the Greek Crisis*. London: Pluto Press.

Kotouza, D. (2018) 'Biopolicing the Crisis: Gendered and Racialized "Health Threats" and Neoliberal Governmentality', in H. Richter (ed.), *Biopolitical Governance: Race, Gender Economy*. London: Rowman and Littlefield, pp. 211–34.

Kourelou, O., M. Liz and B. Vidal (2014) 'Crisis and Creativity: The New Cinemas of Portugal, Greece and Spain', *New Cinemas: Journal of Contemporary Film*, 12 (1–2), pp 133–50.

Koutsourakis, A (2012) 'Cinema of the Body: The Politics of Performativity in Lars von Trier's *Dogville* and Yorgos Lanthimos's *Dogtooth*', *Cinema: Journal of Philosophy and the Moving Image*, 3, pp. 84–108.

Koukoulas, G. (2015) 'Oi meres tis krisis' ('The Days of Crisis'), *Efsyn*, 11 July <https://www. efsyn.gr/nisides/kare-kare/33580_oi-meres-tis-krisis> (last accessed 8 June 2020).

Koumarianou, E. (2012) *To Taxidi tis Zois Mou ('The Journey of My Life')*. Athens: Polichromos Planitis.

Kracauer, S. (1997) [1960] *Theory of Film: The Redemption of Physical Reality*. Princeton: Princeton University Press.

Kyriakos, K. (2017) *Epithymies kai Politiki: I Queer Istoria tou Ellenikou Kinimatografou (1924–2016) (Desires and Politics: The Queer History of Greek Cinema [1924–2016])*. Athens: Aigokeros.

Laclau, E. (2014) *The Rhetorical Foundations of Society*. London: Verso.

Lambie, R. (2018) '*Dogtooth* and the Power of Language', *Den of Geek*, 31 July <https://www. denofgeek.com/movies/dogtooth-and-the-power-of-language/> (last accessed 8 June 2020).

La Porta, D. (2013) '*Miss Violence*: A Family Code of Silence,' *Cineuropa*, 1 September <https:// cineuropa.org/en/newsdetail/243436/> (last accessed 8 June 2020).

Larkin, B. (2009) 'National Allegory', *Social Text*, 27 (3), pp. 164–68.

Latimer, H. (2011) 'Bio-Reproductive Futurism: Bare Life and the Pregnant Refugee in Alfonso Cuarón's *Children of Men*', *Social Text*, 29 (3), pp. 51–72.

Laval, C. (2018) *Foucault, Bourdieu et la question néolibérale*. Paris: Éditions La Découverte.

Lavelle, M. (2019) 'A Year After an LGBTQ Activist's Murder in Greece, His Memory Lives on in 'Our Politics and Our Action', Protesters Say', *The World*, 25 September <https:// www.pri.org/stories/2019-09-25/anti-gay-violence-rise-greece-year-after-murder-lgbtq-activist> (last accessed 8 June 2020).

Lodge, D. (1977) *Modes of Modern Writing: Metaphor, Metonymy, and the Typology of Modern Literature*. London: Edward Arnold.

Lorenz, R. (2012) *Queer Art: A Freak Theory*. Bielefeld: Transcript.

Lübecker, N. (2015) *The Feel-Bad Film*. Edinburgh: Edinburgh University Press.

Lykidis, A. (2015) 'Crisis of Sovereignty in Recent Greek Cinema', *Journal of Greek Media and Culture*, 1 (1), pp. 9–27.

Machosky, B. (ed.) (2009) *Thinking Allegory Otherwise*. Palo Alto: Stanford University Press.

Mademli, G. (2018) 'Not So Weird: The Landscape of New Greek Cinema', *EFA Close-Up* <https://www.europeanfilmacademy.org/EFA_CloseUp-1.759.0.html> (last accessed 8 June 2020).

Mademli, G. (2016) 'From the Crisis of Cinema to the Cinema of Crisis: A "Weird" Label for Contemporary Greek Cinema', *Frames Cinema Journal* <framescinemajournal.com/article/from-the-crisis-of-cinema-to-the-cinema-of-crisis-a-weird-label-for-contemporary-greek-cinema/> (last accessed 8 June 2020).

Mademli, G. (2015) 'The Importance of Being Weird: On Language Games in Contemporary Greek Films', *Filmicon Blog* <https://filmiconjournal.com/blog/post/41/the-importance-of-being-weird> (last accessed 8 June 2020).

Mais, C. (ed.) (2020) 'Idrymata politismou: Mia eisagogi' ('Cultural Institutions [in Greece]: An Introduction'), *Marginalia* 11 <https://marginalia.gr/afieroma/idrymata-politismoy-mia-eisagogi/> (last accessed 14 July 2020).

Marcantonio, C. (2015) *Global Melodrama: Nation, Body, and History in Contemporary Film*. Basingstoke: Palgrave Macmillan.

Marks, L. (1999) *The Skin of the Film: Intercultural Cinema, Embodiment, and the Senses*. Durham: Duke University Press.

Marzec, A. (2015) 'In Limbo, Radically: An Interview with Syllas Tzoumerkas', *Filmicon blog* <https://filmiconjournal.com/blog/post/44/in-limbo-radically> (last accessed 8 June 2020).

Matzner, S. (2016) *Rethinking Metonymy: Literary Theory and Poetic Practice from Pindar to Jakobson*. Oxford: Oxford University Press.

Mavroudi, Z. (2013) *Ruins: Orothetikes gynaikes. To chroniko mias diapompefsis* ('*Ruins: Seropositive Women, Chronicle of an HIV Witch-Hunt*'). Greece: OmniaTV/ Unfollow Magazine.

Mazierska, E. (2015) *From Self-Fulfillment to Survival of the Fittest*. London: Bergahn.

Metz, C. (1977) *The Imaginary Signifier: Psychoanalysis and the Cinema*. Bloomington: Indiana University Press.

Metzidakis, S. (2014) 'No Bones to Pick with Lanthimos's Film *Dogtooth*', *Journal of Modern Greek Studies*, 32 (2), pp. 367–92.

Meuer, U. (2018) 'LabA: Zu austeritärer Politik und Schmalfilm', in E. Büttner, V. Öhner and L. Stölzl (eds), *Sichtbar Machen: Politiken des Dokumentarfilms*. Berlin: Vorwerk, pp. 172–89.

Miller, Hillis J. (1981) 'The Two Allegories', in M. W. Bloomfield (ed.), *Allegory, Myth, and Symbol*. Cambridge: Harvard University Press, pp. 355–70.

Mini, P. (2018) *I Kinimatografiki Morfi tou Ponou kai tis Odiniris Apolafsis: O Monternismos tou Taki Kanellopoulou* ('*The Cinematic Form of Pain and Painful Pleasure: The Modernism of Takis Kanellopoulos*'). Athens: MIET.

Moullet, L. (1959) 'Sam Fuller sur les brisées de Marlowe', *Cahiers du Cinéma* 93 (1), pp. 11–19.

Muhle, M. (2012) 'Imitation of Life: Biopolitics and the Cinematographic Image', *Fillip*, 17 <https://fillip.ca/content/imitation-of-life-biopolitics-and-the-cinematographic-image> (last accessed 8 June 2020).

Mulvey, L. (2006) *Death 24x a Second: Stillness and the Moving Image*. London: Reaktion Books.

Nagib, L. and C. Mello (eds) (2009) *Realism and the Audiovisual Media*. London: Palgrave Macmillan.

Nagib, L., C. Perriam and R. Dudrah (eds) (2011) *Theorizing World Cinema*. New York: I. B. Tauris.

Nagib, L. (2011) *World Cinema and the Ethics of Realism*. New York and London: Continuum.

Neroni, H. (2015),*The Subject of Torture: Psychoanalysis and Biopolitics in Television and Film*. New York: Columbia University Press.

Nichols, B. (2010) *Introduction to Documentary*. Bloomington: Indiana University Press.

Nikolaidou, A. (2020) 'Self-Exoticism, the Iconography of Crisis and the Weird Wave', in P. Panagiotopoulos and D. Sotiropoulos (eds), *Political and Cultural Aspects of Greek Exoticism*, Cham: Palgrave/Macmillan, pp. 139–52.

Nikolaidou, A. (2014) 'The Performative Aesthetics of the Greek New Wave', *Filmicon: Journal of Greek Film Studies*, 2, pp. 20–44.

Nikolaidou, A. and A. Poupou (2018) *I Hameni Leoforos tou Ellhnikou Cinema (The Lost Highway of Greek Cinema)*. Athens: Nefeli.

Nikolaidou, A. and A. Poupou (2017) 'Kapoies post-weird skepseis gia to neo kima tou ellinikou kinimatografou' ('Post-Weird Notes on the New Wave of Greek Cinema'), in *Non-Catalog*. Thessaloniki: Thessaloniki International Film Festival, pp. 88–107.

Noble, A. (2005) *Mexican National Cinema*. New York: Routledge.

Owens, C. (1980) 'The Allegorical Impulse: Towards a Theory of Postmodernism', *October*, 12, pp. 67–86

Page, J. (2009) *Crisis and Capitalism in Contemporary Argentine Cinema*. Durham: Duke University Press.

Pagonis, G. (2018) 'Bougada' ['Laundry'], *Efsyn*, 7 July <https://www.efsyn.gr/nisides/kare-kare/156831_lexiko-tis-krisis-07072018> (last accessed 8 June 2020).

Palioura, M. (2018) 'Zak Kostopoulos: Gia na epivioseis prepei na trecheis' ('Zak Kostopoulos: In Order to Survive, You Must Know How to Run'), *Ladylike* <https://portfolio.ladylike.gr/zak-kostopoulos> (last accessed 8 June 2020).

Panagiotopoulos, P. (2020) 'Demodernise Greece: Sociological Critique on the Construction of an Alternative Country', in P. Panagiotopoulos and D. Sotiropoulos (eds), *Political and Cultural Aspects of Greek Exoticism*. Cham: Palgrave/Macmillan, pp. 53–69.

Panapakidis, K. (2012) *Drag Narratives: Staged Gender, Embodiment, and Competition*, PhD thesis, Goldsmiths, University of London <http://research.gold.ac.uk/7589/> (last accessed 8 June 2020).

Panourgia, N. (2011) 'The Squared Constitution of Dissent', in P. Papailias (ed.), *Beyond the "Greek Crisis": Histories, Rhetorics, Politics, Special Issue of Cultural Anthropology* <http://www.culanth.org/fieldsights/the-squared-constitution-of-dissent > (last accessed 8 June 2020).

Papadimitriou, L. (2018a,) 'Greek Cinema as European Cinema: Co-productions, Eurimages and the Europeanisation of Greek Cinema', *Studies in European Cinema*, 15 (2-3), pp. 215–34.

Papadimitriou, L. (2018b) 'Film Distribution in Greece: Formal and Informal Networks of Circulation since the Financial Crisis', *Screen*, 59 (4), pp. 484–505.

Papadimitriou, L. (2017) 'The Economy and Ecology of Greek Cinema Since the Crisis: Production, Circulation, Reception', in D. Tziovas (ed.), *Greece in Crisis: The Cultural Politics of Austerity*. London: I. B. Tauris, pp. 135–57.

Papadimitriou, L. (2016), 'Politics and Independence: Documentary in Greece during the Crisis', in D. Tzioumakis and C. Molloy (eds), *The Routledge Companion to Cinema and Politics*. London: Routledge, pp. 469–80.

Papadimitriou, L. (2014) 'Locating Contemporary Greek Film Cultures: Past, Present, Future and the Crisis', *Filmicon: Journal of Greek Film Studies*, 2 (1), pp. 1–19.

Papanikolaou, D. (2020) 'Greek Weird Wave: Or, on How to Do a Cinema of Biopolitics', in M. Boletsi, J. Houwen and L. Minnaard (eds), *Languages of Resistance, Transformation, and*

Futurity in Mediterranean Crisis-Scapes: From Crisis to Critique. London: Palgrave Macmillan, pp. 209–30.

Papanikolaou, D. (2019a) 'How Metonymical Are You? Notes on Biopolitical Realism', in O. Andreadakis and G. Mademli (eds), *Non-Catalog*. Thessaloniki: Thessaloniki Film Festival, pp. 104–25.

Papanikolaou, D. (2019b) 'Un overdose d' amore', special issue of *The Passenger: Grecia*. Milan: Iperborea, pp. 110–24.

Papanikolaou, D. (2018a) *Kati Trehei me tin Oikogeneia: Ethnos, Pothos kai Sygeneia tin Epohi tis Krisis* ('*There is Something about the Family: Nation, Desire and Kinship at a time of Crisis*'). Athens: Patakis.

Papanikolaou, D. (2018b) 'Critically Queer and Haunted: Greek Identity, Crisiscapes and Doing Queer History in the Present', *Journal of Greek Media & Culture* 4 (2), pp. 167–86.

Papanikolaou, D. (2017) 'Archive Trouble, 2017', in K. Botanova, C. Chryssopoulos and J. Cooiman (eds), *Culturescapes: Archaeology of the Future*. Basel: Cristoph Merian Verlag, pp. 38–52.

Papanikolaou, D. (2014) 'Athens is Burning', in A. Poupou, A. Nikolaidou and E. Sifaki (eds), *World Film Locations: Athens*. Bristol: Intellect, pp. 28–29.

Papanikolaou, D. (2011) 'Archive Trouble', in P. Papailias (ed.), *Beyond the "Greek Crisis": Histories, Rhetorics, Politics, Special Issue of Cultural Anthropology* <http://www.culanth.org/fieldsights/archive-trouble> (last accessed 8 June 2020).

Papanikolaou, D. (2010a) 'Kati trehei me tin oikogeneia' ['There is Something About the Family'], *The Books' Journal* 1 (November), pp. 96–98.

Papanikolaou, D. (2010b) '*Strella*: Mia tainia gia oli tin oikogeneia' ('*Strella*: A Film for the Whole Family'), in *Strella*. Athens: Polychromos Planitis, pp. 9–24.

Papanikolaou, D. (2009) 'New Queer Greece? Thinking Identity Through Constantine Giannari's *From the Edge of the City* and Ana Kokkinos's *Head On*', *New Cinemas*, 6 (3), pp. 183–96.

Papapavlou, M. (2015) *I Empeiria tis Plateias Syntagmatos: Mousiki, Sinaisthimata kai Nea Koinonika Kinimata* ('*The Experience of Syntagma Square: Music, Emotions and New Social Movements*'). Athens: I Ekdoseis ton Sinadelfon.

Peroulis, K. (2015a) 'To *Lobster* kai i theoria ton dio akron: Apo tin alligoria ton anthropinon scheseon stin kirioleksia tou politismou' ('*Lobster* and the Theory of Opposites: From the Allegory of Human Relationships to Cultural Literalism'), *Unfollow* <http://unfollow.com.gr/print-edition/to-lobster-kai-i-theoria-ton-dio-akron-apo-tin-alligoria-ton-anthropinon-sxeseon-stin-kiriolexia-tou-politikou/> (last accessed 8 June 2020).

Peroulis, K. (2015b) *Automata*. Athens: Antipodes.

Petsini, P. (ed.) (2018) *Capitalist Realism: Future Perfect/Past Continuous*. Thessaloniki: University of Macedonia/Thessaloniki Museum of Photography.

Phillips, J. (2006) 'Agencement/Assemblage', *Theory, Culture & Society*, 23 (2–3), pp. 108–9.

Picard, A. (ed.) (2018) *What is Real? Filmmakers Weigh In*. Paris: Post-Éditions.

Pisters, P. (2014) 'Heart of the Matter: Bodies without Organs and Biopolitics in Organ Transplant Film', *Angelaki: Journal of the Theoretical Humanities*, 19 (4), pp. 23–36.

Plantzos, D. (2019a), 'We Owe Ourselves to Debt: Classical Greece, Athens in Crisis, and the Body as Battlefield', *Social Science Information*, 58 (3), pp. 469–92.

Plantzos, D. (2019b) 'Athens Remains: Still?', *Journal of Greek Media and Culture*, 5 (2), pp. 115–24.

Plantzos, D. (2018) 'Crisis, Austerity Measures and Beyond: Archaeology in Greece since the Global Financial Crisis', *Archaeological Reports*, 64, pp. 171–80.

Plantzos, D. (2017a) *To Prosfato Mellon: I Klasiki Arhaiotita os Viopolitiko Ergaleio* ('The Recent Future: Classical Antiquity as a Biopolitical Weapon'). Athens: Nefeli.

Plantzos, D. (2017b) 'Amphipolitics: Archaeological Performance and Governmentality in Greece under the Crisis', in D. Tziovas (ed.), *Greece in Crisis. The Cultural Politics of Austerity*. London: I. B. Tauris, pp. 65–84.

Plantzos, D. (2012) 'The Glory that Was Not: Embodying the Classical in Contemporary Greece', *Interactions: Studies in Communication & Culture*, 3 (2), pp. 147–71.

Povinelli, E. (2011) *Economies of Abandonment: Social Belonging and Endurance in Late Liberalism*. Durham: Duke University Press.

Pokornowski, S. (2016), 'Vulnerable Life: Zombies, Global Biopolitics, and the Reproduction of Structural Violence', *Humanities*, 5 (3), 71, https://www.mdpi.com/2076-0787/5/3/71 (last accessed 8 June 2020).

Politakis, D. (2019) 'Theloume ki emeis ligi agapi apo to elliniko sinema' ('We, Too, Want Some Love from Greek Cinema'), *Lifo*, 28 February <https://www.lifo.gr/print/short-cut/227999/theloyme-ki-emeis-ligi-agapi-apo-to-elliniko-sinema> (last accessed 8 June 2020).

Ponsard, F. (2014) 'Greek Documentaries are (Not) Still in Crisis', *FIRPRESCI* <https://fipresci.org/report/greek-documentaries-are-not-still-in-crisis/> (last accessed 8 June 2020).

Poulis, K. (2018) 'Zak Kostopoulos was Beaten to Death: So What Do We Do Now?', *The Press Project*, 21 November <https://thepressproject.gr/zak-kostopoulos-was-beaten-to-death-so-what-do-we-do-now/> (last accessed 8 June 2020).

Poupou, A. (2019) 'Social Space, Architecture and the Crisis', in F. Rosario and I. V. Alvarez (eds), *New Approaches to Cinematic Space*. New York and London: Routledge, pp. 27–41.

Poupou, A. (2014) 'Going Backwards, Moving Forwards: The Return of Modernism in the Work of Athina Rachel Tsangari', *Filmicon: Journal of Greek Film Studies*, 2 (1), pp. 45–70.

Preciado, P. B. (2020) 'Biosurveillance: Sortir de la prison molle de nos intérieurs', *Mediapart*, 12 April <https://www.mediapart.fr/journal/international/120420/biosurveillance-sortir-de-la-prison-molle-de-nos-interieurs> (last accessed 8 June 2020).

Preciado, P. (2018a) *Countersexual Manifesto*, trans. by Kevin Gerry Dunn. New York: Columbia University Press.

Preciado, P. (2018b) 'Zackie Oh d' Athènes sort de sa tombe numerique', *Libération* <https://www.liberation.fr/debats/2018/10/12/zackie-oh-d-athenes-sort-de-sa-tombe-numerique_1685015> (last accessed 8 June 2020)

Prodger, P. and T. Gunning (2003) *Time Stands Still: Muybridge and the Instantaneous Photography Movement*. Oxford: Oxford University Press.

Prozorov, S. (2017) 'Conclusion: Whither Biopolitics?', in S. Prozorov and S. Rentea (eds), *The Routledge Handbook of Biopolitics*. London: Routledge, pp. 328–38.

Psaras, M. (2016) *The Queer Greek Weird Wave: Ethics, Politics and the Crisis of Meaning*. London: Palgrave Macmillan.

Psaras, M. (2015) 'Review of *Miss Violence* (2013)', *Filmicon: Journal of Greek Film Studies*, 3 (1), pp. 87–95.

Puar, J. K. (2007) *Terrorist Assemblages: Homonationalism in Queer Times*. Durham: Duke University Press.

Quandt, J. (2004) 'Flesh and Blood: Sex and Violence in Recent French Cinema', *ArtForum*.

Quinan, C. and K. Thiele (2020) *Biopolitics, Necropolitics, Cosmopolitics*: special issue of the *Journal of Gender Studies* 29.

Rajagopal, B. (2015) 'Greece: Welcome to the Third World and Here Are Some Lessons', *Huffpost*, 9 July <https://www.huffpost.com/entry/greece-welcome-to-the-thi_b_7760570?guccounter=1> (last accessed 8 June 2020).

Rakopoulos, T. (ed.) (2018) *The Global Life of Austerity: Comparing Beyond Europe*. New York and Oxford: Berghahn Books.

Rawes, P., S. Loo and T. Mathews (eds) (2016) *Poetic Biopolitics: Practices of Relation in Architecture and the Arts*. London: I. B. Tauris.

Rees, T. (2018) *After Ethnos*. Durham: Duke University Press.

Rees-Roberts, N. (2007) 'Down and Out: Immigrant Poverty and Queer Sexuality in Sébastien Lifshitz's *Wild Side* (2004)', *Studies in French Cinema*, 7 (2), pp. 143–55.

Repo, J. (2015) *The Biopolitics of Gender*. Oxford: Oxford University Press.

Revel, J. (2018) 'Italian Theory and its Differences: Subjectivation, Historicization, Conflict', in D. Gentili, E. Stimilli and G. Garelli (eds), *Italian Critical Thought: Genealogies and Categories*. London: Rowman & Littlefield, pp. 47–58.

Revel, J. (2005) *Michel Foucault: Expériences de la pensée*. Paris: Bordas.

Rich, R. (2013) *New Queer Cinema: The Director's Cut*. Durham: Duke University Press.

Roland, O. (2013) *La Galvanisation du corps: Le Cinéma français et la biopolitique*, PhD thesis, University of Southern California <https://www.scribd.com/document/367949893/La-Galvanisation-Du-Corps-Le-Cinema-Francais-Et-La-Biopolitique> (last accessed 8 June 2020).

Rose, S. (2011) '*Attenberg*, *Dogtooth* and the Weird Wave of Greek Cinema', *The Guardian*, 27 August <https://www.theguardian.com/film/2011/aug/27/attenberg-dogtooth-greece-cinema> (last accessed 8 June 2020).

Rozakou, K. (2012) 'The Biopolitics of Hospitality in Greece: Humanitarianism and the Management of Refugees', *American Ethnologist: Journal of the American Ethnological Society*, 39 (3), pp. 562–77.

Rushing, R. A. (2016) *Descended from Hercules: Biopolitics and the Muscled Male Body on Screen*. Bloomington: Indiana University Press.

Sampatakakis, G. (2018) 'Bodies of Truth: The Terrible Beauty of Queer Performance', *Journal of Greek Media and Culture*, 4 (2), pp. 255–67.

Sampatakakis, G. (2017) 'To theatro os sotiria: Ta *Amaranta* ton bijoux de kant sto Faust' ('Theatre as Salvation: *Amaranta* in Faust Theatre'), *Athens Voice*, 28 January <http://www.athensvoice.gr/culture/theater/338277_theatro-os-sotiria-amaranta-ton-bijoux-de-kant-sto-faust> (last accessed 8 June 2020).

Schonig, J. (2018) 'The Follow Shot: A Tale of Two Elephants', *[in]Transition* 5 (1) <http://mediacommons.org/intransition/2018/03/08/chained-camera> (last accessed 8 June 2020).

Schoonover, K. and R. Galt (2016) *Queer Cinema in the World*. Durham: Duke University Press.

Sederholm, C. H. and J. A. Weinstock (eds) (2016) *The Age of Lovecraft*. Minneapolis: University of Minnesota Press.

Sharpe, K. B. (2016) '*The Lobster*: Debt, Referenda, and False Choices', *Blind Field: A Journal of Cultural Inquiry* <https://blindfieldjournal.com/2016/07/01/the-lobster-debt-referenda-and-false-choices/> (last accessed 8 June 2020).

Shaviro, S. (1993) *The Cinematic Body*. Minneapolis: University of Minnesota Press.

Shohat, E. and R. Stam (2014) [1994] *Unthinking Eurocentrism: Multiculturalism and the Media*, 2nd edition. London: Routledge.

Shonkwiler, A. and L. C. La Berge (eds) (2014) *Reading Capitalist Realism*. Iowa City: University of Iowa Press.

Sifaki, E. and A. Stamou (2020) 'Film Criticism and the Legitimization of a New Wave in Contemporary Greek Cinema', *Journal of Greek Media & Culture*, 6 (1), pp. 29–49.

Simiti, M (2014) 'Rage and Protest: The Case of the Greek Indignant Movement', *Hellenic Observatory Papers on Greece and Southeast Europe*, Paper 82 <http://www.lse.ac.uk/Hellenic-Observatory/Assets/Documents/Publications/GreeSE-Papers/GreeSE-No82.pdf> (last accessed 17 August 2018)

Sisk, C. L. (2019) '*El Castillo de la Pureza* (1972): A Closed Market Represented by a Closed Home', in M. Gutiérrez Silva and L. Duno Gottberg (eds), *The Films of Arturo Ripstein: The Sinister Gaze of the World*. Cham: Palgrave Macmillan, pp. 65–82.

Smith, H. (2017) '"Crapumenta!" . . . Anger in Athens as the Blue Lambs of Documenta Hit Town', *The Guardian*, 14 May <https://www.theguardian.com/artanddesign/2017/may/14/documenta-14-athens-german-art-extravaganza> (last accessed 8 June 2020).

Sobchack, V. (2000) 'What My Fingers Knew: The Cinesthetic Subject, or Vision in the Flesh', *Senses of Cinema* <sensesofcinema.com/2000/conference-special-effects-special-affects/fingers/#31> (last accessed 8 June 2020).

Spatharakis, K. (2011) 'I oikogeneiaki alligoria kai i anazitisi tou politikou' ('Familial Allegory and the Search for the Political'), *Levga*, 17 February <www.levga.gr/2011/02/blog-post_17.html> (last accessed 8 June 2020).

St. Clair, M. (2018) 'Exaggerated Confrontations of Human Behavior: How Yorgos Lanthimos is a Master of Horror Realism', *Vague Visages* <https://vaguevisages.com/2018/12/19/exaggarated-confrontations-of-human-behavior-how-yorgos-lanthimos-is-a-master-of-horror-realism/> (last accessed 8 June 2020).

Stavrides, S. (2016) *Common Space: The City as Commons*. London: Zed Books.

Stewart, H. (2010) '*Dogtooth*'s Infinite Allegories', *The L Magazine*, 28 December <www.thelmagazine.com/2010/12/dogtooths-infinite-allegories/> (last accessed 8 June 2020).

Steyerl, H. (2003) 'Politics of Truth: Documentarism in the Art Field', *Springerin*, 3 <https://www.springerin.at/en/2003/3/politik-der-wahrheit/> (last accessed 8 June 2020).

Steyerl, H. (2012) *The Wretched of the Screen*. Berlin: Sternberg Press.

Stiegler, B. (2019) *Il faut s' adapter: Sur un nouvel impératif politique*. Paris: Gallimard.

Streeck, W. (2016) *How Will Capitalism End? Essays on a Failing System*. London: Verso.

Szeman, I. (2001) 'Who's Afraid of National Allegory? Jameson, Literary Criticism, Globalization', *The South Atlantic Quarterly*, 100 (3), pp. 803–27.

Tambling, J. (2003) *Wong Kar-wai's* Happy Together. Hong Kong: Hong Kong University Press.

Taylor, C. (2012) 'Foucault and Familial Power', *Hypatia*, 27 (1), pp. 201–18.

Taylor, D. (ed.) (2011) *Michel Foucault: Key Concepts*. Durham: Acumen.

Tramboulis, T. and Y. Tzirtzilakis (2018) 'When Crisis Becomes Form: Athens as a Paradigm', *Stedelijk Studies*, 6, pp. 1–11 <https://stedelijkstudies.com/wp-content/uploads/2018/04/Stedelijk-Studies-6-When-Crisis-Becomes-Form-Tramboulis-Tzirtzilakis.pdf> (last accessed 8 June 2020).

Treske, A. (2011) 'Frames Within Frames – Windows and Doors', in G. Lovink and R. Somers Miles (eds), *Video Vortex Reader II: Moving Images Beyond YouTube*. Amsterdam: Institute of Network Cultures, pp. 25–34.

Tsiara, S. (2018) 'On the Surplus Value of a Dream', <https://www.stefanostsivopoulos.com/blog/2018/1/27/on-the-surplus-value-of-a-dreamby-syrago-tsiara> (last accessed 8 June 2020).

Tsilimpounidi, M. and A. Walsh (eds) (2014) *Remapping 'Crisis': A Guide to Athens*. Alresford: Zero Books.

Tsing, A. L. (2015) *The Mushroom at the End of the World: On the Possibility of Life in Capitalist Ruins*. Princeton: Princeton University Press.

Tzouflas, K. (2018) 'Le Nouveau cinéma argentin à la cinémathèque suisse', *Décadrages*, 39 (1), pp. 157–65.

Tzouflas, K. (2017) 'Filmmaking in Economic "Trouble Zones": The New Argentine Cinema and the Greek New Wave', *Cinema* <https://www.cinemabuch.ch/article/620005> (last accessed 8 July 2020).

Tzouflas, K. (2015) 'Cinema (Not) in Crisis, the New Argentine Cinema and the Greek New Wave' <https://www.film.uzh.ch/de/team/postdocs/tzouflas/research.html> (last accessed 8 June 2020).

Tzoumerkas, S. (2017) 'O Syllas Tzoumerkas grafei gia to "Fovo" tou Kosta Manousaki ('Syllas Tzoumerkas Writes About Kostas Manousakis's *Fear*')', *FLIX*, 1 February <https://flix.gr/articles/lost-highway-greek-cinema-fear.html> (last accessed 8 June 2020).

Tzoumerkas, S. (2016) 'Love Letters: Greek New Wave & Revenge Tragedy' <https://syllastzoumerkas.net/greek-new-wave-revenge-tragedy/> (last accessed 8 June 2020).

Urban, G. (2001) *Metaculture*. Minneapolis: University of Minnesota Press.

Vakalidou, Betty (2011) 'I Syngrou sti dekaetia tou 1980' ('Syngrou in the 1980s'), *Roundtable at Passport*, Piraeus, 8 December <https://www.youtube.com/watch?v=A7JSEFjzlIc> (last accessed 8 June 2020).

Väliaho, P. (2014a) *Biopolitical Screens: Image, Power, and the Neoliberal Brain*. Cambridge: MIT Press.

Väliaho, P. (2014b) 'Biopolitics of Gesture: Cinema and the Neurological Body', in A. Gronstad and H. Gustafson (eds), *Cinema and Agamben: Ethics, Biopolitics and the Moving Image*. New York: Bloomsbury, pp. 103–20.

Van Alphen, E. J. (2014) *Staging the Archive: Art and Photography in the Age of New Media*. London: Reaktion Books.

Van Alphen, E. J. (2008) 'Affective Operations of Art and Literature', *Res: Anthropology and Aesthetics*, 53–54, pp. 21–40.

Van Dyck, K. (1998) *Kassandra and the Censors: Greek Poetry since 1967*. Ithaca: Cornell University Press.

Varikos, I. (2013) '*Miss Violence* Director Talks Filmmaking Amongst Greek Crisis', *Greek Reporter*, 14 October <https://hollywood.greekreporter.com/2013/10/14/interview-miss-violence-director-talks-filmmaking-amongst-greek-crisis/> (last accessed 8 June 2020).

Varmazi, E. (2019) 'The Weirdness of Contemporary Greek Cinema', *Film International*, 47, pp. 40–49.

Vint, S. (2011) 'Introduction: Science Fiction and Biopolitics', *Science Fiction Film & Television*, 4 (2), pp. 161–72.

Vourlias, C. (2020) 'No Longer "Weird", Greek Cinema Defies Labels, Borders', *Variety*, 22 June <https://variety.com/2020/film/global/new-greek-cinema-defies-weird-wave-label-1234631203/> (last accessed 30 June 2020).

Weissberg, J. (2012) L, *Variety*, 5 February <https://variety.com/2012/film/markets-festivals/l-1117947010/> (last accessed 8 June 2020).

Westlake, O. (2014) 'Mapping Contemporary Cinema: Short Guide to the Weird Wave' <http://www.mcc.sllf.qmul.ac.uk/?p=1280> (last accessed 8 June 2020).

Whitehall, G. (2013) 'The Biopolitical Aesthetic: Toward a Post-Biopolitical Subject', *Critical Studies on Security*, 1 (2), pp. 189–203.

Williams, R. (1961) *The Long Revolution*. London: Chatto and Windus.

Xavier, I. (1999) 'Historical Allegory', in T. Miller and R. Stam (eds), *A Companion to Film Theory*. Oxford: Blackwell, pp. 333–62.

Xavier, I. (1993) *Allegories of Underdevelopment: Aesthetics and Politics in Modern Brazilian Cinema*. Minneapolis: University of Minnesota Press.

Xydakis, N. (2011) 'I varia fterouga tis oikogeneias' ('The Heavy Wing of the Family'), *Kathimerini*, 9 January.

Youtube (2016) *La Nouvelle vague du cinema grec*-Tracks ARTE (Tracks Arte), <https://www.youtube.com/watch?v=53MsgZz5ipw> (last accessed 8 June 2020).

Zak/Zackie Oh (2019) *Society Doesn't Fit Me But This Little Black Dress Does*, ed. M. Louka. Athens: Rodakio.

Zamora, D. and M. C. Behrent (eds) (2015) *Foucault and Neoliberalism*. Cambridge: Polity Press.

Zaroulia, M. (2015) 'Greece, "Still Remains": Performing "Crisis", Nostalgia and Willfulness' <https://www.academia.edu/12204871/Greece_Still_Remains_Performing_Crisis_Nostalgia_and_Willfulness> (last accessed 8 June 2020).

Zaroulia, M. and P. Hager (eds) (2015) *Performances of Capitalism, Crises and Resistance: Inside/Outside Europe*. Basingstoke: Palgrave Macmillan.

Žižek, S. (2013) 'Redefining Family Values on Film', *The Guardian*, 3 October <https://www.theguardian.com/film/filmblog/2013/oct/03/slavoj-zizek-family-values-on-film> (last accessed 8 June 2020).

Žižek, S. (2007) 'Commentary', *Children of Men* (dir. Alfonso Cuaron), DVD, Universal City: Universal.

Zois, Y. (2012) *Plateau invité: Yorgos Zois*, interview with Court Circuit, ARTE, first shown 6 April 2012.

Zois, Y. (2018) Interview before the first screening of *Third Kind*, ARTE, first shown 8 September 2018.

Filmography

Note: The following is by no means a full index of Greek New Wave films; rather, it is a list of the Greek films as well as international productions by Greek directors mentioned in this book. The English title is followed by the Greek title in transliteration.

A Blast/ I Ekrixi (2014), fiction, 83 minutes. Director: Syllas Tzoumerkas. Screenwriters: Syllas Tzoumerkas and Youla Boudali. Producers: Jeroen Beker, Maria Drandraki, Ellen Havenith and Titus Kreyenberg. Homemade Films, unafilm, PRPL, Bastide Films, Graal, MAMOKO Entertainment, Marni Films Movimento Film, Pan Entertainmet, Prosenghisi Film & Video Productions and Schleswig-Holstein Film Commission, Greece, Germany, Italy and Netherlands.

About Vassilis / Shetika me ton Vassili (1986), fiction, 80 minutes. Director: Stavros Tsiolis. Screenwriter: Stavros Tsiolis. Producer: Stavros Tsiolis. Greek Cinema Center, Greece.

Agora (2014), 120 minutes. Director: Yorgos Avgeropoulos. Producers: Yorgos Avgeropoulos and Anastasia Skoubri. Small Planet Productions, Westdeutscher Rundfunk, Al-Jazeera, Greece, Germany, Qatar.

A Girl in Black / To Koritsi me ta Mavra (1956), fiction, 100 minutes. Director: Michael Cacoyannis. Screenwriter: Michael Cacoyannis. Producer: Anis Nohra. Hermes Film, Greece.

Alps / Alpeis (2011), fiction, 93 minutes. Director: Yorgos Lanthimos. Screenwriters: Efthymis Filippou and Yorgos Lanthimos. Producer: Athina Rachel Tsangari. Haos Film, Hellenic Radio and Television (ERT), Faliro House, Greece, France, Canada, USA.

A Matter of Dignity / To Teleftaio Psemma (1958), fiction, 112 minutes. Director: Michael Cacoyannis. Screenwriter: Michael Cacoyannis. Producer: Anis Nohra. Co-producers: Theophanis Damaskinos and Victor Michaelides. Finos Film and Damaskinos & Michaelides Company, Greece.

Attenberg (2010), fiction, 97 minutes. Director: Athina Rachel Tsangari. Screenwriters: Athina Rachel Tsangari. Producers: Yorgos Lanthimos, Iraklis Mavroidis, Athina Rachel Tsangari and Angelos Venetis. Co-producer: Maria Hatzakou. Haos Film, Greek Film Centre, Faliro House Productions, Greece.

Boy Eating the Bird's Food / To Agori Troei to Fagito tou Pouliou (2012), fiction, 80 minutes. Director and Screenwriter: Ektoras Lygizos. Producers: Giorgos Karnavas, Ektoras Lygizos, Argyris Papadimitropoulos and Elina Psykou. Guanaco and Stefi films, Greece.

Casus Belli (2010), fiction, 12 minutes. Director and Screenwriter: Yorgos Zois. Producer: Maria Drandraki. Squared Square Films, Greece.

Chevalier (2015), fiction, 95 minutes. Director: Athina Rachel Tsangari. Screenwriters: Efthymis Filippou and Athina Rachel Tsangari. Producers: Maria Hatzakou and Athina Rachel

Tsangari. Co-producer: Katerina Kaskanioti. Haos Film, Faliro House Productions, Nova, The Match Factory and Greek Film Center, Greece and Germany.

Congratulations to the Optimists / Sygharitiria stous Aisiodoxous (2012), fiction, 83 minutes. Director: Konstantina Voulgari. Screenwriter: Eleni Mitropoulou. Producers: Fotis Veletzas, Panos Anagnosis and Cleopatra Abatzoglou. MITOS, Greece.

Copa Loca (2017), fiction, 14 minutes. Director: Christos Massalas. Screenwriter: Christos Massalas. Producer: Christos Massalas, Giorgos Karnavas, Konstantinos Kontovrakis. Greece.

Deptocracy / Hreokratia (2011), documentary, 75 minutes.Directors: Aris Chatzistefanou, Katerina Kitidi. Writers: Aris Chatzistefanou, Katerina Kitidi. Producer: Kostas Efimeros. BitsnBytes, Moviementa Productions, Greece.

Dogtooth / Kynodontas (2009), fiction, 97 minutes. Director: Yorgos Lanthimos. Screenwriters: Efthymis Filippou and Yorgos Lanthimos. Producer: Yorgos Tsourgiannis. Co-producer: Katerina Kaskanioti. Boo productions, Greece.

Eastern Territory / Anatoliki Perifereia (1979), fiction, 77 minutes. Director: Vasilis Vafeas. Screenwriter: Vasilis Vafeas. Producer: Vasilis Vafeas. Greek Cinema Center and Sigma Film, Greece.

Electric Swann (2019), fiction, 40 minutes. Director: Konstantina Kotzamani. Screenwriter: Konstantina Kotzamani. Producer: Emmanuel Chaumet, Caroline Demopoulos and Maria Drandaki. Ecce Films, Un Puma, Homemade, ARTE France. France, Argentina and Greece.

Evdokia (1971), fiction, 97 minutes. Director: Alexis Damianos. Screenwriters: John Baldwin and Alexis Damianos. Producers: Artemis Kapasakali and Alexis Damianos. Katamor Productions and Poreia, Greece.

Faster than Light (2018–19), documentary film/live-drag show. Directors: Kentaro Kumanomido and Thomas Anthony Owen. Onassis Cultural Center, Greece.

Fear / O Fovos (1966), fiction, 116 minutes. Director: Kostas Manousakis. Screenwriter: Kostas Manousakis. Producers: Theophanis Damaskinos and Victor Michaelides. Th. Damaskinos & V. Michaelides Productions, Greece.

From the Edge of the City / Apo tin Akri tis Polis (1998), fiction, 94 minutes. Director: Constantine Giannaris. Screenwriter: Constantine Giannaris. Producers: Dionysis Samiotis and Anastasios Vasiliou. Greek Film Center and Mythos Ltd, Greece.

Hector Malot: The Last Day of the Year/ Ektoras Malo: I Teleutaia Mera tis Hronias (2018), fiction, 24 minutes. Director: Jacqueline Lentzou. Producer: Fenia Kossovitsa. Greece.

Homeland / Hora Proelefsis (2010), fiction, 111 minutes. Director: Syllas Tzoumerkas. Screenwriters: Syllas Toumerkas and Gioula Boundali. Producers: Maria Drandraki, Thanos Anastopoulos and Syllas Tzoumerkas. Fantasy Audiovisual, Homemade Films, Greece.

If / An (2012), fiction, 111 minutes. Director: Christophoros Papakaliatis. Screenwriter: Christophoros Papakaliatis. Producers: Kostas Sousoulas and Marielli Lazopoulou. Village Plus Productions Ote tv Universal Music Greece Alpha TV, Greece.

Interruption (2015), fiction, 109 minutes. Director: Yorgos Zois. Screenwriters: Yorgos Zois and Vasilis Kyriakopoulos. Producers: Maria Drandraki, Sinisa Juricic and Elie Meirovitz. Pan Entertainment, Marni Films, Homemade Films, EZ Films and JDP, Greece, France, Italy, Bosnia and Herzegovina and Croatia.

Kinetta (2005), fiction, 95 minutes. Director: Yorgos Lanthimos. Screenwriters: Yorgos Kakanakis and Yorgos Lanthimos. Producer: Athina Rachel Tsangari. Haos Film, Modiano Inc., Top Cut, STEFI Cine & TV Productions, Baby Films and Kino, Greece and Serbia.

Knifer / Mahairovgaltis (2010), fction, 108 minutes. Director: Yannis Economides. Screenwriters: Doris Avgerinopoulos and Yannis Economides. Producer: Panos Papahadzis. Co-producer: Christos V. Konstantakopoulos. Argonauts Productions, Greece.

The Prism GR / Krisis 2011 (2012), documentary, 63 minutes. Directors and writers: Nikos Katsaounis and Nina Maria Pashalidou. N-coded, Greece.

L (2012), fiction, 87 minutes. Director: Babis Makridis. Screenwriters: George Giokas and Efthymis Filippou. Producers: Amanda Livanou and Babis Makridis. Co-producers: Thimios Bakatakis, Efthymis Filippou, Giannis Halkiadakis, Dennis Iliadis and Dimitris Papathomas. Warp Films, Beben Films, Faliro House Productions, Graal, Modiano Productions, Top cut, United Kingdom, Greece and Serbia.

Landscape in the Mist / Topio stin Omihli (1988), fiction, 127 minutes. Director: Theodoros Angelopoulos, Screenwriters Theodoros Angelopoulos. Producers: Theodoros Angelopoulos, Éric Heumann, Amedeo Pahani and Stéphane Sorlat. Paradis Films, Greek Film Center, Greek Television ET-1, Basic Cinematografica, La Generale d' Images and La Sept, France, Italy and Greece.

Letter to Yorgos Lanthimos / Gramma ston Giorgo Lanthimo (2019), promotional fiction video, 2 minutes. Director: Vassilis Katsoupis. Screenwriters: Spiros Kribalis and Zacharias Mavroidis. Producers: Giorgos Papadimitriou, Giorgos Stergiou, Katerina Seferli, Dimitris Tsantilas and Nikos Christopoulos. Dose Ligi Agapi ston Elliniko Kinimatografo, Greece.

Limbo (2016), fiction, 30 minutes. Director: Konstantina Kotzamani. Screenwriter: Angeliki Giannopoulou and Konstantina Kotzamani. Producer: Maria Drandaki and Ron Dyens. Homemade Films, Sacrebleu Films, France and Greece.

Macedonian Wedding / Makedonikos Gamos (1960), documentary, 24 minutes. Director: Takis Kanellopoulos. Screenwriter: Takis Kanellopoulos.

Matchbox / Spirtokouto (2002), fiction, 80 minutes. Director: Yannis Economides. Screenwriters: Yannis Economides and Lenia Spiropoulou. Producer: Yannis Economides. Associate Producers: Spyros Kokkas, Giorgos Lykiardopoulos and Nikos Tsagkaris. Cassandra Films, Greek Film Center, Kino, Max Productions, Strada Productions, Studio ERA, X-Rated Films, Greece.

Microcities / Mikropoleis (2011), documentary series, 14 episodes, 27–30 minutes each. Directors: Giannis Gaitanidis, Thomas Kiaos, Persefoni Miliou. Producer: Hellenic Radio and Television (ERT), Greece.

Miss Violence (2013), fiction, 98 minutes. Director: Alexandros Avranas. Screenwriters: Alexandros Avranas and Kostas Peroulis. Producers: Alexandros Avranas and Vasilis Chrysanthopoulos. Faliro House Productions, Plays2place Productions and Greek Film Center, Greece.

Mum, I'm Back / Mama Gyrisa (2017), fiction, 5 minutes. Director: Dimitris Katsimiris. Screenwriter: Dimitris Katsimiris. Correct Creative Productions, Greece.

Neighbourhood The Dream / Synoikia to Oneiro (1961), fiction, 95 minutes. Director: Alekos Alexandrakis. Screenwriters: Kostas Kotzias and Tasos Leivaditis. Greek Production Company, Greece.

Never on Sunday / Pote tin Kyriaki (1960), fiction, 97 minutes. Director, Screenwriter and Producer: Jules Dassin. Melina Film, Greece and USA.

Next Stop: Utopia (2015), documentary, 91 minutes. Director: Apostolos Karakasis. Writer: Panagiotis Iosifelis. Producer: Marco Gastine and Eleni Chandrinou. Minimal Films, Greece, Germany.

Nike of Samothrace / I Niki tis Samothrakis (1990), fiction, 90 minutes. Director: Dimos

Avdeliodis. Screenwriter: Dimos Avdeliodis. Producers: Dimos Avdeliodis, Makarios Avdeliotis and Nikos Tsangaris. Greek Cinema Centre, Greece.

Norway / Norvigia (2014), fiction, 73 minutes. Director: Yannis Veslemes. Screenwriter: Yannis Veslemes. Producer: Eleni Bertes, Christos Konstantakopoulos, Yorgos Tsourogiannis. Horsefly Productions, Deep Green Sea Productions, Faliro House Productions, Greece.

Not to Be Unpleasant but We Need to Have A Serious Talk / Den Thelo na Gino Dysarestos Alla Prepei na Milisoume Gia Kati Poly Sovaro (2019), fiction, 99 minutes. Director: Giorgos Georgopoulos. Screenwriters: Maria Fakinou and Giorgos Georgopoulos. Producers: Giorgos Georgopoulos, Christos Kontantakopoulos, Antonis Kotzias and Sotiris Tsafoulias. Authorwave, Faliro House Productions, Green Dragon Movies, Multivision, SOUL productions and Yafka Studio, Greece.

Obscuro Barroco (2018), documentary, 60 minutes. Director: Evangelia Kranioti. Producer: Tropical Underground. Anemos Productions, France, Greece.

Oh Babylon (1989), fiction, 90 minutes. Director: Costas Ferris. Screenwriter: Costas Ferris. Producer: George Zervoulakos. Andromeda II and Greek Film Center, Greece.

Park (2016), fiction, 100 minutes. Director: Sofia Exarchou. Screenwriter: Sofia Exarchou. Producers: Christos Konstantakopoulos and Amanda Livanou. Co-producers: Beata Rzezniczek and Klaudia Smieja. Faliro House Productions, Madants and Neda Film, Poland and Greece.

Pity / Oiktos (2018), fiction, 97 minutes. Director: Babis Makridis. Screenwriters: Efthymis Filippou and Babis Makridis. Producers: ChristosKonstantakopoulos, Amanda Livanou, Beata Rzezniczek and Klaudia Smieja. Neda Film, Madants, Beben Films, Greece and Poland.

Plato's Academy / Akadimia Platonos (2009), fiction, 103 minutes. Director: Filippos Tsitos. Screenwriters: Alexis Kardaras and Filippos Tsitos. Producers: Thanassis Karathanos and Konstadinos Moriatis. ARTE, Bad Movies, Das Kleine Fernsehspiel, Eurimages, Graal Digital Creations, Graal, Greek Film Center, Hellenic Radio & Television, MEDIA Programme of the European Union, Medienboard Berlin-Brandenburg, Pan Entertainment and Twenty Twenty Vision Filmproduktion GmbH, Germany, Netherlands and Greece.

Son of Sofia / O Gios tis Sofias (2017), fiction, 111 minutes. Director: Elina Psykou. Screenwriter: Elina Psykou. Producer: Giorgos Karnavas, Konstantinos Kontovrakis. Heretic, Stefi Films, KinoElektron, Greece.

Soul Kicking / Psyhi sto Stoma (2006), fiction, 111 minutes. Director: Yannis Economides. Screenwriter: Yannis Economides. Producer: Panos Papahadzis. Co-producer: Lambros Trifillis. Associate Producers: Nikos Tsagkaris and Panayotis Veremis. Argonauts Productions, Cassandra Films, Giannis Oikonomidis Films, Greek Film Center, Hellenic Radio & Television and Strada Productions, Greece.

Standing Aside Watching / Na Kathesai kai na Koitas (2013), fiction, 98 minutes. Director: Giorgos Servetas. Screenwriter: Giorgos Servetas. Producers: Fenia Cossovitsa, Giorgos Karnavas and Konstantinos Kontovrakis. Blonde Audiovisual Productions, Heretic, 2/35, Feelgood Entertainment, Greek Film Center, Hellenic Radio & Television and Stefi Films, Greece.

Stella (1955), fiction, 100 minutes. Director: Michael Cacoyannis. Screenwriter: Michael Cacoyannis. Millas Productions, Greece.

Still River / Akinito Potami (2018), fiction, 128 minutes. Director: Angelos Frantzis. Screenwriter: Spyros Krimbalis. Producer: Giorgos Karnavas, Konstantinos Kontovrakis, Mathieu Bompoint, Aija Berzina. Heretic, Mezannine Films, Tasse Films, Alatas Films, Greece, France, Latvia.

Stratos / To Mikro Psari (2014), fiction, 137 minutes. Director: Yannis Economides.

Screenwriters: Yannis Economides and Christos Konstantakopoulos. Producers: Christos Konstantakopoulos, Panos Papahadzis and Micheal Weber. Co-producers: Viola Fügen and Eirini Souganidou. Faliro House Productions, Argonauts Productions, The Match Factory, Yannis Economides Films, Feelgood Entertainment, Nerit, Ministry of Education and Culture, Greek Film Center and Film-und Mediensdtiftung NRW, Greece and Germany.

Strella: A Woman's Way / Strella (2009), fiction, 111 minutes. Director: Panos Koutras. Screenwriters: Panagiotis Evangelidis and Panos Koutras. Producer: Panos Koutras. Co-producer: Eleni Kossyfidou. 100% Synthetic Films, Greece.

Suntan (2016), fiction, 104 minutes. Director: Argyris Papadimitropoulos. Screenwriters: Argyris Papadimitropoulos and Syllas Tzoumerkas. Producer: Faidra Vokali. Marni Films and Oxymoron Films, Greece and United Kingdom.

The Attack of the Giant Moussaka/ I Epelasi tou Gigantiaiou Mousaka (1999), fiction, 99 minutes. Director: Panos Koutras. Screenwriters: Panagiotis Evangelidis and Yorgos Korontsis. Producer: Panos Koutras. Co-producers: Ion Constas and Martien Coucke. 100% Synthetic Films, Greece.

The Daughter / I Kori (2012), fiction, 87 minutes. Director: Thanos Anastopoulos. Screenwriters: Thanos Anastopoulos and Vasilis Giatsis. Producers: Thanos Anastopoulos and Stella Theodoraki. Strada Films, Greece.

The Distance Between Us and the Sky / I Apostasi Anamesa ston Ourano ki Emas (2019), fiction, 9 minutes. Director: Vasilis Kekatos. Screenwriter: Vasilis Kekatos. Producer: Eleni Kossyfidou. Co-producers: Panos Bisdas, Guilliaume Dreyfus and Dephine Schmit. Authorwave, BlackBird Productions and Tripode Productions, Greece and France.

The Eternal Return of Antonis Paraskevas / I Aionia Epistrofi tou Antoni Paraskeva (2013), fiction, 88 minutes. Director: Elina Psykou. Screenwriter: Elina Psykou. Producers: Giorgos Karnavas and Eleni Psykou. Elina Psykou, Greek Film Center, Guanaco, Hellenic Radio & Television and Stefi Films, Greece.

The Favourite (2018), fiction, 119 minutes. Director: Yorgos Lanthimos. Screenwriters: Deborah Davis and Tony McNamara. Producers: Ceci Dempsey, Ed Guiney, Yorgos Lanthimos and Lee Magiday. Co Producer: Jennifer Semler. Fox Searchlight Pictures, Film4, Waypoint Entertainment, Element Pictures, Scarlet Films, TSG Entertainment, Investment Incentives for the Irish Film Industry Provided by the Government of Ireland, BFI Film Fund and The Irish Film Board, Ireland, United Kingdom and USA.

The Killing of a Sacred Deer (2017), fiction, 121 minutes. Director: Yorgos Lanthimos. Screenwriters: Yorgos Lanthimos and Efthymis Filippou. Producers: Ed Guiney and Yorgos Lanthimos. Co-producers: Will Greenfield, Paula Heffernan and Atilla Salih Yucer. Element Pictures, A24 and Film4, Ireland and USA.

The Last Porn Movie (2006), fiction, 100 minutes. Director: Costas Zapas. Screenwriter: Costas Zapas. Director: Gregory Athanasiou. Greek Film Center and Minus Pictures, Greece.

The Lobster (2015), fiction, 119 minutes. Director: Yorgos Lanthimos. Screenwriters: Yorgos Lanthimos and Efthymis Filippou. Producers: Ceci Dempsey, Ed Guiney, Yorgos Lanthimos and Lee Magiday. Screen Ireland, Eurimages, Nederlands Fonds voor de Film, Greek Film Centre, and British Film Institute, Ireland, Netherlands, Greece, and UK.

The Matchmaking of Anna / To Proxenio tis Annas (1972), fiction, 88 minutes. Director: Pantelis Voulgaris. Screenwriter: Menis Koumantareas and Pantelis Voulgaris. Producer: Dinos Katsouridis. Katsouridis Productions, Greece.

The Miracle of the Sargasso Sea / To Thavma tis Thalassa ton Sargasson (2019), fiction, 121 minutes. Director: Syllas Tzoumerkas. Screenwriters: Youla Boudali and Syllas Tzoumerkas. Producer: Maria Drandraki. Co-producers: Tomas Eskilsson, Ellen Havenith, Tutus

Kreyenberg, Anthony Muir and Olle Wirenhed. Homemade Films, Unafilm, PRPL, Kakadua Filmproduktion, Film i Väst, ZDF/Arte, Eurimages Greek Film Centre, Film- und Medienstiftung NRW, Nederlands Filmfonds, Svenska Filminstitutet (SFI) Creative Europe Media, ERT and Nova, Germany, Sweden, Netherlands and Greece.

The Ogre of Athens / O Drakos (1956), fiction, 103 minutes. Director: Nikos Koundouros. Screenwriter: Iakovos Kabanellis. Producer: Nikos Koundouros. Athens Film Company, Greece.

The Shepherds of Disaster / Oi Voskoi tis Symforas (1966), fiction, 120 minutes. Director: Nico Papatakis. Screenwriter: Nico Papatakis. Producer: Wirer Samuel. Lenox Films, France.

Third Kind (2018), fiction, 32 minutes. Director: Yorgos Zois. Screenwriters: Yorgos Zois and Konstantina Kotzamani. Producers: Stelios Cotionis, Sinisa Juricic and Antigoni Rota. Squared Square Films, Foss Productions and Nukleus film, Greece and Croatia.

Thread / Nima (2016), fiction, 94 minutes. Director: Alexandros Voulgaris. Screenwriter: Alexandros Voulgaris. Producer: Eleni Bertes. Logline Production and Greek Film Centre, Greece.

True Life / Alithini Zoi (2004), fiction, 119 minutes. Director: Panos Koutras. Screenwriters: Panagiotis Evangelidis and Panos Koutras. Producers: Fabrice Coat, Panos Papahadzis and Athena Sakellariou. Program 33 Argonauts Productions S.A. FilmNet, Greek Film Center, Hellenic Radio & Television (ERT), PPV Athens and Strada Productions, Greece.

Uncut Family (2004), 75 minutes. Director: Costas Zapas. Screenwriter: Costas Zapas. Producer: Gregory Athanasiou. Minus Pictures, Greece.

Unfair World / Adikos Kosmos (2011), fiction, 107 minutes. Director: Filippos Tsitos. Screenwriters: Dora Masklavanou and Filippos Tsitos. Producers: Alexandra Boussiou and Filippos Tsitos. Co-producers: Nikos Kavoukidis and Gian-Piero Ringel. Neue Road Movies, Germany.

Washingtonia (2014), documentary/fiction, 24 minutes. Director: Konstantina Kotzamani. Screenwriter: Konstantina Kotzamani. Producers: Artemis Pattakou and Yorgos Zois. Squared Square Films, Greece.

Wasted Youth (2011), fiction, 122 minutes. Director: Argyris Papadimitropoulos and Jan Vogel. Screenwriters: Argyris Papadimitropoulos and Jan Vogel. Producers: Argyris Papadimitropoulos and Giorgos Karnavas. Co-producers: Dionysis Bougas and Federico Pietra. Stefi Productions, Greece.

Wednesday 4'45" / Tetarti 04.45 (2015), fiction, 116 minutes. Director: Alexis Alexiou. Screenwriter: Alexis Alexiou. Producer: Thanasis Karathanos. Twenty Two Vision, CL Productions, Pie Films, Faliro House, Marni Films, Greece, Germany, Israel.

Winona (2019), fiction, 87 minutes. Director: Alexandros Voulgaris, Screenwriter: Alexandros Vougaris. Producer: Eleni Bertes, Maria Kontogianni. Hellenic Radio and Television (ERT), Logline, Greece.

Worlds Apart / Enas Allos Kosmos (2015), fiction, 113 minutes. Producer: Christophoros Papakaliatis. Screenwriter: Christophoros Papakaliatis. Producers: Christophoros Papakaliatis, Chris Papavasileiou, Dorothea Paschalidou and Kostas Sousoulas. Plus Productions, Greece.

Xenia (2014), fiction, 128 minutes. Director: Panos Koutras. Screenwriters: Panagiotis Evangelidis and Panos Koutras. Producers: Alexandra Bousiou, Eleni Kossyfidou and Panos Koutras. 100% Synthetic Films, Faliro House Productions, Marni Films, Pie Films, Twenty Twenty Vision Filmproduktion, Greece and Germany.

Zorba the Greek (1964), fiction, 144 minutes. Director: Screenwriter and Producer: Michael Cacoyannis. 20th Century Fox, Greece, USA.

Index

CPSIA information can be obtained
at www.ICGtesting.com
Printed in the USA
JSHW011245230323
39371JS00003B/33